The Ethics of Justice Without Illusions

AF734720

The founding premise of this book is that the nimbus of prestige, which once surrounded the idea of justice, has now been dimmed to such a degree that it is no longer sufficient to secure the possibility of a good conscience for those who undertake, in good faith, to make the world a better place in the spheres of politics and law. The many decent human beings who have noticed and experienced this diminishment of justice's prestige find themselves in a thoroughly disenchanted existential situation. For them, the attempt to do justice without the illusion of being grounded in something beyond the sheer facticity of their own performances is a distinctly ethical theme, which cries out to be investigated in its own right. Heeding the cry, this book asks and attempts to answer the following fundamental ethical question: *is a life in the law – even one spent in the pursuit of justice – worth living, and if so, how can a disenchanted person come to bear the living of it without constantly having to engage in self-deception?* If Nietzsche is right that living without illusions is impossible for human beings, then the most important ethical implication of this essentially anthropological fact goes far beyond the question of what illusions we ought to choose. It must also include the question of whether we should succumb to that most seductive and pernicious of all illusions: namely, the belief that exercising great care and responsibility in choosing our illusions – which we might then call our 'principles of justice' – excuses us ethically for what we do to others in their name. The culmination of a 10 year legal-philosophical project, this book will appeal to graduate students, scholars and curious non-academic intellectuals interested in continental philosophy, critical legal theory, postmodern theology, the philosophy of human rights and the study of individual ethics in the context of law.

Louis E. Wolcher is a Professor of Law at University of Washington, USA.

The Ethics of Justice Without Illusions

Louis E. Wolcher

Routledge
Taylor & Francis Group
LONDON AND NEW YORK

First published 2016 by Routledge

2 Park Square, Milton Park, Abingdon, Oxfordshire OX14 4RN
711 Third Avenue, New York, NY 10017

a GlassHouse book

Routledge is an imprint of the Taylor & Francis Group, an informa business

First issued in paperback 2017

Copyright © 2016 Louis E. Wolcher

The right of Louis E. Wolcher to be identified as author of this work has been asserted by him in accordance with sections 77 and 78 of the Copyright, Designs and Patents Act 1988.

All rights reserved. No part of this book may be reprinted or reproduced or utilised in any form or by any electronic, mechanical, or other means, now known or hereafter invented, including photocopying and recording, or in any information storage or retrieval system, without permission in writing from the publishers.

Notice:
Product or corporate names may be trademarks or registered trademarks, and are used only for identification and explanation without intent to infringe.

British Library Cataloguing in Publication Data
A catalogue record for this book is available from the British Library

Library of Congress Cataloging-in-Publication Data
Names: Wolcher, Louis E., author.
Title: The ethics of justice without illusions / Louis Wolcher.
Description: New York : Routledge, 2016.
Identifiers: LCCN 2015049594| ISBN 9781138855649 (hbk) |
ISBN 9781315720234 (ebk)
Subjects: LCSH: Ethics. | Illusion (Philosophy) | Justice.
Classification: LCC BJ1031 .W645 2016 | DDC 172/.2--dc23
LC record available at http://lccn.loc.gov/2015049594

ISBN: 978-1-138-85564-9 (hbk)
ISBN: 978-0-8153-9294-1 (pbk)

Typeset in Baskerville and Gill Sans
by Florence Production Ltd, Stoodleigh, Devon, UK

For Cecelia, Andrew and Logan

Contents

Figures

Acknowledgements

The author previously published certain portions of this book in article form. Permission to use and modify various passages from the following publications is therefore gratefully acknowledged:

Wolcher, L 2012, 'Cultural Diversity and Universal Human Rights', *Cambrian Law Review*, vol. 43, pp. 44–63.

Wolcher, L 2012, 'The Critical Imperative', *The Crit: Critical Studies Journal*, vol. 5, no. 2. Available from: www.uidaho.edu/law/the-crit/issues [May 2015].

Wolcher, L 2011, 'Asking the Right Question in Business Ethics', *Journal of Law, Business and Ethics*, vol. 17, pp. 9–22.

Wolcher, L 2011, 'The Meaning of Justice in the World Today', *National Lawyers Guild Review*, vol. 67, no. 4, pp. 228–245.

Wolcher, L 2010, 'An Inquiry into the Possibility of an Ethical Politics', *Northwestern Interdisciplinary Law Review*, vol. 3, no. 1, pp. 1–21.

Wolcher, L 2010, 'An Inquiry into the Possibility of an Ethical Politics', *Rutgers Journal of Law and Religion*, vol. 11, pt. 1, pp. 383–405. Available from: http://lawandreligion.com/volume-11 [15 May 2015].

Wolcher, L 2010, 'The Problem of the Subject(s)', in *Prospects of Legal Semiotics*, eds A Wagner & J Broekman, Springer, New York, pp. 145–169. With kind permission from Springer Science+Business Media, © Springer Science+Business Media B.V. 2010.

Wolcher, L 2007, 'Senseless Kindness: The Politics of Cost–Benefit Analysis', *Law and Inequality: A Journal of Theory and Practice*, vol. 25, no. 1, pp. 147–202.

Permission to use the following images is also gratefully acknowledged:

Figure 1.1 ('*Politics/Law/Justice* in an unstable society'): Kevin KAL Kallaugher, The Economist, *Kaltoons.com.*

Figure 2.1 ('The sleep of reason produces monsters'): Photo credit: HIP/Art Resource, NY.

Figure 2.2 ('The tragic circle'): Reprinted by permission of the publishers from 'Suffering and Ethical Distress', in *Law's Task* by Louis E Wolcher (Farnham, UK: Ashgate, 2008). Copyright © 2008.

Figure 3.1 ('Mosaic pavement: Apollo and Daphne'): Photo credit: Princeton University Art Museum/Art Resource, NY.
Figure 3.2 ('Liberty leading the people'): Photo credit: Hervé Lewandowski. © RMN-Grand Palais/Art Resource, NY.

The author also thanks his friends and colleagues Kathleen Cavanaugh, Oren Ben-Dor, Marie-Bénédicte Dembour, Costas Douzinas, Michelle Farrell, Adam Gearey, Craig Mason, Andreas Philippopoulos-Mihalopoulos, Alexander Carnera Ljungström, Anèl Boshoff, Annabelle Mooney, Ruth Beardsley, Michael Townsend, Jan Oppermann, Richard Zerbe and Andrew Rutten, as well as his children Edward Wolcher and Sarah Schneider, for their more-than-ample support over the years, and also for the many 'Ah-Hah!' moments of enlightenment that he has experienced in conversations with each of them.

Finally, the author would like to thank Susan Haluk Wolcher for her incredibly consistent support, advice and love, without which this book could never have been conceived or written.

Louis E. Wolcher

Part One

A framework for thinking the ethics of the real

Chapter 1

Indicating the pathway

> The endless path does not have an end that's "infinitely distant"—it has no end.
>
> Ludwig Wittgenstein (2005, p. 486e)

Prologue: Questioning the ethical sufficiency of unity and truth

In one way or another, various conceptions of unity and truth have held sway over Western thought for over two millennia. The impulse to unify and verify is especially strong in matters of law and justice, where the task of ascertaining and judging what happened on the basis of some idea of what ought to have happened seems unavoidable. "In order to be just," writes Levinas (1998a, p. 204), "it is necessary to know: to objectify, compare, judge, form concepts, generalize, etc." One kind of project involves reducing the infinitude of the real to a finite factual statement that can be accepted as true or refuted as false. Another involves producing a normative statement that can be accepted as legitimate or refuted as illegitimate. A concrete (from the Latin *concrescere*, meaning to grow together) case is the effort to construct, dialogically, a unity out of the universe of possible "is statements" (the facts) in relation to another universe of possible "ought statements" (what law or justice demands). Thus, that what happened and what ought to have happened are somehow made into a *thing* (albeit a word-thing called a *legal judgment* or *decision*) that can be inspected for its verisimilitude and validity.

Speaking more generally, the idea of unity attempts to enclose a thing's reality within the soap bubble of its conceptual determination by saying what it is and distinguishing it from what it is not. The idea of *truth*, in turn, motivates people to blow their unifying concept bubbles in the first place, or at least reassures them after the fact that they have done a good job of it. Truth produces these psychosomatic effects by promising the bubble blowers that their verbal determinations of a thing can be intellectually, aesthetically, materially, or emotionally satisfying to them in some way—because either the bubble correctly "corresponds" to the thing (the medieval schoolmen's *adaequatio rei et intellectus*), or it "coheres" prettily with certain other bubbles that have been blown (the modern "coherence" theory of truth), or it produces effects that are "useful" in some way to the blowers (American pragmatism), or it lets the thing itself be "unconcealed" in its truth (the Heideggerian–Greek notion of truth as *alētheia*), or . . . whatever. The point is that according to the Western intellectual tradition, not to mention common understanding, it is always good and fortunate to have unity and truth at one's disposal, and always bad and unfortunate to suffer through disunity and untruth.

Western thought reached the high point of its love affair with unity and truth when Hegel (1977, p. 11) took the radical step of conjoining them. His famous formulation "the true is the whole" (*Das Wahre ist das Ganze*) seems to leave only two options for classifying what is not whole, what is *other-than-whole* (OTW). Either we must say that what appears to be OTW nonetheless actually contains a latent wholeness by virtue of the fact that it is struggling to become whole—that it is but a reflection of "essence consummating itself through its development," as Hegel (1977, p. 11) put it. Or else we must slander and dismiss the OTW by calling it a nullity—"the undetermined immediate" (*das unbestimmte Unmittelbare*) that amounts to a mere abstraction, and therefore is absolutely negative, or nothing (Hegel, 1975, p. 127). To express this point of view in the manner of postmodern neo-Hegelianism: "The knowing subject moves from the start within a horizon of possible experience that is disclosed for it by language. There is no base of brute sensory input prior to, and devoid of, symbolic mediation" (Habermas, 2003, p. 188).

All of which implies, *pace* Heidegger (1998, p. 103), that there can be no such thing as the "pre-predicative manifestness of beings." Nor can there exist, *pace* Kitarō Nishida (1990, pp. 3–10), a state of awareness that is not simultaneously an act of intentionality or discrimination—an act of thinking something *as* something. On this view, the countless teensy-weensy particularities that everyone feels they can and do experience even without cognizing—the "raw stuff of the remainder of the Real" that "cannot be accounted for by any symbolic idealization," as Žižek (1999, p. 156) puts it—are to be treated as less-than-insignificant crumbs that the brush of reason will sweep off the table of world history.

When it comes to morality, the Hegelian viewpoint exhibits the same sort of contempt toward the preconceptual particular that it does in metaphysics. It privileges the unity and truth of the historically developing "ethical order" (*Sittlichkeit*), and dismisses the OTW viewpoint of the individual as inferior at best (Hegel, 1967, pp. 1–13). The immediate particularity of any event, including an ethically charged encounter between human beings, undoubtedly makes for "a first beginning," as Hegel (1975, p. 124) says, but as "pure Being" (*reine Sein*) it "cannot be mediated by anything, or be further determined." Instead of individual morality, which "only expresses the inferior point of view of the individual regarding the ethical world," Hegelian ethics notoriously insists on the primacy of objective right as exhibited in the concrete life of "a people where morality and legality are completely united" (Hyppolite, 1996, p. 48).

The choice on offer is between saying that the OTW is on the way to becoming one with the developing *Sittlichkeit* of an era, and saying that it is absolutely nothing that could ever be worthy of ethical recognition—"shallow thinking" based on "immediate sense-perception and the play of fancy," for example, or a mere "subjective accident of opinion and caprice" (Hegel, 1967, p. 6). In the English language, a sensitive ear can even detect in this dualism of the whole versus the OTW certain normative affinities to the spheres of hygiene and religion, in as much as the words *whole*, *wholesome*, and *holy* all have the same Middle English root: *hool*, meaning healthy or unhurt (Oppen, 2007, p. 172).

Latter-day remnants of Hegel's ethical viewpoint, like bits of ancient DNA in our genes, can be found almost everywhere in conventional Western thought. The belief that ethics is about establishing and internalizing the right norms or rules—the right general expressions of "ought"—remains ubiquitous, even if most people today are somewhat more ambivalent than Hegel was about the wisdom of uniting folkish morality with the positive legal order. "After the demise of strong traditions," as Habermas (2003, p. 273) put it, the West began to experience and continues to experience a post-metaphysical need to create and justify ought statements to itself. His translator's way of describing this need is typical of the large segment of contemporary philosophical thought that equates ethical conduct with conduct that is measured as adequate by the right sorts of norms:

> The fundamental question of morality is how we can legitimately regulate [from the Latin *regula*, meaning straightedge] interpersonal relationships. What is at issue is not the representation of facts, but the appeal to norms [from the Latin *norma*, meaning carpenter's square] worthy of recognition.
>
> (2003, p. 261)

The sheer lopsidedness of the cultural preference for unity and truth over disunity and untruth has served modern science and technology well, especially if wellness is measured by marginal increases in the human capacity to dominate and manipulate natural processes. The effective control and administration of social life also flourishes when the fetish for unity is given free rein to simplify the infinite complexities of human relationships into measurable data and general statements of fact, all of which can then get inserted into the appropriate forms, protocols, and algorithms. The data and statements of fact are performatively produced in particular situations (by individual social scientists, lawyers, government bureaucrats, etc.) according to premade methods whose correct or incorrect application becomes the sole criterion of their truth. Unity that is first produced by method thus becomes the proof of its own previous existence, as method loops back to take a second glance at the accuracy of a particular statement of unity that was born from a previous practical application or misapplication of the very same method. "Einstein: how a magnitude is measured is what it is" (Wittgenstein, 1975, p. 200).[1]

If, however, the concepts of unity and truth are efficient means for pursuing the ends of modern science, technology, and social administration, this does not imply that they are also good for ethics. On the contrary, the care to know in advance how to behave ethically, like the preference for rules over facts, reflects a desire for certainty that can all too easily tranquilize itself with this very certainty (cf. Heidegger, 2005, p. 219). The care for certainty tranquilizes itself by reducing anxiety and fear on account of the pre-cognized reality of what is cared for, in this case the unique, particular situations and vulnerabilities of others. Like Spinoza's *Ethics* (1955, p. 128), it considers "human actions and appetites just as if [it] were considering lines, planes, or bodies," thereby amputating all that is incommensurable in human relationships (cf. Horkheimer and Adorno, 2002, p. 9). Achieving abstract ethical norms "worthy of recognition," as Habermas said, offers people hope that their moral accounts can be rendered neatly once and for all in the name of the future, rather than closed in a messy, ad hoc manner at the end of each day, hour, or minute (cf. Judt, 2012, p. 91). In short, the right normative expressions seem to promise the gift of a good conscience to those who commit in advance to follow them as correctly as possible on every occasion.

The result of ethics being normalized in this way is that human goodness and badness are conceived in juridical terms, which is to say, they are interpreted as products of a unifying, truth-producing act of judgment that can be rendered before and/or after the fact. Acts of judgment in the ethical realm unify, classify, and dispose of the judged. Training in the application of precise ethical categories tends to "manufacture self-confidence" (cf. Dreyfus and Kelly, 2011, p. 6) by offering people escape from "the dismal category of those who, if they had to act in full awareness of what they were doing, would never act" (Beckett, 2011, p. 464). Outcomes produced by behavior judged unethical can be automatically condemned, and moreover, responsibility for these outcomes quickly assigned to individual wrongdoers. Everything else is naturalized and relegated to the category of that for which no one is responsible (e.g., "necessary" or "inevitable" suffering), thereby creating a zone of absolute irresponsibility for everyone (Veitch, 2007).

Given the necessary partiality and selectivity of rule-based normativity, it is little wonder that for millennia what characterized human history most of all was "the great number of people not interested in the sufferings of others" (Camus, 1965a, p. 224). The sheer meanness of suffering—"the dirty, repulsive and slimy universe of pain," as Camus (1965b, p. 196) puts it—always eluded and still eludes the sanitizing politesse that seems to be inherent in the categories of reason.

Since the Enlightenment, however, belief in the proposition that socially necessary human suffering is part of the natural order—a God-given punishment for original sin—has much declined, and the sheer *visibility* of the universe of pain inflicted by human beings on one another has much increased. For some time now, we have been burdened with the suspicion that what is not immediately recognized by the formal idealizations of reason is not nothing—that it can be registered in the human mind-and-heart as *something*, if only un-thematically in the "primordial space of 'wild' pre-synthetic imagination" (Žižek, 1999, p. 52). Idiographic ways of looking at things have now become de rigueur, or at least theoretically respectable. The unique, unrepeatable pseudo-unity of the particular—that which no established concept can capture—clamors for and sometimes even receives our recognition, so much so that we sometimes begin to feel, with Samuel Beckett

(2009, p. 397), that the "classifiers are the [real] obscurantists." Indeed, for quite a while now philosophers have been heard to utter shockingly unity-and-truth-denying sentences like this one: "What many individual things have in common, or what constantly recurs in one individual thing, needs not be more stable, eternal, or deep than the particular" (Horkheimer and Adorno, 2002, p. 182).

This book takes an ethical stand against the holiness and wholesomeness of the whole in Western thought about law, politics, and justice. It unwholesomely frets about (and stands up for) the countless little particularities that are covered over but never truly sublated by the project of perfecting history's categories through rational planning. Its point of view on the value of "progress" is similar to that of the nineteenth-century Russian literary critic Vissarion Belinsky:

> If I ever reached the highest rung on [Hegel's] ladder of development I should then insist on an accounting of all the creatures who have been victims of chance, of superstition, of the Inquisition, of Philip II, etc. . . . Otherwise I should hurl myself head first from that height.
>
> (Camus, 1965a, p. 177).

It offers the very un-Hegelian thesis (if it is proper to speak of theses in a book such as this) that ethics comes from our capacity to notice more than we could ever think or say, and that ethical life—or at least living life with as much decency as possible—depends on a more or less constant effort to exercise that capacity in the spirit of what Horkheimer and Adorno (2002, p. 198) call "steadfastness without a doctrine."

What makes this book ethical is its point, not its subject matter (cf. Phillips, 2005, p. 94). It is ethical not in the narrow sense of a ponderous discussion of ethical rules and duties, but rather in the larger sense that is conveyed by Foucault's term *ethopoetic*: the book attempts to *show* (not merely to say) the context and content of that which furnishes or provides a certain way of doing things with others—someone's *ēthos* in the original Greek sense of the word (Foucault, 2005, pp. 237–238). Not every individual's way of doing things, to be sure, but only that of a particular kind of individual: namely, the kind that has become disenchanted with the ethical sufficiency of even the most unified and truthful gobs and spurts of conceptual language.

For one such person—Ludwig Wittgenstein—ethical disenchantment is connected with the belief that "all propositions stand on the same level" and that "there are no propositions which, in any absolute sense, are sublime, important, or trivial" (1993, p. 39). For another such person—Albert Camus—"it is general ideas that hurt most" (1965b, p. 27), and therefore "I have abandoned the moral point of view" because "morals lead to abstraction and to injustice—they are the mother of fanaticism and blindness" (2008, p. 248). For yet another—Emmanuel Levinas (1999, p. 109)—the best goodness is mad goodness, and "the moment this goodness organizes it goes out." For still another—Alain Badiou—"the ethics of thinking today is to say that it is better to think that all situations are infinite, that it is very difficult to reduce a situation to finite parameters" (2003, p. 182). Then there is Giorgio Agamben, for whom the surest index of "the irreparable ruination of any ethical experience" is the extent to which ethics is confused with juridical concepts (2000, p. 129). And so on and so forth in the same vein, as we shall see.

All of the foregoing examples of ethical disenchantment have at least one thing in common. However different their temperaments and philosophical approaches may have been, every one of the thinkers noted above felt driven, at some point in their lives, to ask themselves some variant of the following question: *Even if a single-minded preference for unity and truth over disunity and untruth can be important and useful for some (or even most) human endeavors, does this mean that it is also good for someone who aspires to live an ethically decent life?*

According to Schopenhauer (1969, vol. 1, p. 24), error is opposed to truth as a deception of reason (*Vernunft*), whereas illusion is opposed to reality as a deception of understanding (*Verstand*). But as we shall see, a disenchanted person looks at both sets of verbal oppositions (error versus truth and illusion versus reality) and never sees more than *particular* determinations of the concepts "error," "truth," "illusion," and "reality" in *particular* situations. A true proposition, on this view, is not a metonym for the reality of an immaterial ideality that would somehow exist apart from it. Nor is a linguistic sign a metonym for a meaning that is any different than a verbal explanation of its meaning would be. Saying "X" and saying " 'X' means Y" are seen to stand on the same level of reality: the event of *saying* as such. Setting aside the admittedly important topic of the causes and conditions of our expressions—the histories of our various "language-games," as Wittgenstein (1953, p. 5e) would have put it—the soap bubbles that determine (and predetermine) the unities of things, ethically speaking, are made up of *words* that people just happen to receive this way or that way, depending on their particular historical circumstances.

This *ēthos* does not generally despise or denigrate the effort to determine things by means of conceptual language, not least because it is always making the same sort of effort itself. It is a profoundly true tautology that only language can attempt to describe what is not language. But what this *ēthos* does try to do—and what accounts for the title *The Ethics of Justice without Illusions*—is deny itself the comfort of a *good conscience* for following any of its own conceptual soap bubbles as they float this way and that through the air of the real.

The structure of the book

This book is the most recent stage of a much larger project. It represents the further extension of a philosophical pathway that the author began to walk in *Beyond Transcendence in Law and Philosophy* (Wolcher, 2005), and continued to travel along in *Law's Task: The Tragic Circle of Law, Justice and Human Suffering* (Wolcher, 2008). As is the case with so many things in life, the fact that it was a *single* pathway, however meandering, became fully visible only in hindsight; or, as another of Hegel's famous bon mots would have it, "The owl of Minerva spreads its wings only with the falling of the dusk" (1967, p. 13). Notwithstanding the unity of the overall philosophical journey when seen from the author's point of view, it must also be said—indeed stressed—that the present book is fully capable of standing alone, and requires no prior familiarity with the author's earlier works to be understood.

The book is divided into two parts. The first is entitled "A Framework for Thinking the Ethics of the Real," and its four chapters comprise the theoretical core of the enterprise. Here can be found certain foundational ideas that have proven themselves essential to the author's project of asking and attempting to answer what the book calls the Fundamental Question. The next section of this chapter explains the overall context and meaning of that question. For now, though, it will suffice simply to pose it: *Is a life in the law—even one spent in the pursuit of justice—worth living, and if so, how can a disenchanted person come to bear the living of it without constantly having to engage in self-deception?*

Essential to hearing what the Fundamental Question is attempting to ask is Part One's development of a radicalized concept of the "speechless particular." It is claimed that the neglected reality that corresponds to this concept can and should lead to a fundamental reevaluation of the relationship between law and justice, on the one hand, and individual ethical responsibility, on the other. Part One also deconstructs and deflates a number of conventional conceptual oppositions that tend to obscure our awareness of the particular, including law versus justice, redeemed violence versus unredeemed violence, moral optimism versus moral pessimism, and the self that is free versus the unfree phenomenal self. Here concepts such as *disenchantment*, *logical transcendence*, the *legal division of suffering*, *ontological particularity*, and *speechlessness* are used to illuminate some of the most important twists and turns in the philosophical pathway that has led to the Fundamental Question.

Part Two, entitled "Some Particular Problems of the Particular," slows down the pace of the journey somewhat, without, however, altering its general direction. The basic style of presentation also changes to become more conversational, in as much as Chapters 5, 6, and 7 were originally presented, and subsequently published, as lectures given before large groups of people in Tehran, Paris, and Seattle, respectively.

Substantively speaking, the second part of the book uses a microscope, so to speak, instead of a telescope: it examines three discrete subject-matter areas of law and policy from the point of view of the same philosophical "eye" (and "I") that in Part One took a perspicuous view of the larger landscape of ethical responsibility in relation to politics, law, and justice. Each of these chapters can be read as a case study, undertaken within a single subject-matter area of law or public policy, of the book's overarching theory of the relationship between justice and ethics. The areas considered are: *international human rights law*, *business ethics*, and *cost–benefit analysis*.

Chapter 5 was first presented in November 2011 in Tehran to Iranian and non-Iranian law students and academics attending an international conference on human rights and cultural diversity. The audience for Chapter 6, in turn, was made up of more than 100 business leaders from various private and public corporations based in France who attended a public program in Paris entitled "Revisiting Business Ethics" in December 2009. Finally, a version of Chapter 7 was given to American academic economists and other social scientists at a May 2006 conference in Seattle on the theme "What Can We Do to Improve the Use of Benefit–Cost Analysis?"

In all three cases, the author attempted to communicate his ideas on individual ethical responsibility as clearly as possible in a way that would make them accessible to non-philosophical, and in some cases non-legal, audiences. Although some of the philosophical arguments in these chapters have been abbreviated, as befits their lecture format, Part One will have already laid the relevant foundations in considerable detail. The resulting gains in the immediacy and ease of readability of Chapters 5, 6, and 7 will hopefully offer adequate compensation to the reader.

The final chapter is entitled "Postscript." First presented at the Forum in Legal and Political Theory of the London School of Economics in October 2009, this chapter is literally an *after*-thought: a thought after the philosophical journey undertaken in the preceding eight chapters. The Postscript's point of departure is a short epigram written by Kafka in early 1918, not long after he had been diagnosed with tuberculosis: "In one and the same human being there are cognitions that, however utterly dissimilar they are, yet have one and the same object, so that one can only conclude that there are different subjects in one and the same human being" (Cisco, 2013, p. 72). Taking its lead from this gnomic text, Chapter 8 traces the rise in post-Cartesian Western thought of the human being conceived of as a "subject" (in the singular): an ethically responsible being that remains the same as itself despite its temporal modifications. Not only is this supposition false, it is argued, but it is also ethically disastrous. The Postscript concludes the book by giving at least some kind of affirmative answer, emotionally uncomforting though it may be, to the Fundamental Question.

"What has been will be again, what has been done will be done again; there is nothing new under the sun," says the preacher in Ecclesiastes 1:9. This admonition is perhaps truest of all when applied to philosophy, which has gone on attempting to answer the same set of fundamental questions since the days of Heraclitus and Parmenides, if not before. These repeated attempts were not failures, in the sense of a technological failure to reach a well-defined goal; for as Heidegger (1984, p. 63) says, "In philosophy there is no 'progress,' hence no regress, either." Progress and regress imply an agreed-upon method for measuring where one is situated in relation to a specified end. But there are and should be no agreed-upon ends or means in philosophy—there are only more or less vital questions that lead to the discovery and rediscovery of more or less significant pathways.

What is true of philosophy in general is also true of this book. The ideas expressed here were foreshadowed in one way or another by more than a few previous thinkers, including especially Theodor Adorno, Hannah Arendt, Walter Benjamin, Jacques Derrida, Vasily Grossman, Martin Heidegger, Max Horkheimer, Emmanuel Levinas, Arthur Schopenhauer, Ludwig Wittgenstein, and, of course, the Buddha. But then again no thinker worthy of the name would ever want to claim that he or she was not trying to stand on the shoulders of giants.

The Fundamental Question

The pathway taken here eventually led to the titular problem of the ethics of justice without illusions because it became apparent along the way that the other promising forks in the path—politics, law, and justice—terminated in existential dead ends. In the final analysis, all three institutions have to do with the establishment and maintenance of systems of duties. Politics leads to law, and therefore to the imposition of legal duties; law leads to justice, and therefore to the moral duty to support just law and overcome unjust law; and justice leads to politics, thereby locking the deontological urge inside the bad infinity of a historical circle. But duties alone do not offer anyone a reason for living, and as Heidegger (2010b, p. 127) says, it is always "more difficult to grapple with life than it is to deal with the world in terms of a system." Difficult as they may be to deal with, the sometimes fervent, sometimes wheezy exhalations of politics, law, and justice ultimately touch upon the infinitely more difficult problems of life itself. The latter problems are more difficult than the former because systems can only anticipate what is generally the case, whereas no living person has ever experienced something in general. Everything that happens in the course of life happens in particular. And this existential truism applies even (or rather especially) to the ever-recurring particular event of repressing one's awareness of particularities by clinging to a comforting (or alarming) general image of what *must* be the case.

The particular in relation to the universal is not equivalent to an object in relation to its concept, though the sense of this contrast is not immediately obvious and will require further development. Suffice it to say for now that Hegelian idealism attempts to refute the foregoing way of thinking by defining the relationship between the universal and the particular with the intention of reconciling them at a higher level of consciousness. Hegel conceived of a "concrete particularism" as an immature, socially unaware internal want or desire; an "abstract universal," on the other hand, he defined as an externally imposed social demand. For Hegel, it is the synthesis of these two moments that represents the apogee of rationality and the spearhead of historical progress. He called this synthesis the "concrete universal," in as much as it converts sociality into an immediate internal desire rather than a mere external obligation that constrains the individual's pursuit of self-interest (Balbus, 1977, pp. 580–581). Sheer, naked particularity on this view is like the inarticulate scream of an infant who has not yet learned how to ask for what it should want, but who someday soon will.

The notion of the particular that is employed in this book is not like this. Rather than constituting an earlier stage in a dialectical synthesis that results in a higher level of awareness, the particular is what is *left over* or *left out* by the concept. Given its concept, an object can be thought about in advance of its appearance. Scientific empiricism, for example, can seek out, observe, and describe "objective" facts—

in the sense of statements about material objects such as the sun and the earth—that refute pseudo-truths based on superstition or dogmatism (e.g., a geocentric universe; a 6,000-year-old earth; the non-existence of humanly caused global climate change). But the particular is not the sort of fact that is accessible to scientific investigation. If it is seen to refute anything at all (a rare enough occurrence in a scientistic age such as ours), the particular refutes factuality's hegemonic claim to be the sole criterion of what is real.

The particular is what Schelling (2000, p. 12) called "the unprethinkable" (*das Unvordenkliche*): it *can* be encountered (or not encountered), but only as a surprise, only when and as it arises. Like Heidegger's "that which is" (2015, p. 4) or Levinas's "there is" (1996, p. 110), the particular is both more and less than a fact. More, in that it overflows or exceeds whatever is included in the concepts that comprise a factual statement. Less, in that it requires no conceptual understanding to be encountered—only awareness, however fleeting.

Viewed as a kind of residue or remainder, the leftover particular is perhaps more visible in the legal process than anywhere else. The idioms of the law operate like cookie cutters, stamping some of the dough of reality into tidy little shapes and leaving the rest of it to be swept off the table as "irrelevant" waste material. A relied-upon commitment is not necessarily a *contract*; a hurtful mistake is not necessarily *negligence*; an unwanted penetration is not necessarily *rape*; an all-white police force patrolling a predominantly black neighborhood is not necessarily *unequal protection of the law*.

Looking backward at the past, many a litigant and law student has learned the hard way that what the law calls "the facts of a case" is not the same as *what happened*. And looking forward to the future, many a lawmaker will eventually come to realize that no mere concept of social reality—no matter how persuasive according to the standards of conventional thought at any given point in history—could ever prevent its own subversion by the inevitably anarchic movements of real, living human beings. Theodor Adorno, whose extraordinary book *Negative Dialectics* anticipated this book's turn to the particular by 40 years, put the matter this way: "Even a robot can learn to copy analytic categories," he wrote, but only a living human being is capable of noticing the "*untruth of identity*," namely, "*the fact that a concept does not exhaust the thing conceived*" (1973, pp. 5, 29–30) (emphasis added).

The untruths of identity in the political and legal spheres have become particularly visible in recent years. An honest diagnosis of today's sociopolitical "mood" throughout much of the Western world reveals a widespread and growing skepticism about the unity and truth of stentorian "ought" and "is" statements made by our leaders—that is, various types of factual-cum-normative putdowns and/or exhortations uttered by politicians, judges, priests, teachers, scientists, business executives, and other high mucky mucks in society. No longer does logically valid reasoning based on authoritative premises about assumed facts enjoy the ancient privilege that traditional rabbinical sources accorded to God's commandments: namely, the privilege of not having their ultimate basis and justification (*ta'amei ha-Torah*) revealed or even inquired-after. Nowadays people are prone to roll their eyes more than ever before in the presence of reasoning that pretends to be universally valid notwithstanding the partiality of its effects.

Mainstream political theorists have even begun to speak about this mood of skepticism in terms such as "political decay" (Fukuyama, 2014), "a deficit of legitimacy" (Meaney, 2015, p. 30), and "democracy's disorientation" (Dunn, 2014, p. 85). They also tend to bemoan the phenomenon and impute it to theoretically correctable institutional deficiencies and unrealistic popular expectations. Alarm-inducing terms such as "decay," "deficit," and "disorientation" paint a picture that is hard to get rid of—one that increasingly tends to "hold us captive," as Wittgenstein (1953, p. 48e) put it, the more these terms are repeated. In this case, the pictured state of affairs is not merely one of a general decline in the perceived trustworthiness of official, authoritative speech. It is, in addition, the picture of a decline that can and should be *reversed* by collective effort aimed at restoring an imaginary state of normalcy.

From the point of view taken in this book, however, names such as Hiroshima and Chernobyl, not to mention Auschwitz, Rwanda, My Lai, Bhopal, Wounded Knee, and Tuskegee evoke experiences and memories that are impossible to reconcile ever again with the possibility of bestowing unwary confidence in what our leaders say and what their prescriptions for progress (or conservation) stipulate. And yet, on the other hand, it is also the case that many (even most) people still keep on getting tricked and fooled on this score by the rhetorically skillful utterance of mere words. Perhaps this is because the language of "ought" and "ought not" tends to take on the same emotional coloring as the reality that it attempts (always unsuccessfully) to subdue, and because in a world that is full of so much suffering it is hard to let go of the will to moral optimism based on faith in clever planning, or planning by the clever.

Like the ascetic Manichaeism of the ancients, various modern-day forms of moral optimism hold that the present world, and human beings in particular, present a mixture of good and bad that can in principle be disaggregated and redeemed in the name of goodness and justice, if only we are prepared to give it the right sort of effort. But somewhere along the pathway leading to this book it became clear, to this author at least, that no truly thoughtful and observant person living in the second decade of the twenty-first century could fail to appreciate the truth of what has become one of postmodernism's greatest contributions to our understanding of politics, law, and justice. Namely, the insight that human beings are always letting themselves be tricked by language and the images they evoke into believing in the inevitability of their limited possibilities and the permanence of the social arrangements that constrain their imaginations. Cultural pessimism—the reactionary view that some agent or agency is responsible for creating the decadence of the present era as compared to some previous golden age[2]—is rooted in this sort of self-trickery. But so too is the opposite narrative of cultural progress, which holds both that the present, however awful it may seem, is still better than the past, and that the future will be better still—not just for some, but for everyone.

Someone who thinks that the grumpiness of cultural pessimism and the Panglossianism of cultural optimism are both caused by the enchantments of language cannot in good faith set his or her motivational compass in either direction. This explains why the aforementioned dead ends of politics, law, and justice were found to be *existential.* To be precise, they are existential in the sense that Camus implied in *The Myth of Sisyphus* (1955, p. 3): "*Judging whether life is or is not worth living amounts to answering the fundamental question of philosophy*" (emphasis added). For it seems clear now that the inchoate concerns keeping the present philosophical journey going all had to do, in one way or another, with the question whether a life in the law—even one spent in the pursuit of justice—is worth living, and if so, how a disenchanted person might come to bear the living of it without constantly having to lie to himself.

Disenchantment is not identical to disillusionment, or at least it should not be confused with the kind of disillusionment that is associated with classical Marxism. Someone who has "lost his illusions and regained his reason" in Marx's sense (1964, p. 44) may be disillusioned with, say, religion, but he remains more than willing to be enchanted by another sort of linguistic enterprise—the language of dialectical materialism, for instance. Disenchantment, on the other hand, can come only to those who have become disillusioned with the ethical claims made by reason itself. Among other things, this implies that disenchantment does not give rise to any superior sort of knowledge or intellectual insight: a disenchanted person does not, for example, see through bourgeois ideology to envision reality as it truly is, cleansed of all false consciousness and purely phenomenal appearances. Disenchantment is not omniscience. It does not even aspire overmuch to that condition—not because it values ignorance more than knowledge, but because it believes, with Wittgenstein (1993, p. 39), that knowing every *fact* there is to know would still end up knowing too little of importance for ethics.

Nor is disenchantment the same as mysticism. The typical mystic, notes Žižek (1999, p. 165), is someone who "wants to isolate the event from the network of its symbolic consequences: he insists on the ineffability of the event, and disregards its symbolic consequences." A truly disenchanted person, in contrast, is someone who fully accepts the fact that *discourse* in all of its many forms (politics, law, justice, religion, high theory—you name it) can and does cause many powerful effects in the world. It's just that such a one views discourse as being no different in principle than any other element in what Max Weber (1949, p. 78) called the "infinite causal web."

Viewed through the lens of causation alone, all linguistic usages show themselves to be "perlocutionary" in Austin's sense (1975, pp. 109–120). That is, they tend to produce certain psychological, social, and material effects that bear no necessary relationship to what the speaker intended by virtue of having employed words to *mean* something (language seen as a "locutionary" act) or *be* something (language seen as an "illocutionary" act). As Foucault showed in context after context, the causal effects of language and the power it embodies are dialectical: that is, the effects become causes of their own, acting back on the world (including discourse itself) to produce still other effects.[3] Once one decides to think of discourse as a mere *cause* rather than a possible *ground* that reason could reliably posit or rely upon as a warrant for right behavior (more on this distinction later), then discourse that aspires to the glorious status of *Logos* or "The Word" starts to look a little bit less . . . *magisterial* than it once did.

It is important to understand that this way of thinking about language-in-reality is not a form of metaphysical behaviorism. It does not claim that the true being of language is nothing other than human behavior, if only because no possible determination of "true being" and "is" can be made outside language. According to Agamben: "Everything that is presupposed for there to be language (in the form of something nonlinguistic, something ineffable, etc.) is nothing other than a presupposition of language that is maintained as such in relation to language precisely insofar as it is excluded from language" (1998, p. 50). Nor does this way of thinking assert that the meaning of a word is the effect it produces in those who receive it. Wittgenstein was right: "We can respond to the causal theory of meaning simply by saying that if someone is pushed and falls down, we do not *call* the falling down the meaning of the push" (2005, p. 35e). Our many uses of the word "meaning," and the myriad effects those uses produce in the world, are far more complicated than that. Noticing that words *affect* behavior is not the same as asserting that they or their meanings *are* behavior, if only because an occurrence (of words, of meaning, or of their being) never shows itself in reality as anything other than this or that particular determination of the concept of "occurrence" (cf. Heidegger, 2010b, p. 117).

Rousseau once wrote, in a letter to the elder Mirabeau: "All the evil I ever did in my life was the result of reflection; and the little good I have been able to do was the result of impulse" (Cassirer, 1963, p. 127). Although undoubtedly intended as hyperbole, his remark does shed interesting light on the relationship between ethics and reason. It suggests that ethics could only become a slave to rational ontology and factuality if it let the *propositions* generated by ontological speculation and *propositions* about the limits of empirical inquiry predetermine what human beings are allowed to notice about their relationships with others. In the sense the term is used here, however, *disenchantment* means, first and foremost, the acquisition and maintenance of a tolerant yet deflationary attitude toward any and all propositions.

Ethical disenchantment is therefore not a logical deduction from some deep ontological knowledge about the way things really are. Rather, it is a psychosomatic consequence of having noticed with horror that rationally and rhetorically convincing uses of the phrase "the way things really are" can lead (and have led) to massacres just as easily as to moonshots. That unsophisticated understandings of the world and rational errors can sometimes lead to kindness and decency in human relationships is also a fact that the disenchanted mind has not failed to notice.

As the subsidiary paths of politics, law, and justice seemed to grow narrower and narrower, the noisy linguistic usages of politicians, lawyers, and visionaries—

however necessary and appropriate to their ends—went from seeming mildly annoying to seeming profoundly disturbing. Indeed, at some point, these usages began to resemble a predator stalking its prey, and with the same intent: to kill the living creature being stalked and consume it from snout to tail, transforming the victim's flesh into the predator's own form while leaving all the inedible bits of its carcass to the mercy of the elements.

Mimicry is a form of apology, since it adopts the gestures, the vocabulary, and eventually even the mentality of that which is mimed. So continuing down the paths of politics, law, and justice meant choosing to engage in what Foucault (2007, p. 3) calls "the politics of truth"—that is, it meant choosing to limit oneself in advance to noticing and saying only what the grammatical conventions governing these practices permit one to notice and say. But for a disenchanted person, the decision not just to participate in, but *to inwardly pledge allegiance to*, any given one of these discourses becomes more than just a possible lifestyle or aesthetic choice. It becomes an inwardly felt ethical impossibility.

The problem is not that individual ethics and the collective pursuit of social justice are de facto incommensurable. To borrow a Wittgensteinean frame of reference, it is clear that a language-game and form of life[4] can exist—indeed does exist—in which sincerely saying the sentence "My own beliefs about justice require me to do *X*" will make uttering the sentence "But my sense of ethics forbids *X*" sound inadmissible or nonsensical. Certainly guilt "deprived of the alibis of reason is hard to carry," as Camus (2008, p. 65) says. And yet what Lionel Trilling (2008, p. 86) wrote about guilt also strikes a familiar chord that a disenchanted person cannot help recognizing: "One cannot 'accept' the suffering of others, no matter for what ideal, no matter if one's own suffering be also accepted, without incurring guilt. It is the guilt in which every civilization is implicated."

Thus, the most pressing existential problem—the one that is most responsible for creating the urgency of the Fundamental Question—is triggered by the temptation to make ethics and justice harmonious in the first place. The problem does not come from some prior theoretical decision to say that there always exists a radical ontological or metaphysical incommensurability between justice and ethics. It comes from noticing what the effort to reconcile them in a given particular case reveals about the one who makes the effort. "Whoever is virtuous must cut off heads," warns Camus (2008, p. 248). Long before any heads are cut off, however, the effort to conform one's conscience to this or that socially approved idea of justice repeats what Tony Judt (2012, p. 91) has called "the intellectual sin of the [twentieth century]: passing judgement on the fate of others in the name of their future as you see it." Passing judgment, one might add, *with a good conscience* is the worst intellectual sin, for it reveals a latent desire to welcome, if not celebrate, other people's pain in the service of one's historically received understanding of a mere concept.

What a terrible thing it would be to forget yourself so completely, so self-confidently, that the distance between your conscience and your historical circumstances is reduced to nothing. And what a terribly sad thing it would be to let your intellectual mastery and acceptance of some "true theory" of being-with-others (Hegelian, Marxian, Freudian, Heideggerian, Foucaultian, or whatever) preauthorize and prepare the way for this sort of forgetfulness in particular situations. The neo-Spinozist idea that all that happens, happens as a matter of necessity, reflects the extreme hubris of the sort of Western thinking that is certain a person's reaction to *the particular* must be explainable in terms of theory, even though it actually knows only that what is *merely true* can be so explained.

Asking a question about the worthiness of one's own life in the law is "egoistic" by definition. But it must also be said that this book's specific engagement with the Fundamental Question is intended to be egoistic in its means, not its ends. This signifies that the Fundamental Question is not designed to secure existential freedom for the purpose of overcoming the kind of "bad faith" that Sartre famously posited in *Being and Nothingness* (1956). For Sartre, self-deception was conceived primarily as a disease of an isolated consciousness: a craven acceptance of the verdicts and stereotypes of others, when in fact one could choose to live "more authentically" by letting Being's "For-Itself" continually challenge and negate its "In-Itself" (Sartre, 1956, p. 628). In contrast, the absence of self-deception that the present work posits is ethical (and therefore social) through and through. Self-deception is bad not because it deprives the self of the chance to live authentically, but because it contributes to the making of a world where others are deprived of the chance to live at all.

If, ethically speaking, the use of words is seen to reside on the same level as landslides, pouncing beasts, and other causal forces, then prudence suggests that it should probably be accorded the same kind of respect that an alert wilderness guide would give to an unstable boulder or a growling mountain lion. But alas, words deserve no greater ethical respect than this. Apart from their effects on our behavior, "no sign leads us beyond itself; nor does any argument" (Wittgenstein, 2005, p. 50e). Considered solely from the point of view of someone for whom reason is neither more nor less than what happens to be *called* "reason" at any given point in time, discourse no longer possesses the consistent power to *beguile*. Indeed, one might say that the extent of a person's enchantment with language can be measured by the degree to which words cause them to imagine and believe that what they happen to be doing is fully justified by what those words "mean"—a point that Chapter 2 will develop in considerable detail.

Although this book will eventually affirm that a disenchanted life in the law can be worth living, it should be noted that a negative answer to this more modest version of Camus's "fundamental question of philosophy" would not imply suicide, as he himself suggested. But it would constitute a warning that continuing to perform the conventional role of a willing functionary in the system (as lawyer, judge, law professor, etc.) would probably make one's life existentially excruciating. Even if Nietzsche (1968, p. 451) is right that we must tell ourselves lies in order to live at all, there are some lies that lose the capacity to convince or reassure us once they are exposed. And who knows, perhaps there is another way to live an ethically decent life in the law that does not require us to deceive ourselves quite as much as we have done in the past.

The triune *Politics/Law/Justice*

The *ēthos* that is displayed in these pages is not the product of some sort of free-floating hope or desire for a kinder, gentler world, however personally welcome the advent of such a world might be. Nor is the book's *ēthos* a mere deduction from a metaphysical stipulation or phenomenological finding, *à la* Martin Buber or Emmanuel Levinas, about the other-regarding essence of the human being. Rather, the first part of the title, "The ethics of justice . . . ," must always be considered from the point of view indicated by the second part, ". . . without illusions." The latter morpheme is meant to indicate a radically deflationary attitude toward the ideas and images that, taken together, comprise the conceptual triune *Politics/Law/Justice*.

To *deflate* is not to dismiss. It must be borne in mind throughout that manifesting a deflationary attitude toward the institutional ideas of politics, law, and justice is not the same as repudiating them, any more than declining to worship Hephaestus, the Greek god of hammers, is the same as deciding never again to make use of a hammer. Questioning whether a disenchanted life in the law is worth living presupposes the possibility that a life spent in the *law*, as opposed to some other endeavor, might be worth living.

By the same token, manifesting an attitude toward justice is not the same as expressing a theory of it. The etymological root of "theory" is the same as that of "theater": the Greek word *thea*, which means the act of seeing something. Just as seeing a play and talking about it are two different sorts of activities, the standpoint of theory in the sense of theoretical discourse is twofold—it can be compared to that of a critic who watches a play in order to write a review of it for tomorrow's newspaper. Theory in this sense manifests the will to identify the particular with the generalizations of knowledge under the constraints of a deadline. Truth conceived as a representation of reality that is adequate to some task (e.g., the enforcement of law) is always in a hurry to divest itself of all that is not identical to itself. The one who single-mindedly aspires to know in order to do is like a "melting pot," as Levinas (1996, p. 13) puts it, where "every Other is transmuted into the Same." The Same is the finite plenum of care filled up by knower-and-task before the task is even begun; the Other, in the present context, is the upsurge in reality of the pre-domesticated particular.

"The history of mankind is the history of the myths with which it covers up reality," observed Camus in his philosophical diary (2008, p. 11). All theoretical discourse about justice is mythological in the precise literary sense of an oft-repeated story or tale containing recurring themes that are meant to convey a significant cultural message about how to control and manage human relationships. Thus, a theory of justice is at once a theory of how to make things always the Same and, conversely, a non-theory of the particular. A *hyper*-theoretical point of view, in turn, thinks it knows for sure what must be preserved as the Same at all costs. Conservative icon Robert Conquest displayed this attitude perfectly when he said "Everyone is a 'reactionary' on things he knows about" (*The Economist*, August 15,

2015, p. 49). To which the *ēthos* of this book replies: the more a disenchanted mind thinks it knows about a given person, situation, or aspect of social life, the *less* inclined it is to want to raise a wall of certainty around it.

The first stirring of human freedom, considered from a purely phenomenological point of view, is the concrete experience of discomfort at the prospect of the particular being absorbed by the Same. This determination of freedom's origin would hold even (or rather especially) when the immediate source of the threat to make something the Same is the resistor's own consciousness, wherein his or her most cherished categories lie waiting, like hungry predators, to consume the particular from snout to tail, leaving behind all the inedible bits for the elements. A deflationary attitude toward justice exhibits existential freedom in this sense, in as much as it reflects a predisposition to be surprised (and perhaps moved to action) by the arrival of a particularity that, being a priori non-identical with the Same already, can also be made *to appear* that way with the expenditure of some effort. The cost of freedom, on this interpretation, would be the psychological and social costs of expending that effort—the effort of resisting the program that the Same insists we impose on reality.

Let it be agreed, with Aristotle (1253^{a}10), that we humans are linguistic beings through and through, social animals endowed with the power of speech and reason (*zoon* or *anthropon logon echon*). Let it even be agreed, with Heidegger (1998, p. 239), that language is the house of being (*Die Sprache ist das Haus des Seins*), in the sense that thinking "lets itself be claimed by being so that it can say the truth of being." In that event, it would still be the case that no agreed-upon statement of anthropological fact (Aristotle) or of ontological conviction (Heidegger) could ever predetermine how the statement itself is or should be *received* in this or that particular circumstance by those who generally accept it as true. Being inclined to accept a statement as true does not establish the ethical value that one sets (or should set) on its truth, or even on the word "true" itself, in a given situation. As was mentioned before, the principal reason for this book's deflationary attitude toward linguistic usages in the theoretical-conceptual sphere is the phenomenon of *disenchantment*—the subjective loss of faith in the magical power of normative language to decisively ground (as opposed to cause) the particular actions it happens to inspire, including above all the infliction of pain on others in the service of a norm-derived "duty" or "preference" to inflict it.

But there is another reason why the book shows a strong inclination to deflate the triune *Politics/Law/Justice*. Intimately related to the phenomenon of disenchantment, this second reason stems from the observation that the triune's constituent members seem to be linked to one another in the bad infinity of a repeating historical cycle. As Chapter 2 will show, the concept of this cycle is derived from a similar set of ideas contained in Walter Benjamin's 1920 essay *Critique of Violence* (1978, pp. 277–300). Here, however, the cycle is not offered as a binding law of history, *à la* Hegel or Marx, or even *à la* Benjamin himself. Rather, it is but another way of expressing the phenomenon of disenchantment, albeit in historical terms.

The concept of this historical cycle focuses primarily on giving an ideal type or model of change in political and legal conditions in those post-Enlightenment societies that eventually came to think of themselves as popular democracies governed by the rule of law—Britain, France, the United States, Australia, Japan, India, etc. The model's dialectical moments can be described in general terms as follows: (a) political struggle routinely leads to laws (or entire legal regimes) that offend the normative sensibilities of some (or many) people; (b) offensive laws, or laws offensively administered, lead to a yearning for a better justice beyond existing law; (c) the yearning for extralegal justice tends toward political action, either reformist or revolutionary; and (d) successful political action leads to the enactment of new laws to secure the permanence of the latest victory over injustice and (incidentally) over the political losers. With the completion of this last movement, the cycle itself is closed and, at the same time, the sequence of its moments is reinitiated.

Sometimes slowly, sometimes all at once, the aforementioned historical cycle (henceforth "the HC") undermines the capacity of any given set of general social procedures to remain fully in charge of anything real for very long. Just as medieval Christian mysticism and the growing availability of scripture in the vernacular made for the exercise of a "counter-power" to the Church's then-dominant model of pastoral power (Foucault, 2007, pp. 191–226), so too various manifestations of the HC in modernity constitute a sort of counter-power to biopolitics. Foucault (2007, p. 120) defines the latter term as "the general procedures for taking charge of life and illness in the West." If we adopt this definition, then it must also be noted, in all honesty, that everyday instances of disgruntlement with the biopolitical system's "taking charge of life" have subverted its tendencies at the margins, both in little ways and big. *Little ways*: consider the challenge to biopolitical power posed by the legions of rebellious, anarchist-minded individual computer hackers around the world. *Big ways*: consider the ongoing political and legal turmoil in America and Europe created by Edward Snowden's recent revelations about the scope and extent of the U.S. government's electronic surveillance in the post-9/11 era (Greenwald, 2014).

At the outset, the HC is characterized by the emergence of politically attractive ideas and images of social arrangements that seem to glow in the soft light cast by labels such as "good," "right," "just," "useful," etc. The ideas need not be attractive to everyone, of course, but only to those (let us call them "the winners") who will in fact succeed, for whatever reason, in instantiating them. But then it almost always comes to pass that the winners mistake the verbal expressions of their ideas and images for what will actually be done with them in particular situations later on—as if reality were like a block of marble that already contained the exact form it will eventually become in the hands of a sculptor whose commission simply states "Carve the figure of a horse." This sort of mistake—taking a linguistic sign for how it will be used—is constantly repeated because the *being of the particular*, as it were, is by definition always disappearing; it therefore exhibits what Badiou (2003, p. 187) calls a "perfect weakness" in comparison to the easily iterable abstractions of ideas and images.

To be completely fair to the winners and those who go along with them, it should be said that the confusion of the ideal with the real is sometimes made on the basis of naïve hope rather than out of venality or carelessness. Perhaps this helps explain why Camus (2008, p. 108) once characterized history as "a long crime committed by the innocent." The intended goal of the winners may even be a state of universally beneficial social harmony and not, say, furthering their own narrow interests or enjoying the sadistic gratifications of oppression for its own sake. They say that, in music, discord is the condition of harmony; if so, then "this may be very profitable and delightful for the music lover, but certainly much less so for the one to whom is assigned the role of discord" (Camus, 1965a, p. 177). The particular as we have defined it is *always* discordant in relation to the universal. Indeed, even winners can become discordant losers when their own previous conceptions of the good and the just are used by the system to grind them down in unforeseen or unforeseeable new situations.

Hence, the official social program established by the temporary winners starts to impose a series of "suffocating closures" (Žižek, 1999, p. 204) on unique particularities in the name of some allegedly universal concept of the good or the right. In the short run, a wide variety of social conditions, including historically derived relations of privilege and the pace of technological change, will determine whether the degree of suffocation inflicted by these closures begins to alarm many people, or only a few. In the long run, however, their cumulative effect nurtures a mood of dissatisfaction that can diminish or extinguish the glow of the original ideas and images, even in the eyes of the winners themselves.

In the greying light of a new reality that some (or many) now see to fall short of the previous ideal, still other ideas and images are ignited to supplement or replace the old ones in the imaginations of those winners (and would-be winners) for whom continually riding the merry-go-round of *Politics/Law/Justice* provides the only possible answer to all that is disappointing in social life. And then behold: some of the new ideas and images are expressed and even enacted; they too get mistaken for what will in fact be done with them in the future; and once again a set of norms is used to manage (and to suffocate) particularities. For the millions who just go along with the HC as the path of least resistance, or for the sake of their careers, "the price for survival is practical complicity" (Horkheimer and Adorno, 2002, p. 178) in what keeps on happening, *always in particular*, in a reality that inevitably exceeds all efforts to reduce it to a set of manageable unities.

This cyclical movement shows itself most visibly in the context of what political commentators are wont to call "unstable" societies—ones that are constantly changing regimes as a result of serial instances of bad government leading to civil unrest, which leads to more bad government and more civil unrest, and so on. Political cartoonist Kevin Kallaugher recently drew an archetype of such a society in a way that makes the aforementioned *circularity* of the process central to the message.

One can infer from the speaker's comment in the middle of the cartoon that he believes some societies are "stuck on a roundabout" of instability, while others

Figure 1.1 Politics/Law/Justice in an unstable society

have managed to "turn the corner." And he is right about this *if* the sole criterion of a society's having "turned the corner" is a relatively long period of time characterized by the absence of overt civil unrest and the presence of routine, orderly political transitions among members of the class of political elites (e.g., parties in and out of power) that are widely accepted (or acquiesced-in) as legitimate in that society. By this criterion, the Soviet Union, for example, began to "turn the corner" to stability by 1923, just after the Russian Civil War ended. And the United States has "turned the corner" numerous times—after the end of the Revolutionary War, after the end of the American Civil War, after the end of the war in Vietnam, and so forth.

As we shall see, however, it is a central theme of this book—drawing on the insights of Benjamin and Foucault, not to mention Marx—that the bad infinity of the HC is a feature of just about every modern society, including even (or rather especially) those which present themselves as being particularly stable in outward appearance. Every Ozymandias likes to boast of the permanence of his works, even (or especially) when the moment arrives for him to begin toppling into the sand. Emphasizing the cyclical nature of the triune *Politics/Law/Justice* is therefore another way of representing the progression of social life through time as "a war without end as the basis of history and the relationship of domination as the explanatory element in history" (Foucault, 2003, pp. 215–216).

It will be noted that the foregoing account of the HC makes politics, law, and justice look like a rotating carousel in which all of the horses move up and down, round and round, in a horizontal circle. This is not the way the carousel looks from an enchanted point of view. The latter sees the ride as spiraling ever upward on a trajectory established by an invisible gyre called "progress." During any given moment or series of moments, it may appear that some horses are stuck in the up position and others stuck in the down position (e.g., masters up, slaves down; bourgeoisie up, workers down; men up, women down; the 1 percent up, the 99 percent down, etc.), but enchanted theory likes to tell a redemptive and ultimately cheerful story about all the horses. It interprets the real interactions among politics, law, and justice as if they traced a primary gyre that, given the right amount of time, commitment, and/or effort, will eventually lead to a better world for everyone.

Enchanted stories of this sort are sprinkled all along the political spectrum. On the right, for example, there is the kind of advice that preaches the virtue of individual fortitude and patience in the face of economic misery and the spectacle of rags, at least once reasonably stable market institutions have been established on the basis of formal freedom and equality for everyone. A rising tide of freedom and prosperity will eventually float all boats, on this view, if only we don't try to channel the water this way or that in the misguided attempt to enact some self-defeating conception of distributive justice (Hayek, 2007).[5] On the left, there is the classical Marxist view that the age-old class struggle, though it has taken different forms during the course of history, will come to a postrevolutionary happy ending with the advent of a worldwide communist society that unites the self-realization of every individual with the needs of the community (Elster, 1985, pp. 446–447). In between left and right on the political spectrum, there are many other enchanted stories, of course. These tend to tell optimistic tales about the need for cautious pragmatism aimed at tolerably progressive (yet fair) goals: the "realistically utopian" political philosophy found in John Rawls's *The Law of Peoples* (1999, p. 11), for example, or the picture of "law as integrity" that is drawn in Ronald Dworkin's *Law's Empire* (1986, pp. 225–275).

No one could rightly claim that there are not enormous political and social differences among the different enchanted stories mentioned above, or that their real practical consequences would not be different if they were adopted as social policy. The point to be made here is not that one's political values, choices, and commitments do not matter—clearly they do. Rather, the point is that precisely *because* they matter, precisely *because* they can have very real consequences, it becomes all the more important to reflect on an ethical assumption that appears to be common to all of them. On the enchanted view—*any* enchanted view—the responsible individual's moral duty is to locate and mount the right expression or image of goodness, justice, or progress, and then to ride it over or through whatever intractable obstacles to its realization may arise. The downfall of the wicked or the undeserving, as determined by doctrine, is to be sought and celebrated (or at least tolerated), as is any perceived general rise in elevation during the journey toward what terms such as "the good," "the just," and "progress" seem to mean.

Paradoxically, the hope for a better future that encourages people to participate in the projects of politics, law, and justice can at the same time lead to the death of hope, and even literal death, for those particular human beings who are sacrificed so that the projects can be realized. The enchanted, for as long as they remain fully enchanted, appear to lack what Keats (1818) famously called "Negative Capability, that is, when a [person] is capable of being in uncertainties, mysteries, doubts, without any irritable reaching after facts and reason." In an enchanted frame of mind, belief in the possibility of gyre-like historical progress toward the images evoked by the words "good" and "just" morphs all too easily into an ethical excuse for remaining indifferent to the cruelties committed along the way. If it thinks about them at all, the enchanted imagination interprets norm-authorized cruelties to others as necessary outputs of a repeatable process—mere examples of how a well-functioning system of goodness and justice *must* work if it is to keep something called "society," or "the nation," or "humanity" moving ever upward in the direction traced by the gyre of progress.

In contrast to the enchanted view of history, the intent behind this book's *circular* description of politics, law, and justice is quite different. Its basic ontological premise, as we have seen, is that whatever content of reality is taken up by any given concept of reality (whether gyre-like, circular, or otherwise) is vanishingly small compared with what remains (cf. Heidegger, 2000, p. 144). Thus, the HC does not pretend to be a comprehensive scholarly "explanation" of world history, *à la* such ponderous tomes as Oswald Spengler's *The Decline of the West* (1996). Its goal is much less pretentious. Its only purpose is to serve as a regulative idea for investigating the possibility of an ethics of the particular.

Not only is such an ethics possible, but its existence might also be a condition of the possibility of having any ethical experience at all. This can be inferred from Agamben's argument about the necessary anti-essentialism of any conception of ethics that rejects the dogmatism inherent in the notion of setting out to perform a pre-given ethical "task":

> The fact that must constitute the point of departure for any discourse on ethics is that there is no essence, no historical or spiritual vocation, no biological destiny that humans must enact or realize. This is the only reason why something like an ethics can exist, because it is clear that if humans were or had to be this or that substance, this or that destiny, no ethical experience would be possible—there would only be tasks to be done. This does not mean, however, that humans are not, and do not have to be, something, that they are simply consigned to nothingness and therefore can freely decide whether to be or not to be, to adopt or not to adopt this or that destiny (nihilism and decisionism coincide at this point). There is in effect something that humans are and have to be, but this something is not an essence nor property of a thing: *It is the simple fact of one's own existence as possibility or potentiality*. But precisely because of this things become complicated; precisely because of this ethics becomes effective.
>
> (Agamben, 1993, p. 42)

Seen from the point of view of the particular—this book's constant frame of reference—neither the struggle for recognition between Master and Slave (Hegel, 1977, pp. 111–119), nor the class struggle (Marx and Engels, 1998, p. 34), nor any other world-historical struggle has ended. It is not even on the way to ending. The particular cannot afford to wait for social struggles and the suffering they cause to cease sometime in the future, at the end of history. Nor can any sort of ethics that cares about the particular. For such an ethics, a compassionately grasped mess, right now, is always truer to the requirements of life than an elegantly reasoned truth about the vector of history (cf. Judt, 2012, p. 270). Channeling Agamben, one might say that if we must insist on thinking of ethics in terms of tasks, then its first and foremost task would be to remain open, *always*, to the possibility of deviating from any pre-given task.

"Attention must be paid"

Historian Fritz Stern (2015, p. 55) recently observed that although post-Napoleonic Europe went a full century without producing any large and catastrophic wars, much of the period was marked by the most appalling sorts of brutality: "Between 1750 and 1913, about 300,000 European and North American soldiers died in battle; they were but a tiny fraction of the indigenous populations that were killed." To be sure, it is also the case that the "corner" mentioned in Kallaugher's cartoon (Figure 1.1) was repeatedly "turned" by many societies during this period. Achieving social stability on the winners' terms can feel a lot better than dying (or worse) in the midst of violent social strife, not only for the winners, but also for the losers. As Hegel (1977, pp. 111–119) reminds us, doubtless many (or most) of the latter would rather live ignobly in "peace" as bondsmen than die valiantly in "war" as defeated would-be lords.

Thus, instability gave way to relative stability after such events as: the dispossession and virtual eradication by whites of the native population in North America during the nineteenth century; Germany's 1907 colonial genocide of the Herero tribes in South-West Africa; Britain's "appalling violations of decency" in response to the Indian mutiny of 1857; and, in "the greatest horror of that century," as Stern puts it, the transportation and exploitation of those human beings who survived the Middle Passage (80–90 percent of 12.5 million souls) only to toil as slaves in European colonies in the Western hemisphere and on plantations in the American South. And yet, even after all these and countless other depredations and murders had been committed in the name of nation, empire, and economic progress, as Stern (2015, p. 56) rightly observes, "it was left to the twentieth century to see how utterly brutal and dehumanizing the world could become."

Unflinching realism about the bloodiness of the past prepares the way for unflinching realism about the sufferings of the present. When combined, these two realisms are consistent with the following regulative idea for thinking about the personal ethical situation of anyone whose life in this or that "peaceful" region of the world happens to coincide with a period of relative political and legal stability: *All apparent social stability is the sign and seal of a previous instability that has been only partially subdued by some sort of conquest.* The successful maintenance of political stability in a society, though it is always more or less temporary on the long scale of historical time, vindicates the last conquerors and conceals what they did to achieve their victories no matter how reasonably it may be expressed and no matter how much it is taken for granted by those who have since come to naturalize its continued existence.

To put it all as plainly, albeit bluntly, as possible: social stability is built atop the dead bodies of history's losers, and it is maintained athwart the living bodies of their descendants, in the largest sense of that term. The category of new losers, descendants of the old, should not be viewed narrowly, *à la* Hegel and Marx. They are not temporarily downtrodden vessels carrying forward the spark of a just future in which the last oppression of man by man will give way to a fully realized universal conception of humanity. As was mentioned earlier, an ethics of the particular cannot afford to wait for the end of history. The new losers are, quite simply, all those individuals and groups that suffer from failing to flourish (or worse) under what Walter Benjamin called, in the seventh of his *Theses on the Philosophy of History*, the prevailing "documents of civilization":

> All rulers are the heirs of those who conquered before them. Hence, empathy with the victor invariably benefits the rulers. . . . Whoever has emerged victorious participates to this day in the triumphal procession in which the present rulers step over those who are lying prostrate. According to traditional practice, the spoils are carried along in the procession. They are called cultural treasures, and a historical materialist [not to mention a disenchanted individual] views them with cautious detachment. For without exception the cultural treasures he surveys have an origin which he cannot contemplate without horror. They owe their existence not only to the efforts of the great minds and talents who have created them, but also to the anonymous toil of their contemporaries. There is no document of civilization which is not at the same time a document of barbarism. And just as such a document is not free of barbarism, barbarism taints also the manner in which it was transmitted from one owner to another.
>
> (Benjamin, 1968, p. 256)

If, as Benjamin suggests, there is a *continuing* taint left over from past barbarisms, this is not because the members of each generation are somehow personally guilty for what their ancestors did. The word "barbarism" comes from the Greek *barbaros*, meaning "foreign," especially with reference to speech. Mimicry is a form of apology, since it adopts the gestures, the vocabulary, and eventually even the mentality of that which is mimed. To reproduce and apologize for a given state of affairs, a mime need not understand the causes of what she mimes—she need only be good at copying what other people do. The taint from past barbarisms is still *here*, in present institutions, because we keep on cluelessly miming the gestures of that past, thereby reproducing its effects in the present. The "documents of civilization" to which Benjamin refers—laws, principles, norms, traditions, etc.—are with (and inside) us today as babblings from a past whose essential foreignness vis-à-vis every present particularity is rarely "heard," so to speak, owing to the fact that we have let ourselves become enchanted with the language that expresses them.

Benjamin does not say that past barbarisms taint the *documents* of civilization, as if the latter, left to their own devices, could somehow magically "determine" unequal and unjust patterns of distribution in the present. He says that the barbarisms taint the documents' *manner of transmission* from one owner to another. To remain perennially deaf to the babbling incoherence of the inherited linguistic sign as such—the inert symbol "*X*" as opposed to what it seems to mean or require—is always to punish, and be punished, "under a foreign code of conscience." This phrase of W.H. Auden's (1972, p. 919) was originally intended to refer to the inability of the dead to control how their words will be received by the living. But it also seems to be an apt way of describing the analogous inability of even the living themselves to control how they will in fact receive those words in particular situations. If there is such a thing as Original Sin, it does not derive from disobedience to God's commands; it comes from the fact that *every* human decision, whether to obey or disobey, "bases itself on something not mastered, something concealed, confusing" (Heidegger, 1971, p. 55). Past barbarisms do not taint our documents; they taint us.

The point is not that the collective pursuit of justice is incommensurable "in fact" with ethics. Surely it is empirically possible for a language-game and form of life to exist in which sincerely saying the sentence "Justice requires me to do *X*" will make uttering the sentence "Ethics does not let me do *X*" seem inadmissible or nonsensical. Even a child knows that guilt deprived of the alibis of reason is hard to carry. Hence, "as long as there is one beggar around, there will be myth" (Benjamin, 1999, p. 400). The biggest myth going is that just or necessary suffering, as somehow "measured" (a mere metaphor, after all) by the norms and standards of the era, is a priori deserved or unavoidable, and therefore that it should be of no ethical concern to those who inflict or benefit from it.

The distinction between enchantment and disenchantment becomes particularly visible precisely at this point in the discussion. An enchanted mind sees no ethical problem in the effort to harmonize its most cherished ethical norms with its most cherished norms of justice—it considers that effort, however difficult it may be, to be part of the solution, not a deeply problematic move in itself. Once harmony is achieved, a commitment always to follow a fully unified canon of *ethics-and-justice* means choosing always to engage in what Foucault (2007, p. 3) calls "the politics of truth." That is, it means pledging to limit oneself in advance to noticing and saying only the kinds of things that the grammatical conventions governing the expression of that unified canon authorize one to notice and say.

The enchanted mind is not necessarily historically naïve. It will perhaps concede that history has *caused* a certain "opportunity set" of social norms and institutions to emerge in today's world, and that this set might have come out differently under different historical circumstances. But having made a brief nod to the role of history in the production of modern normative sensibilities, it will still cling to the illusion that the linguistic expressions of these institutions (legal norms, theories of justice, ethical rules, etc.) are capable of providing rational, supra-historical *grounds* for choosing or not choosing to continue their "meanings" into the future. Faith in the possibility of personal and social progress hangs on maintaining this illusion, as does the possibility of acquiring a good individual conscience on account of doing what the word "progress" seems to require. For what Reinhold Niebhur (2015, p. 28) observed about religious belief is no less true of secular belief: "It is only one step from a vivid image to the touch of magic."

When the disenchanted mind looks at these texts, however, it fails to see any ahistorical "meaning" that is not the immediate result of the hypostasis of someone's particular state of mind into an ephemeral image whose main function is to provide ethical cover for what comes next. For the disenchanted, the decision not just to participate in creating an integrated expression of ethics-and-justice, but *to inwardly pledge allegiance to* that expression, becomes more than just a political or aesthetic choice. It becomes an ethical monstrosity. It is not some radical empirical or ontological incommensurability between justice and ethics that creates the monstrosity, but rather what the effort to reconcile them in any given case reveals about the one who makes the effort. What the effort reveals is a latent desire or willingness to tolerate, if not celebrate, the idea of the other's pain in the name of a fully reconciled sense of justice and good conscience.

The hyphenated noun *ethics-and-justice* indicates a tendency toward subjective reconciliation that is common to legal positivism and natural law theory alike, although its advocacy is somewhat more disguised in the former tradition. Unlike natural law, at least legal positivism's so-called separability thesis makes a preliminary show of separating questions of law from questions of individual morality (Coleman and Leiter, 1996, p. 241). However, positivism does not *also* separate one's ethics from one's extralegal sense of justice. On the contrary, the fact that positivism openly allows for individual moral resistance to unjust laws is the only thing saving the separability thesis from the charge that it advocates the existence of a moral duty to act unjustly if the law requires it (e.g., Hart, 1961, pp. 181–207).

The positivist's plea for "clarity" and "candor" about the relation between law and morals is therefore not a plea to completely ignore the latter in favor of the former. Rather, it is meant to support the claim that individual citizens and officials *should* say, in the face of an unjust law, not that it is not law at all, but rather that "this *is* law; but it is too iniquitous to be applied or obeyed" (Hart, 1961, p. 203) (emphasis added). In legal positivism, as in natural law theory, one's individual ethical responsibility ends once legal rules have been vetted for their consistency with the applicable norms of justice. The possibility that the possession of a "correct" subjective conviction about the rightness of the applicable norms of justice might itself present an ethical problem is not considered.

Although advocacy for the reconciliation between justice and good conscience is present in legal positivism notwithstanding the separability thesis, it is much more visible in the natural law tradition. With the possible exception of Cicero (1999), no thinker in that tradition comes close to rivaling Thomas Aquinas in terms of prestige and influence. "An unjust law," the latter wrote, "has the nature, not of law, but of violence" (1948, p. 633) (I-I Q. 93, Art. 3). Aquinas, following Augustine, believed that only just human ordinances are properly called "law," by which he meant only those rules that conform to the law of nature that God has implanted in human reason.[6] Since, according to Aquinas, natural law is itself supposed to be a reflection of God's own eternal law, it follows that if a human law "denotes a proneness to sin, it is contrary to divine law, and has not the nature of law."

Considered merely as an artifact of history, it is possible to view Aquinas's distinction between the categories "just law" and "violence" as but one stratagem in the centuries-long political struggle between religious and secular authority during the Middle Ages. But his rhetoric also promotes a more subtle kind of mythology—propagated to this day by law and justice alike—about the ultimate value of achieving closure through the unity-bestowing assertion of conceptual correctness. According to this myth, which is quasi-alchemical, the classification of all that happens by means of the legitimate criteria of existing knowledge transmutes every particularity into a mere object ruled by a concept whose own normative status is all that matters. If a given state of affairs is correctly classified as "illegal," "unjust," *and* "evil," the human beings who are found to have participated in making it a reality are tossed into these categories body and soul, so to speak, without leaving any visible remainder to trouble the integrity and permanence of the conceptual jails in which they are imprisoned.

Aquinas's distinction between law and violence thus provides a clue to a presupposition that is common to all forms of natural law theory, whether ancient or modern, religious or secular. Implicit in every theory of natural law is an apology for just suffering, where justice is defined in advance as the correct application of an authoritative concept with the right moral provenance. If an ordinance properly counts as "just law" by whatever conceptual criteria the thinker happens to employ, then it follows on this view that its enforcement in any given case by the just application of violent means is not only morally unproblematic, but also perhaps ethically compulsory.

In short, natural law equates ethics with morality, and both of these with the correct application of just norms. The part of this equation pertaining to *just norms* then takes center stage, while the part about *correct application* is relegated to the lesser status of a mere technique, or, at most, a useful method to test the norm's outer limits of applicability (i.e., casuistry in the traditional sense of the term). The conventional kerfuffle about the acceptability of so-called cultural relativism thus takes place on a terrain that is guaranteed in advance to favor the proponents of natural law in the eyes of the average person. The truth of an abstraction that sounds better in frightened Western ears ("Terrorism is evil and must be stopped by any means necessary") seems almost self-evident; whereas the truth of a countervailing abstraction ("Terrorism is the weapon of the weak whose root causes must be addressed") has the burden of demonstrating itself as true before a skeptical audience.

In thinking about the typical context of this sort of war of norms, it is especially important for present purposes to notice how natural law theory, like all theoretical discourses, tends to extinguish any ongoing awareness or memory of particularities. As Benjamin was one of the first to notice, natural law's enthusiastic endorsement of the *just* application of *just* law makes any particular event of a just law's enforcement appear unremarkable, akin to the swatting of a mosquito:

> It [natural law] perceives in the use of violent means to just ends no greater problem than a man sees in his "right" to move his body in the direction of a desired goal. According to this view (for which the terrorism in the French Revolution provided an ideological foundation), violence is a product of nature, as it were a raw material, the use of which is in no way problematical, unless force is misused for unjust ends.
>
> (Benjamin, 1978, pp. 277–278)

"It is a terrible thing to condemn even a terrible man," said Vasily Grossman (2009, p. 64), thereby contradicting natural law's aforementioned naturalization of the sort of pain that is justly inflicted and suffered. Standing against this view, the abstractions of politics, law, and justice not only encourage us to use their criteria exclusively in deciding whether someone is a "terrible man," but also to take satisfaction (if not pleasure) in doing so.[7] The opinion that it might be a "terrible thing" to condemn such a man comes from somewhere outside the sphere of conceptual correctness, and therefore poses a grave threat to the smooth operation of the existing system of abstractions.

Paying close attention to the agonistic details of any one person's particular encounter with the gears of the social and legal system is unbearable to an authoritarian way of thinking, for it strikes at the foundational principle of all domination. That principle is studied indifference to everything that the canon does not authorize one to notice as a "fact." To ignore the continuing emergence of the particular in reality in favor of a single-minded quest to subsume facts into premade concepts is to engage in what Adorno (1973, p. 172) called "peephole metaphysics." And yet, as Linda Loman said about her husband Willy in *Death of a Salesman* (Miller, 1958, p. 56), there are times when the existential imperative of not lying to oneself means that "*attention must be paid*" to the particular even when its correct conceptual classification seems unavoidable.

The continuum *War–Peace*

Once the guns inflicting overt historical violence fall silent, and the survivors of social conflict manage to crawl out of the ruins, the establishment of even the most just imaginable set of juridical institutions will still have to continue to anoint (relative) winners and subdue (relative) losers. This happens not only within the narrow context of civil lawsuits and criminal prosecutions, but also more broadly throughout society in the form of the pain and gain that are always co-produced by the particular ways in which the legal order distributes rights, duties, privileges, and immunities on the basis of the last effective victory.

Persuasive demonstrations that the law, despite its protestations to the contrary, is not merely corrective in nature, but also distributive and redistributive (in the largest sense of these terms), have been made off and on since Marx's day. They constitute some of the earliest and best contributions to our understanding of the legal order by American legal realism, and by such later movements in legal theory as critical legal studies, feminist legal theory, critical race theory, and queer legal theory. For example, scholars associated with these movements have shown over and over again how facially neutral language in legal rules (e.g., the "reasonable person" in tort law) conceals a historically contingent and socially partial conception of the way the rules should be and are applied (e.g., Bender, 1993, pp. 61–63). The ethical implications of the relentless unmasking of law's political dimension by scholars associated with these movements is best understood from a standpoint that Scott Veitch calls the "sociology of denial." That is, one of law's most important accomplishments is to *conceal its role as a concealer* by pretending to be exclusively about justice between individuals, thereby "obfuscating the effects of power in the structures of social relations" (Veitch, 2007, p. 12).

Like the cartoonists who scold or praise them, would-be lawmakers tend to depict their preferences for the future in the form of more or less crudely constructed tropes, such as Mussolini's "All within the state, nothing outside the state, nothing against the state" (2013), and Ronald Reagan's "It's morning again in America" (1984). Words like these are deployed in the present to gain support for policy prescriptions that are designed either to replace or to reinforce existing socio-legal arrangements. To be sure, not all word-pictures portray futures that are morally equivalent or equally viable. Closely studying and questioning the utopian or mythical[8] images evoked in the minds of true believers by the words that politicians use to describe their ends is undoubtedly an existential imperative for anyone who wants to avoid living in squalor, or worse, in a slaughterhouse.

Also important and necessary are certain forms of active participation in political life, including especially overt resistance to the ongoing oppression of politically weak and vulnerable individuals and groups. It is clear that ethics cannot be so squeamish as to abjure any and all political action, a point that Levinas (that most ethically squeamish of all modern philosophers) made abundantly clear when he said: "If self-defense is a problem, the 'executioner' is the one who threatens my neighbor and, in this sense, calls for violence and no longer has a face" (1998b, p. 105).

There is a difference between an action and its motive, however. Eventually this book's author began to suspect that allowing himself to be motivated by pretty images of a better world might *always* be a form of ethical self-delusion. Images come and go; they rise in popularity and decline in popularity. During different periods in the political history of any given society they will have been successfully marshaled to support the enactment of measures aimed at a huge variety of ends. Despite their heterogeneity, however, the vast majority of these ends can be classified into one of three general categories: (a) the preservation of some cherished golden picture of the past (*conservatism*); (b) the construction of an alternative reality based on some glorious picture of the future (*utopianism*); and (c) the methodical movement from one policy-guiding micro-image to another on the basis of some overarching macro-image that is itself inspired by words like "efficiency" or "what is best on balance for society" (*pragmatism*).

It is obvious, however, that no mere image has ever squirmed and bled the way human bodies do when put to the lash by image-mongers who are eager and willing to make the world look more like their favorite picture of it. Politics, though ethically preferable to overt violence in most cases, thrives on interpersonal struggle and the more or less triumphant overcoming of resistance. The Hobbesian conceptual opposition between peace (as the site of politics) and war (as the site of violence) can make the phrase "peaceful war" sound like an oxymoron to anyone who believes that peace is peace, war is war, and never the twain shall meet (Hobbes, 1914, p. 67). But it is possible to gain a different perspective on the relationship between peace and war if one starts to take seriously two theories that collapse the one into the other from opposite directions. The first is Clausewitz's notorious thesis that "War is not an independent phenomenon, but the continuation of politics by other means" (Clausewitz, 1984, p. 7). The second is Foucault's scandalous reversal of that proposition to read: "Politics is the continuation of war by other means" (Foucault, 2003, p. 15).

It seems probable that a craving for the heart-numbing benefits of a purely *intellectual* sort of peace lies at the root of the Hobbesian view that war and peace are absolute antitheses. This peace—the peace of a good conscience—is threatened by a hypothesis such as Foucault's (2003, pp. 15–16) that:

> the role of political power is perpetually to use a sort of silent war to reinscribe that relationship of force [the effects of power from the last battle], and to reinscribe it in institutions, economic inequalities, language, and even the bodies of individuals.

It would seem that one of the most important consequences of the binary Hobbesian view of war and peace is that it tends to produce a mood of indifference toward the quotidian, "peaceful" suffering of others when armies are not marching. It also produces a mood of resentment toward anyone who dares to disturb the existing state of "law and order" out of a sense of anger, hopelessness, or desperation.

If, however, one views the distinction between peace and war not as a binarism, but rather as a continuum between extremes, then the correct application of these terms becomes not so much a question of "fact" as it is a function of the sensibility or temperament of the person who draws the distinction. Seen from a critical, non-apologetic point of view, military conquest and the pacification of hostilities

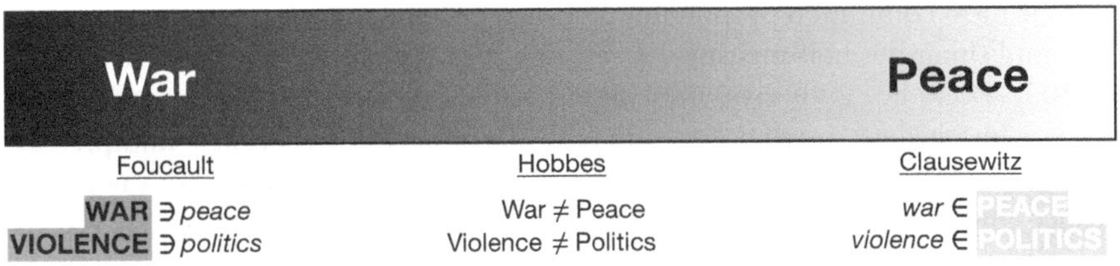

Figure 1.2 War and peace: a continuum

through force of arms bear a "family resemblance," as Wittgenstein (2005, p. 204e) might have put it, to the coercive administration of law and order by the police and the courts.

When viewed exclusively from the Hobbesian midpoint of the continuum shown in Figure 1.2, reality appears to force one to make an either/or, black/white decision regarding any particular instance of socially imposed human suffering that happens to come to one's attention: either it was caused by war or it was caused during a time of peace. If it is the former, there is a presumption that it could and should have been avoided by the establishment of a just peace under the rule of law. If it is the latter, the presumption is that the suffering in question is avoidable only through the peaceful pursuit of legal or political remedies.

If, however, one looks at the real particularities of life and cannot help seeing shades of grey in them, then the conventional classification of a situation as occurring in "peace" as opposed to "war," or vice versa, will not be determinative. Seen from a disenchanted point of view, there always seems to be a political element in war (Clausewitz) and a warlike element in politics (Foucault).

As for what happens during times of "peace," what Scott Veitch (2007, pp. 1, 4) calls the "amnesiac capabilities of legal thought and practice" operate to conceal the consistent and patterned ways that legal institutions operate to "facilitate dispersals and disavowals of responsibility" for certain warlike consequences. Not only does the law discharge the ordinary social function of an ideology that supports relations of power and privilege inherited from the past, law's abstract generality also requires its practitioners to liquidate all unique particularities so as to bring everything under the common measure of its rules and principles. From a disenchanted perspective, however, ethical sensibility simply cannot ignore the particularities that fail to find a foothold in existing legal arrangements—it cannot un-see "the tears that a civil servant cannot see" (Levinas, 1996, p. 23)—without ceasing to be ethics.

Although stable regimes can usually count on the everyday acquiescence of the masses and the active cooperation of collaborators and profiteers, they can also begin to elicit a certain amount of sympathy and solidarity with those who are victimized by their policies. When sympathy and solidarity become overt resistance in the name of justice, and when that resistance succeeds, against all odds, in overthrowing injustice, a kind of reverse alchemy starts to set in.

The most committed proponents of justice are almost never content to rest with accomplishing the half measure of resisting unjust positive law. As Pascal (1941, p. 103) (*Pensée* no. 298) says, they almost always yearn to go further and "make what is just strong, or what is strong just." In order to memorialize and preserve their unexpected victory over injustice, the victors seek to transform the gold of justice into the base metal of new legal arrangements. Thus, it is that the will to justice, if it is to be in any way effective, bends either toward the forcible maintenance of existing "just" legal relations or toward the forcible establishment of a new, "more just" legal regime or law. In the latter case, some losers become winners, some winners become losers, and a new warlike peace breaks out, only to begin boorishly stumbling into the future in much the same way its predecessor did.

The point to be made here is not that the various ethical critiques of law and justice mounted by this book, as well as by thinkers such as Benjamin, Levinas, Foucault, Veitch (2007), Critchley (2014), and Etxabe (2013), are all more or less trying to say "peace is war" in the same general way that *1984*'s country of Oceania used Newspeak to say "war is peace" (Orwell, 1961, p. 7). On the contrary, the intent behind the phrases is completely different in the two cases. Oceania used the latter slogan to suppress certain destabilizing social questions before they could be asked ("Who are we fighting and why are we fighting them?"). The foregoing ethical critiques of law, on the other hand, want to do the opposite: they want to destabilize things by putting into question an everyday answer that most people take for granted ("A state of law and order means that people are not fighting with one another at all").

Nor does paying attention to legally unrecognized particularities imply the proposition that it is always morally bankrupt to construct and rally around inspiring words and images in politics, law, and justice. Human beings *like* and *need* words and images, and there is no point in pretending otherwise. But a linguistic sign or image, though unquestionably real enough to be perceived, is not reality itself. The point of trying to pay attention to pre-domesticated particularities is that expending the effort can allow us to recognize the ways in which our psychological and emotional *attachment* to words and images has lead us into doing (and allowing to be done) many degrading and horrible things to one another—things that the images themselves do not or cannot allow us to recognize *as* "degrading" or "horrible." Evil is not the existence of a state of affairs that violates a norm. Rather, "evil is the will to name at any price . . . the desire for 'everything to be said'" (Badiou, 2003, pp. 66–67).

The main task, so to speak, on the path leading to disenchantment is to destroy idols without replacing them with new ones—not even "the absence of idols" (Wittgenstein, 2005, p. 305e), which is the most seductive idol of all. Once a person has seen, or rather experienced, that this is so—once he or she becomes disenchanted—there is no going back. That is why all of the chapters that follow are concerned, in one way or another, with elucidating the theme of the ethics of justice without illusions as it bears upon the Fundamental Question. Which is, to repeat once again: *Is a life in the law, even one spent in the pursuit of justice, worth living, and if so, how might a disenchanted person come to bear the living of it without constantly having to lie to himself?*

Notes

1. All our space-time verifications invariably amount to a determination of space-time coincidences. If, for example, events consisted merely in the motion of material points, then ultimately nothing would be observable but the meetings of two or more of these points. Moreover, the result of our measurings are nothing but verifications of such meetings of the material points of our measuring instruments with other material points, coincidences between the hands of a clock and points of the clock dial, and observed point-events happening at the same place at the same time.

   (Einstein, 1916, p. 776)

2. Cultural pessimism is as old as human culture and has a long history in Europe. Hesiod thought that he was living in the age of iron; Cato the Elder blamed Greek philosophy for corrupting the young; Saint Augustine exposed the pagan decadence responsible for Rome's collapse; the Protestant reformers felt themselves to be living in the Great Tribulation; French royalists blamed Rousseau and Voltaire for the Revolution; and just about everyone blamed Nietzsche for the two world wars.

   (Lilla, 2015, p. 43)

3. Foucault (1980, p. 98) famously described the dialectic between discourse and its other in terms of a reciprocal cause-and-effect relationship between power and what is generally called "the individual": "In fact, it is already one of the prime effects of power that certain bodies, certain gestures, certain discourses, certain desires, come to be identified and constituted as individuals. The individual, that is, is not the *vis-à-vis* of power; it is, I believe, one of its prime effects. The individual is an effect of power, and at the same time, it is an element of its articulation. The individual which power has constituted is at the same time its vehicle."
4. "I shall call the whole, consisting of language and the actions into which it is woven, the 'language-game' [*das Sprachspiel*]" (Wittgenstein, 1953, p. 5e). "Here the term 'language-*game*' is meant to bring into prominence the fact that the *speaking* of language is part of an activity, or of a form of life [*einer Lebensform*]" (1953, p. 11e).
5. Cf. the advice lampooned in Joe Hill's song *The Preacher and the Slave* (Folk Archive 1997):

   Long-haired preachers come out every night,
   Try to tell you what's wrong and what's right;
   But when asked how 'bout something to eat
   They will answer with voices so sweet:
   You will eat, bye and bye,
   In that glorious land above the sky;
   Work and pray, live on hay,
   You'll get pie in the sky when you die.
6. "As Augustine says, *that which is not just seems to be no law at all.* . . . [I]f at any point it departs from the law of nature, it is no longer a law but a perversion of law" (Aquinas, 1948, p. 649) (II–I Q. 95, Art. 2).
7. "Thomas Aquinas, the great teacher and saint: '*Beati in regno celesti,*' says he, as gently as a lamb, '*videbunt poenas damnatorum, ut beatitude illis magis complaceat*' ['the souls in heaven will be able to enjoy the blissfulness of paradise all the more because they can view the torment of the damned in hell']" (Nietzsche, 1927a, p. 661) (Part I § 15).

9. The radical opposition between utopia and myth was first proposed by the nineteenth-century anarchist Georges Sorel (1999, pp. 28–29), and then adopted, however briefly, by the young Walter Benjamin (1978, p. 292). According to this theory, a utopian movement is well organized and knows what it wants to achieve; it lays down a blueprint in advance that can be evaluated and criticized for its verisimilitude and immediate practicality. Any social movement for justice that carries within itself a well-formed image of the state of affairs that its success would bring into being would fall into the category of the utopian, on this view. However, it is always possible to refute a utopian image by showing that it is inconsistent with the necessary conditions of modern production. It is not the same with social movements animated and organized by a myth. As Sorel (1999, p. 29) put it, "A myth cannot be refuted since it is, at bottom, identical to the convictions of a group, being the expression of these convictions in the language of movement." Mythological movements are unanalyzable as parts apart from their whole to be trivialized on Sunday morning talk shows. They are expressions of pain, of rage at the machine itself, and as such they are just as distant from sophisticated and bureaucratic "programs for change" as the language of the law is from the real life that it aspires to regulate.

Chapter 2

The journey to disenchantment

> Humanism cannot persist simply as love for the victim. It is easy to love the victim.
>
> George Oppen (2007, p. 112)

Generality

The generality of a legal or moral rule is not a material property of the linguistic sign that expresses it. The sign "*Thou shalt not kill*" is colored black, but it is no more general, and no less particular, than "*Mary killed John*," "*Blah blah blah*," or any other configuration of ink marks on paper. This simple, if not banal, observation about language (or better still, pre-language) has many implications for the study of law, justice, and ethics. One particularly important implication, in the words of Wittgenstein, is as follows: "The essential thing about [a rule], its generality, is inexpressible. Generality shows itself in application. I have to *read* this generality *into* the configuration" (Waismann, 1979, p. 154). Or, to put it even more succinctly: *Rule-Sign* "*X*" + *Application of Rule-Sign* "*X*" → *General Scope of Rule X*.

If, over time, a group of people (e.g., lawyers) keep on applying an iterable configuration of signs—say, the string of words comprising a legal rule—in noticeably similar ways, then it becomes possible to describe the customary "meaning" or "general scope" of the rule by abstracting from these applications to make yet another iterable configuration of signs. Or, more simply: "*Rule X means Y*." Indeed, law professors, treatise writers, and Supreme Court justices do this sort of thing all the time. To put it in terms of set theory, these people make lists of some (but rarely all) of the actual applications of a legal rule (the rule's partial "extension" to date), and then, based on their interpretations of the cases on the list, they provide general statements of how the rule is applied (the rule's "intension"). Once again, however, the *generality* of this newly articulated meaning or scope of the rule is not a material property of the linguistic sign that expresses it. "*A rule is not like the mortar between two bricks*," as Wittgenstein puts it: "We cannot lay down a rule for the application of another rule. We cannot apply one rule by means of another rule" (Waismann, 1979, p. 155).

To be sure, people can and often do seek guidance from other verbal prescriptions (including other rules) for how to read and apply a given legal or moral rule. But whatever generality a statement about a rule's generality may have, such generality, like that of the original rule itself, can only be shown by *its* application. That is why Wittgenstein said that if a rule could only be applied by means of another rule, "in this way you would never get off the ground," in as much as the sign expressing the second rule (e.g., "*Rule X means Y*") is no more general, and no less particular, than the sign expressing the first rule ("*Rule X*") (Waismann, 1979, p. 155). If there is any mortar between the brick of a given rule and the brick of how it will actually be applied in a particular case, then it does not consist in yet another splotch of ink—it consists in the very act of application itself.

Thus, no matter how compulsory a given reading of a legal or moral rule may seem to be, the feeling of compulsion comes from someplace other than the words of the rule: "It is not the rule which compels me, but rather, I who compel myself to use the rule in a certain way" (Shanker, 1987, p. 17). If learning what people actually do with a rule is our goal, then we deny ourselves access to important information about reality if we refuse to look at any application of the rule that deviates from what the rule itself—or indeed anyone else's utterance about the rule—seems to "say" about how the rule "should" be applied. Although it is a tautology, it is worth saying out loud that the *actually enacted* scope of a rule is shown by how the rule-sign, along with any relevant additional signs called its "meaning," is in fact applied in case after case after case. Or, simply: "The symbol for a class is a list" (Wittgenstein, 1978, p. 461).

Meanwhile, those who keep on applying the rule to particular situations will in fact notice some things, but not other things, under the aspect of the rule. The practitioners of even the most excellent norm-based systems of control are socially conditioned to ignore the particularities of any human suffering that appears to fall outside a given norm's socially constructed sphere of concern. For example, it probably would not occur to very many prosecutors to charge you with murder for using your own money to purchase a diamond bracelet instead of attempting to feed a starving stranger half a world away. This does not mean that it is logically impossible to notice, as Levinas did, that failing to prevent the deaths of starving strangers might violate the prohibition against killing: " 'Thou shalt not kill'—that means then 'Thou shalt cause thy neighbor to live' " (1999, p. 127). That said, however, it is still unusual in the normative realm for someone to make socially unexpected connections of this sort. The first stanza of *The Power of Custom* by the Greek poet Pindar should come as no surprise to anyone who is reasonably observant about the days and ways of everyday social life: "Custom is the lord of everything, / Of mortals and immortals king. / High violence it justifies, / With hand uplifted plundering." (Higham and Bowra, 1938, p. 296.)

The customary routinization of generality is like the routinization of charisma: it solves the problem of ensuring the continuing succession of the same (especially the same attitude toward authority) by trying to suppress awareness of any potentially destabilizing differences (Weber, 1978, vol. 1, p. 246). It does this in part by offering people the sort of ironclad protection from emotional discomfort that St. Bernard of Clairvaux (Bernard, 1839, p. 2216) was the first to mention in a sermon some nine centuries ago: "What the eye does not see, the heart does not grieve over" (*Quod non videt oculus cor non dolet*).

It is possible to detect a strong tenor of moral disapproval inflecting both Pindar's poem and Bernard's sermon. Reading the two texts together suggests the hypothesis that social custom not only determines what we do and do not notice (and care about) in the world, but also justifies in advance the limits of our awareness and our caring. This reading raises a red flag of warning over customary ways of understanding and applying legal and moral norms. It implies that bad things can happen, and ethical difficulties can arise, when individuals automatically equate widely similar behaviors conditioned by socially approved ways of reading texts with the rational, the true, and the right, instead of cautiously interpreting them as manifestations of the customary, the contingent, and what people tend to call "right."

It should be clear at this point in the discussion that the phenomenon previously denoted as "disenchantment" can bring with it a psychosomatic propensity to see more human suffering than the official canon recognizes, and to grieve more on its account. Although there is no strictly logical requirement that a state of disenchantment alter one's inner sense of individual care or responsibility for the suffering of others, in fact it very often does, and it certainly increases the chances of this happening. After all, what the eye does begin to see, the heart can begin to grieve over. If, with Hobbes (1914, p. 69) (ch. 14), we stipulate that a principal motive for altruism is "to deliver [the] mind from the pain of compassion," then to increase one's sphere of compassion is to increase both one's pain and one's need for delivery from it. And this might furnish a pretty good selfish argument against anyone's becoming disenchanted, if it were the case that disenchantment is a state of mind that could be turned on or off at will.

But in the sense the term is used here, disenchantment is neither a lifestyle choice nor an intellectual argument, neither a duty nor a privilege. It is a state of being—a way of looking at the world of politics, law, and justice. What is at stake is therefore not disenchantment in the conventional post-Enlightenment sense of allowing scientific evidence to convince an otherwise gullible mind not to believe in supernatural explanations of natural phenomena (Weber, 1958, p. 139). What is at stake is the unceasing ethical dilemmas that are created after one has in fact lost faith in the capacity of language as such to provide any secure ground for acting that would be sufficient to justify the possibility of a good conscience.

This deep a level of disenchantment should be familiar to anyone who has ever studied the writings of Agamben, Benjamin, Derrida, Foucault, Heidegger, Levinas, or Wittgenstein, to name just a few of the more notable philosophers of postmodernity. The profound ethical challenge that *this* sort of loss of faith presents to any good faith attempt to pursue a lie-free life in the law is obvious. If the faithful performance of duty according to one's most cherished canons of justice and morality is no longer felt to be sufficient for securing a good conscience, then what else could be? There is, of course, more than one way for a person to address this question—just as there is more than one way for a thinker to become disenchanted and feel the need to ask it. So for the sake of narrative simplicity, the remainder of this chapter describes the particular journey to disenchantment that led to the writing of this book.

Beyond Transcendence and the phenomenon of Logical Transcendence

Beyond Transcendence in Law and Philosophy (Wolcher, 2005) was concerned primarily with bringing to light a phenomenon it called Logical Transcendence ("LT"). Each of the words in LT's name is ordinarily taken to possess a certain cachet, as in such statements as "It's better to be logical than illogical" and "It's good to transcend everyday concerns once in a while." But in *Beyond Transcendence*, the sum intended by combining "logical" and "transcendence" into one concept is less prestigious, and far more mundane, than its parts might seem to indicate.

The movement A→B

Symbolized as *A*→*B*, the phenomenon of LT is "logical" only in the original Greek sense of *logos*, or "the word," as in John 1:1's *En archē ēn ho logos* ("In the beginning was the Word"). It involves "transcendence," too, but not in the quasi-religious sense of somehow rising above the quotidian order of things to achieve a higher realm of consciousness, and still less in the technical Kantian sense of the transcendental conditions of the possibility of experience. Rather, LT entails transcendence in a nearly literal sense that is derived from its etymological origins: it means to climb (*scandere*) across (*trans*). In the phenomenology of LT, thought climbs across the temporal gap separating a given expression or image (*A*) of the ground of a proposed action *to* some expression or image (*B*) of that proposed action itself. For example, *A* might be the text of a legal rule, and *B* the expression or image of a proposed decision that is "based," as lawyers are wont to say, on the rule.

Sometimes the mental process that will eventually gel into LT starts with the image of the action that one wants or hopes to perform (*B*), in whose light one searches for and finds a plausible ground (*A*) from a set of possible justifications. (Mainstream legal theory tends to frown on this mode of decision-making by judges, which it maligns as being "result-oriented.") Other times, ground (*A*) and grounded (*B*) emerge reciprocally from a more or less messy process of mutual discovery (Kennedy, 1986). Still other times, judgment in a so-called "easy case" proceeds without conscious reflection on its grounds (*Law's Task* will come to call this phenomenon "reception"), and the grounding movement *A*→*B* appears only after the fact, by way of self-justification. LT's various modes of appearing are interesting in their own right, of course—indeed, their ethical significance is quite important, as we shall see—but as merely different modes of appearance they should not be confused with the essence of LT as such.

Moreover, it is beside the point whether the action that one *actually performs* immediately after or immediately before this grounding movement of the mind has occurred corresponds to what a knowledgeable observer would call an instance of following the grounding statement "correctly." Considered from the point of view of the actor, a reason that will later be rejected as incorrect is still his or her reason for acting, just as reliance on a misguided ground is still some kind of reliance on a ground. The whole point of describing and elucidating LT is ethical in the more or less traditional sense of *agent ethics* rather than *spectator ethics* (Lacey, 1986, p. 68). Thus, the phenomenology of LT adopts the "internal" perspective of the actor rather than the "external" perspective of someone trying to evaluate or explain what the actor has done. On the other hand, LT's focus on the internal perspective of those who perform legal operations is not meant to bring with it the baggage of normativity that is associated with theories that explicitly or implicitly attempt to *justify* the rule of law from the "internal" perspective of a judge (e.g., Dworkin, 1986, pp. 13–14; Hart, 1961, p. 10). Paying attention to LT is supposed to open up ethical problems and dilemmas rather than closing them down with a programmatic solution.

The prehistory of LT in any given case—that is, an account of why a particular pair of variables following the schema $A \rightarrow B$ was discovered (as opposed to some other pair) and then allowed to congeal into the image of a stable relationship that seems to lead from a ground to an action—has proven itself to be vitally important to the analysis of law by critical legal historians and other scholars (Gordon, 1984). But this sort of prehistory is, strictly speaking, irrelevant to the phenomenology of LT as such. Any given instance of LT undoubtedly has its own causes and conditions, of course, just like every other phenomenal occurrence. What is more, the decisions and actions that accompany LT within a given context (e.g., the judicial system) can be seen to fall into patterns that are accessible to the gaze and classificatory systems of an external investigator—patterns that can be imputed to this or that stereotypical cause or condition generally operative within this or that social theory, be it comprehensive, ad hoc, or even intuitive. Linguistic conventions, shared institutional understandings, economic class relations, attitudes toward race and gender, ideological presuppositions, social-psychological mechanisms such as cognitive dissonance, and so forth—these sorts of social structures have been deployed time and again in legal theory and historiography to explain why a given decision came out the way that it did, rather than some other way.

Nevertheless, the most important feature of LT is not *why* it comes into consciousness on a particular occasion. As Schopenhauer (1999, p. 37) observes, the potential causes and conditions of the will are as many and as arbitrary as the intensity and direction of breezes playing upon a weather vane. Nor does LT's significance lie in the fact that its results are (or should be) counted as correct or incorrect by the criteria of this or that language-game employed in this or that form of life (Wittgenstein, 1953, p. 11e). The key thing to notice about LT, once it takes hold of the mind, is that it tends to provide psychological and emotional *reassurance* to the one who has performed or is about to perform an act that he or she believes to be justified by the ground. Ethically speaking, LT is like a warrant that allows one human being to inflict pain on another in good conscience.

Western thinking tends to overlook LT's purely phenomenal side in order to bestow or withhold encomiums on its products according to various criteria of correct derivation or judgment. Moreover, once everyone within a particular linguistic community (or at least everyone who counts) has accepted that a given result is correct, the corresponding event of LT itself fades into obscurity. If the procession from *A* to *B* is considered at all, it is assumed to have been validated in advance by the principle of sufficient reason—*nihil est sine ratione* ("nothing is without a reason")—and its various corollaries, including the doctrines of logical necessity and causal necessity (Heidegger, 1991, p. 3). By means of a psychological reversal resembling the fetishism of commodities (Marx, 1906, pp. 81–96), the dry abstraction of what is produced *by* LT (e.g., the proposition "Result *B* is well-grounded in rule *A*") is taken to be the living butterfly, and the living movement that produced it (LT itself, or $A \rightarrow B$) is cast off as the dead chrysalis. The correct expression triumphs over the living process, and the true eclipses the real.

The psychosomatic inclination to take hold of and cling to the dead expression of a living process lies at the root of much of what human beings do to one another in the name of the rule of law. The sociological terms for the result of this inclination are *legitimation* and its correlative, the bestowal of *legitimacy* (Weber, 1978, pp. 31–33). Given the political and psychological stakes involved, it is little wonder that modern legal theory has experienced an overwhelming impulse to settle the question of the "true" relationship between word and world, or law and life, once and for all.

Indeed, the impulse for closure on this question bedevils *rule skepticism* no less than its antithesis, *rule fundamentalism*. The first view, to quote Wittgenstein (1953, p. 81e), holds that "no course of action could be determined by a rule, because every course of action can be made out to accord with the rule," and is associated with the so-called "deconstructive turn" in legal theory. Whereas the second view maintains that the proper expression of a rule, *A*, can indeed predetermine its correct application (*B*) by establishing a meaning that "leaps off the page," as Stanley Fish (1989, p. 358) puts it, to overcome all rational opposition. Instead of simply giving a bland report, as Wittgenstein did over and over again, about what the phenomenon of following a rule actually looks and feels like in various settings, both rule skepticism and rule fundamentalism are in a hurry to prove something *absolute* about the nature of legal norms. This is because both points of view spring from a common source: a politico-philosophical obsession with solving, once and for all, the abstract problem of language's "objective" determinacy or indeterminacy (Kripke, 1982).

Even such sophisticated intermediate positions in liberal legal theory as Ronald Dworkin's "Right Answers" thesis (1986, pp. viii–ix) are motivated by a desire to obtain a definitive solution to this problem. Thus, Dworkin gives an elaborate foundational account of legal practice in which various socio-legal factors (e.g., the background principles of law and morality in a given society) are said to objectively constrain the interpretive discretion of decision-makers. His breathless descriptions of law's empire seem meant to vanquish forever the "skeptical thesis that there are no right answers" (1986, p. ix), and to bring an end to "the depressing history of social-theoretic jurisprudence" (p. 14).

During the first two decades of the critical legal studies movement, an exceedingly large share of scholarly attention was devoted to debating the question whether legal rules and principles are logically determinate in Dworkin's or anyone else's sense (compare Schauer 1985 with D'Amato 1989). The early CLS slogan, "Law is politics," was taken on one side of the political spectrum to be the entailment of a deep metaphysical truth about the malleable nature of legal language (e.g., Kelman, 1987, p. 258), and, on the other side, to constitute a false or reckless attack on the metaphysical foundations of democracy and the rule of law (e.g., Carrington, 1984, p. 227). With a few notable exceptions (e.g., Kennedy, 1986), in neither case was much attention paid to the phenomenological structure of LT as such, that is, to how following a legal rule—any legal rule—might show itself concretely in experience.

Still less attention was paid to the *ethical* implications of tracing the Western idea of the rule of law to an underlying phenomenon that shows itself in experience as something less glorious, less intellectually and emotionally reassuring than its hagiologies have always invited us to believe. To be sure, as an ideal type, the rule of law remains distinct enough when compared to other ways of organizing authority in society (Weber, 1978, pp. 215–216). But it is (or should be) ethically disturbing to recognize that the rule of law, though real enough in its own right, at the end of the day rests its claim to validity not on the metaphysically assured (or at least presumed) true meaning of legal rules but rather on what Wittgenstein (1953, p. 81e) characterized as "a way of grasping a rule which is *not* an *interpretation*, but which is exhibited in what we call 'obeying a rule' and 'going against it' in actual cases." For the distance between what one takes to *be* correct and valid and what one merely takes to be *called* correct and valid is infinite, ethically speaking. In the one case, the ethical self allows itself to be submerged beneath its grounding statement, which washes all before it like a tidal wave; while in the other case, there remains a troubling sense of distance between what "we" (the collectivity that calls a thing correct and valid) want to happen and what the ethical self may believe that *it* should want to happen.

The customary

When considered from a purely phenomenological point of view, LT shows itself in experience as the mental and even physiological sensation of being conveyed or carried along by a stable movement from ground to grounded, from *A* to *B*. Perhaps nowhere is this phenomenon more pronounced than in the routine enforcement of the existing legal order, where officials and functionaries tend to think of themselves as bound by antecedent norms. A well-known passage from Chekhov's short story "Ward No. 6" describes one of the characteristic effects that the constant repetition of LT in practice produces on the psyches of those who do the enforcing:

> People who have an official, professional relation to other men's sufferings, for instance, judges, police officers, doctors—in course of time, through habit, grow so callous that they cannot, even if they wish it, take any but a formal attitude to their clients; in this respect they are not different from the peasant who slaughters sheep and calves in the back-yard, and does not notice the blood.
>
> (Chekhov, 2003, p. 56)

The word *custom* denotes the way of being that Chekhov describes. The Greek word *adikia*, usually translated as "unjust," originally meant that something is not right with things as they stand—that the world is "out of joint" somehow (Heidegger, 1975, p. 41). But the origin of the feeling that things are out of joint is not merely this or that bit of normative text—it is custom in the largest sense of the word. Ever since Aristotle (1131^{b}25–1132^{b}20) identified corrective justice with the restoration of an intermediate position between one person's unjust loss and another's unjust gain, the will to justice in the West has operated for the most part on the basis of the psycho-social principle known as "dyadic completion." According to the latter, a perception of victimhood requires that someone be blamed as an immoral perpetrator, and a perception of immorality requires that someone be identified as a victim. And the psychosomatic trigger for having these perceptions in the first place is ultimately pre-theoretical.

The customary is what pretty much everyone comes to take for granted about the rightness and naturalness (or wrongness and unnaturalness) of a given state of affairs. An injustice, like *adikia*, occurs when this rightness and naturalness is seen to be disturbed. William James (1904, vol. 1, p. 120) said that the ethical implications of habit born of custom are "numerous and momentous," remarking that "it alone is what keeps us all within the bounds of ordinance, and saves the children of fortune from the envious uprisings of the poor." His definition is a reminder that it would not be too bad a definition of the concept *critical legal thinking* to say that it is the kind of thinking that tries to take as little for granted as is humanly possible about the customs and habits of the existing legal system.

Unlike the word *law*, which connotes the notion of a choice to follow or not follow what the law commands, customary ways of being do not necessarily or even ordinarily involve a prior decision to adhere to the customs in question. This is why we often say that we do what other people around us tend to do out of "habit" rather than because reason requires it. Properly understood, the relationship between the rational and the habitual, or the legal and the customary, is not antagonistic or antithetical—it is complimentary. The reciprocity between law and custom in this sense is the basis of Pascal's great insight that "custom creates the whole of equity"—not because it is right or just, but rather "for the simple reason that it is accepted" (1941, p. 101) (*Pensée* no. 294) ("*La coutoume fait tout l'équité, par cette seule raison qu'elle est recue*"). For just as there are customary ways of dressing and eating, so too there are customary ways of understanding the texts of the law, not to mention the stereotypical human relationships that they aspire to structure and control.

Conformity with customary ways of reading normative texts can be emotionally comforting. From the standpoint of ethics—the principal theme of the present volume—the experience of LT is particularly significant for those who yearn to have their views and actions validated by something outside the sheer facticity of their own bodily performances. Once this outside thing (the ground) has been formulated, it can be offered as a whipping boy to assume responsibility for any harms that may be caused by what one does in its service. The idea that law and morality occupy distinctly different spheres (the so-called "separation thesis" of legal positivism) overlooks this feature of LT, because it assumes that any potential conflict between behavior required by the law and behavior required by morality is actually a conflict between two different grounding *statements* imposing two different and antithetical *duties*—for example, "Legal norm *L* requires me to do *B* but moral norm *M* forbids me to do *B*" (cf. Fuller, 1958, pp. 648–657).

The dutiful

We owe the belief that duty is the product of the correct reading of a statement to Kant, who conceived of moral duty on the model of the legislative process: morality as self-legislation means that the self somehow lays down the law for itself, and only then proceeds to follow (*B*) what the law "means" (*A*). The Kantian notion of duty is the "apotheosis of lovelessness," said Schopenhauer (2005, p. 24), because it subordinates the empirical self's regard for the Other to its regard for its own imaginary noumenal self (*homo noumenon*), considered as a law-giving inner "ideal person (the authorized judge of conscience)" (Kant, 1996, pp. 560–561). That Kant's secular duty-principle has its roots in the phenomenon of theological awe is apparent from his use of religion as a regulative idea in *The Metaphysics of Morals*: "The concept of religion is here for us only a principle of estimating all our duties as divine commands" (1996, p. 561). That the Kantian notion of duty requires not only the generation of duty-imposing sentences, but also a theory of how those sentences could ever produce any effects in the world of sense—that is, a theory of how language "means"—was explored at some length in *Beyond Transcendence*, which characterized the whole Kantian problematic as a variation on the theme of LT.

The process of doing one's duty is sometimes called "playing by the rules," or "acting on principle," and the offloading of moral responsibility onto the ground (whether chosen or taken for granted), together with the narcotizing effect that this produces on the conscience, are two of its darkest and most important features. Of course, the concept of "offloading" something implies that it was previously loaded somewhere else, and the Western philosophical tradition has tended to locate the original site of moral responsibility in the unified subjectivity of an ethical self that is, somehow, capable of assuming responsibility. The quasi-religious mystification necessary to sustain the previously noted Kantian distinction between the describable *empirical self*—incapable of assuming moral responsibility because all of its actions are determined pursuant to the law of causation—and the morally free but ineffable *noumenal self*—capable of generating uncaused moral commands to the empirical self but incapable of acting in the world—shows how vulnerable the ethical self is to deconstruction and dissolution, especially in a secular age. The notion that moral responsibility requires that a choice must always be made by a stable ethical self among objective grounds capable of being listed, so to speak, on a moral bill of fare, is a theme we will return to repeatedly in this book. For now, it is sufficient to note that one of LT's purely psychological effects on someone who realizes that his or her decision will adversely affect the lives and fortunes of others is akin to the feeling of physical relief that comes when one is able to offload a heavy load one is carrying onto a cement platform.

To summarize the salience of the various distinctions and qualifications that have been made up to this point in the discussion: *Beyond Transcendence* very definitely did *not* attempt or purport to offer a general phenomenology or justification of judgment, *à la* Kant's Third Critique (*Critique of Judgment* 2000) or Hegel's *Phenomenology of Spirit* (1977). Instead, it offered a phenomenology and critique, from an ethical point of view, of the *endmost point* of judgment in legal and moral affairs. In addition to the almost physical relief that comes from offloading responsibility onto the ground, the emotional effect of justifying the deed by externalizing the grounding movement in the form of a statement ("I did *B* because $A \rightarrow B$") begins to resemble what happens in the mind and body of an anxious child whose lost security blanket has been found and returned. Just as the child clings tightly to the blanket in relief, so too the decision-maker clings tightly to his or her justification, thereby soothing the conscience and steeling the will in the face of what will soon become the judgment's real consequences.

The fact that in any given case one may offload responsibility onto the "higher law" of a moral ground instead of onto the lesser authority of a merely legal ground is secondary; the fact that *an offloading* occurs in either case is what is primary. There is a common tendency, nurtured by legal positivism, to conceive of conflicts between law and morality as conflicts between the meanings of two different types of sentences: the expression of legal rules and the expression of moral rules (Hart, 1961, pp. 7–8). If one believes, with Aquinas, that mere humans write the first kind of sentences and God has written the second—either on paper, in right reason, or both (*Summa Theologica*, I–II, q. 91)—then the conflict is theologized and the superiority of moral grounds over legal grounds is assured by religious faith. If, on the other hand, one views all language as humanly produced through-and-through, then the hierarchy between these different types of rules collapses and the psychological dilemma created by the conflict between them is reawakened, as in this passage from Lon Fuller:

> The identification of natural law with a law that is above human laws seems in fact to be demanded by any doctrine that asserts the possibility of an authoritative pronouncement of the demands of natural law. In those areas affected by such pronouncements as have so far been issued, the conflict between Roman Catholic doctrine and opposing views seems to me to be a conflict between two forms of positivism.
>
> (Fuller, 1958, p. 660)

What remains unsolved in either case, however, is the problem of how *any* sort of sentence, whoever its author may be, could provide the definitively understood *A* (the ground) for the movement, within the phenomenon of LT, from *A* to *B*. Of course, it is well known that Fuller conceived of his own project in terms of a search for the "principles that will enable men to live together successfully" (1958, p. 600)—principles such as non-retroactivity and understandability that for him constituted "the inner morality of the law" (1969, p. 39). But if they are to have any effect on human behavior, principles must be expressed in sentences no less than rules. If rules and principles can give rise to *grounds* for acting (according to Fuller's, Aquinas's, or indeed anyone else's theory of law), and if *responsibility* for the consequences of action can be offloaded onto these grounds, then a further question naturally arises: *What sort of thing is a ground in its own right, when considered as an emergent phenomenon?*

The phenomenology of grounding in presence or absence

The answer that *Beyond Transcendence* gave to this question began by disaggregating a sign from its signified. Words considered as strictly sensory objects are but phonemes in the air, pen scratches on paper, and body parts used in ostensive definitions (e.g., the gesture of pointing at something with the finger of a hand); so too are all conceivable explanations of the meaning of words by means of still other words and gestures. Thinking that these ephemera make too weak a reed on which to float such an important weight as the true meaning of language, the mind invents something mightier to call the truth: the word's extrasensory *meaning*. A *ground* is therefore the inner hypostasis of an imaginary solidity that Wittgenstein (1974, p. 54) called a *Bedeutungskörper*, or "meaning-body." This entity is supposed to be unbreakably connected in some way to the assembly of linguistic signs that make up a given syntactical unit of language, such as the words "Thou shalt not kill." Thus, for example, it is felt that the Sixth Commandment's expression of the prohibition against killing is not just an arbitrary aggregation of marks on paper (or stone), but that it also "means" something outside and beyond its own materiality qua linguistic sign.

In the phenomenology of LT, once the meaning-hypostasizing moment has occurred, the resulting image of a meaning-body is inwardly felt to dispel and displace "the Shadow" that T.S. Eliot's poem *The Hollow Men* (1934, p. 80) famously positioned between the conception and the creation, the motion and the act. The behavior that immediately follows this feeling of being carried along by a ground is then said to be *grounded* in the meaning-body of the relevant syntactical unit, for the ethical mind yearns to be supported by something objectively real as well as intellectually and morally compelling. LT can therefore be viewed as the phenomenological origin of the widespread belief that rules and norms need only be accepted as binding in order to begin doing "their" work, as if pieces of paper with ink on them had wills of their own, and were somehow capable of "compelling" human beings to perform actions that might otherwise bother their consciences.

The propensity of legal language to generate euphemisms assists in this process of mystification: *stay of execution*, instead of, say, letting John or Mary continue to live for a while; or *balancing the parties' interests*, instead of noticing the radical incommensurability between, say, the economics of toxic waste disposal and the desire to preserve human health. As Orwell (1954, p. 173) observed about the use of similar phrases in the political sphere—phrases like *pacification*, *transfer of populations*, and *elimination of undesirable elements*—euphemisms like these allow things to be named without calling up mental pictures of them; or to be more precise, they substitute more palatable images for what is about to occur as a consequence of a decision for images that would have been far more disturbing had they occurred to the decision-maker.

Within the sphere of traditional political and legal thought, both liberal and conservative, it is relatively easy to find evidence that a thinker has been carried along by a conscience-relieving movement from a given "rational" or "self-evident" ground to the "well-grounded" advocacy of this or that action or program. Perhaps Kant's open admiration and reverence (*Ehrfurcht*) for "the starry heaven above me and the moral law within me" provides the most famous example of this phenomenon (Kant, 1996, p. 269). But circumstantial evidence for the ubiquity of LT in daily life can also be found every time a person says, in all sincerity, "Don't blame me—I'm just doing my duty." Indeed, the quasi-religious belief that LT has to be more than just a psychological phenomenon—that it must have *metaphysical* validity—is probably what allows many people to believe to this day in the truth of John Adams's old saw about the possibility of having "a government of laws and not of men" (Chapin-Pinotti, 2013, p. 37).

Strangely enough, however, *Beyond Transcendence* also discovered that the same sort of yearning for validation extends beyond the realm of bourgeois conformity to law to encompass certain hypercritical postmodern views about the essential nature of legal texts. One such view is that no formal ground could ever be completely solid—"Formalist or literalist or 'four corners' interpretation is not inadvisable (as Posner seems to suggest); it is impossible" (Fish, 1991, p. 56). Another is that every text is in principle infinitely interpretable, always "open to reinterpretation in the light of social and political realities" (Norris, 1988, p. 166). Numerous concrete examples could be discussed at this point, but it will be sufficient for present purposes to mention just one.

The example is taken from Walter Benjamin's extraordinary 1920 essay, *Critique of Violence*. Synthesizing disparate strands of thought drawn from Marxism, anarchism, and kabalistic Judaism, Benjamin (1978, p. 298) asserts there that the Sixth Commandment's injunction not to kill exists not as a scale or criterion of judgment (*Masstab des Urteils*), but rather as a rough guideline (*Richtschnur des Handelns*) that becomes "inapplicable, incommensurable once the deed is accomplished." This claim is followed immediately by the author's passionate condemnation of the doctrine of the sanctity of life for being naïve as well as "false and ignominious" (pp. 298–299). Judaism has never interpreted the commandment as condemning *all* homicides, he notes, citing the traditional non-prohibition of killing in self-defense (p. 298). What is more, the essay had already earlier assailed, on existential and historical grounds, the kind of "childish" anarchism that refuses to acknowledge *any* constraint toward persons: such a view, he said, "excludes reflection on the moral and historical spheres, and thereby any meaning in action, and beyond this on any meaning in reality itself, which cannot be constituted if 'action' is removed from its sphere" (p. 284).

So far, Benjamin's thesis is unexceptionable. Both history and experience offer to teach us a stark and sobering lesson: the infliction of some amount of pain and death on others appears to be an inevitable and necessary element of human (which is to say *social*) reality. A justice that hesitates ever to cause people pain fears to intervene in the world, which is of course impossible in any case, since being alive is itself always already an intervention. The poet Robert Frost once defined a "liberal" (in the American sense) as someone who is "too broad-minded to take his own side in a quarrel" (Miller, 2015, p. 39). But the avoidance of a quarrel can produce just as many consequences, and just as great ones, as a quarrel can. A posture of absolute nonintervention in matters of justice is therefore a contradiction in terms—a point that Pascal (1941, p. 102) (*Pensée* 295) expressed with admirable clarity when he said that even the simple I-affirming sentence "That is my place in the sun" happens to be "the beginning and the image of the usurpation of all the earth." A timid justice that only wishes and hopes, while never directly intervening in human affairs, is not like the harmless "shadow in a dream" to which the Greek poet Pindar refers in his beautiful meditation on the transience of human life.[1] It resembles more an overmedicated nurse sleepwalking past helpless casualties lying on the ground.

The *justification* for any particular instance of intentional pain infliction is an altogether different matter, however. To "act" at all—that is, to be alive, and therefore always to be acting in *some* manner—is to become fully responsible for the consequences of one's actions, including those consequences that flow from the kind of behavior that law and convention call "inaction." In this one respect, at least, modern conservatives who advise people to take greater personal responsibility for their actions are correct, though probably not in the way that they imagine. "When the privileged classes are happily ensconced in their principles, when they have good consciences," as Sartre (2009, p. 17) puts it, their sense of personal responsibility can retreat behind what those principles seem to "say." Far more than the aforementioned social necessity of inflicting pain on others, which some might classify as a biological or anthropological "fact," the conscience-relieving *justification* for an individual's decision to inflict pain in a particular situation rests on an inchoate magical theory of language. That theory supposes that normative words "stand for" something objectively real and fact-like, something that is capable of deciding on its own that a given portion of someone else's suffering is ethically justified or ethically irrelevant.

In an earlier essay, *On Language as Such and on the Language of Man* (1978, pp. 314–332), Benjamin had already heaped scorn on the "bourgeois conception of language," which treats words and sentences as mere means for communicating factual matter. This refusal to give credence to what Wittgenstein would later call the magical, meaning-body view of language meant that the justification, in any given case, of the need to inflict pain and death on others in the name of justice could not come from the objective "meaning" of normative texts such as the Sixth Commandment. *Critique of Violence* reconfirms this in no uncertain terms by distinguishing between "mythical violence" (*die mythische Gewalt*), whose justifications are always predicated on human texts that at bottom operate ideologically to support the ruling class (laws, principles, moral norms, etc.), and "divine violence" (*die göttliche Gewalt*), which Benjamin says is the "sign and seal" of God's sacred execution in the realm of human affairs.

On the last page of this strange but compelling essay, Benjamin observes that only an inscrutable God (for those who believe in him) can ever know for sure whether a particular killing violates his commandment, and therefore whether it is condemned or justified: "For only mythical [legal] violence, not divine, will be recognizable as such with certainty, unless it be in incomparable effects, because the expiatory power of violence is not visible to men" (p. 300). It therefore comes to pass that the essay stakes everything on the possibility that God *might* be working through the hands of proletarian killers to sanctify the use of history-consummating revolutionary violence.

Critique of Violence is particularly noteworthy for present purposes because it shows how very powerful the yearning for an "external" justification of one's decision to hurt other people can be. If even as radical a proto-postmodernist as Benjamin can reject all of the claims made by conventional normativity, and yet still hunger for the same sort of psychological relief that the latter promises (the possibility of a good conscience from having done the right thing), this shows that LT is no stranger to either point of view. Benjamin appears to have believed that the *absence* of a knowable moral ground for human beings to judge particular instances of homicide, either before or after the fact, actually provides crucial *support* for such deeds as "the revolutionary killing of the oppressor" (p. 298): "If the existence of violence outside the law, as pure immediate violence, is assured, this furnishes the proof that revolutionary violence, the highest manifestation of unalloyed violence by man, is possible and by what means" (p. 300). This is a bit like thinking that, since there are and can be no humanly chiseled perfect marble pedestals to stand on, therefore people should keep trying to walk on water in hopes that someday God will decide not to let them sink. For a nonbeliever, however, there are no holy waters, and all liquid places offer exactly the same amount of support for those who try to walk on them (i.e., none).

Based on this and other similar cases, *Beyond Transcendence* came to the conclusion that an absolute absence that is asserted dogmatically is indistinguishable *phenomenally* (though rarely politically) from other, cruder forms of fundamentalism asserting the existence of an absolute presence. The book fleshed out the phenomenon of LT by giving a close comparative reading, from the standpoint of the Eastern philosophical tradition of Zen Buddhism, to texts written by Martin Heidegger (on being), Emmanuel Levinas (on ethics), and Ludwig Wittgenstein (on language). It tried to expose a certain tendency, found even in these most sophisticated of Western thinkers, to cling emotionally to *some* sort of foundational account of practice—if not the presence of a presence, then the presence of an absence. The primacy of Being over beings (Heidegger), ethics as first philosophy (Levinas), and the distinction between the sayable and the unsayable (Wittgenstein): *Beyond Transcendence* claimed that various subtle forms of LT show themselves in all three cases.

To the extent that "the rule of law," "duty as fidelity to a norm," "being principled," and all the other catchphrases that are associated with unqualified faith in normativity, are not consciously deployed as strategies to achieve the aims of power in particular situations, they rest on a magical view of language. They create the impression that the linguistic signs that express the norms of law and justice (rules, principles, customary practices reduced to writing in helpful legal treatises, etc.) *stand* for something else, something invisible called their "true meaning." It is as if the will to law in all of its many forms (positivistic, natural, moral, ethical, etc.) greatly feared the monsters that might come if it were to fall asleep and let go of these meanings, as in Goya's famous etching entitled "The Sleep of Reason Produces Monsters" (*El sueño de la razón produce monstruous*). (See Figure 2.1).

A state of affairs in which all authoritative constraints on the will to cruelty have been suspended can be a terrible thing to witness, and still more terrible to experience, as recent events in Syria, Iraq, Nigeria, Yemen, the eastern Ukraine, and too many other places on earth will readily confirm. There is good reason to fear the monsters that can come when law-regarding reason falls into a coma, and human life sinks to the level of "bare life" (Agamben, 1998). But the cruelty of irrational lawlessness is not the only kind of cruelty there is. *Beyond Transcendence* tried to show that there is a sense in which reason is *always asleep*, even when it is most awake. It drew attention to the fact that monsters might come no matter what actions the well-grounded subject takes. Seen from the radially disenchanted point of view towards which, in retrospect, the book's arguments were tending, the particular human beings who enforce the law in this or that particular situation look less like Solon, the great lawgiver, and more like Oedipus the King as he stood on the verge of discovering and punishing the murderer of Laius: damned if they do, and damned if they don't.

Figure 2.1 "The sleep of reason produces monsters" 1799. From *Los caprichos*, by Francisco Goya (1746–1828)

Photo credit: HIP/Art Resource, NY

The journey on the pathway to disenchantment is only halfway finished if a thinker rests content with giving or receiving persuasive philosophical demonstrations that the traditional claims of reason are based on the fantastic belief that normative language objectively "means" its correct meaning-body in advance of its application (the "magical" view of linguistic signs in a nutshell). To travel all the way to radical disenchantment, one must also let go of the pretense that the many different ways in which this and other kindred insights have been shown by critical thinkers—whether in Wittgenstein's *Philosophical Investigations* (1953), Foucault's *The Archaeology of Knowledge* (1972), Derrida's *Of Grammatology* (1997), or elsewhere—somehow provide superior insight into *how to be with others* in such a way that one could ever go to sleep in good conscience, without being troubled by any of Goya's monsters.

This first book ended by speculating on the possibility—"however remote" (2005, p. 222)—of a radically deflationary attitude toward law and justice: a sort of Buddhist-inspired "middle way," motivated by compassion, which would experience no compulsion to worship or cling to grounding statements, but also no need to feel contempt for them. *Beyond Transcendence* suggested that the real moral difficulty with the axioms that govern today's dominant juridical discourse in the West is not so much that they are "theoretically weak and crude" (*est d'une fragilité et d'une grossièté théorique*), as Derrida (1990, p. 964) put it. The real difficulty is that human beings keep on doing callous and savage things to one another in a state of consciousness that is trance-like—that is, while having allowed themselves to be invaded and taken over by imaginary incubi (the meaning-bodies) of these or any other axioms, no matter how sophisticated they might be.

Law's Task and the legal division of human suffering

The second book along the pathway to radical disenchantment, *Law's Task: The Tragic Circle of Law, Justice and Human Suffering* (Wolcher, 2008), shifted the focus away from the yearning for grounds to the most important consequence of that yearning in the spheres of law and justice: *the division of universal human suffering by legal means*. The adjective *universal* was chosen to indicate a genus—the vast, undivided body of human suffering as such—that logically and ethically precedes its subdivision into species whose emotive names (*justified* versus *unjustified*, *necessary* versus *unnecessary*, *more serious* versus *less serious*, and so forth) seem calculated to comfort those who do the dividing. Like Benjamin's celebrated angel of history, only an unbiased perspective on the whole is capable of bearing witness to the full costs of what history's winners like to call "progress" (Benjamin, 1968, pp. 257–258). Any narrower viewpoint naturalizes the consequences of historical violence by privileging its own pre-theoretical, pre-critical understanding of which human suffering is acceptable and which is not.

Legal normativity in the eye of some beholder

Since at least the late thirteenth century, when Duns Scotus (2005) delivered his then-controversial lecture on individuation at Oxford, Western legal theory has grasped the fundamental existential fact that no two situations, no two events, are ever identical; otherwise they would be one situation or event, not two. Similarity between cases is the most that can be hoped for by any legal system committed to equality under the rule of law (Stone, 1964, pp. 268–274).

Unlike ipseity, however, similarity cannot even *pretend* to be a self-subsisting unity, if only a unity that further investigation will show to be dependent on human apprehension.[2] Similarity is by definition preceded by the existence of a nascent plurality (*A*, *B*), and hence is the product of an act of grouping ("*A* is similar to *B*"). Even if the status of two different things being similar is regarded as some kind of natural "fact," legal theory also knows that the category of similarity requires the eye of some *beholder* if it is to have any legal consequences. "*Behold*" is more accurate than "*judge*" or "*interpret*" in this context, because the latter two terms suggest, falsely, that a recognizable act of judgment or interpretation must occur whenever a similarity is found. Moreover, the verb *behold* better describes one of the most important phenomenological findings of *Law's Task*, namely, the phenomenon of "reception." According to this finding, even the most careful and self-conscious act of legal judgment ultimately dissolves into a passive beholding of something that is taken for granted. To borrow a well-known distinction drawn by Heidegger (1962, pp. 97–98) in *Being and Time*, similarity shows itself phenomenally as "ready-to-hand" (*zuhanden*), like a hammer in the hand of a carpenter, as opposed to merely "present-at-hand" (*vorhanden*), like a microbe studied through a microscope by a biologist (Heidegger, 1962, pp. 97–98).

The implications for legal normativity of the dependency of the category of similarity on some particular event of beholding are extremely significant. Modern jurisprudence has learned the lesson, first hinted at by Aristotle in his doctrine of equity (1137ᵃ30–1138ᵃ1), that no rule is capable of applying itself. As H.L.A. Hart (1961, p. 123) said, "particular fact-situations do not await us already marked off from each other, and labelled as instances of the general rule, the application of which is in question; nor can the rule itself step forward to claim its own instances." Applying a rule is like crossing a bridge: to say that the mysterious act of "meaning a rule" can already decide a case before it arises is like saying that you can cross a bridge before you even get there (Wittgenstein, 1960, p. 142). Only a particular human judgment, freshly minted on each occasion, can bring a state of affairs within a legal norm or exclude it, even (or rather especially) in so-called "easy cases."

At this point in the discussion, it is worth quoting Derrida's oft-cited comment, in *Force of Law*, about the criterion for any decision that aspires to be just. The comment not only reconfirms Hart's point from a political direction that might be surprising to some readers, but it also entails (or at least brings into view) the category of universal suffering prior to its division by legal means:

> To be just, the decision of the judge . . . must not only follow a rule of law or a general law but must also assume it, approve it, confirm its value, by a reinstituting act of interpretation, as if ultimately nothing previously existed of the law, as if the judge himself invented the law in every case. No exercise of justice can be just unless there is a "fresh judgment." This "fresh judgment" can very well—must very well—conform to a preexisting law, but the reinstituting, reinventive and freely decisive interpretation, the responsible interpretation of the judge requires that his "justice" not just consist in conformity, in the conservative and reproductive activity of judgment. In short,

> for a decision to be just and responsible, it must, in its proper moment if there is one, be both regulated and without regulation: it must conserve the law and also destroy it or suspend it enough to have to reinvent it in each case, rejustify it, at least reinvent it in the reaffirmation and the new and free confirmation of its principle. Each case is other, each decision is different and requires an absolutely unique interpretation, which no existing, coded rule can or ought to guarantee absolutely.
>
> (Derrida, 1990, p. 961)

The philosophical and political orientations of Hart and Derrida could not have been more different. Nevertheless, Hart's remark that no rule can step forward to claim its own instances and Derrida's observation that every new case demands a fresh judgment reflect the same point of view: the egoicity of a decision-maker trying to be just. More precisely, both texts seem more concerned with the responsibility-to-be-just of the one who judges than with the raw, pre-theoretical vulnerability of the one being judged. If there is such a thing as an "ethics of interpretation" in the legal system, as Susanna Lindroos-Hovinheimo (2012) claims, then surely the one who judges is the very site of that ethics. But it is not the *interpretation* as such that imposes ethical responsibility on the decider, for the linguistic sign expressing an interpretation is no more potent in itself than any other linguistic sign. Ethical responsibility comes not from the "meaning" of one's words in relation to some hypothetically just resolution of the case. It comes from the causally painful *effects* of one's words on the lives of particular human beings.

Thus, *Law's Task* was also concerned with the theme of responsibility, but only after something else was revealed, something on top of which responsibility always already stands whether or not it is explicitly aware of it. The book defined the category of universal suffering in order to focus first and foremost on what is included and what is excluded from judgment during every fresh event of judgment. For it is both obviously true, and theoretically significant, that what underlies a prospective judgment has not yet been judged, and may never be.

The tragic circle

A truism can be philosophically helpful if it reminds us of something obvious that we should explicitly notice rather than just take for granted. On the basis of the foregoing simple truisms about the nature of law's enforcement under the rule of law, *Law's Task* invited readers to think of universal human suffering as the unrefined, ever-present raw material, so to speak, of the legal system. Having established that the operations of law and justice begin on every occasion in the midst of an unacknowledged and as-yet undifferentiated mass of human suffering, the book then generalized this point for the legal system as a whole. In particular, it proceeded to describe the constitutive moments of what its subtitle refers to as *The Tragic Circle of Law, Justice and Human Suffering*.

We have already encountered two models similar in intent to the concept of the tragic circle. Chapter 1's notion of a continuum along the axis *War–Peace* (Figure 1.2) illustrated the ethical possibility of noticing that war and peace are not mutually exclusive states—that there are peace-like elements in every war and warlike elements in every peace. Without a prior, disenchanted act of bearing witness in this way, there can be no ethics in the sense meant here. Chapter 1 described the second model as the dialectical triune *Politics/Law/Justice*. Both of these models owe their existence to the metaphorical circle called "tragic" in *Law's Task*. The premise of the tragic circle is that the common origin and product of both the overt violence of war and the covert violence of politics is human suffering in the largest sense of the term: that is, dissatisfaction with the given. Thus, *Law's Task* linked *suffering* to law and justice within the bad infinity of a ceaseless historical process containing three basic moments, or movements.

First, certain instances of human dissatisfaction with the given state of affairs somehow find a way to be noticed by the human collectivity that we call the state, and then to obtain formal legal redress for suffering of their kind. *Second*, the legal system on each new occasion proceeds to divide the vast pool of universal human suffering into parts: parts that it will attend to by enforcing rights and imposing duties, parts that it will ignore, and parts that it will itself co-create. *Third*, and lastly, once the foregoing divisions become routinized, old forms of dissatisfaction are supplemented by new ones, and demands for justice *beyond* the law begin to assert themselves. Some people's demands for justice grow stronger than the institutions that bind them; depending on political conditions, society reevaluates and changes the existing balance between necessary and unnecessary suffering, either by substituting new laws for old laws in an ad hoc manner (reform) or by overthrowing the entire regime and creating an entirely new legal order (revolution).

With the completion of this third moment the circle is closed, and the historical process starts all over again. Readers will recall Kevin Kallaugher's political cartoon, reproduced in Chapter 1 as Figure 1.1 over the caption "*Politics/Law/Justice* in an unstable society." Several years before this cartoon appeared in *The Economist*, *Law's Task* had offered its own drawing to make the foregoing conceptual connections fully perspicuous. Although it was much less skillfully executed than Kallaugher's cartoon, that drawing generalized the dialectic shown there to all modern societies, even those that appear to be relatively stable when viewed at a given point in historical time.

Readers familiar with Benjamin's *Critique of Violence*, discussed earlier in this chapter in a different context, will recognize a strong family resemblance between this diagram and that essay's theory of the "dialectical rising and falling in the lawmaking and law-preserving formations of violence" (1978, p. 300). Generally speaking, violence is *lawmaking* in Benjamin's sense if it initiates a new legal order and does not depend for its legitimacy on any ground other than the sheer fact of its historical success; whereas *law-preserving* violence is the use of force to compel obedience to law once it has been established by lawmaking violence.

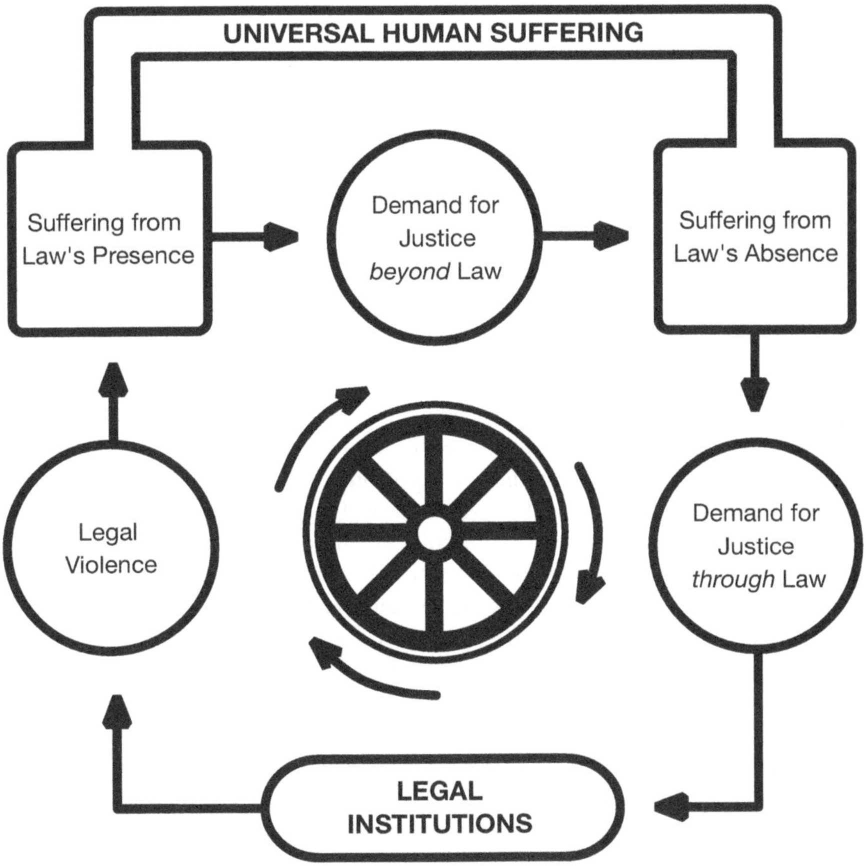

Figure 2.2 The tragic circle. Reprinted by permission of the publishers from "Suffering and Ethical Distress," in *Law's Task* by Louis E. Wolcher (Farnham, UK: Ashgate, 2008)

Copyright © 2008

Only when the two types of legal violence—lawmaking and law-preserving—are viewed together as reciprocal elements of an ongoing historical process does it become possible to notice law's ultimate empirical origin: "violence crowned by fate" (1978, p. 286). Fate, not justice or right. If, now and again, a successful legal regime decides to celebrate its violent roots with fireworks (Independence Day, Bastille Day, etc.), it will never celebrate the *example* that was set by those traitors-cum-liberators who violated then-existing law in order to plant those roots. Benjamin notes that law-preserving violence fears the example set by lawmaking violence not because the latter threatens to derail progress toward legally authorized ends, but because it threatens the very existence of the current legal order (1978, p. 281). He summarized the essential structure of the dialectic between these two forms of violence as follows:

> The law governing their oscillation rests on the circumstance that all law-preserving violence, in its duration, indirectly weakens the lawmaking violence represented by it, through the suppression of hostile counter-violence. . . . This lasts until either new forces or those earlier suppressed triumph [in the name of justice] over the hitherto lawmaking violence and thus found new law, destined in its turn to decay.
>
> (Benjamin, 1978, p. 300)

Figure 2.2, when considered together with Benjamin's diagnosis of the dialectical nature of legal change, paints a picture of the relationship between law and justice that many people would find depressing. This sort of reaction provokes a natural tendency to yearn for evidence or proof of some sort of redemptive closure in the cycle. For Benjamin, the expression of this yearning for redemption took the form of faith in the theological idea of a "divine violence" that would underwrite the final instantiation of a fully just human order (1978, p. 300). For Hegel, the solution was the triumph of the Absolute Idea at the end of history (Kojéve, 1980, p. 148). For Marx (Marx and Engles, 1998, p. 77), it was final proletarian victory in the class struggle and the advent of Communism.

Other theorists look for redemption, not in particular substantive outcomes, but rather in the prospect of achieving the right kind of process or procedure for reaching outcomes, whatever they might be and however much suffering they might produce. Lon Fuller's theory that the rule of law has a non-instrumental moral value independent of its content is a quintessential example of this sort of thing (Fuller, 1969). Eschewing reliance on any substantive legal content that might be called just by someone like Cicero or Aquinas, Fuller's thesis seems to rest on faith in the proposition "If we do things the right way, we'll do the right things" (Fuller, 1948, p. 204). Rawls's "justice as fairness" (1971, pp. 3–53) and Habermas's theory of the "ideal speech situation" (1984, vol. 1, p. 25) also come to mind as examples of hope for the redemption of suffering through a pre-commitment to outcomes that will by definition have been vetted as just by a rigorous application of the right sort of process.

Numerous other Western theorists of the complex relationships subsisting among law, justice, and politics have offered their own redemptive resolutions, though it would be tedious and unnecessary to recount them all here. The intended effect of these theories always seems to be the same: to sell a set of abstractions that, if followed correctly, will produce a better way of doing things. They offer their readers hope for the eventual triumph of justice over injustice by accepting, promoting, and ultimately following a theory. On the other hand, another effect of these theories, whether or not it is specifically intended, is to encourage individual human beings *to act* in the branded ways they recommend, and then to draw a line through the list of casualties that have fallen and will fall in the course of achieving that particular brand of justice. It would appear that *hope for progress* goes hand in hand with *faith in redemption* on account of what must be done in order to get there.

Hope feeds on whatever it is that the image or description of the hoped-for seems to "represent" (e.g., "I hope for a fairer, more just world with attributes A, B . . . etc."). The hypostatized verbal-imagistic lump of *what-is-hoped-for* becomes both the cause and the measure of the hoper's subsequent attitude toward the state of affairs that actually arrives. That attitude is almost always one of disappointment, especially in the political realm. Kierkegaard (1993, p. 62) even went so far as to express the kinship between hope and disappointment in the form of a natural law: "Everything disappoints: Hope, the hoped for does not come, or the hoped for comes—and disappoints."

The banal proposition that human beings need hope in order to live can be traced to Hesiod's misogynistic version of the Pandora legend.[3] It is said that hope keeps despair at bay and inflames action aimed at realizing the hope. Both claims may be true as a general matter, although they do leave open the interesting empirical possibility that a person could act without nurturing hopes and also without *feeling* hopeless. In any event, theories of redemptive closure in the historical cycle of inter-human violence simultaneously *express* the theorist's own hope, and *peddle* particular versions of it to themselves and others. When hope is viewed as an epiphenomenal reaction to human disappointment with the given, it seems benign enough. But when it becomes a motive that is pre-framed by the hypostasis of what-is-hoped-for, and when that motive passes into action, the central problem at stake in this book makes itself felt once again, albeit in a slightly different form: What are the ethics of hope without illusions?

The existential poverty of the idea of redemption through justice

No disenchanted person could ever take comfort from any result, however persuasive, that might emerge from the argument between supporters and opponents of the idea that certain norms of justice are universally valid. For let it be the case that a given norm is accepted as valid by the entire world—the distinctly ethical problem of what to do in just this or that *particular* situation would still loom large. The real difficulty with justice conceived as the conscientious application of just norms is that it pretends that this ethical problem is already solved before it arises, thereby leading its practitioners to the same location as the legal order does: the practice of self-righteous coercion.

If that were all there were to the critique of justice, one might conclude that the search for redemption on account of the social necessity for some individuals to inflict suffering on others—perhaps in the name of universal human emancipation, or a just democratic politics producing a just rule of law—must look somewhere else—somewhere outside the framework of conventional normativity. Benjamin did this, for example, in *Critique of Violence* (1978, p. 292), when he expressed a strong preference for anarchistic uprisings based on myths of emancipation that lack any clear roadmap for the future over utopian social movements characterized by elaborate normative preplanning. Because of the sacrifices that will have led to this hypothetically valid "somewhere else," not to mention the additional sacrifices that will be necessary to maintain its authority into the future, the legitimacy of any principle or image adopted as a guide and justification for individual action ultimately depends on its being seen as *redemptive* (from the Latin *redimere*, meaning to buy back). The memory of past pain and the anticipation of future pain must be seen as somehow capable of being "cancelled" on analogy to the payment of a promissory note.

Cancelled how? Pledging allegiance to justice as a goal is ethically suspect not just because of the latter's questionable provenance or conceptual obscurity in any given case, nor because of its general tendency to ossify into law. After all, it seems probable that human beings will always want and require some sort of coercive system based on abstractions to rule over them. The point is not that law and justice are "bad" and ethics is "good," or that the latter is capable of replacing the former. The point is that the normative aspirations of law and justice must be *deflated* (not abolished) if basic human decency and kindness are to have a chance of breathing. Decency and kindness, not justice: for not only did the ethically redemptive possibilities associated with the idea of justice begin to lose their allure along the way, but at some point the very idea of *redemption itself* began to appear morally dubious, particularly when viewed from a nonreligious perspective.

According to Judeo-Christian theology, a true believer can always look forward to (and fear) a Day of Judgment, when God will settle all moral accounts that have ever arisen from the beginning to the end of time. The "Divine logic" governing the intra-mundane redemption that Judaism associated with the death penalty is similar: as Derrida (2014, p. 14) puts it, "One death, that of the death penalty, reinstates the law or the commandment that the other death (murder) will have violated." Benjamin's aforementioned essay *Critique of Violence* adopts this logic when it argues for the expiatory power of a "Divine Violence" that would somehow manifest itself in the form of a history-consummating and just kind of revolutionary violence (1978, p. 300). A fortiori, however, this sort of logic fails completely if one believes in a fully secularized human history from which any sort of judging God remains wholly absent. If the counting house of history contains no Big Scrooge capable of settling all accounts, then each debt incurred starts to look like a theft, and each payment like a gift that was given to the wrong person.

Thus, no longer was it possible for this nonbeliever to believe in redemption's quixotic presupposition that the blood red color of the balance sheet of human suffering throughout history past, history present, and history to come, could somehow be brought into the black by an unspecified future event that, by definition, will always arrive too late to help those who have suffered and died while waiting for it. The future knows too little about the living who have died before its arrival, but when it slides into the present it will insist on telling us all about the high justice of its triumph. The past, on the other hand, knows all too much about injustice from the point of view of the living who died on its watch, and yet it remains sadly tongue-tied and mute as it stumbles into the present from the other direction.

Contrary to the interest of his own argument, Benjamin left a clue in *Critique of Violence* that indicates why the yearning for redemptive closure must be resisted, or rather, why it will be resisted in this book. It is not only his explicit theism that provides this clue, though it is doubtful that the essay's messianic tone will do much to persuade atheists and agnostics into accepting the theory that certain instances of inter-human violence will eventually be redeemed by the grace of a supernatural being. Rather, the clue comes from Benjamin's choice of *perspective* on the category of universal human suffering.

Benjamin writes that the bad infinity of the dialectic between lawmaking and law-preserving violence (which together comprise the "mythical violence" of law) is visible from the point of view of "a gaze directed *only* at what is close at hand" (1978, p. 300) (emphasis added). This implies that it would be better for human beings to look at what is *not* close at hand, namely, the "divine violence" that "constitutes [legal violence's] antithesis in all respects" (p. 297). Faith in the possibility of redemption for all of the horrible things that people keep on doing to one another in the name of justice requires a broader view, he suggests—a gaze redirected away from history's short-term convulsions and toward the "coming age"—the "new historical epoch" that will arrive when state power is abolished and the cycle of mythical violence is broken (p. 300).

In opposition to this and all other forms of eschatological thinking, George Orwell (2012, p. 385) once had the great inspiration to write in his diary that "perhaps a bird's eye view is as distorted as a worm's eye view." Like a housebound pair of eyes that keeps darting from the task at hand to the street outside the window in the expectation of a visitor, the phenomenology of a good faith legal judgment is characterized by a kind of mental oscillation between, on the one hand, the liquidation of the particular into "the facts," and, on the other hand, the refinement of the universal into "the governing law" (Kennedy, 1986). The *ethically troubled* experience of such a judgment has a similar structure. It shows itself as an oscillation between the perception of the concrete, real individuals being judged and certain abstract images of the norms and practices that together constitute what is called the "legal duty to judge impartially."

This nervous oscillation between looking at what is close at hand and thinking about the whole is probably *the* ethical experience par excellence, as is the choice between them on any given occasion. *Law's Task* used the term *ethical distress* to describe some of the more poignant and dramatic manifestations of this phenomenon. It simply will not do to elide the urgency and difficulty of ethical distress, or to pretend that somehow events will always magically reveal to us which choice (this person or that person; this duty or that privilege) is ethically soundest.

In his excellent analysis of the political theology inherent in Benjamin's idea of divine violence, James Martel (2012) rightly points out that the category of the decision does not require us to make a binary political choice, *à la* Carl Schmitt, between sovereignty and anarchy. He plausibly reads Benjamin to be a critic of *all* idolatrous forms of political representation, whether the idolatry consists in the worshipping of this or that ideal form of polity, or in the pseudo-anarchist conviction that politics can eschew representation altogether and somehow directly enact the "real" self-expression of a people (2012, pp. 2–3). Like Benjamin, Martel is primarily concerned with describing the conditions under which a non-idolatrous, democratic-anarchic form of politics is possible; also like Benjamin, he finds such conditions in the kind of revolutionary action that would embrace the need to represent goals (as in Sorel's earlier-noted category of myth), but would also persistently refuse to represent images of new forms of authority to be superimposed over the community (as in Sorel's category of utopia) (Martel, 2012, p. 3; see Sorel, 1999, pp. 28–29). Elucidating the individual ethical palatability of this sort of politics is a different matter, however. On this last point, Martel throws in his lot with Benjamin's theory of God's redemptive forgiveness, which, however far into the future it may be deferred, promises to give revolutionaries at least *some* emotional comfort on account of their cruelties (2012, p. 147).

Seen from a thoroughly secular, disenchanted point of view, on the other hand, a decision "requires" only what it always already *is*: a particular decider making a particular decision in a particular case. It would not be existentially accurate to say that in the act of decision the sovereignty of the decider replaces the law's sovereignty. The idea that either form of sovereignty exhibits control rests on the illusion that normative statements "stand for" meanings that predetermine, rather than merely reflect, the sum total of their applications. This illusion dissipates like morning mist as the deed is being done. Ethically speaking, the point is not that we do or do not need some form of representation in order to enact democratic politics (clearly we do). Nor is the point that non-idolatrous forms of political representation are generally preferable to idolatrous ones (clearly they are). Rather, the point is that the idea of "representation" itself rests upon an illusion—the illusion that linguistic signs are capable of signifying something "real" that would be any more tangible than they are themselves. Belief in the possibility of redemption through divine forgiveness (or the accolades of future generations) is magical thinking. It is like a child's tattered comfort blanket that somehow retains all of its former power to comfort the adult who holds it now.

On ne saurait faire une omelette sans casser des oeufs: "You can't make an omelet without breaking some eggs," as the old saying goes. Enter the eggs that must be broken to make the redemptive omelet of true justice, in whatever form, and the troublesome possibility that these lowly eggs might cry out in pain against their sacrifice, as Hannah Arendt suggested rather strongly in an essay entitled *The Eggs Speak Up* (Arendt, 1993, pp. 270–284). And there you have it in a nutshell (or a frying pan): The more fervent is one's faith in the possibility of redemptive justice, the more eggs one is (and perhaps ought to be) willing to break in the pursuit of it; while the more eggs actually get broken along the way, the more nauseated one becomes (and perhaps ought to become) at the prospect of consuming the resulting omelet.

The idea that politics is at bottom a tragic enterprise does not sell very well, however. People like to imagine that their omelets have descended to their plates without cost or sacrifice, like manna from heaven. The idea that "there's someone's misery in all we earn," as the poet William Matthews (1995, p. 3) put it, is a downer, and people generally don't like to be reminded of such things, even (or especially) if they are true. If you would like to cultivate the capacity to apologize for the given order of things, however horrible and degrading it may be, you need only believe in Saint Augustine's thesis that on account of Adam's fall human beings are born without *caritas*, or the innate capacity for kindness, and therefore cannot choose to do good on their own (Wiley, 1992, pp. 65–66). The Judaic notion of redemption, when combined with the Christian idea that sin is always in need of expiation, is like a drug that combines amphetamine with heroin: the need to expiate sin is the amphetamine that encourages righteous action (as determined by correct doctrine); while the prospect of redemption is the heroin that soothes the soul and promises eternal relief from the temporal consequences of unavoidable (or unavoided) sin. As Weber (1976, p. 182) was one of the first to notice, the reward of eternal life based on faith in God and the effort to obey his will thus provide modernity with a prototype for believing that the reward of a good conscience will come to those who do their duty—to self, family, employer, state and "society."

Benjamin's famous eighth thesis on the philosophy of history, written 20 years after *Critique of Violence* and discussed at some length in *Law's Task*, goes a long way toward illustrating the ethical consequences of the foregoing quasi-theological model of morality, at least when seen from a disenchanted point of view. In that text, Benjamin imagines the possibility of historical witness as an angel whose back is turned to the future, which it cannot see. All that the angel can see is what has happened in the past—*all* of what has happened—including what continues to happen as the present keeps on relentlessly slipping into the past. Here is how Benjamin characterizes what the angel is forced to witness:

> Where we perceive a chain of events, he sees one single catastrophe which keeps piling wreckage upon wreckage and hurls it in front of his feet. The angel would like to stay, awaken the dead, and make whole what has been smashed. But a storm is blowing from Paradise; it has got caught in his wings with such violence that the angel can no longer close them. The storm irresistibly propels him into the future to which his back is turned, while the pile of debris before him grows skyward. This storm is what we call progress.
>
> (Benjamin, 1968, pp. 257–258)

Benjamin's figure of the angel of history makes a point that should be obvious to anyone: throughout all of human history, one person's or group's progress can be, and usually is, another person's or group's catastrophe. The Ghost Dance of the Oglala Sioux in the late nineteenth century offers a particularly poignant illustration of this historical principle. By means of this dance, certain pitifully small remnants of Northern and Western tribes sought to make peace with the spirits of their countless dead ancestors who had been annihilated during the Western expansion of the white man, and to restore the greatness of all Indian peoples. But this hope for redemption, so to speak, was answered decisively by the U.S. Seventh Calvary's massacre in 1890 of over 200 men, women, and children at Wounded Knee, South Dakota (Brown, 1972, pp. 406–418). Although the elder Benjamin scattered several ambiguous references to redemption in *other* paragraphs in his *Theses on the Philosophy of History* (e.g., Benjamin, 1968, pp. 253–254), the remarkably stark language of the eighth thesis makes it hard (for this author, at least)[4] to hear any echo of the youthful Benjamin's enthusiasm for the possibility of redemption on account of any list of world-historical events that would be long enough to include the massacre at Wounded Knee.

The vexing problem of responsibility for the untold suffering that always seems to lie "close at hand," as Benjamin put it in *Critique of Violence*, for anyone willing to notice it, cannot be solved as easily as two diametrically opposed tendencies of the Western philosophical tradition would have us believe. On the one side are many notable figures in philosophy, including Seneca (1928, p. 439), Spinoza (1955, pp. 224–225), and Kant (1996, pp. 574–575), who have gone out of their way to scold kindheartedness and compassion as moral weaknesses that impede recognition of what reason demands and the performance of moral duty requires. Their point of view is that of Orwell's bird, which sees the worm from far above as something that may have to be eaten. On the other side are figures like Levinas, Grossman, and most of all, Schopenhauer. For them, kindness or compassion, not duty, is the true basis of morality; they believe that "there is no need for abstract knowledge [in ethics], but only of intuitive perception, of the simple comprehension of a concrete case" (Schopenhauer, 2005, p. 117). Their point of view is that of Orwell's worm, which cannot see, and therefore cannot fear, the bird that may be about to swoop down on it.

The phenomenology of reception

To be a bird or a worm? *Law's Task* gave a phenomenology of judgment that described how the micro-phenomenon of LT is fully at work in the legal process, inducing even the most compassionate worms among us to sprout wings and fly up to where a "broader view" on the majesty of law's empire becomes visible, and where the sacrifice of a few (or many) other worms seems but a small price to pay for a well-ordered (and well-fed) world. On the other hand, there are times when even most predatory of legal hawks can be tempted by the spectacle of suffering to take the side of the worm. The book traced the deep-seated ambivalence of these points of view on the binding nature of the rule of law to a fundamental confusion in mainstream theories of legal judgment about the relationship between causes and grounds, contingency and necessity, the socially correct and the immutably true.

In particular, *Law's Task* appropriated Wittgenstein's phenomenology of rule-following to turn the concept of the "easy case" upside down. Instead of proving that law is or can be logically determinate, the so-called easy case is actually the most ethically difficult case. Precisely because it appears to offer no choice, the obvious solution to an easy case is at most "sociologically determinate," that is, an accidental product of history rather than the rationally unavoidable entailment of a valid norm. Socialization and the social pressure to conform may *cause* the easy case to come out the way it does, but this does not imply that the basis of the result is a *ground* that pure reason must respect as unassailably determinate in that or any other case. *Law's Task* claimed that the feeling of choicelessness that characterizes the easy case is best described as a rational or pre-rational *choice* to continue floating along with others on the prevailing tide of conventional social expectations. In the easy case, fidelity to law is not commendable adherence to the invisible meaning-bodies of legal norms. It is better described as going along to get along.

A rigorous phenomenology of the *immediate* reception of language shows that typical legal actors stand in what Heidegger (2002, p. 148) called a "non-regarding" (*hinsichtlos*) relationship to words: people are more or less perpetually losing themselves to the immediate consequences of their perceptions of familiar linguistic signs. Heidegger's imagined protestations to the contrary notwithstanding, the relationship of "losing oneself" also characterizes the immediate recognition of the "as"-structure (*die "als"-Struktur*) of beings, which in Heideggerian thought is supposed to distinguish the human being from the animal (Derrida, 2008, p. 142). The frog sits on a lily pad, for sure, but it would seem that the frog cannot experience what it sits upon *as* a being, *as* a "lily pad," in the way that humans can. Therefore, Heidegger (1994b, p. 176) famously asserted that while beings like the frog are not completely "worldless" (*weltlos*) in the manner of a stone, they are nonetheless "poor-in-world" (*weltarm*), at least in comparison to human beings, who are "world-forming" (*weltbildend*).

However, the Heideggerian concept of the "as"-structure of beings, in this context at least, is a hindrance rather than a help for acquiring a completely disenchanted understanding of legal language. The "non-regarding" relationship of losing oneself to beings goes far beyond merely occasional bouts of human absentmindedness. Nor is that relationship fully explained by the category of the "ready to hand," or unreflective, understanding of and competence with beings, as opposed to those understandings in which beings are distinctly "present at hand" to the cognizing intellect. That is because the non-regarding relationship also characterizes the legal actor's recognition of the material beings called "statutes" and "precedents," all of which first show themselves in the form of legal *expressions*. And in the *final* analysis—after any and all interpretive work on them is done—expressions have no "as"-structure. They just *are*.

Heidegger claimed that humans are the only living beings capable of noticing a given entity, X, *as* X (Derrida, 2008, p. 142). He even thought that encountering X *as* X does not depend on language but rather primordially founds it. This theory creates a problem that Heidegger never fully recognized, let alone solved. For him, language conceived as "the house of the truth of being" meant that it was possible for human beings to choose to be claimed by being *before* they set out to speak (1998, p. 243). Fair enough: we exist before we call it "existing." But the Heideggerian "as"-structure of beings also applies in principle to pen scratchings and phonemes no less than to fountain pens and the hoots of an owl. When seen from the standpoint of the typical legal actor, X in the form of a rule-statement or statement of fact is always only a *statement*—"X"—the material being that we call a linguistic sign. Considered purely as a phenomenon, a legal actor's final *recognition* that sign "X" means or requires such-and-such in any particular situation is not preceded or accompanied by anything at all. "X" is not seen *as* something; *it is just seen*—probably in the same way that the frog just sees the lily pad. *Law's Task* used the term "reception" to describe this ultimately groundless appropriation of legal texts by legal actors.

Groundlessness in this context does not signify some sort of mystical or awe-inspiring existential event of hovering over an abyss. It means, quite simply, that nothing law-like or ground-like, other than the sign "X" itself and the embodied legal actor who clings to it, is present in reality when the actor lets loose the force of law. "In all language there is a bridge between the sign and its application," says Wittgenstein (1980b, p. 67): "No one can make this for us; we have to bridge the gap ourselves. No explanation ever saves the jump, because any further explanation will itself need a jump."

Law's Task quoted the following passage from Wittgenstein's *Blue Book* to further illustrate what can only be called a *negative* fact about the usual way of following an order. What he uncovers there is the complete *absence* of anything approximating an "act" of knowing (or understanding, or interpreting) preceding the event of doing something particular with the expression of an order as to which the recipient experiences no doubt:

> If I give someone the order "fetch me a red flower from that meadow," how is he to know what sort of flower to bring, as I have only given him a word? Now the answer one might suggest first is that he went to look for a red flower carrying a red image in his mind, and comparing it with the flowers to see which of them had the colour of the image. Now there is such a way of searching, and it is not at all essential that the image we use be a mental one. In fact the process may be this: I carry a chart coordinating names and coloured squares. When I hear the order "fetch me etc." I draw my finger across the chart from the word "red" to a certain square, and I go and look for a flower that has the same colour as the square. But this is not the only way of searching and it isn't the usual way. We go, look about us, walk up to a flower and pick it, without comparing it to anything. . . . Now you might ask: do we interpret the words before we obey the order? And in some cases you will find that you do something which might be called interpreting before obeying, in some cases not.
>
> (Wittgenstein, 1960, p. 3)

In light of the foregoing phenomenological observations, it is clear that when Heidegger remarked that "every fact is already understood *as* this and this, that is, it stands under the knowledge of essence" (2002, p. 203), he may have unwarrantedly hypostatized what the word "knowledge" seems to be saying. Knowledge is not a thing or state of awareness—it is a capability. Aristotelian metaphysics holds that a capability (*dynamis*) is always somehow "present" before its enactment (*energeia*) (Heidegger, 1995, p. 157). But even if it is, this does not mean that it is present in the form of an *act of knowing*. The average adult knows what her name is, and that 2 + 2 is 4, even when she is not aware of or thinking about these things, because she is in fact capable of giving that information to anyone who might ask. And the common criterion of her knowing this (i.e., having this capability) is not the presence of some inner "capability-object," for there is no such object that is accessible to the gaze of her or anyone else. It is the fact that she actually gives the information when asked.

The same is true of the capability of applying a given normative text, such as a statute or legal precedent. As the following remark by Wittgenstein suggests, we do not somehow "know" (or pre-know) a linguistic *sign* "as" a *thought* (e.g., sign "X" interpreted as thought X) so much as simply *act* with an image or impression of "X" in mind, albeit perhaps mixed together with other images that have been stimulated into existence by the first one ("Y," "Z," etc.):

> How is it possible even to come up with a thought! Here "How could I have come up with a thought" means: "What does the thought *mean*, to what extent is it a thought anyway, since *nothing* corresponds to it, after all?" As if a thought were magic. What do we mean by the existence of things, that is, what use does this concept have? After all, a thought is just an expression, and there can be no magic hidden behind an expression. What this expression *accomplishes* can only be seen by looking at its use.
>
> (Wittgenstein, 2005, p. 52e)

Phenomenally speaking, "goals" take the form of representations (words and images); and there is a point of view from which words and images can be interpreted as causes that are just as effective as sticks and stones are at breaking bones. The so-called "symbolic order" to which the bodies and minds of individuals are subjected does not primordially consist of signs-endowed-with-meanings; the symbolic order shows itself most immediately as a manifold of words and images capable of producing *effects*. After all is said that must be said in any given situation, and the time has come to act, the legal actor *reacts* but does not *respond* to language: he or she bounces off language, so to speak, without answering it back.

The foregoing phenomenon is easiest to observe in cases in which we react to language automatically or habitually, as in the earlier-noted example of the "easy case" in law. William James's remark about "action grown habitual" gives a succinct description of the phenomenon in question:

> In action grown habitual, what instigates each new muscular contraction [e.g., a judge announcing a result or signing a judgment] to take place in its

> appointed order is not a thought or a perception, but the *sensation occasioned by the muscular contraction just finished.* . . . In an habitual action, mere sensation is a sufficient guide, and the upper regions of brain and mind are set comparatively free.
>
> (James, 1904, vol. 1, pp. 115–116)

Listen, too, to Derrida's description of this same phenomenon in the context of following a rule in what appears to be an easy case:

> When there is a determinable rule, I know what must be done, and as soon as such knowledge dictates the law, action follows knowledge as a calculable consequence: one *knows* what path to take, one no longer hesitates; the decision no longer decides anything but simply gets deployed with the automatism attributed to machines. There is no longer any place for justice or responsibility (whether juridical, political, or ethical).
>
> (Borradori, 2003, pp. 134–135)

Derrida's account of the easy case is correct, so long as one takes care to qualify his use of the concepts of knowing and knowledge in the manner that was suggested earlier—that is, so long as "I know what must be done" is not read to state that an *act of knowing* precedes the doing. The phenomenon of encountering what shows itself as a "determinable rule" is such that a legal actor reacts to the linguistic sign that expresses the rule without any question or hesitation. The typical actor in this sort of situation exhibits knowledge in the sense of demonstrating a capability to use the rule, but he or she does not experience an inner "act" of knowing, or of taking for granted, anything whatsoever about those signs or their meaning. As Wittgenstein (2005, p. 135e) says, this sort of use of language "is better compared to what occurs when, upon pressing a button with the word 'blue' on it, a blue color chip automatically pops up, or doesn't pop up if the mechanism fails."

It would be flattering to reason's sense of vanity to think that the automaticity that James, Derrida and Wittgenstein describe can always be overcome by the application of the right amount of intellectual effort. Indeed, conservative and liberal legal thinkers who detest the postmodern practitioners of deconstruction for casting unreasonable doubt on the rule of law should actually thank them for their efforts. For instance, Anthony D'Amato's "proof," in *Aspects of Deconstruction: The Easy Case of the Under-Aged President* (1989), that a 34 year-old could legally serve as President of the United States, despite the Constitution's requirement that only someone who has "attained to the Age of thirty five years" is eligible to serve, demonstrates more than anything else that it is possible for reason to keep on thinking about the meaning of a linguistic sign long after other people have given up and surrendered to customary ways of understanding. The mainstream legal philosopher Fred Schauer (1985, p. 420) seems to believe that it proves nothing that people like D'Amato are able "to construct weird and fanciful instances in which even the clearest language breaks down," and that it is perhaps even disreputable for them to try. He is indeed right about this, but only if one thinks that the smooth and automatic operation of the rule of law according to customary ways of reading (i.e., according to historical causes, not unimpeachable grounds) is politically, morally and ethically unproblematic.

D'Amato's clever demonstration that there are circumstances under which the linguistic signs "Age of thirty five years" can be used to allow a 34 year-old to serve as President might give the impression that language is infinitely interpretable by reason—that reason can always step in to take control, so to speak, when customary ways of reading are not up to the task. This is an impression that the opponents of deconstruction should welcome and encourage, assuming that they also believe in the Enlightenment principle that human reason is capable of breaking free of its historical causes and conditions to master a reality that somehow keeps on throwing new problems at humanity.

The main difficulty with this Enlightenment view of reason's power to lay down brand new grounds in the form of statements that represent sign-independent entities called "meanings" does not stem from the claim that determinism is true, and therefore freedom of the will is an illusion. The real difficulty comes from the lack of any phenomenological evidence to support it. Thus, *Law's Task* claimed not only that the phenomenon of reception occurs in what lawyers call "easy cases," but also that it eventually comes to pass in *every* case. When the list of justifications for how authoritative legal language (e.g., a statute) "should" be followed comes to an end—when it reaches the bedrock of action, as it always must—the decision-maker's intellectual spade is turned, as Wittgenstein (2005, p. 85e) puts it, for there is then no further event of justifying or grounding to consider.

The scientifically minded might therefore choose to define norm-following as a present disposition or ability created by social custom as it continually co-constructs the identities and typical reactions of individual actors through various processes of socialization (Berger and Luckmann, 1967, pp. 129–183). But this would be a sociological definition, not a phenomenological or ethical one. Custom in this sense is not a *ground* that is consulted by the legal actor. Once the latter has fully internalized custom through learning or imitation, he or she does not then fall back on (i.e., explicitly "follow") the memory-image of some past event of learning or imitation to know how to behave according to custom. As Wittgenstein (2005, p. 162e) puts it, the actor's behavior is "instinctive later on, whatever its origin." That is, the concept of "custom" is but a shorthand way of expressing the idea that the actor and others like him have been *caused* by social conditioning to behave in certain stereotypical ways.

It would be an enormous mistake to interpret the foregoing synopsis of the phenomenon of reception as offering some sort of *explanation* of legal outcomes. Explanations take the form of "A→B," where "B" signifies something to be explained (the *explanandum*) and "A" signifies the cause or the reason (the *explanans*) that explains it. The mental *movement* from A to B that *Beyond Transcendence* called LT represents the phenomenological structure of all explanations, but it does not "explain" the phenomenon of explaining, in the sense of imputing it to a cause or reason. Phenomenology does not explain things—it shows them. In the case of the phenomenology of reception that was offered in *Law's Task*, the main point is to notice what does *not* occur before the very moment of legal decision, not so much what does occur.

What does happen, of course, can be fairly described as an instinctive going-forward-with-symbols. And it is important to acknowledge that it is always possible to try to impute any particular event of this sort to its causes, be they *sociological* (as in Berger and Luckmann's "social construction of reality" (1967)), *psychological* (as in Daniel Kahneman's description of "fast thinking" versus "slow thinking" (2011)), or *physiological* (as in Patricia Churchland's neurological account of "the self as brain" (2013)). But a purely phenomenological description of reception in the legal context does not uncover the presence of any causes; nor does it uncover the presence of any reasons for why a normative expression ("X") is automatically understood one way ("Y") rather than some other way ("Z").

The same thing is true if we look at any particular moment of transition in the process of legal decision-making. If I am unclear about the meaning of the symbol "→" on a road sign, for example, I might consciously interpret it to mean "go to the right." But if I *then* immediately grasp how to go on in the presence of the latter symbols—the ones I have given to myself by my previous interpretation—there is no *further* act of interpretation to be found in consciousness. If a scheme of interpretation is to serve any purpose at all, it must distinguish between what is interpreted (e.g., "*X*," as to which there is some doubt) and the interpretation (e.g., "'*X*' means Y," as to which there is no doubt). And if it then transpires that the meaning of "Y" is also doubted, then there has to be yet another level of distinction in which the interpretation is once again differentiated from the interpreted (e.g., "the words '"*X*" *means Y*' mean Z").

One can choose to keep this process going for a very long time, but not forever. (Indeed, is not this elongation of reason's engagement with linguistic signs the very essence of deconstruction when viewed as a "technique"? Which, of course, was never its point or significance in any case, as Derrida (1990, pp. 921–923) never stopped reminding us.) The regress of signs is not infinite—it is in fact *always* finite, as finite as the length of a person's motivated or unmotivated attention span. This, it turns out, is usually quite short—a fact that mainstream scholars of law unknowingly illustrate whenever they denigrate critical legal thought for its lack of immediate "utility" (Massey, 1992, pp. 821–829). At some point, the interpretation (or the interpretation of the interpretation, or the interpretation of *that*) is simply received and acted upon. On this matter there is no essential difference between a conservative, originalist judge, such as Antonin Scalia (Scalia and Garner, 2012), and a liberal, constructivist one, such as Stephen Breyer (2005), or between a mainstream legal thinker and a radical one. Ultimately all thinking is "thinking fast," as Daniel Kahneman (2011) puts it, because even when we choose to "think slowly" we end up *receiving* our very last thought in a fast sort of way.[5]

The cessation of reason's engagement with the chain of linguistic signs it has created in interpreting a rule is not due to the fact that the rule's sign-independent meaning-body is now completely visible, like a fully intact insect frozen in amber. If some people believe (or have faith) that there is such a meaning-body replicated inside them—and if they even hold this belief up as proof that the rule of law rests on something incontestably objective—then it is sure that a disenchanted, ethically troubled person does not. For the latter sort of person, the word "meaning" refers to nothing more (or less) solid than the word "self" does to Hume in this well-known passage from *A Treatise of Human Nature*:

> For my part, when I enter most intimately into what I call *myself*, I always stumble on some particular impression or other, of heat or cold, light or shade, love or hatred, pain or pleasure. I never can catch *myself* at any time without a perception, and never can observe any thing but the perception. . . . If any one, upon serious and unprejudic'd reflection, thinks he has a different notion of *himself*, I must confess I can reason no longer with him. All I can allow him is, that he may be in the right as well as I, and that we are essentially different in this particular. He may, perhaps, perceive something simple and continu'd, which he calls *himself*; tho' I am certain there is no such principle in me.
>
> (Hume, 1977, pp. 238–239)

Reason's engagement with normative language—that is, the interpretive process—comes to an end only because the actor *stops looking* for any meaning behind the very last linguistic sign upon which he or she acts. "I can, for example, make a scheme [of interpretation] with three [or *n*] levels, the bottom level always being the level of meaning," says Wittgenstein (1960, p. 14), "But adopt whatever model or scheme you may, it will have a bottom level, and there will be no such thing as an interpretation of that." What is more, even if we meticulously comb through each and every moment in the interpretive process—from the naked rule-sign at the top, through each one of the subsequent signs that were constructed by reason's engagement with the topmost one, to the bottommost sign upon which we act—we will find no meaning-body stuck to the nit comb. What appears in phenomenal reality is not some*thing* called "meaning." What appears is (1) a cascade of signs and images, (2) the transitions between them, and (3) the ever-growing feeling that one's next action is what Levinas (2001, p. 31) called *incontournable*, or "that which one cannot get around."

In the previous example of the road sign, it is not just the *meaning* of "go to the right" that is completely absent when I "follow" my interpretation by going to the right (or to the left, for that matter). The *causes* of my ability to immediately act on the words "go to the right" (e.g., the patient efforts of my parents and kindergarten teacher to teach me) are also absent, for the obvious reason that the historical causes of a particular capability temporally precede, but do not coincide with, the exercise of the capability itself in any given case. Neuroscience may have shown definitively that socialization, training, and education produce physical changes in the human brain that are "present" when a given capability is exercised; but it is (or should be) obvious that any such physical changes in the brain are not the same as the causes that produced them.

It should be clear by now that the whole point of drawing attention to the phenomenon of reception is to demonstrate absence, but only in the mundane sense of the *absence of presence*, not in the onto-theological sense of the *presence of absence*. Heidegger exploited the latter idea about absence when he said, in *Being and Time* (1962, p. 264), that "a 'ground' only becomes accessible as meaning, even if it is itself the abyss (*der Abgrund*) of meaninglessness (*Sinnlosigkeit*)," and then again later, in *Contributions to Philosophy* (1999, p. 265), when he said that "Ab-ground is the staying away of ground." In contrast to Heidegger's way of talking about Being in terms of a puissant kind of absence, the foregoing descriptions of the phenomenon of reception do not signify that we are left standing on, in, or before some sort of ontological emptiness or abyss.

In reception, we stand just where we stand in each particular situation, just where history and our own previous efforts have put us. Seen from the internal point of view of a legal actor who happens to be standing here rather than there, there is simply *nothing to be found* that would justify or explain the actor's immediate reaction to a norm-sign that he or she grasps how to go on with. What *can* be found, once again, are (1) mental images of certain symbols, (2) a feeling of certainty, and (3) the deed. Like the famous translating decision made by Goethe's *Faust*, the phenomenon of reception confirms that "In the beginning was the Word" (John 1:1) does not mean that in the beginning there was the meaning (or cause) of the Word. It means: In the beginning was *the deed*.[6]

No wonder *Law's Task* is suffused with a feeling of wary nervousness about the division of suffering by legal means. The agents of law and justice let themselves inflict suffering in the name of "the law" without becoming aware of their own inescapable personal complicity in the continual production and reproduction of mute, groundless (and all too often bloody and hateful) social custom, in case after case after case. Natural law says that there are objective criteria for judging the justice or injustice of positive law in any given situation. It is hard to disagree with this assertion as a matter of purely descriptive ethics. For it happens to be true that lots and lots of people have invoked, and will continue to invoke, what they call "objective criteria" to praise or condemn the positive law of their time and place. The ethical problem with this fact is not that people's criteria are historically contingent and relative. The real problem is that what people call the "objective" (and even "subjective") criteria of justice and injustice are not all that they are cracked up to be, even on the assumption that everyone on earth applied the same ones. A criterion is ultimately a naked symbol, whereas the wordless reality of the particular is not.

Law's Task therefore completed the journey to radical disenchantment on a note that might be characterized as despairing, were it not for the fact that the book also introduced the idea of individual ethical responsibility for the particular. The possibility (or hope) that there could be such a thing as an ethics of justice without illusions seemed just about the only way to give an affirmative answer to the Fundamental Question of whether a life in the law is worth living.

Notes

1. Pindar, "Human Life" (Higham and Bowra, 1938, p. 312): "Man's life is a day. What is he? / What is he not? A shadow in a dream / Is man."
2. Cf. Heidegger (1962, p. 269):

   > Before Newton's laws were discovered, they were not "true"; it does not follow that they were false, or even that they would become false if ontically no discoveredness were any longer possible. . . . To say that before Newton his laws were neither true nor false, cannot signify that before him there were no such entities as have been uncovered and pointed out by those laws. Through Newton the laws became true and with them, entities became accessible in themselves to Dasein. Once entities have been uncovered, they show themselves precisely as entities which beforehand already were. Such uncovering is the kind of Being which belongs to "truth."

3. > Epimetheus, alarmed by his brother's fate, hastened to marry Pandora, whom Zeus had made as foolish, mischievous, and idle as she was beautiful—the first in a long line of such women. Presently she opened a box [actually a *pithos*, or jar], which Prometheus had warned Epimetheus to keep closed, and in which he had been at pains to imprison all the Spites that might plague mankind: such as Old Age, Labour, Sickness, Insanity, Vice, and Passion. Out these flew in a cloud, stung Epimetheus and Pandora in every part of their bodies, and then attacked the race of mortals. Delusive Hope [*Elpis*], however, whom Prometheus had also shut in the box, discouraged them by her lies from a general suicide.
   >
   > (Graves, 1955, vol. 1, p. 145) (synthesizing the accounts of Hesiod and an ancient scholiast)

4. But see Martel (2012, p. 147): "The same storm that Benjamin describes in his 'Theses on the Philosophy of History', a storm that blows out of paradise and fills the world with ruin, is also . . . a storm of divine forgiveness." On the other hand, it is worth noting that 15 years after *Critique of Violence*, and 5 years before *Theses on the Philosophy of History*, Benjamin (1994, p. 486) wrote a letter to Werner Kraft that refers with embarrassment to "the distant past when I thought in purely metaphysical, even theological terms."
5. According to Daniel Kahneman's recent book, *Thinking, Fast and Slow* (2012, pp. 20–21), the current state of psychological research supports the division of the category "thinking" into the following two subcategories:

   > *System 1* [fast thinking] operates automatically and quickly, with little or no effort and no sense of voluntary control. *System 2* [slow thinking] allocates attention to the effortful mental activities that demand it, including complex computations. The operations of System 2 are often associated with the subjective experience of agency, choice, and concentration.

6. > It is written: "In the beginning was the *Word*." Here I am stuck already! Who will help me on? To set so high a value on a "word" is impossible: I must translate it some other way, if the spirit is giving me real enlightenment. It is written: "In the beginning was *Mind*." Consider the first line well, let your pen not move on too fast! Is it by *Mind* that all things are done and made? It should read: "In the beginning was *Energy*." And yet, at the very moment of writing it down, something warns me not to leave it at that. The spirit moves me! I suddenly see the answer, and boldly write: "In the beginning was the *Deed*."
   >
   > (Goethe, 1964, p. 185)

Chapter 3

The rise of the particular

> To generalise is to be an Idiot. To particularise is the Alone Distinction of Merit.
>
> William Blake (de Sélincourt, 1911, p. 131)

The lost nimbus

In olden days, the possibility of acquiring a good individual conscience about prevailing social arrangements was strongly linked to the belief that the overlapping ideas of law, justice, and morality were (or at least someday soon might be) filled with normative contents capable of producing a society—and perhaps even a world—that was good, right, and, above all, fundamentally decent. One could say that the words "law," "justice," and "morality" used to be surrounded with something like a nimbus—the luminous vapor that the ancients said swirled about gods and goddesses when they walked on the earth. This nimbus was often shown in paintings and mosaics as an aureole around the head of a divine figure, as in Figure 3.1's depiction of the God Apollo pursuing the nymph Daphne.

Of course, everybody knew that human beings, fallible as they are, might occasionally create ineffective or even evil governments, enact bad laws, and perform unjust acts. It will be recalled that the first two chapters introduced the conceptual triune *Politics/Law/Justice* in order to help illustrate the bad infinity of a social-historical process that Benjamin (1978, p. 300) called the "dialectical rising and falling in the lawmaking and law-preserving formations of violence." Although history confirms that this process is operative in the long run, its incessant small jolts and incongruities remain largely invisible to most people going about their daily lives in today's (still) relatively prosperous Western democracies—unless, that is, a particularly dramatic rupture with the past (e.g., revolution, civil war, economic catastrophe) intervenes to rend the existing order of things. The wheel of fate can turn every bit as slowly as Longfellow's millwheels of God, especially during extended periods of apparent social stability.

On the other hand, for a long time, a different tripartite constellation was widely accepted by elites and the educated classes as the decorously proper starting point for all serious political and moral discussion, however much the precise contents

Figure 3.1 Mosaic pavement: Apollo and Daphne. Late third century CE. Stone. Roman, Antioch on the Orontes, The House of Menander, Turkey

Photo credit: Princeton University Art Museum/Art Resource, NY

of its constituent concepts might be contested. Ideologically linear rather than dialectical, it was this particular conceptual triumvirate—namely, *Law/Justice/Morality*—that used to be surrounded by a nimbus. It was said to be comprised of: (1) a *legally* well-regulated polity; (2) *justice* as what the law is already doing, for the most part, unless something unusually awful comes to the attention of enough of the voting public, in which case the idea of justice beyond the law steps out of the shadows to help rally support for incremental reform; and (3) *morality* as a proper guide to righteous individual behavior in all cases.

The olden days are gone. Wittgenstein (1980b, p. 2) once remarked to his students that "the nimbus of philosophy has been lost." By this he meant that faith in the answerability of the traditional "big questions" of philosophy (What is being? What is justice? etc.) has been replaced by an ever-growing skepticism about the adequacy and binding validity of universals. He also meant that a kind of craftsman-like pride in working out the details of various clever techniques for doing philosophy had replaced the overconfident rationalism that had motivated most of the great philosophical systems of the past. Just as astrology became astronomy, and alchemy became chemistry, so too political economy became economic modeling and econometrics, and philosophy has been replaced by academic philosophy, which all too often seeks refuge from social ontology in the history of ideas or the scholastic analysis of texts.

God is dead (Nietzsche)

Like the meaning of Nietzsche's aphorism "God is dead" (1927b, p. 6), the deepest meaning of the loss of faith in the moral invincibility of reason's various systems of control is not to be found in persuasive theoretical demonstrations that law, justice, and morality lack all foundations, or in the obviously false empirical claim that no one today would ever write a book claiming to have discovered the true foundations of these practices. Plainly the idea of justice beyond the law still can, and often does, function as a secular theodicy, promising that present pain will be relieved in the hereafter of a more just worldly existence to come. In this respect, secular belief in justice resembles religious belief, which Marx (1964, p. 44) famously characterized as both the sigh of an oppressed creature and the opium of the people.

Just as there are many different religions, so too modern theoreticians of justice have understood their theme (and peddled their opium, in some cases) in many different ways. To mention just a few of these, justice has been understood: *liberally* as an idealized kind of fairness (e.g., Rawls, 1985); *conservatively* as the enforcement of justified expectations to entitlements (Nozick, 1974, p. 153); *pragmatically* as pitching in with others to do the hard civic work of shaping our future (Rorty, 1997, pp. 106–107); *comparatively* as a theory aimed at reducing injustice rather than creating perfect justice (Sen, 2009, pp. 400–401); *globally* as the struggle to place international human rights above localized claims of power and interest (Glendon, 2001, p. 241); *psychologically* as a noble human yearning for transcendence from an unjust status quo (e.g., Balkin, 1998, p. 162); and even *paradoxically* as the aporia of a decision with the greatest urgency that is never present but always to come (*á venir*) (e.g., Derrida, 1990, pp. 255–256).

There is little doubt that justice has—and probably always will have—plenty of priests, acolytes, and parishioners. Social life sucks, and there will always be Big Thinkers who are willing and able to offer little followers glittering abstractions for making it seem less sucky. Nevertheless, it is also fair to say that justice, like God, has lost its nimbus, and that it has lost it for basically the same reason that God lost his.

It is important to remember that God is not dead in the Nietzschean sense because someone finally came up with overwhelming proof of his nonexistence (proof that only a fool could disbelieve), or because no one in fact believes in him anymore. This is not to say that modern-day scientists and philosophers do not keep on trying to prove (increasingly, it seems) that God does not exist and that it is both socially and individually harmful to believe in him (e.g., Dawkins, 2006; Grayling, 2013; Hitchens, 2007). *Mutatis mutandis*, the existence of billions of people who still worship this or that deity does not prove that skeptics like Dawkins, Grayling, and Hitchens are wrong about God and religion.

Paradoxically, the mere fact that the truth of God's existence and status is in fact so radically *contested* and *contestable* in so many different parts of the world is sufficient proof in itself that he is dead in Nietzsche's sense. To be more precise and parochial, the real reason the Abrahamic God lost his nimbus throughout Western culture is that belief in him became *optional*—a mere personal choice, in other words, rather than a socio-legal compulsion. With freedom of religion came freedom from religion, for God could no longer reliably count on the whip of the state to herd bodies into his churches and, more importantly, to force obedience to his will. As Leszek Kolakowski (2013, p. 184) put it in a 1981 essay bearing the evocative title *Anxiety About God in an Ostensibly Godless Age*, "The God who once guaranteed a stable order of values and social relations, rules of reasoning and mechanisms of the physical world, and who functioned as the culmination of that order, no longer exists, *for that order no longer exists*" (emphasis added).

The secular state tolerates religion in general, but it does not endorse any religion in particular, nor indeed any other systematic set of beliefs. Once God became a mere preference or choice that individuals considered themselves free to accept or reject (i.e., once people were no longer imprisoned or burned at the stake for not believing in him), his reign as the universally acknowledged ultimate ground of the universe was finished. As early as the seventeenth century, Pascal's wager (1941, pp. 79–84) (*Pensée* no. 233) had paradoxically affirmed God's existence *and* his dethronement at the same time, in as much as the wager attempts to prove the value of belief in God to a human subject open to being "cured" of unbelief if that would be in his rational self-interest. If God had to go a-begging, so to speak, among human beings—if believing in him was optional—then the one who is free to believe or not believe in the first place steps forward to become the ultimate (i.e., final) arbiter of what is or should be universally believed.

In a word, the concept of subjectivity was elevated to a cosmic principle, the very ground of grounding itself. But the supposedly unitary Kantian subject of the late eighteenth century eventually broke like a wave on the rocks of history during the next two centuries—wars, genocides, the ceaseless hypertrophy of technologies, economic crises, economic and cultural globalism, consumerism, the information revolution, etc. Left behind when the wave receded were millions and billions of individual subjects, each with its own particular set of "preferences" about what is and should be believed about God, morality, politics, and everything else. To compensate for the "missingness of God" (*Fehl Gottes*) (Heidegger, 1976, p. 105) as a social universal, humans gave themselves the overdetermined presentness of their countless individual opinions and choices.

The shattering of the rational unitary subject into a plethora of administratively aggregated individual subjects (consumers, voters, liberals, conservatives, Baptists,

Sunni Muslims, etc.) whose preferences cannot in principle be deduced from first principles, but can only be comprehended statistically through scientific research and opinion polls, is a social phenomenon of world-historical significance. Its occurrence goes hand in hand with what Foucault (2008) called the rise of biopolitics. But in addition to creating social circumstances favorable to the management and control of "populations" by government and capital, the shattering of the one true transcendental subject into countless different contingent subjects also created conditions favorable to the spread of what previous chapters called disenchantment. In particular, it meant that the universality of belief in the possibility of being rationally well-grounded in *Law/Justice/Morality* would suffer a fate similar to that of the universality of belief in God.

It's not that the concept of being well-grounded in what is universally true is provably false, any more than the most cherished tenets of Judaism, Christianity, or Islam are provably false. When a nimbus dims, it is not because something true has been ostentatiously negated (the scholastic notion of *nihil privativum*); it is because something real (a universal feeling of compulsory universality) has become a *nihil negativum*, has gone out of existence (Schopenhauer, 1969, vol. 1, p. 409). By the same token, the real reason that the secular triumvirate *Law/Justice/Morality* lost its former prestige is not its proven falsity—rather, it is the sheer existence of far too many people who openly disbelieve the traditional claims of law, justice, and morality.

In this regard, Marx's early critical essays on law and morality, especially *On the Jewish Question* and *Critique of Hegel's Philosophy of Right* (Marx, 1964, pp. 3–31, 43–59), let loose a rivulet of skepticism about the prestige of the triumvirate that eventually became a flood with the advent of such twentieth-century jurisprudential movements as legal realism, sociological legal theory, critical legal studies, feminist legal theory, critical race theory, and queer legal theory. Giving a catalog of all the modern and postmodern nimbus-dimming literature about legal theory would be a truly monumental task. Suffice it to say that the mere fact someone can not only publish a book on feminist jurisprudence with chapter titles like "Justice as Fairness: For Whom?" and "Whose Traditions? Which Understanding?" (Okin 1991), but also can have selections from the book included in a prestigious undergraduate anthology about justice (Solomon and Murphy, 2000, pp. 332–339), is enough to show that the nimbus surrounding the word "justice" is not what it used to be.

Skeptics do not necessarily disbelieve the claim that one set of linguistic norm-signs is "better" or "more just" than some other set. Rather, they are inclined to disbelieve the claim that norm-signs stand for *universally* valid meaning-bodies, and that conformity to official or elite expectations about how to follow a regime of linguistic normativity is always a moral imperative. Arthur Leff (1979, p. 1239) gave voice to the attitudinal shift underlying this sort of disbelief when he said: "The aim of ethical discourse is ethics, not discourse, and a piece of lousy thinking is not necessarily 'immoral'."

In short, the nimbus of *Law/Justice/Morality* grew dimmer and dimmer the more people there were who came to disbelieve in the proposition that the language expressing even the most excellent of norms is not only the existential *boundary* (in a Heideggerian sense) of social justice and individual ethical responsibility, but also their firm metaphysical *limit.* "Limits" (*Schranken*) in this context refer to the beyond-which that something (e.g., a normative expression) dare not go if it wishes to keep on being recognized as what it has always heretofore been. "Boundaries" (*Grenzen*), on the other hand, constitute something's ontological starting point, the topological and temporal "wherefrom" from which an expression is constantly starting afresh in each new situation in which it is used. "A boundary is not that at which something stops [a limit] but, as the Greeks recognized, the boundary [*horismos,* in Greek] is that from which something begins its presencing" (Heidegger, 1971, p. 154).

Convention interprets a normative expression such as a rule of law or a rule of morality as both a boundary and a limit—that is, it is taken to be both the valid starting point for normative practice (a boundary) *and* an entity that is somehow capable of "saying" in advance how it must or must not be applied in particular situations (a limit). In set-theoretical terms, the meaning of a limit is *intensional* (meaning-full), whereas that of a boundary is *extensional* (a mere list). The belief that a rule-statement can impose metaphysical (as opposed to merely socially conditioned) *limits* in advance on what can be correctly done with it is what Wittgenstein called the magical view of language (Phillips, 2005, p. 173).

Underlying the magical view in the normative sphere is something resembling Aristotle's notion that prior to the enactment (*energeia*) of every actual event is its possibility (*dynamis*). If the essence of every actuality consists in its prior possibility (Heidegger, 2008, p. 194), then the possible can be seen to enjoy a kind of constant "presence" that makes it accessible in principle to the objectifying gaze of reason (Heidegger, 1995, p. 186). This thesis gave rise to the Aristotelian and medieval conception of science as an exercise in deduction about how things *must* exist in nature, according to reason's interpretation of the "purpose" of every phenomenon as revealed by a careful diagnosis of all its possibilities. Modern, post-Newtonian science has completely abandoned this teleological view of nature, of course, in favor of direct observation and the construction of models that are not required to fit any preexisting metaphysical criterion of what a thing "must" be in order to fulfil its purpose (Weinberg, 2015). In contrast, modern legal and moral teleology—the view that rule-signs are always intensional before they are extensional—makes it seem that the difference between a boundary and a limit is simply a function of the ability to perceive the rule's correct metaphysical "possibilities" before they are applied.

Unfortunately for the conventional proponents of *Law/Justice/Morality*, the most corrosive aspect of disbelief in their claims is not the existence of widespread doubt about the *boundary-status* of many (or even most) anodyne normative expressions. "Thou shalt not kill," "Thou shalt not steal," and so forth are perfectly acceptable starting points for moral judgment. What is subject to doubt is the *limit-status* of these and any other general normative expressions when applied by a particular human being in a particular situation—that is, their ethical sufficiency qua abstractions. In sum, the most corrosive form of disbelief in *Law/Justice/Morality* rejects the neo-Kantian thesis that it is possible to acquire a good conscience solely through conformity to social expectations about how to apply abstract norms. Just as the ever-increasing possibility (in the West) that one can publicly choose to be an atheist or "unaffiliated person" is enough to show that God's prestige is no longer what it once was (Pew Research Center, 2015), so too the fact that one can choose to deny and publicly refute the self-congratulatory claims of the triumvirate *Law/Justice/Morality* is enough to show that it has lost *its* nimbus.

This is one of those cases in which a battle is already lost just because it has to be fought, as when disgraced American president Richard Nixon lost his battle for respectability the very moment the words "I am not a crook" came out of his mouth. The ancient struggle of *Nomos* against *Chaos* no longer promises to soothe the anxiety of the privileged mind with the comforting appearance that its schemes for ordering the disordered are self-evidently entitled to unanimous approval, to the benefit of us all. Too many people now see *Nomos* for what in any case the oppressed classes have always felt it to be: how "they" see the world, as if the elite were attempting to pour a gallon's worth of reality into a teacup of historically contingent order.[1]

After Auschwitz (Adorno)

There are no longer any "happy atheists," says Kolakowski (2013, p. 184), for just "as the certainty of faith collapsed, so did the certainty of un-belief." Especially "after Auschwitz," as Adorno (1973, p. 361) puts it, there is something sanctimonious if not obscene about squeezing any kind of rational sense out of the fate of the world's many victims; for in light of what happened in that place, we simply cannot in good conscience say any more "that the immutable is truth, and the mobile, transitory is [mere] appearance." The phrase *after Auschwitz* in this context does not denominate a period of chronological time that began January 27, 1945, when the Nazi camps in Poland that went by that name were liberated by the Red Army. Instead, *after Auschwitz* names a certain *state of awareness*, always very personal and intimate, of what can happen—namely, the worst—when the difference between the real and what is called "the true" is radically suppressed or forgotten.

The cozy relationship between the concept of ethical responsibility and the faithful performance of one's legally and socially approved (or mandatory) duties is no longer as secure as it once was. Consider the much-diminished nimbus surrounding the words "doing my duty." It is known that the SS used to reward good performance by its camp personnel with a trip to Solahütte, a resort located 30 kilometers south of Auschwitz. A personal photo album kept by SS *Obersturmführer* Karl Höcker contains numerous photographs of smiling SS officers and guards enjoying festive meals, lifting pints of beer, and generally celebrating their well-earned time off (United States Holocaust Memorial Museum, 2007). These photos are in many ways more chilling than those depicting the extermination process itself, for they portray the individual perpetrators as ordinary human beings having an ordinary good time after a hard day's work. They illustrate why Adorno's phrase "after Auschwitz" does not just put into question the decency of continuing to write poems after 1945; it also puts into question the decency of continuing to heap praise, *à la* Kant, on the performance of any norm-derived duty for duty's sake.

Two interrelated notions have begun to seep into what might be called, for lack of a better term, *postmodern ethical consciousness*. The first is the idea that a world completely defined in advance by words is a sterile, hateful place for humans to live. The second is the idea that making the world livable again requires paying special attention to those particularities of human suffering that keep escaping the net of official recognition. The plausibility of these two ideas is probably due to the fact that the countless degradations and horrors repeatedly perpetrated in the name of reason during the last 100 years also happened to coincide with the rise of unprecedented technological means for widening and deepening our awareness of them. For example, it is one thing to know intellectually that "collateral damage" is an inevitable consequence of war, even of what is widely regarded as a just war; it is quite another thing to be constantly bombarded with film footage and photographs of burning children or mutilated villagers on television and on the Internet.

By the same token, the main barrier blocking widespread popular awareness of the squalid and degrading situation of the underclasses during "peacetime" used to be the relative emotional poverty of the written word. In 1937, for instance, George Orwell (2010, p. 38) stressed just this factor to explain the difficulty that bourgeois readers must have had in trying to grasp the reality of the living conditions experienced by the unemployed and working poor in the North of England:

> Words are such feeble things. What is the use of a brief phrase like "roof leaks" or "four beds for eight people"? It is the kind of thing your eye slides over, registering nothing. And yet what a wealth of misery it can cover!

Words are still feeble things, of course, and they still cover over a wealth of misery. But now the difficulty in understanding that Orwell noted can at least be partially overcome by access to images on television and the Internet. These days, very few members of the middle and upper classes do not know that wrenching narratives and documentary videos and films showing the kind of misery that Orwell put into "mere words" in 1937 are but a mouse click away on YouTube.

Like the pea under the stack of mattresses that disturbed the princess's sleep in Hans Christian Anderson's fairytale, the particular has somehow grown capable of making its ethical significance truly felt beneath the dead weight of centuries of abstractions and casuistries on the subject of our general moral and juridical duties to one another. *Felt*, not read or represented. The possibility of having an unrepresented awareness of the particular is stressed by Jean Genet in the following passage from *Prisoner of Love*, which attempts to describe the indescribability, so to speak, of the reality of Palestinian life in the occupied territories:

> If the reality of time spent among—not with—the Palestinians resided anywhere, it would survive between all the words that claim to give an account of it. They claim to give an account of it, but in fact it buries itself, slots itself exactly into the spaces, recorded there rather than in the words that serve only to blot it out. Another way of putting it: the space between the words contains more reality than does the time it takes to read them. Perhaps it's the same as the time, dense and real, enclosed between the characters in Hebrew.
>
> (Genet, 2003, p. 5)

Adorno, whose book *Negative Dialectics* (1973) remains to this day the most important treatment since Hegel of the idea of irreducible particularity in its relation to abstractions, uses the metaphor of long division to generalize the ethically troubling meaning of Genet's theory of the space between words: "objects do not go into their concepts without leaving a remainder" (1973, p. 5).

No rational ethical system ever devised has come up with a theory of the remainder. That is because conventional conceptions of ethics define themselves by "ought" and "ought not"—that is, they seize conceptual terrain in advance (i.e., in general terms) in order to warn of potential juridical responsibility for certain particularities that have not yet arisen. The Hobbesian theory that man, in his innermost nature, is wolf to man (Plautus: *lupus est homo homini*) views the establishment of this sort of juridical responsibility as a good and necessary constraint on our natural inclination to hurt one another.

But there is another side, as it were, to the advance seizure of conceptual terrain by "ought" and "ought not": namely, what the seizure encourages or allows to go on in the territory that is excluded. As Agamben (2012, p. 21) observes, it is now possible to say that ethics is rationalized "not in order to assume another kind of responsibility, but to articulate zones of non-responsibility" (see also Veitch, 2007). Like the West Bank Barrier, the high wall thrown around the terrain of juridical responsibility—whatever else it may do, however many people it may protect from harm—*also* serves to protect the good conscience of individual actors on the hither side of the wall from the spectacle of suffering lying beyond it.

When it comes to the ethical state of awareness called *after Auschwitz*, Adorno (1973, p. 362) admitted that he had probably been wrong to say that "after Auschwitz you could no longer write poems"; but this was only because he thought that "perennial suffering has as much right to expression as a tortured man has to scream." Pragmatic realism, which holds that only knowable truths matter and that the possibility of other truths should not concern us (Leiter, 2002, p. 278), encourages an ethically unseemly degree of haste in attaining closure. Unseemly because the pragmatist, in contrast to those who refuse to understand at all, "wants to understand too much and too quickly," as Agamben (2012, p. 17) puts it; the pragmatist thus overlooks the only decent way forward, which is not to choose between ignorance and immediate utility, but rather to investigate "the space between these two options."

"The realist confuses the established reality with reality itself" (Marcuse, 2011, p. 167). His universal rule of knowing is what Descartes called a *clara et distincta perceptio* ("clear and distinct perception") giving rise to *certum aliquid* ("something certain") (Heidegger, 2005, pp. 152, 175). But the *sense* of any certainty, in keeping with the etymological roots of "sense" (*sent* and *set* in Indo-European), is "always the direction (*sens*) of a road" (Derrida, 1989, p. 90)—it is not the open space of reality that the road happens to transect. Reality is neither true nor false, certain nor uncertain, sensible nor senseless—it simply *takes place.* To borrow an image from Walter Benjamin (1978, p. 6), the fan of reality, like the fan of memory, never comes to an end of its segments. A scrupulous person knows that only inside its folds does the truth of the particular lie, and moreover, that the fan *could* always be unfolded further.

This implies a conclusion that pervades virtually all forms of postmodern critical theory: what seems to be graspable "as" this or that is always in some sense betrayed by the very act of grasping it. The particular in this sense returns to the sphere of reason in the form of a revenant that is always disappointed and saddened by its betrayal by language. The point to be made here is not captured by the familiar right-wing caricature of postmodernism: that somehow there is no reality "out there," but only interpretations, only discourse. Rather, the point is that there is always *too much reality* out there for the concepts of "the factual" and "the true" to handle. What is, is always more than it is.

The ghost of the particular

As far as the instrumental use of language is concerned, what lies between the spaces that are mentioned by Genet and Agamben is immaterial by definition—one could say that it is even spectral, given the fact that this particular immateriality has to do with unnoticed human pain rather than some abstract Platonic idea. In short, a specter is haunting the temple of law and justice, and reason has increasingly begun to notice it. Not the old specter of a Communism that would imply the eventual withering-away of the state and all its institutions, including the law, but rather the fresh revenant of an irreducible particularity that no longer submits to being corked-up like vapor inside the specimen bottle of language.

Law *and* justice: the ghost of the particular does not rattle its chains against the rule of law in angry impatience for justice to be done. Instead, it silently reproaches the serial cruelties that seem to accompany just about every legal and political effort to manage people and populations, no matter whether the intent of the managers is to preserve the past in the name of law, or to perfect the future in the name of justice. The difference between law and justice, when seen from the point of view of the particular, is less like the difference between earth and heaven than it is like the difference between being ignored today and being ignored tomorrow.

The particular is not exactly silent in the face of injustice—it is speechless. As will be explained more fully in Chapter 4, the ability to keep silent belongs only to those who are used to speaking ("the speechful"), only those whose silence can be "heard" to mean something, such as reticence or acquiescence, if they decide not to speak. The noises made by the speechless, on the other hand, sound a priori meaningless in the ears of the makers and shakers of the world, even when they are noisier than a waterfall.

The implications for ethics of the opposition between the speechless particular and those who speak will be greatly diminished if the concept of speechlessness is interpreted according to conventional empirical categories alone. To be sure, those who are completely inexpressive—comatose persons, for example, and those living with end-stage Alzheimer's disease—are undeniably without speech. On their account, the law has even created special categories of persons ("guardians," "caretakers," etc.) to speak on their behalf while operating under the burden of an enhanced, or "fiduciary," legal duty. But in this book, the empirically voiceless are but the tip of an iceberg. Beneath them lie two additional layers. First, there are the *politically speechless* human beings whose voices are never listened to or heard within the institutions that determine their fates. And then, holding up all the rest, there is the massive base of the iceberg: the category of *ontological particularity*. Both types of particularity will be discussed in this chapter, and sometimes they will even be intermingled for rhetorical effect. At the end of the day, however, it will be the notion of ontological particularity that bears most directly on the central theme of the ethics of justice without illusions.

The ethics of punching (Levinas)

Without the state-sanctioned authority of God to validate and solidify social hierarchies and their associated relations of domination and subordination, exploitation and obedience, the legitimation of inter-human violence becomes a purely secular problem for which the image of a social contract among self-interested rational actors is one of the more notable and enduring proposed theoretical solutions. For its part, however, critical theory has traditionally relied on the different image of an historical struggle for recognition in the dialectic of master and slave (Hegel, 1977, pp. 111–119), morphed into that of resistance to oppression in the class struggle (Marx and Engels, 1998, pp. 34–35), to represent inter-human violence as a *temporally bounded* natural fact, like a geological era that will one day come to an end.

If social contract theory portrays inter-human violence as an aspect of human nature that must be eternally restrained by some sort of agreed-upon Leviathan, then critical theory is inclined to represent such violence, or rather certain forms of it, as a necessary condition for its own eventual erasure from world history. As Marx put it in his essay *Private Property and Communism*:

> Once the essence of man and of nature, man as natural being and nature as a human reality, has become evident in practical life, in sense experience, the quest for an *alien* being [God, the State, moral laws, etc.], a being above man and nature (a quest which is an avowal of the unreality of man and nature) *becomes impossible in practice.*
>
> (1964, pp. 166–167) (emphasis added)

In short, it is stipulated (or hoped) that at the end of history the progressive violence of the past will have made any future oppression and violence unimaginable.

Thus, critical legal theory, in one way or another, has tended to represent those who employ one or more of the dialectical moments in the triune *Politics/Law/Justice* to "punch *down*" (as the saying goes) in the social order as despicable oppressors. Rich slumlords punch down when they evict long-term tenants of modest means to develop high-end condominium projects; bosses punch down when they pay minimum wage (or less) to their workers and then aggressively obstruct the latter's efforts to unionize; the government punches down when it seeks to punish its whistleblowers for treason instead of holding to account the demonstrably culpable high officials on whom the whistles were blown. *Mutatis mutandis*, critical theory is viscerally inclined to approve of anyone who succeeds, against all odds, in using the same triune (*Politics/Law/Justice*) to "punch *up*" at the elite and their many privileges. Critical thought is predisposed to valorize most of those who punch up as progressive reformers, heroic resistors, selfless communitarians, or revolutionaries on the right side of history.

For what it's worth, the author of this book agrees that the general psychological inclination to draw the distinction between punching down and punching up is essential to the effective pursuit of what progressives like to imagine, and conservatives like to scorn, under the heading "social justice." It is also a progressive political imperative of the highest order, one with which the author agrees (again, for what it's worth). It might even be the case that the distinction between punching up and punching down will show itself as ethically decisive in many (or even most) situations, although it is hard to see how anything *in general* can be meaningfully said on the subject of our *particular* ethical responses.

But it is worth repeating that the subject matter of this book is neither social justice nor any other form of justice. It is the ethical situation of a disenchanted person involved in the work of justice. As previous chapters have attempted to demonstrate, politics, law, and justice are not the same as ethics. Punching down and punching up are both forms of punching. If the ethical critique of violence is to avoid falling into pre-critical dogmatism, it must always begin by acknowledging without equivocation that they belong to the same class: *the infliction of suffering on others.*

Having demonstrated over and over again that what once appeared to be the silk purse of justice is really the sow's ear of interest or ideology, critical legal scholars can hardly be surprised when their own cherished silk purses are likewise turned inside out by their political opponents. It is as if 40 years of critical legal thought had succeeded all too well in demonstrating the metaphysical groundlessness of all traditional conceptions of law, justice, and morality, which is to say their logical indeterminacy and infinite political malleability. What else are we to make of the fact that oppressors can and often do so readily assume the garb of the oppressed in the popular imagination (and vice versa), and, more generally, that the grammar and rhetoric of justice and human rights can so easily and plausibly be flipped by interested parties to support just about *any* reproach to the law's tendencies?

We live in an era in which the discourse of justice and human rights has been put into the service of high-level bombing campaigns and drone strikes (Douzinas, 2000, pp. 133–137); American oligarchs can publicly assert with a straight face that political critiques of income inequality have placed the richest 1 per cent of the population in a position similar to that of German Jews on the verge of *Kristallnacht* (Perkins, 2014); activist Christian lawyers can, also with a straight face, invoke the historical example of heroic judicial resistance to *Dred Scott v. Sandford*[2] to support the argument that religious liberty gives public officials the right to deny marriage licenses to gay couples despite the Supreme Court's decision in *Obergefell v. Hodges*[3] (Blinder and Fausset, 2015); and far-right French politicians in neo-fascist parties win considerable public support for their anti-Muslim and anti-immigrant policies by using the language of civil rights and *laïcité* to defend (or pretend to defend) the victims of misogyny and homophobia (Alduy, 2014, p. 20).

Today's political struggles are no less important than they used to be, but they are no longer about the true or evolving meaning of universals. Instead, they take place on a featureless terrain from which the idea that universals *must be* universally binding has withdrawn forever. The point to be made is not the familiar one, associated with George Orwell and W.H. Austin, that hypocrisy is no longer possible because language has been corrupted by politics, propaganda, and capitalism to such a degree that it is no longer capable of expressing the difference between what is true and what is false. Rather, the point is that postmodernity has at last awakened to the fact (if it is right to call it a fact) that "true" is just another word that is used in many different language-games of truth, each with its own special criterion of correctness (Foucault, 1972). Or, if you will, more than a few human beings living in the twenty-first century look at the word *true* and, whether rightly or wrongly, conveniently or inconveniently, *do not see a nimbus.*

Emmanuel Levinas was one of the most notable thinkers of the twentieth century who did not and could not see a nimbus surrounding the word "true." Again and again, he famously described the phenomenology of "facing" during the ethically charged moment when the Other first appears to the I; that is, *while* the particular is appearing to us but *before* it congeals in language and thought into a determinate being about which something true or false could be said. He typically characterized the phenomenon of face-to-face discourse this way, for instance:

> I do not just think that he is, I speak to him. He is my *partner* in a relation that was only to have made him present to me. I have spoken to him, that is, I have overlooked the universal being he incarnates in order to confine myself to the particular being he is.
>
> (Levinas, 1998a, p. 5).

Levinas's analysis of justice, which since the 1980s has exerted considerable influence on critical legal theory, involves what the present author has called elsewhere "the problem of the passage" between the infinite ethical responsibility generated by facing and the finite social necessity of imposing suffering on particular others in the name of justice (Wolcher, 2005, p. 121). Although Levinas did not write extensively about law as such, the typical *temporal* focus of the jurisprudence that he did write, as of that of his followers, is ethics during the very moment of doing justice. From the point of view of a Levinasian analysis of "ethical justice," the most important task during that moment is to soften its necessary harshness by making the agents of justice "more knowing in the name, the memory, of the original kindness of man toward his other" (Levinas, 1998a, p. 229).

Nevertheless, and *pace* Levinas, we are not concerned here with the possible perfection of justice against its own harshness, however ethically and politically desirable this may appear to be. Instead, the titular theme of "the ethics of justice without illusions" seeks to investigate an important dimension or consequence of this very aspiration: namely, *the haunted situation* of anyone who tries in good faith to do the perfecting without receiving any comfort from conventional understandings of how linguistic norms mean what they seem to mean. We care most of all about what can happen in (and to) the disenchanted human heart as a consequence of the ever-increasing awareness that there may exist an irreparable scission between individual ethics and social justice.

Neither a victim nor an executioner (Camus and Levinas)

Camus's famous ethical aspiration to be "neither a victim nor an executioner" (1947, pp. 141–146) rests on the clear-eyed recognition that the sword of justice has two edges, not one, and that it cannot redeem a wounded world without opening new wounds that themselves stand in need of redemption. This recognition is the consequence of the reflux, so to speak, of irretrievable past cruelties that at one time could be swallowed (or gagged down) on the belief (or half-belief) they were ethically irrelevant, because just about everybody agreed they were "necessary" to enforce the rule of law, to preserve the health of society, or to hasten the inevitable victory of justice over injustice. Once the feeling of justification in any given case is exposed as but an effect-cum-cause in the infinite causal web—that is, once the idea of *justice-as-ground* has been disenchanted—the ethical problem of attempting to do justice without the illusion of being grounded in anything beyond the sheer facticity of the attempt itself begins to loom large.

One of France's most celebrated artists, Eugène Delacroix, once remarked that genius does not consist in the production of new ideas, but rather in continuing to advance the one dominant idea that what has already been said once or twice, or even many times, has not yet been said enough (Camus, 1965a, p. 237). Every schoolchild in France probably would be able to recognize his most famous painting, *La Liberté guidant le peuple*, which celebrates the July 1830 revolution toppling King Charles X of France (see Figure 3.2). But there is one particular image in this painting that conveys an idea that the will to justice would like to suppress. The idea in question is *not* the one represented in the top half of the picture, where French Romanticism, at the very height of its power and influence, celebrates the gloriousness of freedom's victory over tyranny, and of justice over injustice, in a manner that could not be more stirring to the emotions.

The idea that most threatens the conscience of the will to justice—and therefore the one it would most like to suppress—is not about glory and transcendence. It is about the suffering and death of those who must be overcome for justice to be done. Its image peers out at the viewer malignantly from the *bottom* part of the

Figure 3.2 "Liberty leading the people" 1830. Oil on canvas, by Eugene Delacroix (1798–1863)

Photo: Hervé Lewandowski. © RMN-Grand Palais/Art Resource, NY

painting, where the ghastly, half-naked bodies of the dead are lying. Liberty and her companions are just about to trample these bodies under foot, and it would appear that they *must* trample them under foot to get where they are going.

Who are the dead and dying in this picture? Whatever the historical facts may be, one cannot bring oneself to believe that as sensitive an artist as Delacroix intended to depict only heroes and martyrs at the bottom of his painting. The sufferings of heroes and martyrs are redeemed by the future success of their cause. Eventually marble monuments and bronze statues will raise them from the dead, so to speak, like Lazarus. The anonymous millions whose sufferings and deaths are merely deemed necessary or useful for the great and glorious cause to succeed, or who just happen to be in the wrong place at the wrong time, have no such luck. The memory of *their* sufferings is lost to history. *Their* shattered lives become the cobblestones over which history's winners march in triumph.

These lowly cobblestones include not only history's long list of failures and also-rans, but also the countless innocents—the so-called "little people" of the earth—who always seem to get caught in the crossfires of historical change. Not only the literal crossfire of wars and revolutions, but also the figurative crossfire of economic crises and upheavals, social dislocations, and environmental catastrophes. Their unspoken political opinions may be progressive, conservative, reactionary, or simply nonexistent. Their unknown personal characteristics and past deeds may be admirable, despicable, or both. It doesn't matter: they will all fall victim to the crossfire. Military officers have given an antiseptic name to these sorts of victims—"collateral damage"—and just like quicklime thrown into a mass grave, this terrible term is intended to sanitize and hide what lies beneath it.

Levinas provides a quintessential example of the haunted situation of someone who tries in good faith to do what is right and just without receiving any comfort whatsoever from the illusion that the hand which wields the sword of justice is somehow ethically distinguishable from his or her own hand. Lest his conception of ethics be confused with dogmatic pacifism or even cowardly quietism, Levinas unequivocally rejected the idea of non-resistance to evil: "If self-defense is a problem, the 'executioner' is the one who threatens my neighbor and, in this sense, calls for violence and no longer has a Face" (Levinas, 1998a, p. 105). It is therefore worth noting that Levinas (1998a, p. 231) publicly celebrated (crying "Honor to the West!") the justice of France's decision to try Klaus Barbie, a notorious old Nazi, in 1987 for war crimes and crimes against humanity committed some four decades earlier.

On the other hand, it is also true that Levinas chose to qualify his praise for the Barbie trial, and hence undercut its political effectiveness, by giving an unqualified affirmative answer to the question whether "the S.S. man has what I mean by the face" (1998a, p. 231). The Roman playwright Terence's most famous aphorism describes Levinas's ethical outlook perfectly: "I am human; nothing that is human is alien to me" (*Homo sum; humani nihil a me alienum puto*) (Terence, 1976, p. 29). By agreeing with the scandalous proposition that even a member of Hitler's dreaded *Schutzstaffel* has an ethically relevant "face," Levinas effectively hedged his praise of the Barbie trial in a manner that might seem conflicted if not sacrilegious to those for whom justice is a supreme value, especially in the context of the Holocaust. Despite his painful personal experiences during and after the Holocaust, or perhaps because of them, Levinas's answer expresses the surprising psychological fact that he could not help caring ethically about the fate of even those human beings responsible for perpetrating the worst sorts of crimes.

All known ideals of justice have tolerated and even demanded a certain amount of necessary violence and suffering so that "justice may be done," as the saying goes. Justice must reject in principle the tortured sentiment expressed by Samuel Beckett: "I can't bear the thought of giving any more pain" (2011, pp. 493–494, n. 1). The wooden scaffold that was specially erected at Auschwitz to hang (on April 16, 1947) Rudolf Höss, the first commandant of that unspeakably vile place, remains to this day a sobering reminder of a profoundly simple truth (see Figure 3.3). *Justice does not and cannot declare war on universal human suffering because the infliction of pain is one of its necessary instruments.*

And yet, to paraphrase Vladimir Jankélévich (2005, p. 19), thinkers like Levinas are burdened by the nagging realization that every particular real person we collectively or individually punish today infinitely exceeds the sin in which our sense of injustice (or *ressentiment*) wants to imprison him. Levinas knew that the minute

Figure 3.3 Gallows used to hang Rudolph Höss. Auschwitz, Poland

Photo: Louis Wolcher

we begin to think of *any* particular human being as less than this, we are lost. To understand this is to know that the classical problems of law and justice are also problems of an individual moral nature. Their apparently social or political hue masks an ethical core because in fact there is no such thing as a social contract or *volonté générale* that is not always first interpreted and administered by a particularity: a human being that inwardly counts as a "Me Myself" before he or she dons the uniform of a functionary (an idealized self) in this or that system of collective repression.

To put the matter the way Walter Benjamin (1978, p. 278) did in *Critique of Violence*, no critique of violence can be genuinely *critical* if it does not suspend belief, for purposes of the critique, in the ideological formula that "just ends can be attained by justified means, justified means used to just ends." Although Benjamin was referring here to a "common dogma" uniting the jurisprudential theories of positive law and natural law, the ethical salience of his comment is far more radical. As the previous chapter's discussion of disenchantment suggests, any ethical critique of "just ends" and "justified means" will always remain fatally incomplete unless it is prepared to confront and demystify the phenomenon of *self*-enchantment. It suggests that ethics cannot declare that peace has arrived so long as there remains any amount of pain inflicted by one person on another that is routinized and accepted as natural.

Ontological particularity

Awareness without personhood or knowledge

Not lying to oneself is not the same as not lying to one's *self.* The reader will find no neatly packaged metaphysical description or theory of individual identity in these pages. That is because the philosophical problems that are usually identified with words such as "the self" and "the ego" belong to the larger problem of *conceptuality* as such. That is, they arise from the ways in which the structures of language encourage one to believe that a substance must correspond to every substantive, and an event to every verb. The conventional sense of the question "Who says 'I'?" overlooks the possibility that it is only the mouth pronouncing the word "I" that is saying the word "who" on any given occasion.[4] *The self* is therefore one of the very categories (along with concepts such as "law" and "justice") that this book seeks to unpack and demystify. Nevertheless, since the ethics of participating in the projects of politics, law, and justice is our primary focus, the vocabulary of selfhood will be impossible to avoid, and at times might even present certain advantages.

Thus, Aristotle's famous definition of the human being as *zōon logon echon*—the animal (*zōon*) that has language (*logos*) (*Politics* 1253^{a}9)—points toward a profound duality in the everyday experience of being human. On the one hand, the human being seems to be an embodied, psychosomatic bundle of flesh, bone, nerves, and blood, no different from any other sentient animal subject to the rigors of natural processes. But on the other hand, the human being is also a speaking being capable of thinking, naming, and describing things in the world, including most especially its own subjectivity as an "I."

The well-known Cartesian modification of this unresolved duality draws a firm metaphysical distinction between body and mind—*res extensa* and *res cogitans*—within the unifying medium of linear time conceived as a sequence of homogeneous moments (Descartes, 1984, vol. 1, pp. 223–224). Although Aristotle also thought of time as a sequence of moments, Descartes's two-substances answer to the question of what it means to be human accentuated the fact that the so-called "mind–body problem" is primarily a consequence of its presumed temporality. In particular, the presupposition is that an immaterial mind and a material body actually go hand in hand with one another from one moment of time to the next, like a holographic thumb and a real forefinger moving from bead to bead along a string of prayer beads. This gives rise to the classical enigma of how these utterly different types of entities could ever "communicate" with one another at (or in) the "same" time.

"Freedom," said Heidegger (2010a, p. 149), "rests in being able to let [*Lassenkönnen*], not in ordering and dominating." We need not worry about Descartes's two substances can comminicate with one another if we let go of how the obsessive metaphysical craving for a unitary self. If we can let something like the self as *res extensa* and the self as *res cogitans* occupy two different, and ultimately incommensurable, temporal contexts, then the possibility that the latter would be unable to *definitively dictate* to the former would no longer be felt to be a problem. Each self would be a sort of sovereign, so to speak, in its own sphere, or rather, in its own time. Indeed, recognizing that the *res cogitans* cannot completely master the *res extensa* with words in the temporal milieu that is most proper to it might actually represent an ethical advance rather than the evasion of an ethical problem, especially if one's disenchantment with normative language leads one to agree, with Badiou (2003, p. 66), that "Evil is the will to name *at any price*." Chapter 5, which explores a phenomenon called "senseless kindness," will return to and sharpen this very point.

For now, though, it is sufficient to state that the concept of *ontological particularity* rests on the methodological decision to disarticulate the distinction between the speaking individual and the psychosomatic individual by drawing attention to their *different temporal modes of appearance*. In a nutshell: the concept of the speaking individual finds its home in the linear milieu of what Benjamin calls "homogeneous, empty time," whereas that of the psychosomatic individual keeps on furiously erupting, over and over again, in the horizontal medium of "time filled by the presence of the now [*Jetztzeit*]" (Benjamin, 1968, p. 261). An active speaker's syntax and its purported semantic content can only unfold, like music, sequentially along a horizontal "span" of moments. In contrast, the ceaseless flow of non-intentional, "hyletic data" is immanent to the more or less passive consciousness of the psychosomatic individual who is continually being bombarded with it (Husserl, 1962, pp. 226–230). Benjamin's opposition between *homogeneous time* (spread along a horizontal line) and the *now-time* (enclosed within a horizon) is a convenient way to characterize this phenomenological difference.

It is important to understand that the point of performing this sort of disarticulation of the double self's temporal modes of appearing is not to prove that time conceived as a horizon surrounding an eternal now is somehow metaphysically "truer" than time conceived as a linear sequence of moments, or vice versa. It is not the true nature of time that needs to be exposed—it is, rather, the phenomenon of disenchanted ethical trauma that needs exposure. And paying close attention to the logical and phenomenological incommensurability of these two concepts of time is the key to that exposure, for this procedure highlights—and more importantly, *dignifies*—the experience of ethically relevant realities that the thinking, speaking individual does not in fact "know," and therefore cannot say. The tears that Levinas (1996, p. 23) says the civil servant cannot see are actually tears that the civil servant qua speaking individual is rigorously trained not to witness and acknowledge; they are not, thank God, tears that he is utterly incapable of experiencing qua psychosomatic individual.

As Agamben has already observed, the real advantage of disarticulating the bodily self from the speaking self is to show that there is a fundamental *ethical* incommensurability between, on the one hand, the more or less continuous flow of vital functions in the body and brain of the psychosomatic individual (respiration, digestion, hearing, dreaming, etc.) and, on the other hand, the only intermittent eruption of language from the conscious, speaking individual. Since the one is continuously mute and the other is only occasionally verbose, it is really quite astonishing, says Agamben (2012, p. 122), that "subjectivity and consciousness, in which our culture believed itself to have found its firmest foundation, rest on what is most precarious and fragile in the world: the event of speech." It is also quite worrying, because it shows that every attempt at subjectification by the speaking individual enacts a kind of constitutive falsehood: any subjectification in language, no matter how honest (e.g., "This is who I really am . . .") is simultaneously a de-subjectification of the pre-linguistic, living, breathing, experiencing psychosomatic individual (Agamben, 2012, p. 123).

The notion of ontological particularity contradicts the ultimately deistic thesis that all things derive their natures from a common source (e.g., God) that has placed them in the "same" space and time, and therefore that they have a natural "mutual orientation" to one another that makes it possible for true knowledge to take the form of a remainderless merger of mind and thing—*assimilatio intellectus ad rem* (Heidegger, 2005, p. 120). But of course everyday experience confirms that the body is capable of sensing what no amount of reasoned speech can say. As a phenomenological finding, ontological particularity owes its discovery to the distinctly *ethical* choice to pay attention to the experience of the same radical incommensurability between the psychosomatic individual and the speaking individual that Agamben mentions.

The concept of ontological particularity allows for the psychosomatic individual to *become aware* of something (the reality of the particular) that the speaking individual does not and cannot "know" or express. Walter Benjamin's theory of experience provides a clue about the nature of this difference, in as much as there is a latent ambiguity in the English word "experience" that a distinction drawn in German helps to clarify. *Erfahrung* and *Erlebnis* can both be translated as "experience," but as Andrew Feenberg observes, for Benjamin they signified two different *types* of experience:

> He distinguished between *Erfahrung*, experience shaped by a deep relationship to reality, and *Erlebnis*, experience as a momentary response to passing sensation. *Erfahrung* registers the real at a subconscious level and changes the person who undergoes it, while *Erlebnis* is a defensive response to the speed and shock of daily life in a modern society. *Erlebnis* has no resonance and quickly slips out of consciousness as new experiences challenge the subject. These characteristic modern experiences leave few traces in contrast to *Erfahrung*, which has a kind of existential depth.
>
> (Marcuse, 2011, pp. 238–239)

The ontologically particular, in the phenomenological-ethical sense used here, is accessible only to the kind of pre-articulate awareness associated with *Erfahrung*; in *Erlebnis*, it flits by everyday consciousness without leaving a trace. On the other hand, it must also be acknowledged that *Erfahrung* as such does not enclose the particular in the prison cell of any sort of "knowledge," and furthermore, that any subsequent passage from *Erfahrung* into propositional language represents another sort of betrayal of the real. The concept of ontological particularity thus reflects an ethically troubling truth that is hidden within Hegel's great insight that the particular cannot assert itself, or be asserted by others, without the universal—that is, without language. As Agamben (1998, p. 50) puts it, language "holds man in its ban insofar as man, as a speaking being, has always already entered into language without noticing it." It follows that the particular can never acquire "its" voice, but only *a* voice, not its own, in which event it ceases to be itself, it ceases to be particular.

From what has been said already, it is clear that the concept of ontological particularity should not be confused with the concept of a particular person or type of person, downtrodden or otherwise. The word "person" comes from the Latin *persona*, which referred to the mask worn by actors in the theater. And while the etymologically related Greek term *prosopon* did not denote a mask, it did mean the typical facial characteristics of the individual—the "face," so to speak, that one presents to others in the *agora*. Both words implied that their respective personhoods, so to speak, were relatively fixed and constant.

As we shall see in the next chapter, a downtrodden and forgotten "person" in this conventional sense speaks and is heard much, much less than a high and mighty "person," and therefore experiences political speechlessness much more often. However, the intermittent manifestations of personhood that happen to be noticed by oneself and others, though politically and legally important, do not furnish the contents of what we have called *ontological particularity*. Instead, these manifestations of personhood are best understood as traces. A trace is a present remainder (but not a representation) left over from a past particularity—for example, a lipstick stain on a cocktail napkin or a footprint in the flowerbed. Levinas (2003a, p. 41) once said that "the significance of the trace consists in signifying without making appear." In keeping with this definition, the ordinary manifestations of personhood are best viewed as *traces* of ontological particularity rather than as representations of it.

Though empiricism registers only representable facts, everyday experience confirms that it is possible to become aware of something without grasping it in thought or reducing it to a proposition—just as one can touch a mountain without being able to put one's arms around it (Descartes, 1984, vol. 2, p. 32 n.1). This type of awareness sometimes leaves a trace of itself in language that evokes the memory (whether voluntary or involuntary) of having experienced something that in itself is tiny and insignificant. Proust's famous "episode of the madeleine" in *Remembrance of Things Past* (1934, p. 34) is a case in point, as is Orwell's account of getting to know the progress of individual crumbs left on a dirty tablecloth in the down-and-out boardinghouse where he lodged while doing research for *The Road to Wigan Pier* (2010, p. 4). By the same token, every time we say "I think (or want or believe or hope or . . .) such and such," the little word "I" leaves a trace of something real that is presently happening psychosomatically that is not identical with any description of some "person" to whom the grammatical subject of the sentence might seem, on later reflection, to refer.

Like a sweat stain on an old letter written by one obscure person to another, both of whom are long since dead, the trace of a quotidian experience that is deposited in casual language expressing conceptually insignificant memories is not the same as a proposition of fact. Does the stain suggest that the day was hot? That the writer was nerve-wracked? That the writer started writing just after having done vigorous exercise? That an ancient reader (not the writer) left the stain when she read it on a hot day? Etc. No one can or will ever know. The very indeterminacy of the trace as a signifier is its greatest strength in the present context: no one doubts that *something real happened* as the letter was being written that the letter itself does not (or at least need not) describe, just as no one doubts that no amount of determinate speech could ever decide exactly what that something was.

Casual, everyday speech is to the proposition what the sweat stain is to the letter: a trace that there was something non-propositional or non-literate *going on* in reality as and when the proposition or letter was being produced. "Language and statements are not at the same level of existence," says Foucault: "However banal it may be, however unimportant its consequences may appear to be, a statement is always an event that neither the language nor the meaning can quite exhaust" (1972, pp. 28, 85). In short: the oft-mentioned postmodern distinction between *saying* and *said* gestures at something the awareness of which belongs to the category of ontological particularity without also belonging to the category of knowledge. The speaking individual "takes time," as it were, to say what is *said*;

the psychosomatic individual, however, is the one who experiences the now-time of *saying* as such.

The difference between an experience and the memory of it, or more broadly, the difference between the real and the true, has not gone unnoticed by philosophy. Indeed, the distinction between what can be understood in thought and described in language (*the knowable and sayable*), on the one hand, and, on the other hand, what can only be *named* from an awareness of it that lies beyond (or falls short of) knowledge (*the real but unsayable*), has always played a major role in Western thought. One can find it just about everywhere in the Western canon. Some of the more notable examples include: Plato's distinction between objects of knowledge and the idea of the good (*hē tou agathou idea*) (*Republic VI*, 508e–509b); Kant's distinction (1998, p. 112) between the Thing-in-Itself (*Ding an Sich*) and objects of consciousness (phenomena); Heidegger's distinction between Being (*Sein*) and beings (*Seindes*) (1962, p. 62); and Wittgenstein's Delphic remark, in the *Tractatus* (1974, p. 74), about the imperative of remaining silent in the face of those aspects of reality that we cannot speak about ("*Wovon man nicht sprechen kann, darüber muss man schweigen*").

However, unlike the distinctions drawn by Plato, Kant, Heidegger, and Wittgenstein, the concept of ontological particularity that is at stake here does not gesture at the unity of something that transcends propositional speech in order to ground, or be grounded by, metaphysical or ontological speculation. To be sure, the particular is "infinite" in the precise etymological sense of being not *finitus*, that is, not finished or determined by limits set in advance. However, this does not imply that the particular is conceptually very large, so to speak, like Descartes's God[5] or Heidegger's Being.[6] Nor is it very small, like the infinitesimal atoms of Leucippus and Democritus,[7] Duns Scotus's indivisible haecceities,[8] or Leibniz's extensionless monads.[9]

In the Western philosophical tradition, the concept of God or Being is supposed to explain the origin of beings in the world—from the top looking down, as it were. Whereas the concept of ineffable tiny entities is supposed to explain, from the bottom looking up, that which makes up the substance of the world, or, as in Wittgenstein's picture theory and logical atomism, that which accounts for the possibility of representing something in language.[10] Either way, the particular as such is requested to step aside, like a bit actor in a movie, so that *something else* can be explicitly noticed and cognized, whether it be God, Being, World, or Language. In contrast, the ontologically particular in the sense used here seems, shall we say, rather trivial when seen from the point of view of either ontological largeness or metaphysical smallness. More's the pity.

The discovery that the sensibility of the ontologically particular, like that of God in theology, is not subject to the *principium individuationis* ("principle of individuation") is one of the great triumphs of the human spirit. At long last it offers to liberate the ethics of the real from the ethics of the true. Insofar as its pragmatic significance is concerned, the discovery that the particular is not exhausted by any attempt to subsume it under a correct concept, or describe it in a true proposition, subverts the primacy of what was once taken to be the traditional ethical question par excellence. No longer is ethics exclusively, or even primarily, the study of "how men ought to act in general, not as a means to a given end" (Lacey, 1986, p. 66), or even about how the individual called "I" ought to act in a given case. Generally speaking, "Ought" is confident that it knows all that it needs to know about reality, having already fitted it into the Procrustean bed of an "Is" statement. Prior to *Ought* (which is impatient to establish norms and get things done), and prior to *Is* (which feels certain in its knowledge of the world), looms a far more disturbing ethical question—one that takes infinite patience to answer: *Whom and what will I have* failed *to notice?*

What lies between the lines

In disarticulating the speaking individual from the psychosomatic individual, the previous section considered the phenomenology of *becoming aware of* (without "knowing") the ontologically particular in the course of exposure to the kind of experience that Benjamin called *Erfahrung.* Chapter 7's discussion of the phenomenon of senseless kindness will complete this part of the analysis, which is intimately related to our attempt to answer what we have called the Fundamental Question: whether it is possible for a disenchanted person to live a lie-free life in the law. The present section, however, brings out a different ethical dimension of ontological particularity: namely, its tendency to be missed altogether while we are undergoing the kind of existentially shallow everyday experience that Benjamin called *Erlebnis.*

The latter aspect of ontological particularity belongs to the category of that which is not in fact presently noticed by a particular individual (whether considered psychosomatic *or* speaking) during any given event of noticing something. It has three defining characteristics. First, it has the property of being something that cannot in principle *be* noticed by the individual in question, in as much as it is defined as that which he or she *does* not notice, though of course someone else might notice it (e.g., "He gave her an engagement ring containing a blood diamond, and she doesn't even suspect it"). Second, it can be understood by the actor, but only *after* the fact as something that was previously overlooked (e.g., "It never occurred to me that homeless people were sleeping underneath the bridge that I drove over this morning; now I see that they have been camped there for weeks"). Third, to the extent that it is characterized presently by others, or afterward by the actor as something that was previously overlooked, it is always characterized "as" this or that ("blood diamond," "homeless people")—which is to say never in the form of Adorno's post-conceptual remainder, but only as an epagogic instance of a general concept.

In principle, the eidetic reduction (i.e., the methodological bracketing of all ordinary ontological categories of understanding) (Husserl, 1990, pp. 33–42) allows the phenomenologist to observe not only what is present in consciousness, but also what is absent. The sort of ontological particularity with which we are now concerned can therefore be described privatively as what the ethical "I" *does not presently doubt* about his or her present situation, that is, about reality. It owes its ethical significance to the phenomenal fact that each and every one of us *is* such an ethical "I" during each and every moment of our lives. It is important to realize that in failing to notice what we do not doubt about a situation, there is no inner "decision" not to doubt. Instead, the binary decision to *doubt-or-not-doubt* something "is simply absent," as Wittgenstein puts it (2005, p. 248e). Others can presently characterize what we do not doubt. Later on, we can take note of the fact that we did not doubt something before. But in the very moment that counts most—the lived ethical moment of choice and action—what we do not doubt is just *not to be found in us*, no matter how hard we may try to look for it.

The category of what the ethical "I" does not doubt about a situation thus adds an important qualification to Heidegger's well-known observation that "in the instant when I have chosen, I am no longer free" (2005, p. 115). By this, he meant that if the most genuine sense of being-free is to be placed indifferently before two or more possibilities of acting, then "freedom is cancelled" once one possibility is seized to the exclusion of all others. But the phenomenological category of what the ethical "I" does not doubt about a situation (the ontologically particular), as we have determined it, shows that the much-vaunted "freedom to choose amongst possibilities" is always already *unfree*. No one is free to choose a possibility, however ethically imperative, that can only be revealed by an impossible "awareness" of what one does not doubt.

In this context, the earlier mentioned metaphors of the space between words (Genet) and of the space between the options of understanding quickly and not understanding at all (Agamben) bring to mind another important metaphor of spatiality: Wittgenstein's image of a network (*ein Netzwerk*) laid over a surface, which he used in the *Tractatus* to illustrate the contingency of the relationship between language and reality. We shall use this metaphor to create a model, so to speak, of the notion of not-doubted ontological particularity in order to make its peculiar ethical status as perspicuous as possible:

> Let us imagine a white surface with irregular black spots on it. We then say that whatever kind of picture these make, I can always approximate as closely as I wish to the description of it by covering the surface with a sufficiently fine square mesh, and then saying of every square whether it is black or white. In this way I shall have imposed a unified form on the description of the surface. The form is optional, since I could have achieved the same result by using a net with a triangular or hexagonal mesh. Possibly the use of a triangular mesh would have made the description simpler: that is to say, it might be that we could describe the surface more accurately with a coarse triangular mesh than with a fine square mesh (or conversely), and so on. *The different nets correspond to different systems for describing the world.*
>
> (Wittgenstein, 1974, pp. 67–68) (Prop. 6.341)
> (emphasis added)

A few years later, in one of his lectures at Cambridge, Wittgenstein refined this metaphor further by saying that propositional language—the language of "facts"—must have the "right multiplicity" to be able to describe what lies underneath the network or grid. Using the figure of a reticulated grid with numerous points falling along its lines, but with one other point, *z*, located *inside* one of the squares of the grid, he said: "And if language can only describe a route which follows the lines, then it will be impossible to describe or prescribe a route to a point *z* which is not on the lines" (1980b, p. 2).

Figure 3.4 combines the network metaphor of the *Tractatus* with the grid metaphor of different routes specified in advance to illustrate a central feature of this book's theory of the particular:

The drawing shows two different labeled pathways for getting from point *X* to point *Y* inside the shaded area in the middle: *X-a-b-c-Y* and *X-d-e-f-g-c-Y*. These two pathways correspond to two different linguistic systems, or grammars, for

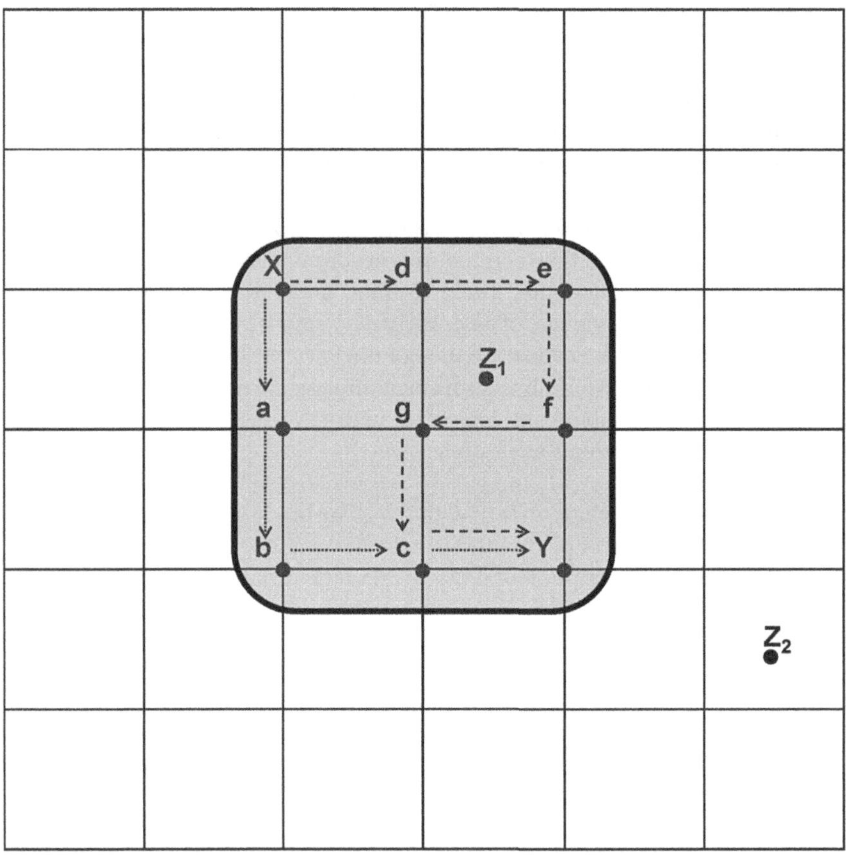

Figure 3.4 The grid and the particular

describing and dealing with the reality that lies underneath the grid. The shaded area represents what Wittgenstein (1953, p. 5e) would have called a particular "language-game" that some people use (and are used by) in interacting with the reality that underlies it. Within this general language-game (e.g., the language of the law), there can be and usually are several different sub-games (the language of criminal law, the language of contract law, and so forth) in which different actors may specialize. Not only that, some of these sub-games may actually compete with one another socially and politically to control those aspects of reality that find themselves within the reach of legal power.

To cite a familiar example drawn from an ongoing judicial debate within American constitutional law: let one pathway in Figure 3.4 represent the grammar of construing a constitutional provision in terms of something called its "original meaning" (cf. Scalia and Garner, 2012), and let the other represent the grammar of interpreting the same provision in terms of something called its "general purpose" (cf. Breyer, 2005). In the example shown in the diagram, both methods just happen to lead to the same result—point *Y*—though the two ways of getting there are different, and therefore different things are noticed about reality along the way. The ontological particularities that comprise the total real situation in which the parties to this hypothetical "case" find themselves is shown as point Z_1. These particularities are in principle unrepresentable, except in the form of "factual" propositions, which themselves take their bearing and acquire their syntax from the method that a given judge uses to decide the case. So method *X-a-b-c-Y* (e.g., "original meaning") notices and stresses certain aspects of the situation (Z_1) that method *X-d-e-f-g-c-Y* (e.g., "purposive interpretation") misses or discounts as irrelevant, and vice versa.

So far so good. Every particularity that attracts the attention of legal actors in the form of something that they feel the need to deal with officially must perforce be expressed and understood "as" something. The idea of speaking about something "as such" can be traced to the late Middle Ages, where the equivalent terms *ut tale* and *qua tale* were used to indicate the what-being, or essence, of the thing in question. Heidegger (2008, p. 105) would greatly expand this idea into the phenomenological structure of always noticing something as something on the basis of what is already known and familiar (*die Struktur des Etwas als Etwas*). Although Derrida (1989, p. 51) notes that Heidegger's "as-structure" is preverbal and "not to be confused with the 'as' of a statement," it is obvious that nothing can be *said* about any pre-predicative *as* that is not first and foremost the "as" of some statement. It is a profound tautology that there is *no language but language* to express the nonlinguistic.

That said, it is important to notice that the official interpretation of the total situation corresponding to Z_1 is to a large extent out of the hands of the real human beings who are living it. That is, the ultimate power to control the binding linguistic expression of their situation is given to other people (legislators, lawyers, witnesses, judges, stenographers, etc.). Chapter 4 will return to this point in analyzing speechlessness, and especially the ethical difficulties that are associated with what it calls *motivated ventriloquism*. For present purposes, however, it is more important to pay close attention to the situation indicated by the other *Z*-point in the drawing. For if the "case" associated with Z_1 was at least noticed in *some* way by the legal system, the same cannot be said about the situation that is labeled Z_2.

It will be observed that *neither* pre-established pathway from *X* to *Y* (i.e., neither method of describing and dealing with reality) passes through or even near point Z_2, which is located outside the shaded area. In fact, Point Z_2 is essentially invisible as far as the grammatical situation of the legal system now stands. In Figure 3.4, *Point* Z_2 *represents the idea of the not-doubted ontologically particular in relation to the language of reason and control.* Point Z_2 is also the metaphorical correlative of the fate of all speechless particularities in the bureaucratic state, as described by Levinas in this incomparable passage taken from his essay *Transcendence and Height*:

> For me, the negative element, the element of violence in the State, in the hierarchy, appears even when the hierarchy functions perfectly, when everyone submits to universal ideas. There are cruelties which are terrible because they proceed from the necessity of a reasonable Order. There are, if you like, the tears that a civil servant cannot see: the tears of the Other (*Autrui*).
>
> (Levinas, 1996, p. 23)

It must be stressed that this book's *concept* of the pre- or non-rational particular is not completely separate from whatever rational linguistic system may be interpenetrating the environment of the real in which a given ontological particularity arises. Like any proposition that negates something positive, the concept of the non-rational remains a function of the rational, which is its proper other, as the very existence of this or any other book proves. Or, as Adorno (1973, p. 85) puts it in his own continuation of the net or grid metaphor: "what slips through the net is filtered by the net."

Adorno's point is that it is foolish, not to mention ethically dangerous, to believe that one's own hypersensitive mind and heart are capable of noticing and describing particularities "as they really are," uninfected by one's social conditioning and linguistic conventions. Any way of thinking that opts for the particular so completely that it treats the conceptual as a mere soap bubble (cf. Adorno, 1973, p. 199) deludes itself about its powers of perception. It also risks overlooking the causal (and hence ethical) significance of different ways of speaking or remaining silent. Marcuse stressed the same point in a manner that has become anodyne in social theory:

> The factuality of a fact does not yet justify its appropriateness to serve as starting point and principle of theory. The facts are not undifferentiated material, they are in and of themselves structured . . . by the fundamental interests of the theory and practice that "apprehend" them. For a true theory

> facts are "signs" for particular tendencies in whose context the meaning of a fact, its factuality, becomes intelligible.
>
> (Marcuse, 2011, p. 77)

Nevertheless, non-doubted ontological particularity in its ethical significance is quite different from the ethics of speaking or remaining silent in a given situation. If the reader will forgive the proffering of yet another metaphor, the ethical eye is like a flashlight in the dark: in principle, it could be pointed in any direction, but at any given moment it sees only what actually happens to be illuminated within its field of vision. All else, however pitiable and deserving of notice it may be, lies unseen in the darkness. The ethical heart, in turn, can throb only for what the flashlight lets the eye notice.

If, as was said earlier, we define an overlooked ontological particularity privatively as that which the ethical I *does not doubt* about a situation, then it follows that there can be no question in principle of making such a particularity "more noticeable," or of responding to it "more authentically." It is paradoxical but true that in the twenty-first century what the ethical I does not doubt in this sense has increasingly come to haunt the sphere of what the ethical subject thinks it knows. After Auschwitz, we now realize more than ever before that ethical attention is linked to prior ethical recognition—a simple but easily forgotten linkage that the American poet George Oppen (2007, p. 127) managed to distill to its essence: "Brick in the wall, the heart seizes it because the eye has picked it out." Conversely, we also realize that ethical indifference is linked to prior ethical *in*attention—another simple but easily forgotten linkage that St. Bernard even took to be worthy of a sermon: *Quod non videt oculus cor non dolet*; "What the eye does not see, the heart does not grieve over" (Bernard, 1839, p. 2216).

When considered together, these two connections—ethical attention linked to ethical recognition, and ethical indifference linked to ethical inattention—suggest that ethics as a subject for philosophical inquiry is fundamentally different from metaphysics and jurisprudence. To the extent they acknowledge particularities at all, the latter two disciplines can do so only in the form of metaphysically essential suppositions, or empirically contingent facts. The same cannot be said about ethics, at least as the term is used here. Critical ethical inquiry encompasses not just what is noticed "as" a fact, but also what *will not be noticed at all* because of the blinkered and partial ways we have of noticing things.

The previous century, in addition to greatly increasing the visibility of instances of human suffering that used to be hidden from view, also gave birth to an argument about the nature of evil and those who are capable of committing it that is seldom explicitly stated, at least in polite company, but that nonetheless pervades our current intellectual climate. Literary theorist Edward Mendelson has expressed the nature of the argument perfectly:

> On the one side are those who, like W.H. Auden, sense the furies hidden in themselves, evils they hope never to unleash, but which, they sometimes

> perceive, add force to their ordinary angers and resentments, especially those angers they prefer to think are righteous. On the other side are those who can say of themselves without irony, "I am a good person," who perceive great evils only in other, evil people whose motives and actions are entirely different from their own.
>
> (Mendelson, 2014, p. 6)

Just like all particularities, countless different manifestations of these two psychological types or styles have undoubtedly existed throughout human history. Indeed, more than 200 years ago, Hegel (1977, p. 383) invented a special term of scorn—"beautiful soul" (*schöne Seele*)—to describe individuals who are unable to reconcile their personal sensitivities about inflicting righteous violence on others with the claims imposed on them by reason in the form of their socially conditioned sense of duty.

But that was then. This is now. The argument for the idea of the inevitability of human progress toward the Absolute Idea and the end of history no longer appears as convincing as it once was. The legacies left by imperialism, colonialism, and other forms of chauvinistic exceptionalism during the past two centuries have cast a pall on the idea that everyone on earth ought to participate (or be made to participate) without reservation in some sort of universally valid Hegelian *Sittlichkeit* ("ethical order"). Whatever the ratio may once have been between the two styles of thinking that Mendelson describes, it is a central premise of this book that, after Auschwitz, the ratio has changed to the disadvantage of the self-righteous. Without investing a stupendous amount of time and energy in self-deception, it is no longer easy for an intelligent and ordinarily decent individual to sustain the illusion that he or she belongs to the class of those who are unqualifiedly (or at least reasonably) good, and that committing or tolerating an ethical outrage or a gross injustice is only the kind of thing that other people do.

Notes

1. Cf. Wittgenstein (1993, p. 40): "Ethics, if it is anything, is supernatural and our words will only express facts; as a teacup will only hold a teacup full of water [even] if I were to pour out a gallon over it."
2. 60 U.S. 393 (1857) (holding that African Americans, whether slave or free, could not be American citizens).
3. 576 U.S. ___, 135 S.Ct, 2071 (2015) (holding that same sex couples have a fundamental right to marry under the U.S. Constitution).
4. "As Dogen said, 'Who says "I"? It is "I" who says "who"' (Keizan, 2001, p. 174).
5. I clearly understand that there is more reality in an infinite substance than in a finite one, and hence that my perception of the infinite, that is God, is in some way prior to my perception of the finite, that is myself.

   (Descartes, 1984, p. 31)
6. Thus if being [*Sein*] itself is to be disclosed and grounded in *its* original differentiation from the essent [*das Seiende*], an original perspective must be opened. . . . In accordance with the hidden message of the beginning, man should be understood,

> within the question of being, as the site which being requires to disclose itself. Man is the site of openness, the there. The essent juts into this there and is fulfilled.
>
> (Heidegger, 1959, pp. 204–205)

7. > Initiated in the fifth century BC by Leucippus and Democritus . . . [physical] atomism [is] a theory of the physical world, according to which it is constituted by an infinite number of indivisible corpuscles moving randomly in an infinite void.
   >
   > (Honderich, 1995, p. 64)

8. The thirteenth-century philosopher-theologian Duns Scotus (2005, p. 83) invented the Latin term *haecceitas* ("thisness") to denominate what he took to be the absolute but indeterminate unity of an individual entity that, once its reality has been assured, could then perform the work of tying what he took to be the metaphysical reality of common natures (*natura communis*, or universals) to individual members of a species. Haecceities as such were important to Scotus only insofar as they provided conceptual hooks for attaching the universals that determine the *quidditas* of a thing: *what* a being is as opposed to *that* it is. (See Cross, 2014).

9. > 1. The *monad*, of which we shall speak here, is nothing but a simple substance which enters into compounds; *simple*, that is to say, without parts. 2. And there must be simple substances, because there are compounds; for the compound is nothing but a collection or *aggregatum* of simples.
   >
   > (Leibniz, 1934, p. 3)

10. Wittgenstein's *Tractatus* assigns to the concept of nameable but otherwise indescribable simple "objects" (*Gegenstände*) the role of being the condition of the possibility of something else, namely, the representation of combinations of such objects (states of affairs) in primitive propositions (Wittgenstein, 1974, § 4.0312, p. 22). This idea lies at the root of the Wittgenstein's "picture theory" of language, which he later abandoned, and it helped to inspire the movement in twentieth-century philosophy known as logical atomism (Honderich, 1995, pp. 63–64).

Chapter 4

On speechlessness

> To will to surmise the undoubtable and therefore to represent it as undoubtable would make as much sense as straining to see a sound.
>
> Martin Heidegger (2010a, p. 29)

An individual's relationship to what he or she "does not doubt" about the real, in the sense indicated in Chapter 3, can be profitably compared to what psychology and neuroscience call a perceptual deficit. The general criterion that unites red-green color blindness (deuteranopia), face blindness (prosopagnosia), word blindness (pure alexia), the inability to form mental images (aphantasia), and tone deafness (amusia), is that someone who suffers from any of these conditions is not able to notice or perceive something that most other people are able to notice or perceive. In other words, deuteranopia, prosopagnosia, alexia, aphantasia, and amusia are what the average doctor would call "abnormal" conditions (McCloskey, 2009, pp. 3–4). Aspect blindness—the inability to continuously perceive different aspects of an ambiguous image of the sort that is used in Gestalt psychology (e.g., a schematic cube or the figure of a duck–rabbit)—is quite similar (Wittgenstein, 1953, pp. 213e–214e).

Our inability to become aware of the ontologically particular that we do not doubt resembles the foregoing abnormal conditions, in as much as what one person does not doubt about a given situation can in fact be doubted and noticed by others, even many others. The main difference, of course, is that *everyone* suffers from blindness to undoubted ontological particularities at *every* moment of their lives. Although it is as "normal" as never being able to see the back of your own head, it also constitutes what might be called *universal ethical blindness*. Its manifestations are ubiquitous in mass consumer societies. Consider, for example, the countless instances of undiluted, untroubled satisfaction that the average middle class shopper feels when he or she purchases a shiny new iPhone, a trendy pair of designer jeans, or a crisp head of lettuce, without ever once experiencing conscious awareness of the actual working and living conditions under which these particular products were produced or brought to market.

The existential fact that you might become aware of some particularities of a situation that I am not *presently* aware of (and vice versa), and therefore that you can conceive and speak about a situation "as" this or that in ways that I am not *presently* able to do (and vice versa), is of enormous ethical significance. The present chapter discusses why this is so by paying close attention to the kind of concept-resistant particularity that was earlier called "political speechlessness."

The speechless particular

The articulate, who are used to having their words heard and opinions respected, often mistake their techniques for describing what is present and past and predicting what is to come for a pair of magic spectacles. They believe that only the perspective afforded by a rigorous pre-commitment to true discourse will allow them to observe and navigate the morally correct course through the messy flow of reality that somehow keeps appearing in what Benjamin (1968, p. 261) called the *Jetztzeit*, or "now-time." In truth, however, the articulate are more like myopes trying to read from afar an entry in the miniaturized two-volume edition of the *Oxford English Dictionary*: at best they would see and understand only the largest and darkest words and images, while everything else on the page would appear as irrelevant and incomprehensible as a cluster of flyspecks.

The politically speechless

Things are different when seen from the point of view of the politically speechless, for their lives *are* the flyspecks. That life is hard and the world a cold and unforgiving place is a judgment with which millions (or billions) of luckless human beings would agree, assuming against all odds they were ever asked to render an opinion.

Raggedly dressed children digging for scraps in the garbage dumps of great cities; crazed lifers staring at the walls of their tiny prison cells during months, years, or decades of solitary confinement; sleep-deprived seamstresses toiling 12 hours a day, 7 days a week, in dingy sweatshops in high-rise buildings prone to igniting or collapsing; aged, demented residents of rundown nursing homes kept all day and night on their beds, tranquilized by drugs and in diapers, because no one wants to pay attention to them; illiterate, brutalized girls and boys made to service sex tourists in grubby hotel rooms or in the back seats of cars; hapless women whose bodies and instincts tell them that their partner is an incorrigible wife-beater or child-abuser, but who nonetheless feel trapped in abusive situations that they dare not acknowledge to themselves; the inveterately shy ones with darting eyes and downcast demeanors who remain tongue-tied and inarticulate when asked to speak because they have spent their entire lives being yelled at or ignored; the perpetually insecure who are ashamed to say anything when someone claiming to have lofty credentials or a superior intellect tells them that they should detest what they like, or like what they detest: This ad hoc listing of some of the world's quietly desperate and forlorn will serve to give a preliminary indication of the meaning of political speechlessness.

As was already noted, Aristotle (1253^{a}10) famously characterized the human being as *zōon logon echon*: the living being with the gift of *logos*, or rational speech. But speech consists not merely of "a multiplicity of tone-data" (Heidegger, 1962, p. 207), nor even a multiplicity of meaningful tone-data. Those who speak can also choose to remain silent. Indeed, reticent silence can make some things just as manifest as the most eloquent torrent of words, perhaps even more so. Many a jury has interpreted a criminal defendant's decision not to explain himself as an admission of guilt, notwithstanding the formal legal validity of the privilege against self-incrimination (Frank and Brochard, 2006). Likewise, the silence of a legislature in the face of a long-standing judicial interpretation is often "read" by judges to express acquiescence in that interpretation (Eskridge, 1988).

In everyday life, pauses in the speech of the loquacious resemble punctuation marks between written clauses more than they do blank pages. More generally, one could say that keeping silent, when considered from the standpoint of Aristotle's definition of the human being, is mostly what speakers do while they are waiting to speak. Going even further, if Plato's thesis that thinking is essentially a soundless dialog between me and myself (*eme emautō*) is accepted as valid (*Sophist* 263*e*; *Theaetetus* 189*e*), then even voiceless, solitary reflection can be interpreted as a form of speech.

Heidegger (1962, p. 208) managed to elevate the various connections between speech and silence noted above into a general ontological principle when he said that keeping silent is "another essential possibility of discourse," while adding the rather elitist qualification that in order to keep silent "authentically" (*eigentlich*) one must first have something to say. Heidegger's way of describing the relation between speech and silence brings into view an important social and political question that he himself did not consider: Who or what determines whether someone's speech *or* silence is loud enough to be heard, or rather, important enough to be listened to?

Possibility and actuality

We owe the idea that possibilities are as real and knowable as actualities to Aristotle, who said that "everything that comes to be moves towards a principle, that is, an end [*telos*]" (1050^{a}7). Indeed, he thought that a being's possibilities—its *dynamis* (Latin: *potentia*)—characterize the very essence of its reality, including the universal essence of the human conceived as the end toward which every individual member of the species strives (1050^{a}15–16). On this view, a being's possibilities-of-being (*dynamis*) at any given moment are like marbles in a box: they constitute in advance its very essence. In the Aristotelian system, mere actuality—*energeia* (Latin: *actus*)—becomes the enactment of one among the manifold of possibilities that make up a being's essence as it strives toward its purpose, as if at each moment of its existence one and only one marble is and must be drawn out of its essence-box.

Putting this all together, for Aristotle there could have been no such thing as speechlessness, since the *dynamis* of speaking by definition belongs to *all* human being as a determination of their essence at every moment of their lives, whether or not they actually do speak. Unfortunately, this way of thinking about the relationship between possibility and actuality has influenced our tradition in myriad ways. It licenses us to believe that there is no essential distinction between the speechless and those who speak ("the speechful"), since the *dynamis* of speech belongs to both, even if the *energeia* of actually speaking in this or that particular situation does not.

When considered from a neo-Aristotelean point of view, the speechless are always on the way to speaking, and if they do not in fact speak, they have only themselves to blame. Thus it is that those who talk and write a lot about weighty and important matters of social and political life often blame the speechless themselves for their plight. Sometimes conservative authors assert that only traditional virtues, harnessed by the power of mind and will, can allow individuals to rise above the burden of circumstances, and therefore that failure must be a sign of inferiority and personal weakness rather than a consequence of chance, or of the way that current political and economic institutions happen to be structured (Bennett, 2013). On other occasions, conservatives attempt to occupy the ethical high ground by claiming that basic morality requires letting people take personal responsibility for their own bad choices, including the choice not to speak up (Fried, 1981, pp. 20–21). Still other members of the fraternity of the speechful believe that their own failure to notice any audible complaints coming from the sphere of speechlessness means that all of its inhabitants have acquiesced in or implicitly agreed to existing social arrangements. They even have special terms to describe their certainties about what the speechless have "consented" to endure: *the social contract*, *the general will*, and *representative surveys of opinion*.

"Motivated blindness," which social scientists sometimes invoke to explain how people can hurt others without specifically intending to do so (Nguyen, 2014, p. 11), thus finds its aural analog in *motivated deafness* to the inarticulate moans of the speechless. Perhaps the pithiest and best known remark on this general theme from a political point of view is Upton Sinclair's: "It is difficult to get a man to understand something, when his salary depends on his not understanding it" (Sinclair, 1994, p. 109). Like Blanche DuBois in *A Streetcar Named Desire*, the unheard, unnoticed speechless are fated either to rely on the kindness of speechful strangers, or else perish from their indifference (Williams, 2004, p. 178).

Motivated ventriloquism

If motivated deafness leads to ethical indifference, then its doppelganger, *motivated ventriloquism*, tends to produce ethical verbosity. In the latter phenomenon, certain speechful politicians and experts do indeed eagerly express concerns about this or that segment of the world's speechless masses, but they do so by speaking about *their own* concerns *for* these others. Here one can find the sort of socialist that Orwell (2010, p. 124) described in *The Road to Wigan Pier*:

> The truth is that, to many people calling themselves Socialists, revolution does not mean a movement of the masses with which they hope to associate themselves; it means a set of reforms which "we", the clever ones, are going to impose upon "them," the Lower Orders.

Also included in the category of motivated ventriloquists are today's cadres of technocratic "experts," who are paid by national and international agencies and NGOs to decide what to build, what to supply, and what "development" to pursue on behalf of the Third World's poor, oftentimes with disastrous results (Easterly, 2006).

Then, there are the partisans of "plain language," who attempt to stake out a neutral place on the political spectrum by claiming that abuses of language on the part of both the powerful *and* their critics are the root of all evil. For them, the universal use of concrete, easily understood speech and prose is the road to all social salvation (Cutts, 2000, p. 11). Their standard-bearer is Orwell (1954, p. 177), who famously said, in his influential 1946 essay *Politics and the English Language*, "Political language—and with variations this is true of all political parties, from Conservatives to Anarchists—is designed to make lies sound truthful and murder respectable, and to give an appearance of solidity to pure wind."

Although Orwell's thesis sounds plausible, especially in an era of "soundbite politics," the supposition that the speechless always prefer plain speaking to convoluted speaking is no less a unilateral projection by the speechful on the speechless than the supposition that they always prefer central planning by the state to unfettered markets, or vice versa. "Speaking truth to power," by means of which speechful progressives deconstruct the cant and uncover the hypocrisies of the politically powerful, often fulfills an ethical imperative of the highest order. But sometimes it winds up benefiting the agendas of other speechful progressives more than it benefits the particular lives of the speechless themselves. This can be especially galling if said truths are seasoned with the argument that the inarticulateness of the speechless is irrelevant to politics and ethics because the hegemony of ruling-class ideology prevents them from recognizing where their own true interests lie (Gramsci, 1971, p. 161).

The notion of speechless suffering is therefore quite different from Hannah Arendt's idea (2004, p. 376) that those who do not already have the right to have rights as members of a political community cannot enjoy human rights in any meaningful sense. The speechless remain speechless even (or rather especially) when articulate and compassionate others sympathetically notice and describe their plight and mount political campaigns to end their suffering. It is impossible, strictly speaking, for anyone trying in good faith to be just by following this or that chosen method of justice to uncover the truths that lie *inside* the sufferings of the speechless. This is a definitional (i.e., grammatical-logical) point, not a metaphysical one. Any *talk* about what the millions and billions of speechless human beings *want* is a hypothesis that can be verified only by speculation or opinion polls. Which is to say, mere generalizations about speechless needs and desires will probably be a priori false in some, even many, particular cases. And it will be recalled that, for a disenchanted person, it is always in *particular* cases that ethical responsibility lies.

Viewed from the standpoint of Agamben's figure of *homo sacer*, speechlessness can be interpreted as a logical corollary of the concept of bare life. The ancient Roman legal category of *homo sacer* originally applied to convicted criminals who had lost all legal rights, including the right not to be murdered by a citizen, and hence were too spiritually polluted even to be sacrificed to the gods. In *Homo Sacer: Sovereign Power and Bare Life* (1998), Agamben famously applied the practical result of this legal status—that *homo sacer*, like a wild animal, possessed only "bare life"—to the inmates of Nazi extermination camps. The absolute rightlessness of *Muselmänner* in a place like Auschwitz, like that of *homo sacer*, meant that the decision to kill them or let them live was completely arbitrary and out of their hands.

Moreover, the descriptive utility of the concept of bare life need not end with those whom the law has explicitly categorized as rightless outcasts. "In a different yet analogous way," says Agamben (1998, p. 180), "today's democratico-capitalist project of eliminating the poor classes through development not only reproduces within itself the people that is excluded, but also transforms the entire population of the Third World into bare life." Even those who are possessed of notionally formal rights, if they lack the voice to create, invoke, or enforce them, can be viewed under the aspect of *homo sacer*. For such people, the decision to kill or let live, and on what terms, belongs exclusively to the fraternity of the speechful.

Blaming the speechless, assuming things about them, and even interpreting them as fragile others who need and want saving by means either of clever lies *or* plainly told truths, is really the unilateral imposition of an un-chosen narrative by those who speak on those who do not. Orwell (2010, p. 32) observed that his bourgeois status gave him a peculiar privilege that was absent from the lives of the members of the working class of his day, despite the fact that for a long time he did not earn much more than a miner earned. This was the privilege of having *some* expectation of getting what he wanted, within reasonable limits. It was to this very privilege that he attributed the historical fact that progressive and revolutionary movements have usually been led by the *speechful* on behalf of those whom we have called the *politically speechless*:

> Hence in times of stress "educated" people tend to come to the front; they are no more gifted than others and their "education" is generally quite useless in itself, but they are accustomed to a certain amount of deference and consequently have the cheek necessary to a commander. That they will come to the front seems to be taken for granted, always and everywhere. In Lissagaray's *History of the Commune* there is an interesting passage describing the shootings that took place after the Commune had been suppressed. The authorities were shooting the ringleaders, and as they did not know who the ringleaders were, they were picking them out on the principle that those of better class would be the ringleaders. An officer walked down a line of prisoners, picking out likely-looking types. One man was shot because he was wearing a watch,

> another because he "had an intelligent face." I should not like to be shot for having an intelligent face, but I do agree that in almost any revolt the leaders would tend to be people who could pronounce their aitches.
>
> (Orwell, 2010, p. 32)

The movers and shakers of the world—the powerful talkers among us—can have no greater confidence in their opinions of what the speechless really think and believe than they can have in their opinions of what lions really think and believe. Wittgenstein (1953, p. 223e) once said that if a lion could talk, we could not understand him. But a slightly different proposition is more obviously true: Lions *do not* talk to us, and never have; therefore, we have absolutely no right to assume they would agree with what we say about them if they could speak. If an adult thinker attributes humanlike thought and speech to a lion we dismiss the move as crude anthropomorphism. But whenever a point of view is attributed to the speechless in general (a constant occurrence), we really ought to call it what Nietzsche (1968, p. 407) would have called it: an expression of the speaker's own will to power.

At least those who think they hear the voice of God inside their heads can cite scripture for the proposition that there *is* such a thing as God's making his voice audible to humans (e.g., Exodus 6:1–8). The speechful who imagine that they "hear" the voices of the speechless can lean on no such authoritative doctrinal crutch. This does not imply that motivated ventriloquism on behalf of the politically speechless is necessarily a bad or ignoble thing to do. But it does imply that it is a bald-faced lie to tell *oneself* that one's rhetoric is but the selfless execution of a wish inaudibly whispered into one's ear by the speechless themselves.

The signifying face versus the enigmatic particular

We earlier encountered the Aristotelian-Heideggerian thesis that remaining silent is not the negation of speech—that speaking and keeping silent are both variations on the theme of *Logos*. If this observation is correct, then the proper antithesis to discourse in general would not be silence, but rather what we have been calling speechlessness.

The concept of speechlessness gestures at something that is denied both to the word expressed *and* to the word withheld. Speaking figuratively, one could say that speech and silence, qua discourse, lie in a perpetual state of reciprocal suspension and tension vis-à-vis speechlessness. The one does not "support" the other—it's all a matter of the observer's perspective. Much as the base of a triangle can be seen, depending on a shift in one's perspective, either as suspend*ed* below the apex, *or* as suspend*ing* the apex and sides from above.[1]

As we shall see in a moment, the concept of origin or ground is irrelevant to the relations depicted in Figure 4.1. The speechless realm, or better still the mute real, does not somehow "give rise" to discourse in the manner of a cause, origin, or first principle. Rather, the relationship between speechlessness and discourse is

Figure 4.1 Two perspectives on discourse and its antithesis

more or less dialectical. Most of the time, discourse dangles the speechless like a stylish and well-ironed coat dangles an unnoticed bit of lint; while every now and then an element of the speechless realm can intrude, like a carelessly managed cigarette, to scorch the fabric of discourse, at least on the part of those speechful human beings who can bring themselves to notice what has happened.

If we adopt the foregoing perspective on discourse's proper antithesis, might it not be possible to gain critical ethical insight into the nature of an appropriately enlarged concept of speechfulness by comparing its discourse, not with what convention takes to be the "subject matter" of language (e.g., beings), not with what language is typically thought to be "about" (e.g., this or that state of affairs), but rather with . . . *something else*?

The usual practice in Western philosophy has been to compare language with an ineffable Big Other whose name is frequently capitalized to signify its lofty status as the ultimate vis-à-vis of all human speech: "God," "Being," "the Noumenal World," "the Real," and so forth. The felicitous term "Big Other" is borrowed from Lacan, although its use here is quite narrow and is certainly not meant to allude to the full panoply and richness of Lacanian philosophy (Žižek, 1999, pp. 87, 288, 314–315, 330). As used here, *Big Other* simply indicates a thinker's decision to create or adopt a *name* for something that he or she conceives (often grandiosely) to be the condition of the possibility of all language, and yet, at the same time, something that language cannot *describe*. Whereas this book's concept of ontological particularity might be called a "little other," and is motivated by ethical concern at the level of the humbly corpuscular, most concepts of the Big Other in Western philosophy are motivated by the desire to truthfully say, picture, or evoke the grounded nature of existence as a whole *before* getting down to the business of investigating this or that philosophical sub-theme (jurisprudence, aesthetics, ethics, etc.).

For present purposes, the main problem with the usual way of proceeding is not so much that its theoretical target is too large, but that it posits a more-or-less undifferentiated conception of the human being involved in some sort of generic relationship with a Big Other. Consider, for example, the unitary Kantian "transcendental subject" standing *opposed* both to an ineffable Noumenal World and to a homogeneous field of universally effable phenomenal objects; or the generic Heideggerian "being of the human being" (*Dasein*) standing *within* what the ontological difference classifies as an indescribable Being as such (*Das Sein*). Paying attention in these ways to the relationship between something that is universally conceived of as "the human being" or "the human situation" and its corresponding Big Other draws no fundamental distinctions *within* the sphere of humanity as such. But since we have already posited an ethically important distinction between the speechful and the speechless, this makes the usual way of proceeding—that is, establishing metaphysical Truth about "the human being" so as to properly ground ethical truth—unsuitable for the project of investigating the relationship between the relentless gabbiness of the speechful and the utterly non-discursive situation of the speechless.

Fortunately, the philosophy of Emmanuel Levinas provides a useful starting point for our investigation, since it distinguishes within the category of the human between the ethical self as "I" and the face of the Other (usually capitalized) standing opposite this I during the event of "facing" that characterizes the quintessential "ethical moment" for Levinas (1996, p. 148). His project of privileging ethics as "first philosophy" in comparison to ontology (1989, p. 75) famously upended the traditional hierarchy between knowledge and ethics, and without a doubt the radicalness of this gesture prepared the way for many fruitful investigations into the relationships among ethics, justice, and politics (e.g., Diamantides, 2010).

Nevertheless, Levinas (1996, pp. 9–10) *also* claimed that the ethical moment is co-equally the "situation of discourse." By this he meant that it is a situation characterized, first and foremost, not by some content-laden "celebration of being" (the *said*), but rather by *saying*. That is, by "a relationship with him to whom I express the expression, and whose presence is already required for my cultural gesture of expression to be produced" (1996, p. 52). The central position that is accorded the event of saying in Levinasian ethics is thoroughly in keeping with the Aristotelian definition of the human as an essentially speechful being. Unfortunately, this tradition tends to hinder more than advance the task of thinking through the phenomenon of speechlessness in relation to the fraternity of the speechful.

Levinas employed the term "discourse" (*discours*) to say two completely different things. First, he noted that the face of the Other is "discourse" in the sense that it can be *comprehended* by the I as belonging to a particular "being." This sort of discursive comprehension of the face is utterly conventional: it shows itself within the horizon of ontology, which is to say, within the overlapping categories of *language* conceived of as a vehicle for conveying knowledge, and *reason* conceived as a medium for receiving it. Since Levinas, like Adorno, thinks that the immediate particularity of the face is always irreducible to its concept, this suggests that for one's face to be given to and received in language in the conventional manner "is to signify on the basis of what one is not" (1996, p. 10). If I cannot ever "know" the being I call "you," then ethics, conceived by Levinas as the relationship between the I and the face of the Other, must be "otherwise than being, or, beyond essence," as the title of one of his books puts it (1998b).

His deep-seated mistrust of the ethical sufficiency of any conventional meaning that could be conveyed by a mere linguistic sign leads to the second sense in which Levinas (1996, p. 10) interprets the phenomenon of the face-to-face encounter between the I and the Other as a situation of discourse: "To comprehension and signification grasped within a horizon, we oppose the signifyingness of the face." But by evoking the idea of *signification* beyond and outside all propositional truth values, it would appear that Levinas wants both to have his postmodern cake and eat it too. A *sign* (from the Latin *signum*, meaning mark or token) need not "represent" in the sense of describing something else, but it must at least communicate something that is other than itself *to* some observer. Positing a face that signifies in the forest when no one is around to see it makes just as much (or as little) sense as positing the sound made by the apocryphal tree falling in the forest when no one is around to hear it.

Hence, Levinas will propose or speculate on the curious thesis that the moral consciousness which arises in the I's encounter with the face is not so much a function of "the vision of the face" as it is the result of "audition and speech" (1996, p. 10). According to this way of thinking—or rather, according to the odd trope of nonvisual audition, or of vision morphing into audition—the face of the Other somehow speechlessly *signifies* directly into the mind's ear of the I as it is being seen. And *what* the face signifies in appearing, without saying it out loud, is an oft-recurring theme in Levinas's work: the face always broadcasts a "temptation and impossibility of murder" (1996, p.10), according to which " 'Thou shalt not kill' signifies . . . 'thou shalt do everything in order that the other live' " (2001, p. 272).

What and how can the face of a speechless Other *signify* to a speechful I? It is by no means clear what it means to have (or even imagine) a signifying "discourse" with someone who does not speak and is never heard. For example, it remains frighteningly obscure, to this author at least, whether the naked face of a person in a persistent vegetative state, or with end-stage Alzheimer's disease, signifies the Levinasian imperative of letting or causing the other *to live*, or the contrary imperative of letting or causing the other *to die*. More generally—and keeping in mind our previous reflections on the striking ethical prominence of the temporal present—it is unclear how *any* kind of signification (of the face or anything else) could ever arrive soon enough to close the logical and ontological gap between what we just happen to be aware of (right now) and what-we-do-not-doubt (right now). In grappling with the moral dilemmas raised by the prospect of keeping the speechless alive or letting them die inside an ever-renewed *right now*, it is hard to envision how an ethics of the face conceived of as a kind of "signifier" would be of much assistance.

Or rather, one can indeed imagine such an ethics, but in that case a disenchanted mind might still question whether it would be ethically sufficient to treat the face as always wordlessly signifying the same general sort of message. There seems to be a troubling inconsistency between the view that every true proposition "*S is p*" falsifies *S* when considered as the name of some unique particularity (Levinas, Adorno), and the view that the unique particularity that is the face of the Other nonetheless *always* silently signifies "extreme exposure, defenselessness, vulnerability itself" (Levinas, 1989, p. 83). A scorn for all forms of dogmatism except one still represents a kind of dogmatism.

If speechlessness is equated with extreme exposure and vulnerability in *every* situation, then one would have gotten rid of one illusion only to replace it with another. The metaphysical illusion that the linguistic sign of a true proposition stands for an objective meaning-body would have been dispelled only to be replaced by another, uncomfortably comparable illusion: the belief that the face as such communicates an infinite vulnerability that is as eternally compelling in the sphere of ethics as what "1 + 1 = 2" communicates in the sphere of arithmetic. Please do not misunderstand: in that case, Levinas's phenomenology of the face would remain no less cogent, no less self-evident. But intellectual honesty would require that it be reclassified as the merely regional phenomenology of looking at the face *in a certain way* (e.g., with a distinct feeling of compassionate concern).

The foregoing reflections suggest that what is required for the sort of comparison to speechfulness that is wanted here is something that *never* occupies the order of discourse or signification, not even in theory, and yet still somehow manages to be ethically troubling. Moreover, the opposing entities or terms of the comparison should not establish or presuppose any hierarchy between them, such as the ontological relation of origin-to-originated that subsists between *Being* and *beings*, or *God* and *creation*, in traditional accounts of these Big Others, or the normative relation of *need* to the *duty of hospitality* that subsists between the face of the Other and the I in the Levinasian account of ethics.

If the speechful speak in what Lacan (2007, p. 81) rightly called the master's discourse, or the discourse of mastery, then any comparison we employ plainly cannot be heard to imply the metaphysical priority or normative superiority of that discourse over the non-discursive comportment of those who are not speechful. On the other hand, nor can it be heard to imply the opposite priority. An utterly unsentimental concept of speechlessness that construes it as a pre-signifying, enigmatic particularity will offer just the object of comparison we seek. To put the matter bluntly, ethical trauma, when considered from the point of view of a disenchanted mind, is a consequence of minding that the particular face of the Other might very well "show itself" (so to speak) as *invisible or inscrutable*, rather than being aware that the face always signifies something morally universal that one is tempted to ignore.

The speechlessness of nature

Benjamin on the sadness of nature

The first use of speechlessness as a concept, at least in something like the sense in which it is used here, appeared in a letter written by Walter Benjamin to Martin Buber in July 1916 (Benjamin, 1994, p. 80). The letter's purpose was to explain why Benjamin had declined an invitation to submit a contribution to the new journal *Der Jude*, a German magazine on Jewish affairs founded earlier that year by Buber and Salman Schocken. Interpreting the editorial policy of the magazine as one of encouraging "politically engaged writing," Benjamin states that he cannot bring himself to think of language in instrumental terms, as a mere means for determining political motives and actions. Many of the articles appearing in the first volume of *Der Jude* took pro-war positions on the ongoing European conflict with which Benjamin intensely disagreed. But far more important than this, he asserts, is the lack of "coincidence" between the journal's inchoate stage of development and Benjamin's own. Language, writes Benjamin, is not effective through the transmission of its content, but rather through "the purest disclosure of its dignity and its nature." He declares that his own "concept of objective and, at the same time, highly political style and writing is this: *to awaken interest in what was denied to the word*" (emphasis added). And what is denied to the word, Benjamin tells Buber, constitutes the sphere of "speechlessness" (*Sprachlosigkeit*).

At roughly the same time that he wrote this letter, Benjamin (1978, pp. 314–332) was working on a strange and enigmatic text bearing the ungainly title of *Über Sprache überhaupt und über die Sprache des Menschen*: "On Language as Such and on the Language of Man." Unpublished during his lifetime, the essay gives an unabashedly theological interpretation of language, in keeping with an interest in Judaism and the Kabbalah that at the time had only recently awakened in him. This interest, in turn, can be traced in large measure to the author's newly established (and ultimately lifelong) friendship with Gershom Scholem.[2] Peter Demetz (1968, p. xxxv) characterizes the essay as a whole as a form of belated Romanticism; and Benjamin (1994, p. 486) himself, after his turn to Marxism and dialectical materialism, seems to have discounted the value of the essay's overall perspective. From a purely philological standpoint, Demetz (1968, p. xxxvii) is probably correct in concluding that when seen from the point of view of the later, Marxist Benjamin, this early essay on language is "reactionary" for suggesting "the possibility of restoring the original glory of language without totally revolutionizing nature."

Curiously enough, it is this peculiar combination of theological mysticism and reactionary humanism that makes Benjamin's youthful essay on language so interesting and productive. Given what is at stake in the present investigations, it would be both unnecessary and unwise for us to attempt to untangle and inspect all of the many strands of thought contained in this exceedingly complex and difficult text. *On Language as Such and on the Language of Man* is valuable for our purposes for two reasons only: first, because it applies the concept of speechlessness to the situation of nonhuman nature; and second, because it relies on the religious notion of redemption to characterize the relationship between those who speak, defined universally as *Menschen* (human beings), and speechless nature. "Because she is mute," the text states, "nature mourns"; but at the same time it asserts that the dialectical inversion of this proposition is also true, for "the sadness of nature makes her mute" (Benjamin, 1978, p. 329).

The reason the text gives for why nonhuman nature is sad is theological through and through. Human beings conceived atheistically as unprivileged elements of the natural order can no more know that speechless nature is sad than they can know that Wittgenstein's speechless lion (1953, p. 223e) is sad. "Sad" (*traurig*) is only a paltry human word. The sense of its having transcendent objective validity as a true description of nature requires a point of view standing outside all merely contingent human "perspectives." Not only must this point of view see and know things as they really are, it must also have given human beings certain special privileges vis-à-vis nature. In short, only a firm belief in the ultimate *audibility* of mute nature from an omniscient and caring perspective—in this case, that of the supernatural entity Judaism calls *YHWH*, *Elohim*, or *Adonai*—authorizes Benjamin (1978, p. 329) to declare: "It is a metaphysical truth that all nature would begin to lament if it were endowed with language."

For Benjamin, as for the deity himself, the language of truth is not the same as the language of true propositions. As we saw in Chapter 2, convention holds that words are tools of communication through which content (called "meaning") is conveyed from one speaker to another. The view that propositions "stand for" something else called their "meanings" Wittgenstein (1978, p. 54) stigmatized as the *Bedeutungskörper* ("meaning-body") theory of language, and he famously railed against it throughout his later career. Benjamin, however, cared very little for the demonstrations of analytic philosophy. The distinctions that Frege (1948) drew between the sense and the reference of a word or proposition may have been useful for solving formal enigmas such as whether the phrase "the morning star" means the same thing as "the evening star" just because they both refer to the same planet (Venus). But Benjamin's desire to give a theological interpretation of discourse required that he cast aside the view that the essence of language is propositional. The theological language of names, Benjamin tried to say, is the only language suitable for the thinking about the temporal present, for names do not describe something "about" what is named—instead, they summon forth what is named into phenomenal appearance.

This shows why Benjamin does not claim, in *On Language as Such*, that nature told him or proved to him scientifically that it is speechless because it is sad and sad because it is speechless. Instead, he takes care to employ the device of a second conditional clause to advance the claim that nature is sad: "Nature would begin to lament *if* it were endowed with speech." The use of the conditional suggests that Benjamin knew full well he was speaking *for* nature in making this claim, not somehow channeling its voice in the manner of a spiritual medium.

On the view that nature lacks something that has been withheld from it (i.e., speechfulness), the essay asserts that nature's sadness and propensity to mourn have to do, first, with its alienation from the originally creative word of God, and second, with its subsequent enslavement (*verknechtung*) to the "prattle" (*Geschwätz*) of instrumental human speech. Benjamin therefore refines the concept of speechlessness that was initially sketched in his letter to Buber from that which is denied to *the word in general* to that which is denied only to the *human word*:

> Things have no proper names except in God. For his creative word, God called them into being, calling them by their proper names. In the language of men, however, they are over-named [*überbennant*]. There is, in the relation of human languages to that of things, something that can be approximately described as "over-naming": over-naming as the deepest linguistic reason for all melancholy and (from the point of view of the thing) of all deliberate muteness. Over-naming as the linguistic being of melancholy points to another curious relation to language: the overprecision [*die Überbestimmtheit*] that obtains in the tragic relationship between the languages of human speakers.
>
> (Benjamin, 1978, p. 330)

The reference in this passage to the "deliberate muteness" of nonhuman things is no accident. Earlier in the text, Benjamin had stated, "There is no event or thing in either animate or inanimate nature that does not partake of language, for it is in the nature of all to communicate their mental meanings" (*seiner geistigen Inhalt mitzuteilen*). Just to be clear about the thrust of his intentions, he adds that "this use of the word 'language' is in no way metaphorical." Thus, the overall picture of language drawn in *On Language as Such* is one in which everything in the universe is either *speaking* or mutely *wanting to speak*, albeit without being able to do so.[3]

Hence Benjamin will state unequivocally, near the end of the essay (p. 329): "Speechlessness: that is the great sorrow of nature" (*Sprachlosigkeit: das ist das grosse Leid der Natur*). What Demetz calls the text's "reactionary humanism" begins to surface in the very next sentence, enclosed in parentheses almost as an afterthought: "*And for the sake of her [nature's] redemption the life and language of man—not only, as is supposed, of the poet—are in nature*" (emphasis added). For the young, pre-Marxist Benjamin, God's decision to give man dominion *over* speechless nature (Genesis 1:28), while situating him *in* nature as a speaking being, can only mean one thing. Nature, whose very ground God cursed after Adam's Fall (Genesis 3:17), must depend for its ultimate salvation on man and his ability to speak.

The ineffable language of God prepares the way for identitarian thought

The Judeo-Christian thesis that God has given human beings mastery over nonhuman nature is comparable to legislation authorizing a judge to appoint a guardian over the affairs of a legally incompetent person. On this analogy, just as the law supervises guardians according to a special, fiduciary standard, so too does God stand in judgment over humans for the ways in which they implement their mastery over nature's beings. Crucial for understanding Benjamin's theory of nature's circuitous path to redemption through both divine and human language is a theme modeled on those Kabbalistic strands of Judaism that emphasize the esoteric meanings of the words and characters in the Hebrew Bible (Matt, 1996, pp. 101–108). In place of the latter's emphasis on the hidden theological meanings of linguistic signs, Benjamin substitutes the hidden theological meanings of nature's beings. In *On Language as Such*, he contends that entities like trees and rocks and chipmunks are, in addition to just being themselves, always mutely "communicating" themselves—at first to human beings, and then through humans to God.

Summing up what it calls a "purified" (though still "imperfect") concept of language, the essay's final paragraph states:

> The language of an entity is the medium in which its mental being [*sein geistiges Wesen*, which in this context is better translated as "spiritual essence"] is communicated. The uninterrupted flow of this communication runs through the whole of nature from the lowest forms of existence to man and from man to God. Man communicates himself to God through name, which he gives to nature and (in proper names) to his own kind, and to nature he gives names according to the communication that he receives from her, *for the whole of nature, too, is imbued with a nameless, unspoken language, the residue of the creative word of God, which is preserved in man as the cognizing name and above man as the judgment suspended over him.*
>
> (Benjamin, 1978, p. 331) (emphasis added)

The Jewish tradition holds that the coming of the Messiah will eventually redeem mankind and its long history of less-than-righteous behavior. According to Benjamin's essay, until that spectacular moment arrives, perhaps sometime in the remote future, the design of creation set forth in the Torah signifies that nature's *own* path toward redemption passes through the mediating efforts of human beings. God has given humans the power to prepare nonhuman creation for the arrival of the Messiah by deploying righteous language and behavior during the course of their lives—including especially speech and action aimed at scrupulous adherence to the Halakhah—just as God will ultimately judge humans for their many failures in this regard.

Oddly enough for a theological text coming out of this tradition, *On Language as Such* appears to be more concerned with the ultimate fate of speechless nature than it does with the ultimate fate of speechful human beings. Indeed, the amount of sympathy that Benjamin displays for the plight of nature as it waits in mute silence to be redeemed is really quite extraordinary. In one way or another, the essay repeatedly stresses the fact that nature, like a comatose person, lacks any power to say yea or nay concerning the events that determine what will become of it. God has bound his nonhuman creatures to wait in speechlessness, and in sorrow, while human beings keep on inadequately discharging the fiduciary responsibilities vis-à-vis nature that God has imposed on them.

On the account of creation provided in Genesis, and accepted without question in Benjamin's essay (p. 322), nonhuman nature first arises before and beyond the realm of human speech. God creates all that is not human *before* he creates man, and he does so by uttering divine language. After bringing forth the heaven and the earth, God begins to speak: *Vayomer Elohim* ("And God said . . ."). In verse after verse, divinely uttered language speaks beings into existence, each according to their "kind" (*mîn*, in Hebrew). In the initial phases of creation—*before* God makes man in his image (in the first version of creation in Genesis 1:26) or breathes life into man's nostrils (in the second version in Genesis 2:7)—God speaks in the language of finitude, the language of entities: "Light," "waters," "grass," "cattle," "winged fowl," and the like. After having first created an earth that was only initially "without form and void" (Genesis 1:2), God's words then proceeded to formalize a plethora of unified entities to populate it.

Notably, the book of Genesis does not say that God created beings by speaking commands containing contents. It is not the "meaning" of God's words that create and organize entities into unities, as if divine meanings were like a cadre of worker-angels employed to mediate between God's words and their intended result. For Benjamin, "*There is no such thing as a meaning of language; as communication, language communicates a mental* [geistiges] *entity, that is, something communicable per se*" (p. 320) (emphasis in original). To be precise, *divine* language is immediate rather than mediated by meaning. Genesis does not say that God created man and other entities "through the word" (p. 322). Instead, it says that God speaks, and then things leap into existence fully formed, as it were, bearing the invisible imprint of the names God gave them (p. 322).

This biblically derived image of the unmediated, pure, and immediately productive language of God gives Benjamin the idea of interpreting language in general as a manifestation (a saying) rather than as an instrument (a said). Long before language produces a speaker's intended meaning, long before it becomes enslaved in the "prattle" (*Geschwätz*) of instrumentalism and planning, language is manifestation: "Its linguistic being, not its verbal meanings, defines its frontier" (1978, p. 317). In short, all language, divine or human, communicates (i.e., manifests) *itself* before it communicates anything else. What language communicates in the case of human speech is "the linguistic being of man," which for Benjamin signifies that human beings communicate their own mental-and-spiritual life (*Geistesleben*) *in* (and not merely by means of) their use of language.

Nonhuman beings, however, are speechless. Among other things, this means that God did not endow them with the capacity to utter the names that he had given them when he spoke them into existence. His decision to let Adam name every living creature (Genesis 2:19) lowered an impenetrable curtain between human and nonhuman beings, obscuring the absolutely pure and immediate language of God with the mediating language of man. Nature mourns, says Benjamin, because things have lost touch with the names with which God created them. On the one hand, "Things [*Die Dinge*] have no proper names except in God" (p. 330); but on the other hand, "The absolute relation of name to knowledge exists only in God" (p. 323). This implies that human language names things in a mediated and inferior way: humans proceed from thing to thing according to knowledge acquired from beings in an ad hoc manner, rather than according to knowledge that is possessed absolutely in the manner of the deity (p. 323).

"In man, God set language, which had served Him as medium of creation, free" (p. 323). Though this freedom took the form of the creative human power to acquire knowledge about things, it did not include the power to know them *ab initio*, as God does (p. 323). The new *knower* (man) was created in the image of the creator, but man's power of knowing was not. Humanly bestowed names are "no closer to the word [of God] than knowledge [is] to creation" (p. 323). After Adam's Fall, "the eternal purity of names was violated," and "the sterner purity of the judging word [of God] arose" (p. 328). The *judging* word: God eternally sits in judgment over the impure use of human language. This state of affairs explains why Benjamin is able to reach the startling conclusion that "The tree of knowledge did not stand in the garden of God in order to dispense information on good and evil, but as an emblem of judgment over the questioner" (p. 328).

The biblical story of the tower of Babel reconfirms this interpretation of the relationship between divine and human language and knowledge. Genesis 11:1–9 tells of the postdiluvian unity of the earth's people, as well as the planned magnificence of the city and tower they wanted to build. But God realizes that this unity and magnificence depend on the power to name in one voice. He says: "Behold, the people *is* one, and they have all one language; and this they begin to do; and now nothing will be restrained from them, which they have imagined to do." So he denies them this power, which might come to resemble his own, by confounding and multiplying their languages—"that they may not understand one another's speech"—and by scattering them abroad on the face of the earth. Ever since that time, the beings of nature have had to go under the yoke of a multiplicity of human languages, where they are hopelessly "over-named" (*überbenannt*) (p. 330).

In *The Task of the Translator*, written 5 years after *On Language as Such*, Benjamin (1968, p. 77) credits Mallarmé for the thesis that the overabundance of different languages in the world prevents human beings from making the unity of truth manifest. This is because "the supreme idiom is lacking" (*manque la suprême*), and the "immortal word" (*l'immortelle parole*) remains silent. Mallarmé's thesis gives voice to a desire (or obsession) that is no less powerful or persistent for its constantly having been frustrated. Noting that this desire has given rise to "the great motif of integrating many tongues into one true language," Benjamin stipulates that this one true language, if it existed, would also have to be the language of truth—"the tensionless and even silent depository of the ultimate truth which all thought strives for" (1968, p. 77). The philosopher yearns for this one language of truth, as does the translator seeking to faithfully convey the sense or effect of the original that she is seeking to translate. But alas, says Benjamin in *The Task of the Translator*, "There is no muse of philosophy, nor is there one of translation" (1968, p. 77).

Poor speechless nature. Even a muse could not help her articulate her needs and desires. For a speechless being to be named at all, "even when the namer is Godlike and blissful," is bittersweet, for the speechless must simply sit by and accept whatever they are called. "But how much more melancholy [it is]," says Benjamin in *On Language as Such* (1978, p. 330), "to be named not from the one blessed, paradisiac language of names, but from the hundred languages of man, in which name has already withered."

Although Benjamin devalues ordinary instrumental language as it is actually used by humans, his decision to valorize another *type* of language (the originating language of divinely uttered names) is tellingly conventional. In fact, scripture's account of creation, which equates God's use of language with creation as such, offers Western thought its first purely theoretical solution to the problem of how to link thought and language, on the one side, and nonrepresentational reality, on the other. That problem, which is prior to the so-called "epistemological" question of how we can know things, concerns the supposed unity and self-identity of what thought is aiming at in the pursuit of true discourse about any entity, any *X* whatsoever. The problem is conventionally divided into three parts: (1) whether a thing is the same as itself through time (the *unity* question), (2) whether a thing is itself and not some other thing at a particular moment in time (the *identity* question), and (3) whether a thing is the same kind of thing as others of its type (the *identity of indiscernibles* question).

It will be recalled that the first chapter of this book began by questioning the ethical sufficiency of the ideas of Unity and Truth in Western thought. The hypothesis was that traditional solutions to the foregoing sorts of problems are either *stipulated*—and hence embarrassingly conventional rather than transcendent —or else *naturalized* as something to be accepted as obvious. Not even Plato could prove the reality of his unity-giving Ideas, on which everything else in his system depends, without appealing to pre-rational faith in an Idea of the Good that, by surpassing being itself (*epekeina tēs ousias*), gives the rest of the Ideas the unity and self-identity they need to do their jobs properly (*Republic* 508*d*–509*b*).[4] No wonder the early Church was attracted to Platonism and Neo-Platonism (Weinberg, 1964, pp. 9–29). If the absolute identity of each and every being with itself can be theologically assured in advance—if it is believed on faith that each being *naturally* falls into its own God-given category—then human beings have a basis for claiming that the entire world is but a plenum filled with already-unified entities available for them to dominate and exploit.

To be sure, one might doubt (as Benjamin does) that humans have the ability to cognize these objects as they really are. But this sort of doubt concedes only that one's knowledge of reality is limited and fallible. It in no way denies that each entity possesses a transcendent unity that exists prior to human cognition. At the end of the day, the most important principle espoused in *On Language as Such*, despite its unconventionality in other respects, is that each and every being is in fact a unity corresponding to a God-given name. Religious faith in the ultimate unity and self-identity of beings thus lays the foundation for believing that humanity can collectively hope and aspire to experience, think, and describe the real as it is, *without remainder*, despite the admitted fallibility and finitude of any given particular human being.

This was certainly the conclusion reached by traditional Christian natural law theory, which found in scripture proof of what Aquinas called an "eternal law" whose divine light God has imprinted on our minds in the form of the universal natural law (*Summa Theologica*, I-I q.93 a.3). Religion thus prepared the way for the secularization of the unity-principle in the form of what Adorno (1973, p. 148) calls "identitarian" thinking. Descartes, in proving the reality of the real, took a step away from the literal text of Genesis by reasoning to the same conclusion from the idea of an infinite God alone (Descartes, 1984, vol. 2, pp. 1–62). And Kant, although not denying God's existence, was content to locate the source of the unity of thought's objects entirely within a fully secularized faculty of understanding belonging to a transcendental human subject—one whose pre-given categories are immune to the ravages of time, history, and chance (Wolcher, 2005, pp. 108–114). While Hegel and Marx, for their part, could take comfort from their belief in the unifying processes of history, which allegedly insure the inevitability of an end state for humanity in which all beings will have been shorn of everything extraneous to their ultimate truth.

Despite the radicalness of its ethical concern for nonhuman nature, Benjamin's early essay on language exposes but does not question the deepest root of speechlessness. Its perspective remains wedded to the quintessentially Western notion that metaphysical unity and self-identity govern absolutely in the sphere of the real. Like most other manifestations of Western thought, the essay is able to suppress the suspicion that there might be an irredeemable ethical difference between the true and the real so long as it can believe that any apparent difference between them is merely *epistemological*, that is, a consequence of our imperfect ability to know entities. And as a general matter one can believe in the latter proposition so long as one believes that *some* magical entity (God; Nature; the transcendental subject; the Arc of History) stands as surety for the unbreakable *ultimate* unity and self-identity of every real particularity.

Discourse and its antithesis

Immanent to the practice of the political is the hubristic belief that knowledge can make an absolute whole out of what is essential to every particularity (Lacan, 2007, p. 31). The same can be said about the practice of law and justice, as a brief remark on "the mythical origin of law" in *On Language as Such* suggests. Law's origin, says Benjamin, is marked by the "immense irony" that the tree of knowledge in the garden of Eden was not put there to dispense information on good and evil, but rather stands "as an emblem of judgment over the questioner" (p. 328). The irony is immense, for Benjamin, because the legal order is hopelessly deluded about the origin and value of what it does. The law believes that the possible excellence of its judgments is based on true knowledge about the facts of a case and the meanings of the norms that are applicable to it; whereas in reality, the very act of human judgment itself has already been judged negatively by God, who, after forbidding Adam and Eve to eat of the fruit of the tree of knowledge, drove them out of Eden for violating his command and thereby coming to "know" about their nakedness (Genesis 3:1–24).

Benjamin to the contrary notwithstanding, the Abrahamic God's furious judgment on the human act of judgment creates an irony that is no longer perceived as biting in today's technocratic world. Indifferent to the threat of divine judgment in secularized societies, today's discourses of politics and law both strive, albeit each in their own special way, to create the impression that nothing of real importance that can be said has not already been said, weighed, and properly evaluated. Humans now imagine that the entities they aspire to know and manipulate possess a natural unity that "corresponds" without remainder with their own correct acts of cognition, in much the same way that God's originating language of names forever clings to his speechless creatures in the biblical account of creation. This modern perspective on knowledge is what Adorno (1973, p. 148) called "identitarian," by which he meant the kind of thought that in one way or another identifies the conceptual with the real.

Identitarian thought relishes itself as fully adequate to the particularity that it suppresses, which is why Adorno could call it "the primal form of ideology" (1973, p. 148). In a word, identitarian thought is profoundly authoritarian. It lends a harmonizing perspective to history and experience that fosters an intolerant attitude toward disorder (cf. Leslie, 2007, pp. 156–157). It supposes that the structures and representations that the speechful find in their own consciousness constitute the limit of what can be experienced in reality; that knowledge consists in putting (or allowing to fall) the data of consciousness into correct categories within a system of knowing that can be affected by the real only on its own terms; and that truth is the correctness or coherence of propositions within a pre-given system of knowing.

In identitarian thinking, the real is allowed to surprise human beings only for the briefest of moments, following which its novelty must immediately be domesticated and subsumed as an instance or extension of the already known. Identitarian thought makes history seem continuous by ignoring or filing down the rough patches of reality that are constantly irrupting in the now of this or that particular moment to challenge the integrity of the dominant conceptual apparatus into which, at any given point in time, all facts must fit if they are to be recognized as real.

On Language as Such is identitarian in this sense precisely because it draws no meaningful distinctions *within* the category of the anthropologically human. Like Aristotle, the text presupposes that to be human at all necessarily means to possess the power of discourse, if only the lesser power (compared to God's) of producing instrumental speech and inconsequential prattle. In sum, Benjamin's identification of every member of the species *homo sapiens* with speechfulness overlooks the possibility that speechlessness, considered as a burden and sorrow of the existentially impotent, is not limited to the sphere of nonhuman nature.

Human speech, silence, and speechlessness

Our discussion of the opposition between speechlessness and speech will now discard its Benjaminian reference to the relation between, on the one hand, non-human nature, and, on the other hand, the human being determined universally (*à la* Aristotle) as a speaking being. Aristotle's famous co-definition of the human being as *zōon politikon* ("political [or social] animal") (1253^{a} 3–6), though anthropologically correct, suffers from a failure to distinguish *within* the politico-social sphere according to the degree or extent to which a particular person has real access to speechfulness, to being heard. In keeping with previous indications about the important category of political speechlessness, henceforth the opposition *speechfulness versus speechlessness* will refer to a distinctly political and ethical relationship *between* human beings that arises within the context of social life as people actually (and not merely theoretically) experience it.

What allows for this comparison to proceed fruitfully, and what gives it its ethical salience, is the recognition that the sort of distinctly hierarchical relationship that *On Language as Such* describes as subsisting between the speech of humans and the speechlessness of nonhuman nature applies with equal force to the relationship in the now-time between human beings who speak and those who, *for whatever reason*, in fact do not. That is, the top–bottom hierarchical privilege that is implied by the semiotic relation between "humanity" and "nature," rooted as it is in Judeo-Christian theology and traditional Western thought, can be seen as perfectly homologous to the relation between speechful humans and speechless ones (see Figure 4.2).

Speechless human beings may understand speech; they may know how to speak; and they may even want to speak. But at the end of the day they simply *do* not speak, or at least they do not speak audibly. Earlier in this chapter, we cataloged numerous examples of this phenomenon. Those who in fact never dare (or are never asked) to speak about the state of the social world and their relationship to it are not exactly silent. As was noted earlier, silence can be meaningful when it is injected into being by those who are used to being heard. But the power to express oneself by way of suspending *or* withholding meaning is irrelevant to those who, for whatever reason, are never in fact listened to by anyone in a position to care and/or do something about their fate.

The expressions of the speechful already count, or are somehow made to count. Like everything else the socially and politically privileged or lucky do, *their* silence is legible. Speechless humans, however, like deer and other nonhuman creatures, may leave behind traces of their passing, but never articulate signs that anyone cares to look at. Their silence is inaudible, both before and after the grave. Even the minute traces of their being so-and-so, and not otherwise, remain for speechful others either to notice or to overlook, either to bring to language or to leave

HUMANITY	::	SPEECHFUL HUMANS
nature		speechless humans

Figure 4.2 Homologous relations of dominance

eternally unexpressed. Motivated ventriloquism can give the speechless realm the simulacrum of a voice, but in that case the "voice" speaks in the idiom of the speechful about only those elements of the speechless realm that the speechful care to mention.

Indications of this last point can be found everywhere in social life. Consider, for example, the meaningless refuse that is created whenever hired or careless hands tip the contents of dresser drawers owned by recently deceased "ordinary" persons into the dustbin. That refuse can be compared to a buried monument, never to be unearthed, of a forgotten civilization. Faded ribbons from a long-lost lover's hair; a torn theater ticket saved as a memento of a favorite performance attended long ago; a cheap plastic baby rattle once used by a child who grew up, moved away, and completely lost touch with her parents; an expired first driver's license earned when cars still had transmission stick-shifts located on the steering wheel—in short, all the precious (to *someone* at *some time*) little bits and pieces of a quotidian life once lived and now *forever* lost to speech and memory.

The anonymous existence of these pitiful bits and pieces corresponds to the anonymous existence of pebbles on the uninhabited shore of a distant sea, which is to say, theirs is an existence that is destined to oblivion. The esoteric seventeenth-century English author Thomas Browne expressed more or less the same idea in theological terms near the end of his extraordinary essay *Hydriotaphia, Urne-Buriall* (1658, ch. 5): "Oblivion is not to be hired: The greater part must be content to be as though they had not been, to be found in the Register of God, not in the record of man" (Browne, 1658, ch. 5). But whereas Browne allows that the anonymity of the speechless in the human world will at least be somewhat offset by the attention that will be paid to them by an omniscient God, a disenchanted and thoroughly secular human mind can take no such supernatural comfort.

Presumably the kind of God that knows even when a sparrow falls also counts the hairs on the heads of the speechless and speechful alike (Matthew 10:29–30). If human beings of the latter sort can reassure themselves that God is their ethical wingman, so to speak—that he will always take compassionate notice of the category of those whom *they* do not notice—then their guilt on account of ignoring the pain of countless anonymous others is much lightened. In a thoroughly secular context, on the other hand, there is no imaginary wingman to notice and care about the speechless. There is only the disenchanted ethical I, whose anxiety and sorrow on account of what he or she does not doubt in the ethical sphere cannot be laid off on anyone else. The ethical burden of attempting to do justice without illusions does not lighten when man ceases to revolve around the illusory sun of religion and starts to "revolve about himself as his own true sun" (Marx, 1964, p. 44). On the contrary: once it became clear that the death of God was leading to a deflation of Truth to the status of a mere technique, that ethical burden grew considerably heavier.

The category of speechlessness thus suggests the possibility of a kind of secular ethical concern that arises *before*, or at least coequally with, Levinasian "first philosophy." The latter stresses ethical recognition of a mortality that shows itself in the face of this or that particular Other (Levinas, 1999, pp. 157–158). But the phenomenological facts of the case—or at least the particular case of a disenchanted person—suggest that another origin of ethical concern lies in something like an *awareness of unawareness*. That is, it lies in the dawning of the shocking recognition that it is extraordinarily easy not to know, or to forget, that the Other ever existed in the first place, and, even if one does notice or remember the Other, that it is so very easy (and tempting) to put one's own words into his mouth. On this score, Aleksandr Solzhenitsyn once gave a warning about the inherent limitations of bearing witness that is disturbingly relevant to the idea of an ethics of justice without illusions:

> All those who drank of [the experience of the Soviet Gulag] most deeply, who learned the meaning of it most fully, are already in the grave and will not tell us. No one will now ever tell us *the most important thing* about these camps.
>
> (Grossman, 2010, p. 296)

Let us be clear: it's not that the speechless lack the power to generate noise through their mouths or gestures with their hands. It's not that they are somehow fated by their genetic or cultural makeup to be lesser beings than those who can speak—Hegelian slaves, for instance, unwilling to risk their lives in a battle for recognition with their masters (Hegel, 1977, pp. 111–119). The central, defining point of the concept of speechlessness will be lost if, like Hegel, we hurry to impute it to natural or metaphysical causes. The speechless are speechless simply because they *do* not speak, or, if noise does come out of their mouths, it *is never in fact heard* as speech by those who speak to, of, or for them.

From what has already been said, it is possible to derive the following general determination of the concept of political speechlessness: The politically speechless are those who do not in fact audibly speak up *or* remain silent in the critical moments when their fates are determined. The speechless in fact mount no verbal defense against even the most hackneyed and banal forms of speech, including the flattened-out discourse of management and control that consummates, and to a large extent constitutes, modern technological thinking. For the speechful are not necessarily (or even often) eloquent and profound. Their speech can be as boringly ordinary as a one-minute telephone call from someone like Adolf Eichmann to a station master trying to arrange for the departure of a train from Budapest to Auschwitz.

Not for nothing did Hannah Arendt take pains to clarify that her concept of "the banality of evil," first deployed in her controversial coverage of the Eichmann trial in Jerusalem, was not some doctrine or theory, but rather was a *factual* statement. Whether or not the phrase "the banality of evil" always accurately described the mentality of Eichmann himself (it probably did not, given what we now know about his actual motivations, which generally were much more fanatical than Arendt supposed), the *concept* of banality remains useful in the present context. It helpfully describes "the phenomenon of evil deeds, committed on a gigantic scale, which could not be traced to any particularity of wickedness, pathology, or ideological conviction in the doer, whose only personal distinction was perhaps extraordinary shallowness" (Arendt, 2003, p. 159). Experience shows that the careless babblings of the speechful can be just as stupid and shallow as the needs of the speechless are deep, and yet still manage to wreak the kind of terrible suffering that will, in actual fact, remain forever unspoken and unheard.

Of course, this does not imply that the speechless are utterly defenseless against the predations or casual thoughtlessness of those who speak. Every now and then, their inarticulateness gives rise to a rage that bursts forth in acts of wanton crime, riot, or anarchy. In such extreme cases, what Benjamin (1978, p. 292) said in *Critique of Violence* about the modern economy as a whole applies with equal vigor to the entire speechless realm: "It resembles much less a machine that stands idle when abandoned by its stoker than a beast that goes berserk as soon as its tamer turns his back." As we saw in Chapter 2, occasionally these spasms of violence may even induce the speechful to change political and social arrangements to mollify the masses. More often than not, however, the disorganized and uncoordinated misbehaviors of the speechless are simply repressed in the name of crime control or preserving social order.

No redemption through language

The concept of the speechless unsaid is not mysterious. Properly understood, the quasi-mystical opposition between the sayable and the unsayable is unsuitable for describing the category of what the politically speechless do not say or are not heard to say. It would be better just to indicate that the speechless unsaid is purely and simply that which happens to be left unsaid or unheard during the critical moment when the fate of the speechless is determined by the discourse of the speechful.

The term "speechless unsaid" denotes a subset of the concept of ontological particularity described in Chapter 3. Imagined in terms of the illustration shown in Figure 3.4 ("The grid and the particular"), the speechless unsaid always falls "between the lines" of intelligibility that have been established by the discourse of the speechful, no matter how caring and compassionate their motives may be. It is that which empirically *is not said* amid any given event of saying, and that which *is not understood* by the speechful even during their most insightful moments of understanding. The speechless unsaid represents the stillborn discursive content, so to speak, of reality as it is actually lived by the politically speechless. "Discursive" and "stillborn" because the content in question *could* have been spoken about by the speechless, or heard by the speechful, but in fact was not. "Content" because the speechful *do not doubt* (in the sense intended in Chapter 3) that the speechless unsaid is not real, even though it is.

Despite its amorphousness, the realm of speechlessness is quite real. Indeed, it co-constitutes what is called reality itself, for reality is not "made up" of the discourse of the speechful alone. Levinas's name for the totality of the speechless realm—human and nonhuman alike—is *il y a* ("there is"), which he characterized, a little too grandiosely for present purposes, as "being's energy of being" (Levinas, 2003, p. 11). Instead of identifying the speechless with being as such, let's just say that their manner of being is to drone on and on like the faint but unheeded hum of a transmission wire or, better still, like the state of unarticulated "quiet desperation" in with Thoreau (1937, p. 7) said the mass of people lead their lives.

The possibility of arranging for more and more people to speak, however politically attractive that strategy might be for making the world a more democratic place, fails to deal with the most important ethical implication of the concept of speechlessness. To be sure, when speechless human beings somehow manage to "find their voice," as the saying goes, they leave their speechlessness behind and enter the realm of discourse. But their doing so no more abolishes the category of speechlessness as such than the material successes of the boys in Horatio Alger's rags-to-riches stories helped lift all (or even many) poor children out of the gutter in nineteenth-century America.[5]

All meaning, political or otherwise, within the sphere of speechlessness is a priori infinite in the very precise etymological sense of lacking *finitus*, which in Latin means "having definite or definable limits." Limits give unity, and unity is the precondition of all intentionality. But limits and unity are a function of what we earlier called the "as"-structure of beings, which is to say, they are dependent on the language and thought of the speechful. Any finitude and unity that may (or may not) arrive to determine the social reality behind the political structures that manage the speechless realm necessarily come from the *outside*, from those who speak, rather than from the *inside*, from the speechless themselves.

Doubtless it is noble and praiseworthy to care deeply about the injustices created by current political and legal arrangements, including the kind of injustices that come from too few people having the right or the power to speak about those arrangements in ways that could make a real difference. Thus, for example, global food-rights activist Raj Patel is probably right to criticize the pro-development "philanthrocapitalism" practiced by such rich "hyperagents" as the Bill & Melinda Gates Foundation for their inclination to "play God" with African food policy. "There has to be something problematic," he said recently, "about a few big brains in Washington State making decisions about an entire continent. At the very least, shouldn't this make any small-'d' democrat queasy?" (Rieff, 2015, p. 19).

Indeed, it should. In fact, Patel's question does make this particular small-"d" democrat queasy. But no *general* moral commitment, however imperative, should ever be confused with what we have been calling the ethics of justice without illusions. A conscience that allows itself to be soothed by committing to a general critique of injustice is also one that prepares itself to be anesthetized against the effects of the ungeneralizable particular. A real starving child whose particular life, right now and right here, depends on real food that happens to be in the hands of a real philanthrocapitalist is a lot easier to overlook or ignore if one inflexibly pre-categorizes all of the latter's programmatic efforts as ignoble or unjust.

In the course of the philosophical journey that culminated in the writing of this book, the author came across Michael Löwy's striking paraphrase of one of Benjamin's last (and greatest) insights: "*So long as the sufferings of a single human being are forgotten there can be no deliverance*" (Löwy, 2005, p. 34). That this insight is Benjaminian through and through is self-evident to anyone who has ever read his rigorously sad but hopeful *Theses on the Philosophy of History* (Benjamin, 1968, pp. 253–264). In this context, the phrase "the sufferings of a single human being" refers to the sufferings of each and every human being—what *Law's Task* called "universal human suffering"—without prior discrimination on account of the sufferer's badness or goodness according to conventional criteria of justice or morality. Of course, to actually notice and remember on a scale that is vast enough to include everything from the suffering of Jesus on his cross to that of Rudolf Höss on his scaffold would be humanly impossible. However, to be temperamentally *inclined* to notice and remember, without prior discrimination, within the circle of universal human suffering is a different matter. Not only is this a possibility, but also Löwy's paraphrase of Benjamin suggests that it is a condition of the possibility of "deliverance," that is, redemption.

The notion of deliverance/redemption gets its rhetorical power from religion, where the image of a Last Judgment by God reigns supreme as the ultimate criterion of the moral worth of an individual's life. Redemption's appeal is considerably lessened in a world viewed atheistically. What is done in that world is done forever and will never be erased or offset by good deeds recorded in some invisible deity's account book. It seems clear, therefore, that the secular translation of the injunction-cum-reminder contained in Löwy's statement would have to evoke an "ethics" in something like the sense that Levinas meant when he wrote about ethics as a secular phenomenologist, that is, not in the theological mode of being a "Jewish philosopher."[6] Here would be an ethics whose temporality shows itself as an infinite responsibility that the I always already bears *right now* (cf. 1996,pp. 18–19).

A thoroughly disenchanted person has lost the psychological ability to wait or hope for supernatural forgiveness at the end of days. Löwy's statement, when read in the purely secular context of an ethics of justice without illusions, thus resonates as "ethical" in the curiously aesthetic sense that Wittgenstein employed in the *Tractatus*:

> When an ethical law of the form, "Thou shalt . . .," is laid down, one's first thought is, "And what if I do not do it?" It is clear, however, that ethics has nothing to do with punishment and reward in the usual sense of the terms. So our question about the consequences of an action must be unimportant. – At least those consequences should not be events. For there must be something right about the question we posed. There must indeed be some kind of ethical reward and ethical punishment, but they must reside in the action itself. (And it is also clear that the reward must be something pleasant and the punishment something unpleasant.).
>
> (Wittgenstein, 1974, pp. 71–72) (Prop. 6.422)

It is important to understand that the word *consequences* in this passage does not refer to the debate within academic philosophy between those who measure "ought" by the concept of duty (e.g., Kant and the so-called "deontologists") and those who measure it by the social consequences that a given action produces (e.g., Bentham and the so-called "consequentialists"). Instead, Wittgenstein's ethical aesthetic focuses exclusively on the *immediate* consequences of an action *for the ethical I as such.*

Seen from the latter point of view, the task of witness and memory that is recommended by Löwy's statement ("So long as the sufferings of a single human being are forgotten there can be no deliverance") can have nothing to do with punishment and reward in the theistic or even legal sense. Rather, it must entail the kind of reward and punishment that resides immediately and immanently within the singular performance of ethical actions in particular situations. *This* sort of task would have to be borne in each and every case by no one other than a "Me-myself," who would then experience reward or punishment *eo instante*, as the common law might put it (Blackstone, 1979, p. 168), for what he or she is doing.

Despite appearances, it would be wrong to think of this aesthetic as a form of ethical solipsism. The true ethical solipsist is someone who cannot summon the courage to act without nurturing hope for *his own* deliverance or redemption on account of any potential misdeeds. Wittgenstein's ethical aesthetic no longer indulges in this fantasy. It leaves hope for redemption behind in order to experience heaven and hell in the here and now. Neither the abstraction "Thou shalt . . ." nor the prospect of future judgment for having violated its command is definitive anymore. The only thing that matters ethically is what happens between the I and the Other *right now*, when everything real has to happen if it is to happen at all.

An ethics that somehow managed to synthesize Wittgenstein's ethical aesthetic with Levinas's "ethics as first philosophy" would be the antithesis of Nietzsche's aesthetic ideal of living one's life in such a way that one would willingly choose to live it over and over again as part of the eternal recurrence of the same (1992, p. 69). Nietzsche's "Higher Man" is someone "who wants to have *what was and is* repeated to all eternity" (1966, p. 56). The fact that Nietzsche's Higher Man has "reverence" (*Ehrfurcht*) for himself above others (1966, p. 287) certainly distinguishes Nietzsche's ontological aesthetic from Levinas's other-regarding conception of ethics. But what makes Nietzsche's principle of the willed recurrence of the same uniquely different from this book's idea of an ethics of justice without illusions is not the formal distinction between a self-regarding aesthetic ethics and an other-regarding ethics of care. The significance of that distinction pales in comparison with another difference—one that stems from the seemingly trivial grammatical observation that the verb forms of "willing" and "wanting" are *transitive.*

To will or want something means to will or want some *X*, where the criterion of *X* consists of the words and/or images that one would truthfully use to describe the "what" that one wills or wants. But willing is not "an immediate non-causal bringing-about" (Wittgenstein, 1953, p. 159e). To will the recurrence of event *X* is *to do* something at some particular moment in time. In the case of Nietzsche's willed recurrence of the same, this doing involves undergoing an experience in which certain words and images associated with the linguistic sign "*X*" hang in the air, so to speak, both after the earlier-willed event itself and in advance of its willed recurrence. However, the relationship between willing *X* at t_1 and *X* actually coming about at t_2 is empirical and contingent, not logical. For those who are inclined to notice or be affected by them, countless unwilled particularities will always intrude between t_1 and t_2 to disrupt the continuity and self-identity of what the willed word "*X*" imperiously seems to name.

The essential transitivity of willing and wanting is no small thing. Nietzsche's advocacy of willed attachment to a mere image of the self's own actions belongs to the same logical category as the arguments made by politics, law, and justice for willing attachment to the images that *they* inspire. To pledge allegiance to words and images that I make of and for my own actions, and to pledge allegiance to words and images that "they" make for me, are both forms of pledging allegiance to an eyeless idol made of paper and ink. Whereas the sort of ethics that this book is trying to track down would somehow involve participation in the protean operations of law and justice without ever once nurturing the self-righteous illusion that the idea of justice, however resplendent it may seem, is anything more or less real than a pretty but transient hallucination.

The Benjaminian aspiration to make human language more genuine, more Godlike, offers to redeem too little. In bestowing what seems to be a primal unity to human beings—if only the "unique" unity of the "one of a kind," as Levinas (1999, p. 122) puts it—a human *Logos* modelled on the creative Word of the Judeo-Christian God eternally misses what is different in an unseemly haste to anoint what is the same. To be blunt: experiencing the face of the Other "as" belonging to a self-identical God-created being, *à la* Benjamin, or experiencing it "as" signifying "Thou shalt cause the other to live," *à la* Levinas, is not the same as experiencing what one does not doubt about a situation. Experiencing *that* is far more disorienting than emotionally challenging or reassuring, for it means awakening to the darkness of the world. It means becoming aware of one's unawareness about the underlying social reality of a situation, its ontological particularity as such.

Nietzsche once said: "To impose upon becoming the character of being—that is the supreme will to power" (1968, p. 330). When it comes to politics, law, and justice, he was right. In those spheres, at least, identitarian thinking of *any* sort always seems to show itself as a strategy that is deployed in a ceaseless war of wills, a war of domination and resistance. Listen to speeches at a political rally or debate; watch the progress of a courtroom trial; attend an academic conference and observe the panicky egoism of those who are presenting papers and those who are trying to tear them down. Struggle is what identitarian thinking accomplishes, and that is probably what it should accomplish if the human world is to become a more (or less) "just" place to live. But despite its admitted value as a tool or weapon in the fight for what is called "justice," at the end of the day that is all identitarian thinking can accomplish. It cannot redeem the infinite sufferings of humanity, and still less the sadness of nature, for the simple reason that it is this very sort of thinking that is constantly creating an unfulfillable need for redemption in the first place.

Notes

1. "A triangle can really be [seen as] *standing up* in one picture, be hanging in another, and can in a third be [seen as] something that has fallen over" (Wittgenstein, 1953, p. 201e).
2. Benjamin first met Scholem in Munich in March of 1915, when the former was 23 years old and the latter was 17. Interestingly, Benjamin sent Scholem an early draft of the essay on language under cover of a letter dated November 11, 1916, only four months after he had written about the "sphere of speechlessness" to Buber (Benjamin, 1994, pp. 81–82).
3. In 1933, Benjamin would analogize or equate nature's language with human language in a short textual fragment called *On the Mimetic Faculty*. There, however, it was a matter of comparing similarities that are "created by nature" (there is no mention of God) with those created by human speech. The fragment claims that these are founded ultimately on the maintenance of both sensuous and "non-sensuous" similarities between human language and reality (Benjamin, 1978, pp. 333–336). This thesis bears an interesting resemblance to the early Wittgenstein doctrine that language can create a "picture" (*Bild*) of reality only because it is possible for the former to exhibit the same "form" as the latter (Wittgenstein, 1974, pp. 7–12).
4. See Heidegger (1998, p. 175): "The expression 'the idea of the good'—which is all too misleading for modern thinking—is the name for that distinctive idea which, as the idea of ideas, is what enables everything else."
5.

    > Horatio Alger, Jr. (1834–99) was a prolific writer of dime novel stories for boys. From the debut of his first novel, *Ragged Dick*, in 1867, Alger was instrumental in establishing a new genre of dime novels known as the "city story." The genre arose out of the wide-spread urbanization that followed the Civil War and paralleled the rise of industrialism. Alger's stories heroicized the young street urchins living in poverty among large, urban centers such as New York, Boston, and Philadelphia. With uncommon courage and moral fortitude, Alger's youths struggle against adversity to achieve great wealth and acclaim. These rags to riches stories were enormously popular with the public and flourished in the decades from 1870 to 1890.
    >
    > (Stanford University Libraries n.d.)

6. "I am not a Jewish thinker. I am just a thinker" (Levinas, 1987, p. 83).

Part Two

Some particular problems of the particular

Chapter 5

International law

Universal human rights and cultural diversity*

> The general designation "culture" already contains, virtually, the process of identifying, cataloguing, and classifying which imports culture into the realm of administration.
>
> Max Horkheimer and Theodor Adorno (2002, p. 104)

The origins of "diversity"

This international conference in Tehran has created an important opportunity for rethinking the relationship between universal human rights and cultural diversity.[1] In the West, there is a tendency to think about culturalism and universalism as antitheses in the human rights arena. Indeed, one's expressed attitude toward the concept of "cultural relativism" has become a kind of shibboleth. All too often it is taken to signify the existence of a stark political–moral division between those who are *for* universal human rights and those who are *against* them.

By way of contrast to this either/or mentality, the title of the present conference, "Cultures in Support of Humanity," seems to elide the antithesis. It contains three distinct terms that purport to work in harmony (not in conflict) with one another: the plural noun *cultures*, the singular noun *humanity*, and the participial phrase *in support of*. The word "cultures" implies a *plurality* of different and diverse things; the word "humanity" indicates the *unity* of something that always remains the same as itself; and the words "in support of" imply that the first can or should help to advance the goals of the second. This arrangement of terms echoes the spirit, so to speak, of UNESCO's *Universal Declaration on Cultural Diversity* (1991). The Declaration's official website summarizes that spirit well when it says that "cultural diversity is a 'common heritage of mankind' and . . . its safeguarding [is] a concrete and ethical imperative, inseparable from respect for human dignity."

Article 2 of the Declaration uses the term "cultural pluralism" to name this ethical imperative, and the organizers of the Tehran conference must have had something like that in mind when they promulgated the title "Cultures in Support of Humanity." UNESCO's decision to characterize cultural pluralism as an *ethical* imperative is quite interesting, for ethics is not the same as justice. Ethics concerns the conscience of each and every *me*, personally and individually, rather than what *we* collectively should do. At the most basic experiential level, ethics involves the ever-urgent problem of how the unique ethical subject, in every case a "Me-myself," will reconcile his or her right to exist with the equally valid and imperative right to exist of the Other. At bottom, ethics poses what might be that most important of all moral questions: not *What should I do?* but rather *Who* am *I in relation to the Other?*

Today, I hope to unpack the meaning and significance of the concepts conveyed by the intriguing title "Cultures in Support of Humanity" for the discourse and practice of international human rights. The goal is to move the discussion of cultural diversity in the sphere of human rights to a deeper level than that which is allowed for by the usual (and in my view sterile) verbal opposition between "universalism" and "cultural relativity."

As I see it, the most fundamental question in this sphere is *not* how a liberal preference for individual human rights can be reconciled with the illiberalism that is often necessary to achieve cultural self-preservation. It is, rather, the problem of how the entities called "the individual" and "culture" are constituted (or co-constituted) in the form of *unities* that are worth protecting and preserving in the first place. What is at stake is not particularly complicated. This does not make it easy to see or understand, however. Often the simplest insights are the hardest to achieve, owing to the extreme difficulty of thinking about what we usually take for granted, as well as to the fact that any language we might use to converse with one another contains within it many obscure sediments from the past that remain unacknowledged or unrecognized.

Take the origin of the word "diversity" itself. Article 1 of the UNESCO Declaration makes diversity sound like something noble and good, "as necessary for humankind as biodiversity is for nature." But in Old French, the noun *diversité*, from which the English word is derived, also signified the quality of "oddness, wickedness, and perversity." The negative connotation of this medieval word for diversity existed in English from the late fifteenth century, when diversity began to mean "contrary to what is agreeable or right; perversity, evil." The archaic notion that diversity is something unpleasant (or worse) is fully in keeping with the concept's Latin root, *diversitatem*, which signifies "contrariness, contradiction, [and] disagreement" (Harper, 2012).

This brief etymological survey reinforces the need for us to be brutally honest with ourselves about the troubling ambiguities surrounding the project of respect for cultural diversity. Throughout most of human history, readily noticeable physiological, linguistic, and/or behavioral differences among members of the species *homo sapiens* have been interpreted in ways that are much less charitable toward diversity than UNESCO's Declaration is. In fact, "diversity" has usually signified something good and fortunate for *US* (i.e., *our* group) and bad and unfortunate for *THEM* (i.e., *their* group). Normatively speaking, *THEY* were traditionally excluded from the concept of justice, that is, from the sphere of those beings whose treatment could rightly be called *either* just *or* unjust. At the same time, *THEIR* exclusion accomplished the inclusion of *US* as the only proper subjects of legal and moral rights. One of *US* might *choose* to treat one of *THEM* with respect, but as Aristotle put it in the *Nicomachean Ethics*, this would only be a sort of justice "by analogy"[2] or "metaphorically"[3]—a matter of *OUR* discretion rather than *THEIR* right. All too often *THEY* have appeared to *US* in the form of what the philosopher Giorgio Agamben (1998, p. 83) calls "bare life"—living beings that *WE* can notice or ignore, kill or let live, without incurring culpability.

The 1948 *Universal Declaration of Human Rights* was supposed to put an end to this way of thinking and dealing with the *THEMs* of the world. Now, for the first time, everyone on earth was supposed to be the subject of a limited kind of universal justice solely by virtue of the fact that he or she is a "member of the human family," as the Declaration's *Preamble* puts it. But human languages are like tar: their past usages persist in sticking to our fingers no matter how hard we try to shake them off. Thus, even the word "human" resonates with the sort of exclusivity that the U.N. Declaration and all subsequent human rights instruments have aspired to overcome. The point is not just that this word distinguishes human life from animal life in a way that might be (and has been) seriously questioned from an ethical standpoint (Derrida 2008, p. 186). I mean to say in addition that the word "human" has a dubious history even if the focus of one's moral concern is limited to our own species.

As my friend and colleague Costas Douzinas (2000, p. 186) has observed, the word *humanitas* appeared for the first time in the Roman Republic as a translation of *paideia,* the Greek word for education and cultivation. But, of course, no one would say that the haughty Romans recognized all people on earth as equally educated and cultivated—far from it. The Latin word for human being is *homo,* not *humanus.* The concept of *humanitas* in its original Roman form was based on the juridical and moral distinction, drawn by Stoic philosophy, between two different types of people: *homo humanus* and *homo barbarus*—the civilized, educated, and fully human man of rights (*US*) *as opposed to* the uneducated, uncivilized, and therefore non-"human" barbarian (*THEM*). In ancient Rome, the idea of *US* meant exclusively the educated and virtue-loving Roman citizen, a divisive usage that was resurrected in the fourteenth and fifteenth centuries during the Italian Renaissance. This so-called "rebirth" of knowledge and art called itself the *renascentia romanitatis*—that is, a rebirth of classical *Roman* culture—and notwithstanding its undeniable excellence, Renaissance thought continued to draw a firm distinction between civilized *US* (*homo romanus*) and uncivilized *THEM* (*homo barbarus*) (Heidegger, 1998, p. 244).

This abbreviated history of the word "human" casts new light on some of the most important language used in the 1948 *Universal Declaration of Human Rights.* In particular, it shows that when the Declaration recognizes the "inherent dignity and . . . the equal and inalienable rights of *all members of the human family*" (emphasis added), it does not make a moral and legal claim about a preexisting empirical classification called "all members of the human family." Rather, it endeavors to officially *constitute* all members of the human family as a juridical entity for the first time since the eighteenth century, when the French *Déclaration des droits de l'Homme et du citoyen* had attempted—albeit with little success, as Hannah Arendt (2004, pp. 369–384) reminds us—to elevate the "Rights of Man" to a level that was at least somewhat commensurate with the "Rights of the Citizen."

The dialectics of unity and diversity

If the international law of human rights counts the human family as one, then the notion of "cultural differences" reconstitutes this one into many. The Preamble of the UNESCO Declaration defines culture as "the set of distinctive spiritual, material, intellectual and emotional features of society or a social group, and . . . it encompasses, in addition to art and literature, lifestyles, ways of living together, value systems, traditions and beliefs." Seen from the inside by its individual members, each such distinct society or social group shows itself as an *US* whose existence is co-constituted by the recognition that it is different from other societies and groups considered not-*US*, that is, *THEM*.

In fact, there can be no *US* without a *THEM*. There is an important sense in which a culture cannot be itself—that is, a distinct, self-aware human culture—unless and until it comes into decisive contact with other, different cultures. Consider an example drawn from the history of my own country, the United States. Until Europeans began to arrive en masse on the North American continent, there were no "Indians," no "Native Americans." There were only people who thought of themselves as Mohawk, Arapaho, Lakota Sioux, Cheyenne, and so forth. The very idea of an indigenous "native people" (in the singular) in North America could have arisen only after white settlers began to intrude on local culture*s* (plural) that had always before thought of themselves as essentially different from their foes and neighbors in other tribes. Unity and diversity are not just logical correlates: they are also parasitic on one another at the level of their substantive content.

If we do not take too distant a view of day-to-day experience, the truth is that we drift through our lives most of the time without ever taking *explicit* notice of many (or even any) of the historically contingent features of our social environment that have gone into making us who we are. Heidegger (1962, p. 174) famously called this phenomenal oblivion to what counts as a state of normalcy in everyday life *Geworfenheit*, or "thrownness." Within the comfort of our own social environments most of us are able to swim around thoughtlessly like pet fish thrown long ago into a community tank—the aquarium, so to speak, that history and culture have pre-constructed for us. If we *do* happen to notice a "unique" aspect of our own culture, this is usually because we have become consciously aware of something in it that contrasts with analogous features of other cultures, past or present. I will confess, for example, that I never really explicitly thought about the fact that I spoon sugar into my tea *before* drinking it until the first time I visited the Middle East and saw what was, for me, the remarkable sight of people drinking tea through lumps of sugar held between their teeth.

So on the one hand, what is diverse must see itself as unified, must constitute itself *as* "itself," before it can recognize itself *as* "different" from something else.

But on the other hand, what sees itself as itself can only do so if it takes the form of what Hegel (1975, p. 168) called "self-relating negativity": that is, only if it reflects itself back onto itself as a unity that stands opposed to something else that it is not. The idea of absolute unity, the ancient dream of Western philosophy since Parmenides (1984, p. 55), is no more intelligible to us than the idea of absolute difference. To be recognized and understood as something unique, every *THIS* requires a contrast: it needs to stand opposed to at least one *THAT* that it is not.

This implies that the idea of the *absolute* diversity of cultures is no more intelligible to us than the idea of the *absolute* unity of humanity. When Heraclitus (1987, p. 13) said, "The sun is not only new each day but forever continuously new," he quite literally did not know what entity he was talking about. That is because nothing can be called *forever continuously* different from itself without first being called itself, however momentary and transient its self-identity is taken to be. *Pace* Heraclitus, it might be better just to lay down the rule that the poet Wallace Stevens did in "Notes Toward a Supreme Fiction": "The sun / Must bear no name, gold flourisher, but be / In the difficulty of what it is to be" (Stevens, 1990, p. 381). Unity and diversity are not like an apple and an orange—they do not offer two different material possibilities between which one could choose once and for all, thereafter discarding what remains as personally unpalatable. Unity and diversity are more like the two arms on a pair of kitchen tongs: you can't use the tongs to lift up apples or oranges (or suns) without squeezing both of its arms together.

What then are we to make of the phenomenon of change? How can an individual or culture be the *same* as itself, and yet also somehow *different* from itself from one day (or year or decade) to the next? Ever since Hegel's day, the formal philosophical name for the strange (but I think ultimately emancipating) idea that a thing can be both itself and not-itself is "dialectics." Theodor Adorno (1973, p. 5) described the essential insight of all dialectical thought, well enough for present purposes, as follows: "The name dialectics says no more . . . than that objects do not go into their concepts without leaving a remainder [and] that they [eventually] come to contradict the traditional norm of adequacy." An even simpler way to express this same point would be to say that a concept, just like every other abstraction, "does not exhaust the thing conceived" (Adorno, 1973, p. 5)—and thus the category of the true is not coterminous with that of the real. At any given moment in historical time, whatever we call *US*, for example, is much bigger and unrulier than the tidy little concept of "*US*" (or "our culture") invites us to believe.

It is of course true that the average person lives with a more or less automatic sense of worldly permanency, and that being in possession of this sort of automatic sensibility is probably indispensable to the conduct of ordinary life (Arendt, 1993, p. 259). But a practical sensibility that allows us to navigate within reality should never be confused with reality itself, lest we come to have faith in the extremely dangerous proposition that believing a thing is so always makes it so. The real is no more identical to the conceptual than ambient noise is identical to the English words "ambient noise." The one keeps droning on and on in the background, whether or not we notice it, in a way that Levinas (2003b, p. 11) has called *il y a*, or "there is"; the other lingers in existence only in the highly abbreviated form of "that-which-is-recognized-*as-X*." The many different historical experiences of humankind converge on at least one enduring truth about social arrangements: *nothing lasts forever*. Like a liter of water poured slowly but inexorably over a little teacup, eventually the real will escape whatever conceptual container is placed beneath it.

The implications of this insight for the would-be conceptual unities called "culture," "cultural diversity," and "the individual" are profound. Take the idea that a given group of people have *a* culture (in the singular). It is convenient, perhaps even necessary, for sociologists and cultural anthropologists to adopt this notion as a sort of Kantian regulative ideal[4] to govern their research. Science needs to make certain simplifying assumptions about reality in order to say anything coherent about it. But as Max Weber's concept of the ideal type (1949, pp. 49–112) reminds us, there always is in principle an identifiable social scien*tist* to hold responsible for whatever simplifying assumptions happen to be made in a given research context. In contrast, when an international human rights instrument such as the UNESCO Declaration calls for "genuine dialogue among cultures" (Article 7), the inherently political question of who *speaks* for each culture—that is, who gets to define its traditions and set them in opposition to the traditions of other cultures—is left hanging in the air.

In Chapter 27 of his *Essay Concerning Human Understanding*, John Locke suggests the following solution to the metaphysical problem of unity and diversity amidst change: "An entity of any sort can remain the same throughout its changes provided that the changes that take place in it are characteristic of entities of that sort and are allowed for in their concept" (Penelhum, 1967, p. 96). Although rather dry in its formulation, Locke's solution does offer the great advantage of bringing into the foreground the interesting notion of what a concept "allows." What, for example, do the concepts "Iranian culture" and "American culture" *allow for* in the "entities" that correspond to these phrases?

It is a truism that a concept cannot allow or disallow anything unless someone first formulates it. Concepts are like the laws of the state in that respect: they cannot take effect, so to speak, until they are promulgated.[5] Yet everyone knows that those who happen to be socially dominant within a given group of people have a much greater opportunity to speak and be heard than do less privileged members of the group. The opinions of the relatively few (let us call them the "speechful") who define a given culture, especially to those outsiders who praise cultural diversity, do not necessarily express the views of the masses, most of whom remain speechless and unheard while the important work of cultural definition is going on. Must we assume that the louder a given voice is, the more clearly and correctly it articulates the truth to us about some monolithic unity that goes under the name "*THEIR* culture"? And must we also assume that the absence of any nuance or vocal dissent emanating from the politically speechless within a given group of people implies that *THEIR* culture really is what those who speak for it say it is?

I will return to the enigma of a culture's simultaneous unity and disunity in a little while. For now, however, permit me to drop a small hint about the ethical significance of this enigma: If cultural diversity is something precious, as I truly believe it is, then it is also the case that no human culture has ever really remained itself for very long.

The problem of linguistic diversity

The various means by which human beings distinguish *US* from *THEM* are never *just* procedures for determining the value-free "facts" of a situation, as if we were red balloons that one day casually decided, in a ho-hum sort of way, that we were colored red only because we had come into contact with otherwise identical balloons colored green and blue. There is also a certain degree of *condescension* in the practice of group self-identification, no matter how open-minded and personally free from contemptuousness a given observer might be. Judging from the historical evidence alone, any group of individuals that insists on calling itself *US* also tends to bring with it a judgment about the normatively subordinated (not just factually different) status of what it calls *THEM*. That this is true in the case of all forms of racial, ethnic, national, and religious chauvinism is obvious. But it also holds true even when the most progressive members of a particular social group sincerely conceive of all human beings in universal terms. There are always limits to our toleration of the culturally specific behaviors of those who are not-*US*, no matter how much good faith we display and no matter how widely we may throw the net of our tolerance.

However much it may praise cultural diversity, for example, the UNESCO Declaration shows plainly enough where it stands on the question of conflicts between cultural diversity and individual human rights. Article 4 states, unequivocally, "No one may invoke cultural diversity to infringe upon human rights guaranteed by international law, nor to limit their scope." It would seem that what the Declaration takes to be a universal human right and what it takes to be tolerable (or even essential) under the heading "respect for cultural diversity" are necessarily conceived from the point of view of some *US* or other. That is, from *some* point of view on the outer limits of what *WE*, who happen to support the Declaration in a certain culturally inflected way, are prepared to tolerate about *THEIR* culture.

The explicit or implicit hierarchy established whenever *WE* speak about *THEM*—to reproach, to tolerate, or even to praise their behaviors—can be found everywhere in the discourse of human rights. By way of illustration, consider the unconscious condescension that is exhibited in *The Law of Peoples*, where John Rawls distinguishes between what he calls decent and indecent "hierarchical peoples." To illustrate this distinction, Rawls constructs what he calls "an imaginary decent hierarchical Muslim people" by the name of "Kazanistan" (1999, p. 64). After describing its basic political structure (the details of which need not concern us here), he has this to say about his imaginary culture's final normative status:

> I do not hold that Kazanistan is perfectly just, but it does seem to me that such a society is decent. Moreover, even though it is only imagined, I do not think it is unreasonable that a society like Kazanistan might exist, especially since it is not without precedent in the real world. . . . Readers might charge me with baseless utopianism, but I disagree. Rather, it seems to me that something like Kazanistan is the best *we* can realistically—and coherently—hope for.
>
> (Rawls, 1999, p. 78) (emphasis added)

To whom was the word "we" meant to refer in this last sentence? This exegetical question is not difficult to answer, for Rawls is not shy about saying why he drew the decent/indecent distinction in the first place. Although undoubtedly well-meaning, Rawls explicitly conceives of his dualism from the point of view of a proponent of Western liberalism for whom the most pressing political and moral task is, as he puts it, "to specify how far liberal peoples are to tolerate nonliberal peoples" (1999, p. 59).

On the flip side of things, consider some of the distinctions discussed in Dr. Saleh Hussain Al-Aayed's treatise *The Rights of Non-Muslims in the Islamic World*. After noting that Islam guarantees freedom of belief for non-Muslims, including the right to build and attend non-Muslim places of worship, Al-Aayed (2002, pp. 63–70) concedes that the case is otherwise in the special situation of the Arabian Peninsula. There shariah law has been interpreted (rightly in his view) to forbid the public proclamation of any religion other than Islam. Elsewhere, we find Al-Aayed (2002, p. 9) referring to the distinction between "people of the Book [i.e., Christians and Jews] and polytheists," and it seems quite clear that he does not mean that the Abrahamic religions differ from polytheistic religions, such as Hinduism, in the same way that red balloons differ from blue ones. Instead, the former are said to be entitled to more respect than the latter. Like Rawls, Al-Aayed is speaking normatively about the outer limits of his tolerance for religious diversity, albeit in his case from a distinctly Islamic point of view.

"Perspectivism" is the name for the idea, made famous by Nietzsche (see 1968, p. 272), that every human being's epistemological and normative stance—whether it consists in a claim couched in terms of trans-cultural validity or a demand that cultural differences be respected—necessarily proceeds from *someone*'s particular point of view. This is so even (or especially) when the claimant asserts that his or her point of view is not a point of view at all, but rather what Catherine MacKinnon (1983, p. 635) has called "the standard for point-of-viewlessness."

The great German sociologist Karl Mannheim transformed Nietzsche's philosophical theory of perspectives into the scientific discipline that we know today under the name "sociology of knowledge." In his seminal 1929 book *Ideology and Utopia*, Mannheim described the essential task, as well as the peculiar difficulty, of such a science in the following way:

> Once we recognize that all historical knowledge is relational knowledge, and can only be formulated with reference to the position of the observer, we are

> faced, once more, with the task of discriminating between what is true and what is false in such knowledge. The question then arises: which social standpoint *vis-à-vis* history offers the best chance for reaching an optimum of truth? In any case, at this stage the vain hope of discovering truth in a form which is independent of an historically and socially determined set of meanings will have to be given up. The problem is by no means solved when we have arrived at this conclusion, but we are, at least, in a better position to state the actual problems that arise in a more unrestricted manner.
>
> (Mannheim, 1985, pp. 79–80)

It is important to recognize that Mannheim was not the sort of crude cultural relativist who maintains that just because "everything goes" (or has gone on) in human history, therefore anything goes, morally speaking. His most important epistemological insight is far subtler. It is just this: while knowledge seems relative because there are so many competing versions of it, each human perspective exhibits an *objective* relation between the social location of the knower and his or her particular object of knowledge (Mannheim, 1985, pp. 264–311). Hence, each perspective is indeed entitled to call itself "true," or rather, to say that it provides *a* (not *the*) correct criterion for truth, albeit only from the perspective of the knower's own social and historical context.

It might seem strange that a factual truth about a simple custom such as the best way to drink tea with sugar, or which side of the road to drive on, can be both objective *and* relative at the same time—strange, I should emphasize, without being particularly controversial. One can find the same sort of relatively noncontroversial strangeness in the field of translation. In his well-known essay *The Task of the Translator*, Walter Benjamin gives the simple example of the difficulties presented in translating the German word *Brot* into French, or the French word *pain* into German. Drawing a formal distinction between the *intended object* of a word (in logical terms, the word's "reference," or in the case of a proper noun, its "bearer") and the word's *mode of intention*, Benjamin states:

> The words *Brot* and *pain* "intend" the same object, but the modes of this intention are not the same. It is owing to these modes that the word *Brot* means something different to a German than the word *pain* to a Frenchman, that these words are not interchangeable for them, that, in fact, they try to exclude each other. As to the intended object, however, the words mean the very same thing [namely, a piece of cooked dough].
>
> (Benjamin, 1968, p. 74)

Any sensitive observer who has ever spent more than a little time in France and Germany will be able to grasp Benjamin's point immediately. The average Frenchman's total social relationship, so to speak, to bread is substantially different from the average German's. To be sure, people of both nationalities seem to genuinely *savor* their bread, whereas Americans (at least Americans like me) mostly just chew and swallow it. But it is also the case that the French savor their bread in substantially different ways than the Germans do. Thus, to mechanically substitute *Brot* for *pain* in a German translation of, say, a French novel is to leave out and distort the full significance and resonance that the French word for bread originally projected to its intended audience. All good translators know that translation is an art, not a technique. They realize that a successful translation is more like painting someone's portrait than it is like painting by numbers in child's activity book (cf. Pinsky, 1994, pp. xxi–xxiv).

It is a grave philosophical mistake to think that every word must stand for what Wittgenstein (1974, p. 54) called its *Bedeutungskörper*, or "meaning-body": that is, a context-transcendent, metaphysically unified entity for which different languages provide functionally equivalent linguistic signs. Properly understood, translation does not create a facsimile of the original in a different tongue—it creates a *new original* whose meaning bears a more or less strong relationship to what it translates without ever being wholly equivalent to it. That is because the real use of language does not consist in a sort of arm's length manipulation of two external objects: linguistic signs and their objective meanings. Instead, it involves the use of words with what Benjamin (1968, p. 74) called a "mode of intention," and it always is embedded in what Wittgenstein (1953, p. 11e) called some "form of life" (*Lebensform*). In other words, speaking and writing is in every particular, real case a historically contingent *activity*—a dialectical whole whose essential moments are: *words ↔ actions ↔ social context ↔ words.*

The relativity of universality

The Preamble to the *Universal Declaration of Human Rights* expresses the uplifting principle that certain fundamental, inalienable rights belong to "all members of the human family." It thus heralds, on behalf of the world's many governments, the beginning of an international era in which the long history of legalized intra- and cross-cultural predation is closed forever. Unfortunately, this universal commitment often brings with it the naïve belief that linguistic meaning is also universal—that the content or scope of a human right is indifferent to the language in which it is expressed. For example, it is one thing to say, as do the *Universal Declaration* (Article 5), the *International Covenant on Civil and Political Rights* (Article 7), and the *Convention against Torture and Other Cruel, Inhuman or Degrading Treatment or Punishment* (Article 16), that no human being should be subjected to cruel, inhuman, or degrading treatment or punishment. But it is quite another thing to say that the English phrase "cruel, inhuman or degrading treatment or punishment," like the English word "bread," possesses the exact same mode of intention (to use Benjamin's term) as its translation into, or translation from, the words of some other language.

Take Article 7 of the ICCPR. It most definitely forbids cruel, inhuman, or degrading treatment; but at the same time it also states, in Article 53, that "the Chinese, English, French, Russian and Spanish texts are equally authentic" versions of its provisions. If a word like *Brot* can signify bread differently to a German than the word *pain* signifies it to a Frenchman, then it is not implausible to think that the phrases 残忍的、不人道的或侮辱性的待遇 in Chinese, *cruel, inhuman or degrading treatment* in English, *traitements cruels inhumains ou dégradants* in French, *жестокого, бесчеловечного или унижающего достоинство обращения* in Russian, and *tratos crueles, inhumanos o degradantes* in Spanish all overlap substantially in their potential coverage (else there would be no point to having such a treaty) without being exactly equivalent in their culturally specific modes of intention.

Article 33(3) of the *Vienna Convention on the Law of Treaties* states misleadingly that when treaties are authenticated in two or more languages, "the terms of the treaty are presumed to have the same meaning in each authentic text." That is like saying that the meaning of bread is presumed to be the same in both France and Germany, when everybody knows that it is not. One wants to ask: "same meaning" (or bread) as it is expressed in which language? You will not be able to determine what various governments around the world have *actually* agreed to do and refrain from doing in Article 7 by just staring at the foregoing words or looking them up in dictionaries. Nor will you find this out by reading the views of the Human Rights Committee, the ICCPR's official monitoring body, since it has no effective power to enforce its interpretations against governments that disagree with it. Instead, to learn the real meaning of Article 7—its meaning as practiced in reality, that is—you must investigate how the officials of each government concretely apply the words in *particular* situations. Only then will you be in a position to accurately describe the cross-cultural similarities and differences that exist when differently situated peoples try to make the prohibition against cruel, inhuman, or degrading treatment a reality in and for their own societies.

More generally, it seems to me that to simply assert in English (or any other language) that different cultures display something called "cultural diversity" is not to venture deeply enough into the problem of culture in relation to language. Such a claim does not penetrate to the most basic level of all outward manifestations of cultural diversity. That substrate is just this: any given observer, at least if he or she is not fluently bilingual, will notice, understand and express the apparent oddities of another culture in his or her own culturally specific language. But the latter language will always convey the noticed cultural differences in a manner that is inflected by its own unique history, which is to say, only imperfectly when compared to the language of the alien culture that it purports to describe. *Pain* is not the exact equivalent of *Brot*; indeed, *pain* in France is probably not the equivalent of *pain* in Haiti, just as *Brot* in Germany is probably not the equivalent of *Brot* in Austria. Moreover, it is also likely that even the word *Brot* in Germany is not used with the identical mode of intention from region to region, town to town, or, for that matter, from household to household. At best, only the linguistic sign "*Brot*" considered as a purely *material* entity in written language has remained pretty much the same as itself throughout a relatively long stretch of time. (Not forever, though: *Brot* used to be written **𝔅𝔯𝔬𝔱**, after all.)

Most modern scholarship about the opposition between universalism and cultural relativism in human rights is tone deaf, so to speak, to the problem of *linguistic relativism* that is inherent in any attempt to express universal concepts in different languages, that is, in the context of different forms of life. Professor Donnelly's influential article *Cultural Relativism and Universal Human Rights*, for example, distinguishes between personal rights, civil rights, and social rights on the basis of what the text calls a "certain core of 'human nature'" that it takes to be "relatively universal" (Donnelly, 1984, p. 415). Based on a conception of that core human nature *as expressed in the English language*, Donnelly opts for a form of "weak cultural relativism" (p. 419). That is, the text concludes that basic personal rights (e.g., the right to life, liberty, and security of the person) "come very close to being fully universal"; that civil rights (e.g., freedom of conscience, speech, and association) are "a bit more relative"; and that social rights (e.g., the right of free and full consent of intending spouses) are "subject to much greater cultural relativity" (pp. 417–418).

Here is not the place to judge whether Donnelly's theory of weak cultural relativism is right or wrong, good or bad. My point is more basic than that. Before it can be evaluative by the world's many different peoples, his thesis must first be translated into a language that they can understand. Thus, suppose all non-English-speaking people on earth were to accept the general principle that there exists a universal core of human nature, and that it implies a normative continuum stretching from human rights that are relatively universal to those that are relatively relative (Donnelly, 1984, p. 419). Would they not necessarily be accepting this very thesis as it, as well as the particular human rights continuum in question, are expressed in Chinese, French, Russian, Spanish, etc.? If so, it is not at all obvious that, say, linguistic signs such as "liberty" (English), 自由 (Chinese), *liberté* (French), *свобода* (Russian), and *liberdad* (Spanish) all have the very same mode of intention within each and every society and cultural milieu where they might be used to convey the hard core individual right that Donnelly thinks is expressed in Article 3 of the *Universal Declaration of Human Rights*. In fact, it is quite obvious to me that they do not, and that the concept of liberty is not so much "contested" from place to place as it is inarticulately taken for granted in many different ways.

Becoming sensitive to the ineluctable problem of translation between cultures—that is, the phenomenon of linguistic relativism—allows us to notice that there are at least two kinds of cultural diversity when it comes to the creation and protection of individual human rights in international law.

The first is relatively straightforward: given their social and political backgrounds and context, a nation's leaders may object to a particular human rights declaration or treaty because they reject the universalization of its rights as the latter are expressed in the leaders' *own language*. For example, the conservative, pro-free-market Reagan and Bush administrations did this on behalf of the United States when they opposed the *International Covenant on Economic, Social and Cultural Rights* on the ground that recognizing economic and social goals as rights would, as they put it, "lead governments to deny civil and political rights in the search for distributive justice" (Weissbrodt et al., 2009, p. 158). Overt political "diversity" of this sort is perhaps the clearest illustration of the above-noted sociopolitical distinction between speechfulness and speechlessness within a given society. It brings out the ethical difficulties that can arise whenever decisions are made about *who speaks* what *OUR* culture believes in, as well as *who is heard* abroad about the contents of *THEIR* culture. In any case, this first kind of cultural diversity shows itself as a self-conscious rejection of the possibility of achieving even a small overlap in coverage among the different ways in which an instrument's official languages express the rights in question.

The second kind of cultural diversity is less obvious, but in many ways has much greater importance for understanding the phenomenon of cultural difference. Human rights lawyers already know that there is a "material" element to customary international law—that is, uniformities in the actual *behaviors* of states—in addition to the "psychological" element of *opinio juris*, or the subjective feeling of "oughtness" that has to attend such uniformities of behavior if they are to become binding international norms (McDougal et al., 1977, p. 269). The distinction between the materiality of behavior and the psychological immateriality of *opinio juris* points toward another, equally compelling distinction: a mere verbal agreement ("We all agree to do or not do *X*") is not the same as a consensus of behavior in applying the linguistic sign "*X*" to real cases. It is quite possible for the representatives of different nations to agree with one another *in good faith* to adopt the linguistic signs contained in a human rights instrument, and yet still proceed, again in good faith, to interpret and apply them differently. The latter differences, in turn, stem from cultural differences that have been woven into their bodies and hearts from birth, and are reflected in the various ways in which they actually use the words of their own languages in dealing with particular situations. For every situation is always first and foremost a particular situation before it falls into one or more idioms.

The idea that language and truth can be both objectively correct *and* culturally relative at the very same time is easy to understand in the context of everyday activities like drinking tea and eating bread. As the case of the prohibition against cruel, inhuman, or degrading treatment or punishment may suggest, however, this idea presents an altogether different aspect when viewed in the context of the deeply held *moral* values that are associated with the international protection of human rights.

The point here is not that the concept of "truth or falsity" applies only to statements of fact, not to statements of value, or that the words "good," "right," and "just" are simply indefinable (Moore, 1993, pp. 61–62). The kind of cultural relativism that maintains that there is no single moral truth in the world but only different moral truth*s* is not so much true or false as it is a category mistake. Its only real claim to utility lies in the undeniable truth that differently situated people often really do in fact differ about the content and application of moral norms, and have done so throughout history. This implies that there is at least one limited kind of truth or falsity in the realm of what we call "moral action" that all reasonable people ought to be able to acknowledge: namely, sometimes morally charged differences in the behaviors of different groups of people actually exist, and sometimes they do not exist.

For example, it is surely a *fact* that very many people in the world today say and believe, with complete sincerity, that cutting off someone's hand as a punishment for theft is both morally wrong and a legal violation of the *Convention against Torture and Other Cruel, Inhuman or Degrading Treatment or Punishment* (Human Rights Committee, 1993, pp. 11–14). At the same time, however, candor also requires the admission that many *other* people in the world say and believe, with equal sincerity, that this punishment is not only legally right,[6] but also morally mandatory,[7] and furthermore, that its enforcement is not a violation of the Convention (Human Rights Committee, 1992, pp. 1–2, 18–19).

To state truthfully that different groups of people just happen to say and believe different things about morality and law is first and foremost to state a *fact*. This sort of fact belongs to the subject matter studied by descriptive ethics and comparative jurisprudence. But in itself this fact, just like any other fact, is neither right nor wrong, neither good nor bad. Rather, it expresses what Wittgenstein (1993, p. 38) called the merely "trivial or relative sense" of our judgments about right and wrong, as opposed to the emotionally deeper sense that is involved whenever we stop objectively reporting on other people's beliefs and actions and begin to evaluate them for consistency with what we think they *ought* to be.

The deeper sense of morality to which I refer will have been experienced by anyone who has ever disapproved of what someone else did on the ground that they really ought not to have done it. Which is to say: it has been experienced by pretty much everyone who has ever lived. While perspectivism may be useful as a regulative ideal for sociological research, this idea completely fails to capture the virtually *universal* feeling of disapproval and even outrage that characterizes the concrete phenomenology of making negative moral judgments about other people's practices.

The philosopher O.K. Bouwsma describes an interesting conversation he once had with Wittgenstein about the translation of morally charged words that illustrates this last point rather well:

> Imagine a [group of human beings] who when they viewed things that were horrible, loathsome to us, clapped their hands, their faces bright, and now they always uttered the word "doog." And now you are to translate the word "doog." How will you translate it? Will you hesitate about this? Wittgenstein was trying to bring out the unsatisfactory character of "I approve." [This group] apparently approves. Will "good" do? I suppose that this involves that the use of the word "good" is affected in some such way as this: That . . . the use of the word "good" comes to serve also in naming things that are good. One might be horrified not simply at people's regarding such things [as] good but also at their calling them good. . . . If we were to translate "doog" into "good," we should be suggesting not simply that they approve of certain things but also that these things are justified by our law. . . . The use of the word "good" is too complicated. Definition is out of the question.
>
> (Bouwsma, 1986, p. 42)

It is important to notice what this passage does *not* say. It does not say that the definition of the word "good" is out of the question because there are many different abstract "conceptions" of goodness and none of them can be shown to be absolutely correct (the claim of vulgar cultural relativism). It says, rather, that the word "good" brings with it *feelings* on the observer's part that make it morally unsuitable as a translation in this context. Feeling morally queasy about something that other people are doing is a phenomenal fact, not a value. And it simply won't do to deny the existence of this kind of fact merely because one suspects that the queasiness cannot be justified (or refuted) with formal arguments producing conclusions that are or ought to be universally valid and binding.

The probability that words expressing the very same human rights norm might be received and applied differently by different cultures was well understood by the framers of the *Universal Declaration of Human Rights*. Professor Mary Ann Glendon (2001, p. 69) has observed that René Cassin, one of the *Universal Declaration*'s principal architects, understood clearly that "a 'universal' document would have to leave an ample degree of pluralism in the understanding and implementation of many of its rights." And while "many" does not necessarily mean "all," she quotes Cassin as saying: "It is not necessary for one conception [of every human right] to triumph over another conception." Glendon uses similar terms to describe the subjective intent of the members of the drafting committee in May of 1948, as they went about the task of putting the *Universal Declaration* into its final form:

> They were striving now to make the document clear enough to be readily understandable by men and women everywhere, as well as to achieve a level of generality that would leave each country and culture an appropriate degree of flexibility in interpreting and implementing its provisions.
>
> (Glendon, 2001, p. 111)

If uttering encomiums to pluralism and flexibility (i.e., cultural diversity) in the interpretation of universal human rights was politically necessary to induce governments to agree to them, then it is also quite revealing that there was a need to engage in such a strategy in the first place. It would seem that the words of the *Universal Declaration* were not intended to be completely "universal" (as this term is understood in English) where it might matter the most to the real individuals whose rights were being specified: namely, at the level of *how those words, as translated in good faith into their own languages, would actually be applied to them in the innumerable particular situations that would arise in their own societies.*

After all, the U.N. was not going to compel the judges and politicians of the world's many states to attend a reeducation camp where they would all be drilled (in Esperanto?) for months or years in the one, monolithically correct method of applying the *Universal Declaration*'s general terms—terms such as "cruel, inhuman or degrading treatment or punishment" (Article 5) and "freedom of opinion and expression" (Article 19). The U.N. did not embark on this sort of massive indoctrination project in 1948, nor has it done so since. The interesting question remains, however, whether it should have aimed at something far more radical than obtaining multinational agreement to the various linguistic signs that express the text in different languages: the total erasure of cultural differences in order to create a univocal, universal consensus about the actual *methods of application* of those signs.

The haunting

Generally speaking, a method of application is a technique for connecting one thing to another thing. A bricklayer applies a particular method for mixing and troweling mortar to join a brick to a wall. Another, analogous concept is called a "method of projection": a technique for creating one thing (an image) on the basis of another thing (the imaged) (Wittgenstein, 1960, p. 53). A geometer, for example, can project a two-dimensional figure in one plane onto another plane by applying a mathematical formula to it. When it comes to language, what serves to connect a bare linguistic sign to reality (or project reality into language) consists of a variety of culturally specific techniques for using words according to certain more or less long-standing grammatical conventions. In most cases, these conventions have become second nature to those humans who use (and are used by) them. Like the material element in customary international law, these conventions exhibit themselves first and foremost as regularities of *behavior*, not merely as regularities of speech about what the conventions "mean" or "require."

If two groups of people adopt a single rule-expression in English, such as "Always drink tea with sugar," but then proceed to employ two different *methods of applying* the rule to reality—for example, one group dissolves sugar in tea before drinking it and the other drinks tea through a cube of sugar held between their teeth—then clarity would be better served if we thought of them as following, not one rule, but two different rules. If clarity about what is actually happening in reality is what we seek, then we should not say that the two groups "interpret" the same rule differently. Instead, we should "restrict the term 'interpretation' to the substitution of one expression of the rule for another" (Wittgenstein, 1953, p. 81e, 201), and then notice that ordinarily neither group of people does that. They just *behave differently* in relation to the same linguistic sign, namely, "Always drink tea with sugar." Actually following a rule in a certain way is *not* an interpretation. It is, as Wittgenstein (p. 81e, 202) says, a "practice" (*eine Praxis*).

But in that case, the two different ways of applying the rule-sign in question would not be universal. To be sure, the two groups would "universally" use the same linguistic sign if they ever talked about the proper way to drink tea. But that would be like a financial institution and the boundary of a river sharing the linguistic sign "bank." In order for everyone's method of applying the sign "Always drink tea with sugar" to be identical in reality, one group's method for drinking tea would have to conquer or otherwise prevail over the other's. If one recalls the depressing history of European colonialism, perhaps this example will begin to illustrate why, as Glendon (2001, p. 221) remarks, "The problem of what universality might mean in a multicultural world haunted the United Nations human rights project from the beginning."

And so it has. But I do not think that being haunted is necessarily a bad thing, for not all spirits are evil and out to do us harm. In this particular case, I think that it is actually good for the ethical sensibilities of human beings that the discourses of universality and diversity keep on haunting one another, so to speak, in the sphere of human rights.

If "cultural diversity" purports to name the overarching unity of every unique culture or subculture that is gathered together under its concept, then it is also the case that this unity is constantly being contradicted by the diversity injected into reality by ontological particularities as they arise *within* each culture. Individuals look to their culture to reassure themselves that their world is grounded in something solid and enduring. At the same time, culture amounts to nothing at all unless some (or many) individuals, by choice or by habit, keep on reproducing it. To paraphrase Michel Foucault (1980, p. 98), the individual that culture has constituted is at the same time also its vehicle. On the other hand, it is always possible—perhaps even ethically necessary—to step out of the vehicle in which you happen to be journeying, especially if the bumpiness of the ride on a particular occasion makes you feel morally queasy.

Following the foregoing train of thought leads one to the conclusion that the constant unity of *culture* is logically and empirically dependent on the constant unity of the always unique particular *individual* human beings who reproduce it. Listen, for example, to what Nietzsche had to say on the origin, the pragmatic utility, and the ultimate ontological insecurity of what human beings take to be unified in everyday life:

> We need "unities" in order to be able to reckon: that does not mean we must suppose that such unities exist. We have borrowed the concept of unity from our "ego" concept—our oldest article of faith. If we did not hold ourselves to be unities, we would never have formed the concept "thing."
>
> (Nietzsche, 1968, p. 338)

If the unity of culture is a thing, then it seems to me that it must be counted as a particularly protean kind of thing. For when the individuals who sustain a given culture change, the culture itself changes. Who would deny the readily verifiable empirical proposition that individuals can and do change their behaviors and values in the course of history, including their own personal histories? Clinging to the notion that the empirical Self possesses a constant and consistent self-identity and unity is a very dubious metaphysical position, to say the least, as thinkers as diverse as David Hume (1977, pp. 38–39), Nietzsche (1968, p. 149), Freud (1962), and William James (1904, vol. 2, pp. 316–317) have attempted to demonstrate over and over again.

History teaches us that the self is especially susceptible to change the more it comes into contact with people who are not like it. And it is both obvious and historically significant that the opportunity for *US* to come into contact with *THEM* (and vice versa) has never been more extensive than it is today. Globalism is not just about economics. It is about the unity and disunity of culture itself, as well as the unity and disunity of the very selves of the individuals who comprise it.

According to a recent article (*The Economist*, October 22, 2011, p. 27), in 1950 the whole population of the earth (2.5 billion) could have stood, shoulder to shoulder, on the Isle of Wight (381 square kilometers); whereas quite soon the earth's more than seven billion people will require an island the size of Zanzibar (1,554 square kilometers) to stand on. Contact with cultural diversity is no longer a choice; it is a necessary fact of life for just about everyone. I take it that the UNESCO *Declaration on Cultural Diversity* tries to make a virtue out of this necessity when it says: "Cultural diversity widens the range of options open to everyone; it is one of the roots of development, understood not simply in terms of economic growth, but also as a means to achieve a more satisfactory intellectual, emotional, moral and spiritual existence" (Article 3), and "Creation draws on the roots of cultural tradition, but flourishes in contact with other cultures" (Article 7).

But, at the same time, the Declaration also demands that care be exercised so that "all cultures can express themselves and make themselves known" (Article 6). All but the most extreme cultural universalists would probably be inclined to agree with the sentiment behind this demand. If respect for different cultures means anything at all, it means to respect each individual who bears the culture in his or her body, mind and heart; for without the living individual human being, culture would be nothing but a historical curiosity. This shows why the Declaration considers respect for cultural diversity to be a distinctly *ethical* requirement, for ethics is always about some particular *ME*'s respect for some particular *YOU*.

On the other hand, however, the Declaration itself does not seem to be troubled by the apparent contradiction that it introduces into its project of preserving cultural diversity by extending the universal right of self-expression and self-publication to "cultures" themselves. The more frequently different cultures exercise their right to make themselves known to one another in this increasingly globalized world of the Internet and the cell phone, the multinational corporation and an interconnected global economy, the less likely it is that the individuals who together comprise a given culture will remain securely themselves. For in that case, they will have been exposed to features in other cultures that can lead them to doubt the value of certain features in their own. Therefore, the less likely it is that the culture itself will continue to have something unique to express.

The deepest antinomy contained within the international human rights movement to reconcile respect for the dignity of the individual with respect for the cultural differences that he or she embodies is not, as is sometimes imagined, the conflict between the West's cultural commitment to the importance of individual rights and certain non-Western cultural conceptions that value the wellbeing of the group more highly than that of the individual. These are static and petrified characterizations of an antinomy that always shows itself as being fundamentally dialectical in nature. To put it all in a nutshell: the unity or diversity of the individual (whether in West or East, North or South) is inseparable from the unity or diversity of the culture in which he or she lives—change or maintain one, and you change or maintain the other. The dynamic unpredictability of this historical dialectic is the *real* antinomy of universalism versus cultural diversity today.

Xerxes whips the Hellespont

Ancient Greek historian Herodotus (1997, p. 525) gives an interesting account of how the great Persian King Xerxes reacted when a great storm blew up and broke to pieces a bridge he was building between Asia and Europe. "So when Xerxes heard of it," writes Herodotus, "he was full of wrath, and straightaway gave orders that the Hellespont should receive three hundred lashes, and that a pair of fetters should be cast into it." Those who would *force*, by language or by arms, a permanent reconciliation between the value of respect for universal human rights and the value of respect for cultural diversity are very much like Xerxes. They would whip a sea consisting of billions of human beings embedded in thousands of different cultures until it promised to quieten its waters and submit to their abstractions.

But abstractions, like bridges, eventually fall down. The will to impose unity is also the will to deny the ontological particularity that belongs to each and every real individual, each and every real culture. To set too high a value on *the unity* of the individual person (I did not say "to set too high a value on the individual person") is to set too low a value on culture. Likewise, to set too high a value on *the unity* of culture (I did not say "to set too high a value on culture") is to set too low a value on the individual. Either way, it is certain that the ceaseless historical dialectic between the particular and the universal will make sure to knock down whatever bridges our puny faculty of reason might venture to build.

Notes

* An earlier version of this chapter was published in the *Cambrian Law Review*, vol. 43, pp. 44–63 (2012), under the title "Universal Human Rights and Cultural Diversity."

1. An international human rights conference under this title was convened in Tehran on November 24–26, 2011.The conference was cosponsored by the Non-Aligned Movement Center for Human Rights and Cultural Diversity (NAMCHRCD), headquartered in Tehran, the International Committee of the Red Cross, the Irish Centre for Human Rights, Curtin University's Centre for Human Rights Education, Tehran's School of International Relations, and the Iranian National Committee of Humanitarian Law.
2. 1134^{a}29 (referring to relations between free and equal citizens of the *polis* and those who are not free and equal to them).
3. 1138^{b}7 (referring to relations between master and servant and husband and wife).
4. > [T]he ideas of reason have an important function in the conduct of natural science if they are understood *regulatively*, that is, if they are taken to represent not metaphysical beings or entities whose reality is supposed to be demonstrable, but

> rather goals and directions of inquiry that mark out the ways in which our knowledge is to be sought for and organized.
>
> (Guyer and Wood, 1998, p. 18)

5. Cf. Heidegger (1962, p. 269):

> Before Newton's laws were discovered, they were not "true"; it does not follow that they were false . . . To say that before Newton his laws were neither true nor false, cannot signify that before him there were no such entities as have been uncovered and pointed out by those laws. Through Newton the laws became true, and with them, entities became accessible in themselves to Dasein.

6. Amputation is imposed for what Islamic law calls a *hudud* crime, or one for which the Qur'an itself specifies the penalty (Entessar, 1988, pp. 96–98).
7. Cf. *Qur'ān* 24:2 ("As to the thief, Male or Female, cut off his or her hands: a punishment by way of example, from Allah, for their crime: and Allah is exalted in power.").

Chapter 6

Business

Asking the right question in business ethics*

> One cannot "accept" the suffering of others, no matter for what ideal, no matter if one's own suffering be also accepted, without incurring guilt. It is the guilt in which every civilization is implicated.
>
> Lionel Trilling (2008, p. 86)

Bon soir, mesdames et messieurs. And thank you, Your Excellency, for your very kind and generous welcome. On behalf of all the panelists here tonight, I would also like to thank *France-Amerique*, the Commission Franco-Américaine, the France-Fulbright Association des Anciens, and the Université de Cergy-Pontoise for organizing this event.[1] I am hopeful that our program this evening will produce an interesting conversation, both theoretical and practical, on the advertised theme: *Regards Croisés sur l'Ethique des Affaires*, or, "Revisiting Business Ethics."

I probably should make my own particular orientation to tonight's topic as clear as possible at the outset. It has been nearly a quarter century since I gave any real legal advice to actual business clients. In those days, I thought of business and business litigation as a kind of war and was generally inclined to take no prisoners in the battles I fought. Time and reflection have mellowed me since the fierce days of my youth, however, and now my own thoughts on the relationship between ethics and business tend to be more philosophical than pragmatic. Nevertheless, I believe with all my heart that the distinctly ethical dimension of how we human beings interact with one another as individuals is (or should be) the most important issue confronting each one of us during our brief journey together on this earth. From this point of view, ethics truly is "first philosophy," as Emmanuel Levinas (1989, p. 75) puts it. And I, for one, think the problem of ethics in the business context is as confused and confusing as it is profound, and that it could do with a great deal of serious meditation and clarification on the part of anyone who cares deeply about it.

So I hope you will forgive me if my remarks are placed at a different level than one might expect to find in a typical "how-to" seminar on business ethics. By this I mean the kind of self-improvement extravaganza that people sometimes attend (and even pay to attend) in order to learn how to make as much money as possible without getting into too much legal and ethical difficulty. I say that I will speak at a different level, not necessarily a higher one, for in the matter of how we human beings behave in the economic sphere, far too much is at stake—far too much avoidable human suffering—to pontificate at the beginning of a conversation about whose perspective promises to be more important or noble.

"Can we harmonize ethical questions?"

I have been asked by the organizers of these proceedings to begin the discussion by focusing on a particular question pertaining to business ethics. That question is: *Peut-on harmoniser les questions éthiques?* ("Can we harmonize ethical questions?"). My esteemed colleagues from the business world, on the other hand, have been asked to focus on a slightly different question: *Peut-on harmoniser les pratiques éthiques?* ("Can we harmonize ethical practices?").

In English, as in French, the word harmonize comes from the Greek term *harmonia*. In ancient Greece, the noun *harmos* had an anatomical meaning—it denoted "joint" or "shoulder." When translated literally, therefore, the etymologically related word *harmonia* signifies a means of joining two things together, on analogy to the way that the muscles and tendons in someone's shoulder join her arm to her body. Of course, this literal signification of the word has long since given way to the notion we have today that harmony is an agreement or concord of sounds. But I cannot help hearing an echo, so to speak, of the old meaning of *harmonia* in the way tonight's questions are formulated.

I could be mistaken, but I also can't help detecting something akin to a powerful feeling of yearning in the way these two questions are expressed. I sense the presence of a fervent desire or hope that somehow human beings might be able to join together what is *different* in the ethical sphere to make what is the *same.* The image of this larger sameness seems to be one in which human beings achieve a consensus in word and deed that allows them to strive together—as integral members of the social body, so to speak—for the promotion of something called "the ethical conduct of business" in a manner that will be as effective and efficient as the way healthy individuals are able to move their arms in their shoulder joints. For reasons that I will soon explain, I am somewhat troubled by this hope. Or perhaps it would be better just to say that I think it would be dangerously premature to yearn for harmony in the matter of ethical questions and ethical practices before investigating what *kind* of questions we should be asking in the first place.

As someone who attempts to think as deeply as I can about the relationship between law and ethics, I was immediately struck by the fact that there is a third question missing from these other two, namely, *Peut-on harmoniser les réponses éthiques?* ("Can we harmonize ethical answers?"). I, for one, do not regard this omission as a mistake. On the contrary, I think that the organizers' decision not to obsess over the task of getting immediate answers to ethical questions is not only wise, but also an absolute precondition for gaining a proper understanding of what is at stake in the matter of "business ethics."

I admit that, at first glance, what I have just said seems to be untrue. According to common sense, the right questions are supposed to lead to the right answers, and these in turn are supposed to lead to the right kinds of behavior. An ethical practice, on this view, consists in permanently linking four terms in such a way that the behavior governed by that practice becomes lawful in the Kantian sense of being rule-governed. Ever since the European Enlightenment turned us all into rational subjects (or control freaks), many (if not most) thinking people have come to believe that the only plausible ethical equation ought to read something like this: *right question* → *right norm* → *right answer* → *right behavior* = *right practice*.

It seems, therefore, that there must be some sort of mistake in the way tonight's questions are formulated, since they talk about questions and practices but not about answers. In general, it has been my experience that businesspeople and their lawyers want to get as clear an answer as possible to the question of what limits there are, both legal and ethical, on their pursuit of gain for themselves and their employers. They want to understand in advance the rules of the game they are playing, just like players in a game of Monopoly want to know exactly what is supposed to happen when someone passes "Go" or lands on the square marked "Go to Jail." People want to know the answers, or at least the rules that will give them the answers, because they are rewarded in their business and in their profession—and most especially in that precious currency called self-respect that we pay to ourselves—by how competently they perform their jobs and how well they play the roles allotted to them by their chosen careers.

Consider the ethical rules of lawyers, for example. In my country, like many other places in the world, lawyers are required by the rules and principles of legal ethics to zealously represent the interests of their clients within the bounds of the law. "Zealously" is the very word that the American Bar Association (2007, Preamble) uses to express this idea in its *Model Rules of Professional Conduct.* You will immediately recognize that ethics in this context frequently means being zealous on behalf of a client's interests as opposed to (if not against) someone else's interests. Thus, if any *other* ethical limits inhibit this ethical duty of zeal in pursuing a client's interests—as indeed there are and should be—then lawyers undoubtedly would like to know exactly what they are. This helps explain why a course called "Professional Responsibility" is taught in just about every American law school, and why State Bar Examiners routinely administer a multiple-choice legal ethics examination whose presupposition is that the rules can be made to yield a correct answer to just about every ethical situation a lawyer is likely to confront (Terry, 2000, pp. 61–74).

The same sort of burning desire to know all the relevant ethical limits and boundaries holds true in the case of the business executive whose compensation and career advancement depends on how zealously she pursues the ends of the firm she represents. She wants to be given immediately useful answers to practical ethical questions so that she can get on with playing the money-and-career game all the more effectively. American social theorist C. Wright Mills (2008, p. 197) once observed that a "panic for status" has come to replace "the prodding of poverty" in the motivational apparatus of today's business and cultural elite. Sadly enough, I think he is right. And, of course, we all know from personal experience that those whose status is under attack by chaotic events yearn most of all for the comfort of a predictable order that will give them a better chance to preserve or enhance their place in the hierarchy.

I believe that I understand, and I know that I sympathize with, those whose primary motivation is practical in the way I have just described. Although it has become somewhat of a cliché, it is nonetheless true that we are living during a time of intense global competition among voracious international firms that are inclined to interpret the entire world as a vast warehouse full of exploitable resources, not least of all "human resources," as well as an enormous bazaar for buying and selling things. Martin Heidegger (1977, p. 21) characterized the world that we have made in this image as *Der Bestand* ("standing reserve"), while C. Wright Mills (2008, p. 176) called it, rather more evocatively, I think, "society as a salesroom." While I may be wrong once again, I fear that many, if not most, executives experience their careers in business as a kind of rat race, as we used to say in the 1960s. In this race, the best and biggest cheese goes to those rats best able to navigate the complex maze of formal and informal constraints on the pursuit of self-interest that social institutions have placed between them and *le fromage*.

Nevertheless, tonight I would like us to consider the possibility that it can be morally disastrous to yearn for answers to ethical questions without first investigating what the right questions are, and that this risk is particularly great in the field of business ethics. As the English philosopher G.E. Moore remarked in the preface to his monumental treatise *Principia Ethica*:

> In Ethics, as in all other philosophical studies, the difficulties and disagreements, of which its history is full, are mainly due to a very simple cause: namely to the attempt to answer questions, without first discovering precisely *what* question it is which you desire to answer.
>
> (1993, p. 33)

Privileging the question "What *exactly* are my ethical duties?" tends to produce an answer that effectively legalizes ethics in the interest of clarity. That is, it creates pressure to spell out ethical rules in detailed codes intended to make them "enforceable" in one way or another—if not through law, then through social and economic pressures and penalties the costs of which can be calculated in advance. The businessperson who only cares about what limits others will impose on his or her self-interested behavior conceives of ethics as an external constraint, like the threat of legal punishment, rather than an internal constraint, like the feeling that one should not cheat a friend. Metaphorically speaking, such a one wants to know how to skate as closely as possible to the thin ice in the pond so as to achieve all the more effectively her primary goal, which is to make money and advance her career without falling into the freezing water.

If, in any given case, such a person behaves the way other people would call "ethical," she merely acts *in conformity with* conventional ethical rules and expectations. She does not act this way *because* she has made those rules and expectations part of her own personal *ēthos* in the original Greek sense of the word: namely, the cultivation of one's character so as to always manifest the proper way of being-with-others (Foucault 2005, pp. 237–238). In other words, she acts in a certain manner not because being "ethical" constitutes the ultimate ground of her behavior, but because she feels she is compelled to do so in order to get ahead.

Ethics for such a person is a means to a non-ethical end—it is not an end in itself. Her definition of unethical behavior might be expressed this way: "Unethical behavior means doing something that other people will disapprove of in a way that will harm my interests if they find out about it." I am reminded in this connection of the ancient fable of the Ring of Gyges. This magical ring allowed its wearer to become invisible at will, and I wonder, as Plato did more than two millennia ago (*Republic* II 360*c*), whether someone who could put it on would behave the same way if she knew that she never had to fear being reproached by others on account of the consequences of her actions.

Standard of conduct versus standard of review

At this point, I think it would be useful to introduce a distinction between two of the most important concepts in the theory of corporate ethics: a standard of conduct versus a standard of review (Bainbridge, 2002, pp. 408–438). A *standard of review* adopts the "external" perspective of an observer—a referee, if you will—evaluating the past or present conduct of someone else; whereas a *standard of conduct* adopts the "internal" perspective of someone who is about to perform an action that may or may not be evaluated by others. The behavior in question could be a physical action like personally dumping toxic waste in the ocean or handing over money to a charity. But it could also be the prior *decision* to perform (or order the performance of) such an action, for making a decision is also a kind of action.

Strictly speaking, the act of deciding is the most relevant type of "behavior" to consider from the point of view of corporate ethics. In that context, we are usually interested in learning not just *what* a particular firm has or has not done, but also *that* those in charge of the firm made (or neglected to make) a decision to do it. In looking at the theory and practice of corporate ethics from the outside, sometimes we want to know how judges and other people make a "decision about a decision" that corporate officials have already made, in which case they are probably employing some sort of *standard of review*. Other times, however, we are interested in knowing what *standard of conduct*, if any, actually guided the officials in making the decision that they did.

In the American law of corporate governance, for example, we know that if shareholders legally challenge a business decision made by management, the judge will usually employ a rather forgiving standard of review—one that gives extremely broad deference to management's expertise and exercise of discretion.

We lawyers call this the "business judgment rule," and virtually all theorists of corporate governance agree that the rule permits (but does not require) management to make decisions that seem to be altruistic or socially responsible, but only on the condition that their so-called "ethical" decisions serve the long-term best interests of the corporation and its shareholders (Marens and Wicks, 1999).

Corporate lawyers (and executives in the know) sometimes refer to this attitude toward ethical business practices as "enlightened self-interest," or "doing well by doing good" (Marens and Wicks, 1999, p. 280). Thus, one often reads or hears the following kind of sentiment expressed about the relationship between human decency and corporate profitability: "The primary objective of the corporation is to conduct business activities with a view to enhancing corporate profit and shareholder gain, albeit *subject to the qualification that 'long-term shareholder gain' may require 'fair treatment' of non-shareholder constituents*" (National Association of Corporate Directors, 1995, p. 601) (emphasis added). Please note: "*may* require fair treatment," not must. "May," that is, if and only if treating non-shareholder constituents decently happens to be in sufficient demand in the marketplace at the time and place in question.

Forgive me for saying so out loud, but I cannot help feeling that the "doing well by doing good" theory of corporate ethics is similar to the point of view held by certain sociopathic personalities. By definition, a sociopath is someone who is unable to actually experience empathy (*Antisocial Personality Disorder Symptoms*, 2014). But if a sociopath is smart, he can learn to pretend to empathize with others in order to achieve his goals, whatever they may be. As ugly as this comparison might seem, it does have the virtue of showing that the business judgment rule is a standard of external review, not a standard of conduct. Before they actually make corporate decisions, executives no more employ the business judgment rule as the only reason for their business judgments than judges make a prediction of how they might decide a case as the reason for why they decide it the way they do (Hart, 1961, p. 10).

Of course, this is not to deny that businesspeople and their lawyers will (sometimes) take the business judgment rule into account when making assessments about the various legal risks of pursuing a proposed course of action. Prudence often requires that we take account of what others will think about our behavior, especially if they are in a position to punish us if we make a choice that they don't approve of. If the business judgment rule does enter into management's pre-decision analysis of legal risks in this way, then to that limited extent the rule affects their conduct. Strictly speaking, however, a standard that others might use to evaluate a given decision is analytically distinct from the basis of the decision itself. That is, a *business judgment* is one sort of thing and the *judgment of a business judgment* is another.

A standard of conduct is the criterion that a decision-maker consults explicitly, or is guided by implicitly, before she makes a decision. This standard actually determines (or at least co-determines) her real subjective motive for acting before the fact. In the phenomenology of ethical decision-making, understood conventionally, a standard of conduct shows itself as a constellation of words or images inwardly experienced as binding by the actor at time t_1, just before performing the action in question. An ethical standard of review, on the other hand, arrives some time later, at t_2 or t_3, in the form of the criterion that a referee (or any other observer) uses to evaluate the decision that was made earlier. (By the way, the concepts of "referee" and "observer" are large enough to include the actor herself if her conscience compels her to reflect on the rightness of her past decisions.)

Seen from the outside by a referee, a decision-maker tends to be a "what." That is, the referee stands to the decider in the kind of relationship that the philosopher and theologian Martin Buber famously called "I-It" (*Ich-Es*) rather than "I-Thou" (*Ich-Du*) (Buber, 2000, p. 20). From the referee's point of view, the person being judged exists a cool distance away during the time it takes to consider and render judgment: the individuality of the latter appears to be completely bound up with her past corporate decision and the criteria the referee uses to evaluate it. In theory, the referee reduces the decision-maker to the "relevant facts" of her past—a mere defendant in the dock, so to speak, to be judged and then praised or condemned for *what she has done* rather than for *who she is*. The typical referee's tendency to depersonalize others in this way helps to explain why *Dikē*, the scale-holding Greek goddess of justice, is usually shown wearing a blindfold in the classic iconographies of justice that adorn so many Western courthouses.

Seen from the inside, however, the distance between the decider and an impending decision keeps on closing until the point at which it disappears completely. A decision-maker is always a "who" to herself—a "myself," not some indifferent person or other. She is a "me" who inevitably must keep answering, by her decisions and her conduct, that most fundamental of all ethical questions: "*Who am I?*" (cf. Heidegger, 2009, pp. 32–36). For in the matter of how we choose to treat other people, we do not experience ourselves as machines that are merely the sum of their past determinations and inputs. Instead, each one of us is always a *ME MYSELF* confronting a future that is, ethically speaking, a *tabula rasa* that we are always just on the verge of filling up with the ceaseless scribble of our deeds. If we *are* the sum of what we *do*, then it could be said that the problems of ethics, business or otherwise, are always teetering precariously (and all too often invisibly) on the leading edge of each and every moment of our life.

The business judgment rule as ethical cover

In theory, the standard of conduct of a corporate executive is supposed to be derived, at least to some degree, from the law of corporate governance. This is due to the oft-spoken sentiment that businesspeople, just like everyone else, "ought" to comply with all applicable legal norms, even in those cases where disobedience is not likely to be discovered or punished. For example, when a U.N. Special Rapporteur asked the world's largest international business associations to comment on the problem of corporate involvement in human rights abuses in places in the world where there is little or no enforcement of domestic laws, the associations responded in unison: "All companies have the same responsibilities in weak governance zones as they do elsewhere. They are expected to obey the law, even if it is not enforced, and to respect the principles of relevant international instruments where national law is absent" (Ruggie, 2010, p. 14, ¶ 14). The existence of this sort of feeling (or at least the propensity to express it, as vice's way of paying tribute to virtue) is not negated by the fact that it is not always clear to the average person just where the general duty to obey the law comes from.

Most contemporary moral theorists would agree that you have no moral duty to obey the laws of an unjust regime (e.g., Hitler's Germany or Stalin's USSR), and that under some circumstances you may even have a moral duty to affirmatively disobey such laws. But it will not surprise you to hear that the averagely patriotic person in many, if not most, prosperous countries these days (including especially France and the United States) is inclined to consider her nation's laws and institutions, taken as a whole, as being reasonably just. That said, abstract philosophical disagreement about whether or not there is a moral duty to obey the positive laws of a reasonably just government (compare Finnis (1984) with Raz (1984)) has not yet discombobulated the widespread social expectation that everyone should at least try to do so.

In America, as elsewhere, the law says that directors owe a special, fiduciary duty to the shareholders. The word "fiduciary" comes from the Latin verb *fidere*, meaning "to trust." The legal separation of ownership from day-to-day control is a pivotal feature of the modern corporation, and this arrangement gives rise to what economists call "agency costs." That is, the interests of the managers of a firm and the interests of the owner-shareholders are not perfectly aligned. To compensate somewhat for this asymmetry of interests, the law tells the managers that they must act solely for the benefit of the shareholders and must avoid any conflicts of interest between themselves and the corporation they serve. This has been interpreted by most lawyers and businesspeople to mean that managers have a legally enforceable fiduciary duty to "maximize shareholder value" in all cases (Brigham and Ehrhardt, 2010).

To be sure, every now and again a progressive argument is made that firms should be required to declare their intention to deliver goods and services that serve societal needs and not just shareholder interests (Hutton, 2015). But then, inevitably, comes a rhetorical and political backlash, usually in the form of the conservative counterargument that the shareholder value model is "the defining feature of the modern corporation. Change it and you wreck the entire machine" (*The Economist*, March 21, 2015, p. 62). Whether or not socially redefining the ends of capitalism to include at least *some* measure of corporate social responsibility (CSR) would necessarily wreck the economy, it is a fact that the conservative counterargument almost always prevails in the nitty-gritty world of corporate litigation. This is especially true in Delaware's Court of Chancery,[2] whose opinions matter a lot to large multinational corporations on account of the fact that a disproportionate number of them are incorporated in Delaware.

If this is how the law is received in most places, or in the places that count, then it follows that what is called "corporate ethics" and "corporate social responsibility" cannot be acknowledged as proper ends of the corporation, but rather must be justified as mere means to a non-ethical (or at least pre-ethical) end. If, as Milton Friedman (1970) once declared, "the social responsibility of business is to increase its profits," then acting to benefit non-shareholder interests (including the interests of what people sometimes call "human rights," or even "society as a whole") becomes an option that corporate managers can and should pursue *if and only if* it can be made to pay more than acting contrary to those interests would pay.

Seen from this perspective, a corporate executive's legally mandated internal standard of conduct requires her to maximize the discounted net present economic value for shareholders of every decision she makes on behalf of the firm. Since politicians, regulators, and prospective customers can, and often do, make moral judgments about those with whom they deal, appearing to be a good corporate citizen can produce considerable value in the marketplace. This means that "doing what is good" can sometimes make more money for the shareholders in the long run than "doing what is bad," owing to the resulting increase in market value of the firm's cachet for social benevolence. If CSR is never a proper end in itself, but *can* in the right circumstances become a proper means to the end of greater shareholder value, then it would seem to follow that evaluating the propriety of a given company's CSR expenditures is functionally indistinguishable from evaluating the propriety of how much it spends on advertising.

A recent paper by Harrison Hong and Inessa Liskovitch (2015) on the "halo effect" of having a corporate reputation for good behavior underscores this last point rather well. The authors looked at recent bribery prosecutions under America's Foreign Corrupt Practices Act (FCPA). Their study found that among those firms that were prosecuted and convicted under this Act, those with the most extensive and visible CSR programs tended to get the most lenient penalties. The correlation in the case of two particular subject-matter areas of CSR was fairly significant: "We estimate that either eliminating a substantial labor-rights concern, such as child labor, or increasing corporate giving by about 20 percent, results in fines that generally are 40 percent lower than the typical punishment for bribing foreign officials."

It would appear that not all good deeds are created equal, though, since the authors also found that corporate spending on employee and community relations had a much bigger impact on reducing the size of the penalty for an FCPA violation than spending for such activities as promoting diversity or championing the environment. Based on the results of this study, the concept of *doing well by doing good* seems to include the Monopoly game equivalent of drawing a corporate Get-Out-of-Jail card, at least if the company ostentatiously throws a little money in just the right charitable direction. If the Hong–Liskovitch study is correct, it suggests that the corporate opportunity to maximize profits by gaming the ethical–legal system as a whole is much bigger than any cloistered academic like me could have imagined.

Be that as it may, it is not *always* the case that doing good (or even certain kinds of good) will pay more than doing the exact opposite of good. If we consider things from the standpoint of Oliver Wendell Holmes Jr.'s famous Bad Man, "who cares only for the material consequences which [knowledge of the law] enables him to predict" (1920, p. 171), then even violating the law and running the risk of a criminal fine or an adverse civil damages award begins to look just like any other economic cost. In that case, the legal and reputational risks associated with socially harmful and illegal corporate behavior would resemble mere factors of production whose costs can be calculated and compared with the potential economic benefits that would accrue from incurring them.

Whether it is *ethical* (and not just illegal) for corporate officials to incur, or run the risk of incurring, adverse legal consequences for themselves and their firms while acting solely in the interest of maximizing shareholder value is an interesting and important question. It is not, however, a question I intend to talk any more about tonight, both because my time is limited and because I think that the most interesting and difficult questions in business ethics are triggered by a different kind of case.

I am referring to the common situation in which legal risks are correctly regarded as being minimal or even irrelevant, and yet it is still possible (indeed likely) to maximize shareholder value by acting in a way that most people—including especially the corporate decision-makers themselves—would call "doing bad." I will give a couple of examples of this shortly. For now, however, please note that in the kind of case to which I am referring, even the most law-abiding managers imaginable would find themselves ensnared in what most people would call an "ethical dilemma."

The dilemma is easily expressed, but not so easily resolved. On the one hand, a manager's fiduciary duty to the company and the shareholders implies its own kind of morality—the kind that says you should not betray a trust that you have voluntarily undertaken to honor. Diverting money from your employer to benefit yourself personally and diverting money away from your employer to benefit or protect needy or vulnerable others seem disturbingly similar from this point of view. But on the other hand, the executive's own sense of self-respect as an ethical person, or at least a person who aspires to be decent, implies that she should not engage in behavior that she herself regards as immoral.

Making money is like making omelets—somewhere, somehow, the chef has to break some eggs. And I, for one, am glad to observe that not everyone involved in the affairs of business has the stomach for breaking any and every egg in the world exclusively for the sake of turning a profit. Indeed, in a recent book evocatively titled *The Moral Underground: How Ordinary Americans Subvert an Unfair Economy*, Lisa Dodson shows that there exists in the business world today at least *some* increasing measure of human aversion to unceasingly performing the task of egg-breaking for profit. Dodson empirically uncovers numerous particular instances in the American economy of "ordinary people who chose to act upon injustices in their midst" (2009, p. 188). Among these are more than a few cases in which corporate managers practiced what she calls "moral disobedience" to institutional norms:

> I discovered [a subset of managers] who acknowledged that they not only tried to be flexible with employees but also intentionally broke company rules. This moral disobedience differed in form according to their industry, their status within it, and the particular work conflicts that arose, yet the results were similar: time, food, fuel, education, clothes, vacation, and health care were informally added to some low-wage workers' compensation only through breaking rules.
>
> (Dodson, 2009, p. 71)

Dodson's investigation into acts of moral disobedience by business managers reveals that the lowly eggs destined to become a particular corporate omelet are sometimes heard to "speak up," as Hannah Arendt (1993, p. 270) once put it, to the chefs. It is especially significant that most of the instances of moral disobedience that Dodson mentions fall into the category of the randomly particular. That is, these cases erupt every now and again in poignant and unique face-to-face encounters between particular managers and particular subordinates. They happen exceptionally—not as a rule, but despite all rules.

This kind of case does not put into question the business necessity of having generally applicable internal corporate rules. Instead, it puts into question the ethical sufficiency of adhering to the rules in every conceivable situation. "Ethical sufficiency," I should add, not when considered from the standpoint of the firm, but rather from the standpoint of a manager who thinks of herself as a moral human being: a living, breathing, particular *ME MYSELF* who has to look at her face in the mirror every morning.

Whenever I have lectured on the subject of corporate governance in law schools, I have typically offered the hypothetical example of a company's pending decision whether or not profitably (and lawfully!) to sell weapons to one or more warring factions within some failed Third-World state. The question I then ask is really quite simple: What if, all things considered, the conscientious executive actually concludes that the shareholders and the company will do much better, in the short run *and* in the long run, if the firm goes ahead and sells the weapons, even though she knows the weapons will be used to perpetrate morally abhorrent acts?

It is interesting that students often seek to evade this question by "fighting the hypothetical," as we law professors say. That is, they doubt whether the executive's assessment of the economic situation could possibly be correct. But I try to remind them that "doing well by doing good" is not a natural law, and that there are indeed cases (many, many cases) in which engaging in morally questionable practices can be made to pay better than acting decently, all things considered.

Should the conscientious executive in my hypothetical refuse to sell the weapons even though she understands that deciding to squelch the deal does not maximize shareholder value? And if she does refuse to sell, how is she supposed to explain herself to her colleagues and her shareholders? Should she be honest and say that she made the decision she did because a contrary decision would be immoral according to her, despite the fact that it would generate greater shareholder value? Or should she lie to everybody and say that she believed her decision really did maximize shareholder value by improving (or not tarnishing) the company's "image," despite the fact that she actually believes that any long-term threat to the corporation's public image would be more than offset by the sale's attractive short-term gains?

The latter course—lying about her actual motives, her actual standard of conduct—might very well insulate her decision from legal attack under the business judgment rule. Here it would be more than a little enlightening to read what two respected scholars of corporate governance have to say concerning questions of this sort:

> No competent attorney would allow her client to argue in court that their corporation made a decision because it "was the right thing to do" in the face of evidence that management knew of legal alternatives whose impact[s] on the bottom line, short term and long term, were indisputably superior. It may smack of moral cowardice, but given the uncertainty of what sustains and makes a business profitable over a period of years, virtually any act that does not financially threaten the survival of the business could be construed as in the long-term best interest of shareholders.
>
> (Marens and Wicks, 1999, p. 281)

In my example of a proposed arms deal with a Third-World warlord, would it be ethical to conceal one's real motives from shareholders and colleagues in the way that this text seems to tolerate (or invite)? Kant's famous (or infamous) argument (1996, pp. 611–615) that it would be immoral to lie even to a murderer at the door suggests that this course of conduct would be unethical. And even if Kant's argument is qualified to allow lying in some situations (Varden, 2010), there is an added complication in this particular case: lying to deceive a dangerous and malevolent stranger is one thing; lying to deceive people to whom you have voluntarily promised to act as a trusted fiduciary is something else.

On the other hand, the executive in my example might also think that she has a personal moral duty not to help her customers kill people in an unjust civil war, and that her legally and morally binding fiduciary duty to turn a quick profit for her firm and its shareholders is clearly outweighed by this other, purely moral duty. Indeed, with all due respect to Kant, I, for one, cannot help thinking that it might be immoral *not* to lie or conceal one's true motives in this situation, especially if innocent human lives would be lost in the event the true basis of the corporate decision were found out and the decision not to sell the weapons overturned. A lawful contract is not necessarily a just or moral contract. Indeed, even the ironclad legality of a deal does not always guarantee that its makers will never be legally punished for it, as many directors and executives of I.G. Farben A.G. learned, much to their chagrin, at the war crimes trials of German industrialists held in Nuremburg after the Second World War (Jeffries, 2008).

Corporate social responsibility versus individual ethical responsibility

Perhaps now it is easier to see why I said earlier that, in matters of ethics, slowing down to consider what the right question is can be more important than rushing out to find the right answer.

In Alexandre Dumas' iconic novel *The Count of Monte Cristo* (2003, p. 274), the protagonist remarks that a "worried capitalist is like a comet, he always presages some disaster for the world." Those who oppose the whole idea of CSR believe that the sort of worried corporate manager whose tender heart bleeds for non-shareholder interests portends great misfortune for the world—not because she shows too little ethical concern, but because she shows too much. This does not imply that anti-CSR advocates think of themselves as moral monsters. It would be kinder and more accurate to say that the ethical index they employ is marked with a different scale than are the indices that many others use.

Philosophers sometimes express this sort of difference by distinguishing between teleological and deontological ethical systems. The former take their name from the Greek word *telos*, meaning "purpose or result," and are perhaps best exemplified by classical utilitarianism's idea that morality means doing what produces the greatest good for the greatest number (Mill, 1895, p. 31). The word "deontological," on the other hand, derives from *deon*, Greek for "that which is binding." Instead of estimating at the *ex post* consequences of a proposed course of action, deontic moral systems stress the *ex ante* duty to perform or not perform the action in question. An extreme example of this attitude is Kant's notion (1993, p. 187) of always following the moral law regardless of what may happen—a principle famously encapsulated in a Latin proverb that he quotes: *Fiat iustitia, pereat mundis* ("Let there be justice even if the world should perish as a result") (Kant, 1996, p. 345).

It is true, of course, that most people are not philosophers—a demographic fact that you will probably be quite relieved to hear. Most individuals possessing at least an ordinary amount of decency rarely exhibit consistency, or even thoughtfulness, in the way they make ethical decisions. Putting aside those instances in which selfishness overwhelms ethical sensibility so completely that it would not be correct any more to say that the framing of the decision is "ethical" in any meaningful sense, sometimes people help others out of what they perceive to be their duty, without thinking about the consequences. Other times, they let themselves be guided by the mental "balance" between the anticipated beneficial effects of a proposed course of action and its anticipated detrimental effects. And still other times (the vast majority of times, I would say), they act without any reflection at all, just doing what feels right to them.

In contrast to the average person, the sincerest opponents of CSR tend to take a consistently teleological approach to ethical problems. In a manner that is closely analogous to so-called "rule utilitarianism,"[3] they define morality in the economic sphere as simply allowing the invisible hand of the market to magically increase net overall social welfare, rather than trying to plan bureaucratically for the doing of good on a case-by-case basis. This theory holds, for example, that if you want a society in which there is consistently enough food to feed the population (certainly a moral goal no less than a political one), then you had better take Adam Smith's well-known aphorism to heart: "It is not from the benevolence of the butcher, the brewer, or the baker, that we expect our dinner, but from their regard to their own interest" (Smith, 1937, p. 14). Expressed in cruder terms, I take it that this sort of thing is what Gordon Gecko, a character in the motion picture *Wall Street* (1987), meant when he uttered the famous line, "Greed—for lack of a better word—is good." It also seems to be what the influential libertarian writer Ayn Rand (1992, p. 752) meant when she praised the virtues of what she called a "utopia of greed."

For those who subscribe to the Gecko/Rand view of corporate ethics, the laws of corporate governance can be interpreted as an enforceable promise according to which the shareholder wealth maximization norm is, as law professor Stephen Bainbridge (2002, p. 424) puts it, "a bargained-for term of the board-shareholder contract by which the directors agree not to make Kaldor–Hicks efficient decisions that leave shareholders worse off." In economic theory, "Pareto optimality" means a distribution of wealth such that any redistribution or other change that is beneficial to one individual is detrimental to one or more others. The Kaldor–Hicks version of efficiency, on the other hand, relaxes the rigor of the last criterion: it lets there be losers from a change in distribution so long as the winners could (in theory) compensate the losers and still remain winners (Posner, 2011, pp. 17–20). A Kaldor–Hicks efficient decision is therefore one that makes it plausible to say that *society as a whole* would be better off with it than without it—so long as "better off" is understood cardinally, that is, as the positive mathematical sum of the amounts that some individuals in society would willingly pay in order to obtain that decision minus the amounts that others would willingly pay to avoid it.

Bainbridge's economistic description of the law of corporate governance is a dry way of saying something that the average person might have difficulty swallowing. It presupposes the existence of situations in which doing what most people would call the "right thing" is *also* socially valuable in the precise economic sense of increasing net social welfare as measured by the microeconomic criterion of willingness to pay. Even in such cases, says Bainbridge, corporate managers are duty-bound legally (if not also morally) *not* to pursue that course of action if it will lose their shareholders even so much as a penny compared to another outcome that is at once socially inefficient *and* morally inferior. If the law of corporate governance and the tenets of fiduciary ethics can conspire together against customary morality and social welfare in a way that is this precise, calculating, and comprehensive, then surely this would put us all well on the way toward achieving the kind of utopia of corporate greed that even the most fervent followers of Gordon Gecko and Ayn Rand could admire.

On the other hand, economists will tell you that net overall social welfare calculations can be exceedingly uncertain and difficult to perform. Where high transactions costs prevent the observation of actual market transactions (a very common situation), the Kaldor–Hicks formula creates an illusion of precision that is rarely confirmable in practice. Better just to rely on the wisdom of the marketplace in all cases, say the Geckos and Rands of the world, than to trust the flawed (and probably biased) calculations of individual do-gooders who are spending other people's money. Considered from the point of view of those who hold that the single-minded pursuit of corporate profitability will eventually maximize utility in the long run for *everyone* in society (Schumpeter, 2009), it is clear not only that for-profit corporations *are* not charities, but also that they should never try to *act* like charities. Unless, of course, management's careful business calculations show that a particular investment in charity will produce a higher net rate of return than spending the money on something else, such as a factory upgrade or a new corporate jet.

It is true that a few eggs will inevitably get broken along the way to corporate profitability. But that, say the apologists for this point of view, is an inescapable feature of beneficial competition itself, where "chance and good luck are often as important as skill and foresight in determining the fate of different people" (Hayek, 2007, p. 134). Friedrich Hayek, widely regarded as a leading apostle of the free market, vehemently opposed socialism on the ground that it is better for everyone to let chance and countless numbers of self-interested market transactions determine who gets what in society than it is to put the matter into the hands of bureaucrats who are in a position to redistribute social wealth according to God-knows-what idiosyncratic interpretation of fairness (Hayek, 2007, pp. 134–146). It is not much of a stretch to say that the same argument applies to any CSR initiative that would loosen the constraint of the profit motive on corporate decision-making. To someone like Hayek, a corporate manager who redistributes shareholder wealth according to her own interpretation of right and wrong must look a lot like an elected official redistributing wealth through tax-funded social programs.

Any corporate manager who consistently applies the Gecko/Rand/Hayek theory of morality must think there are two and only two ethical questions that she ever ought to ask herself in any situation in which she finds herself acting on behalf of the company. (The answers to these questions are pretty much self-evident, by the way, which is an interesting fact in its own right.) The questions are: *First*, should I make this decision solely to further my own selfish financial and career interests rather than the interests of the shareholders and the company? And *second*, should I make a decision that I and others might praise as being ethical if, in my well-considered opinion, it will not ultimately maximize the long-term economic value of the company to the shareholders?

The most stalwart opponents of CSR tend to believe that the only rationally defensible answer to both of the foregoing questions is "No." Stealing and other forms of self-dealing by management, they say, impose "agency costs" that undermine overall confidence in the market and thereby threaten to make everybody worse off (Bainbridge, 2002, pp. 35–38). For them, business ethics is mostly about reminding corporate officials not to steal from the firm to feather their own personal nests. Apart from that, they believe that if a corporation cannot do well economically by doing good morally in any particular situation, then its managers not only have no legal or moral right to do something good for its own sake, they have a distinctly *moral* obligation not to do so. Stealing from rich Peter to pay poor Paul is no different than stealing from Peter to pay yourself, on this view.

Not only that, what is supposed to count as "doing good morally" if the behavior in question does not also maximize the financial interests of those who own the company? Moreover, who is supposed to decide this very question in those cases in which *moral* disagreement—and not just business disagreement—breaks out within the ranks of management?

For example, suppose Director *A* thinks that using cheap child labor to manufacture widgets in the Third World is morally bankrupt, whereas Director *B* thinks that doing so is morally justified because at least it gives poor children and their families some extra income that will help them survive the daily grind of their hardscrabble existence. After all, says *B* (a utilitarian), in some places in the world the only real, immediate alternative to putting children to work in a factory is letting them starve, or else subjecting them to the horrors of human trafficking. In response to this line of argument, Director *A* (a Kantian) rejoins that he is quite sure there is an objective moral duty not to exploit child labor under any circumstances, regardless of the consequences.

If a fully informed calculus of legal and reputational risks does not compel one result or the other—if, hypothetically, it is very unlikely that exploiting Third-World child labor in this situation will ever be discovered and sanctioned by the law as "illegal" and by customers as "immoral"—then whose moral compass is supposed to determine what the ethical conduct of business looks like in this context? Is it simply a matter of counting heads, so that if six teleological-minded directors think that using child labor is morally justified, and five deontological-minded directors do not, then we will say that it is justified? And vice versa if the vote goes the other way? If the ethically right thing to do is subjectively contestable in this case, then it probably can also be contested in a lot of other cases. If this is so, say the Geckos and Rands of the world, perhaps it would be best always to follow the simpler and seemingly more objective demands of fiduciary morality alone.

Every good lawyer knows that it is highly advantageous to be given the power to frame the question, for the way a question is asked largely predetermines the range of answers that will be regarded as reasonably responsive to it. It seems to me that if the only two questions relevant to corporate ethics are expressed in the way I just did a moment ago, then the answers appear both obvious and inescapable: you have an ethical obligation to steer the company toward doing what you personally think is good and moral if and only if you think this course of action would maximize the firm's economic value to the shareholders. Otherwise, you should just swallow hard, try to suppress your gag reflex, and get on with the task of performing your fiduciary duty to make the most possible amount of money for them.

What is a conscientious corporate official supposed to do if she cannot help finding the foregoing conclusion morally repugnant? An interesting development on this score emerged recently from the student body of the Harvard Business School, of all places. The sentiments expressed by the vast majority of these students tend to cast considerable doubt on the inevitability of the Gecko/Rand/Hayek way of asking and answering ethical questions about how business decisions should be made.

In June of 2009, 400 members of the business school's graduating class stepped forward to take the following oath:

> As a manager, my purpose is to serve the greater good by bringing together people and resources to create value that no single individual can build alone. Therefore, I will seek a course that enhances the value my enterprise can create for society over the long term. I recognize that my decisions can have far-reaching consequences that affect the well-being of individuals inside and outside my enterprise, today and in the future. As I reconcile the interests of different constituencies, I will face difficult choices. *Therefore, I promise*: (1) I will act with utmost integrity and pursue my work in an ethical manner. My personal behavior will be an example of integrity, consistent with the values I publicly espouse; (2) I will safeguard the interests of my shareholders, co-workers, customers and the society in which we operate. I will endeavor to protect the interests of those who may not have power, but whose well-being is contingent on my decisions; (3) I will manage my enterprise in good faith, guarding against decisions and behavior that advance my own narrow ambitions but harm the enterprise and the people it serves. The pursuit of self-interest is the vital engine of a capitalist economy, but unbridled greed can be just as harmful. I will oppose corruption, unfair discrimination, and exploitation; (4) I will understand and uphold, both in letter and in spirit, the laws and contracts governing my own conduct and that of my enterprise. If I find laws that are unjust, antiquated, or unhelpful I will not brazenly break, ignore or avoid them; I will seek civil and acceptable means of reforming them; (5) I will take responsibility for my actions, and will represent the performance and risks of my enterprise accurately and honestly. My aim will not be to distort the truth, but to transparently explain it and help people understand how decisions that affect them are made; (6) I will develop both myself and other managers under my supervision so that the profession continues to grow and contribute to the well-being of society. I will consult colleagues and others who can help inform my judgment and will continually invest in staying abreast of the evolving knowledge in the field, always remaining open to innovation. I will mentor and look after the education of the next generation

> of leaders; (7) I will strive to create sustainable economic, social, and environmental prosperity worldwide. Sustainable prosperity is created when the enterprise produces an output in the long run that is greater than the opportunity cost of all the inputs it consumes; (8) I will be accountable to my peers and they will be accountable to me for living by this oath. I recognize that my stature and privileges as a professional stem from the respect and trust that the profession as a whole enjoys, and I accept my responsibility for embodying, protecting, and developing the standards of the management profession, so as to enhance that trust and respect. This oath I make freely, and upon my honor.
>
> (Harvard Business School MBA Oath, 2009)

This is quite a list of promises, many or most of which are likely to make the average profit-seeking fund manager on Wall Street roll his eyes (or worse). Protect the interests of "those who may not have power, but whose well-being is contingent on my decisions"? Strive to "create sustainable economic, social, and environmental prosperity worldwide"? Goodness gracious! "*My purpose is to serve the greater good*," they all said, as if each one of them were answering the ultimate ethical question that I posed to you earlier: "*Who am I?*"

The media attention and publicity surrounding the graduates' oath-taking was considerable at the time. Predictably enough, the conservative counter-reaction to the Harvard MBA Oath was not long in coming. Typical of the kind of criticism that the oath received was the following passage from an article by Matthew Bishop, the Globalization Editor of *The Economist* magazine:

> One of the two main criticisms of the oath and of the whole idea of turning management into a profession, particularly in business-school faculties, is that it is either unnecessary or actively harmful. Crimes such as embezzlement are punishable by law. Shareholders who feel that managers have not acted in their best interests can sue them. Meanwhile, by promising to "safeguard the interests" of colleagues, customers, and society, are the future captains of industry simply shortchanging their shareholders?
>
> (Bishop, 2009, pp. 67–68)

I cannot help reading the question at the end of this passage as being purely rhetorical. That is, it does not seem to invite inquiry or expect an answer so much as assume a "yes"-answer that it thinks is or should be obvious to the reader. The question compares the exercise of individual moral autonomy in the making of what a business manager personally regards as a socially responsible (but relatively less profitable) business decision to "shortchanging" shareholders. A cashier shortchanges you if you give him $100 to pay for $90 worth of groceries and he gives you back $5 in change. If the cashier is greedy, he might slip the other $5 you are entitled to into his pocket; if he is like Robin Hood, he might pass the money along to a homeless person. Either way, you (and by analogy shareholders) have been shortchanged. The exact form that a Harvard MBA Oath-guided decision takes—whether it is to divert corporate assets or to decline otherwise profitable opportunities—seems morally irrelevant to Bishop. From his point of view, it would appear that Harvard's oath-taking "future captains of industry" have promised to violate their fiduciary duty of loyalty to the shareholders by threatening not to "act *solely* for the interests of his principal within the business area for which he is employed" (Seavey, 1964, p. 243) (emphasis added).

It is important to understand that the critique of the Harvard MBA Oath that I have just described is not really about what particular actions or types of actions are ethical or unethical, right or wrong, in a transcendent sense, or even in a commonsensical, everyday sense. Nor does the critique speak to the very real moral dilemmas that are faced all the time by corporate officials, a few examples of which I have already mentioned. Instead, anti-CSR critiques are at bottom always about moral agency. They are about *who* should have ultimate power in the ethical sphere—who should be allowed to say, authoritatively and definitively, what it means for a corporate employee to behave ethically.

Command-and-control ethics

During his trial in Jerusalem, former SS officer Adolph Eichmann declared with great emphasis that he had lived his whole life according to Kant's moral precepts. The philosopher Hannah Arendt, who covered the trial for *The New Yorker* magazine, had a hard time making sense of this part of Eichmann's testimony, which she called "outrageous on the face of it, since Kant's moral philosophy is closely bound up with man's faculty of judgment, which rules out blind obedience" (Arendt, 1965, p. 136). She therefore speculated that Eichmann's enthusiastic and extraordinarily effective wartime effort to help destroy the Jews of Europe was grounded in an unconscious distortion of Kant's categorical imperative.

As Kant had originally formulated it (1993, p. 187), the categorical imperative requires each individual to "*act as if the maxim of your action were to become by your will a general law of nature.*" But as Arendt notes (1965, p. 136), Eichmann seemed to have interpreted the command to read, instead, "*Act in such a way that the Führer, if he knew your action, would approve it.*" On this reading of his testimony, Eichmann let his internally constructed image of another person's will control all of his moral choices, as if the Führer's will was so unimpeachably right that Eichmann's only remaining ethical task was to unreservedly let his own will be identified with it.

Now I hasten to say that I do not mean to draw any direct moral comparison between what Eichmann and his ilk did in Europe during World War II and what today's MBA graduates and corporate managers are doing every day, in countless venues around the world. That would be worse than a cheap shot—it would constitute an unconscionable affront to the memory of the millions who died by Eichmann's hands. It would also ignore all of the good and decent things that businesspeople have done for humanity, of which the wartime activities of Oskar Schindler (Crowe, 2004) represent a particularly notable example.

Nevertheless, I think that Arendt's analysis of the way Eichmann preconstructed the intellectual environment in which he made his moral choices sharpens to a fine point the one ethical question that by its very nature must always precede any discussion about the contents of one's moral duties. That question is not about what is or is not morally right. It is about agency. It asks: *Who will I let control my moral actions, me or someone else?*

I recently ran a Google search on the term "corporate ethics codes." It returned nearly 21 million hits. The drafting of corporate ethics codes has become a business in its own right, complete with elaborate advice on how the corporate elite can control their employees and satisfy their shareholders by laying down the law, so to speak, of permissible corporate tactics. Websites with titles like "How to Write a Code of Ethics for Business" promise to bring down several birds (not all of them ethical) with one stone: not only will an ethics code help your company determine its priorities and values, they say, but "it can also help you down the line if one of your employees or vendors drags you into legal trouble" (Spiro, 2015).

Made up of internal rules enforced by "compliance officers," corporate ethics codes purport to constrain employees who might otherwise be tempted to cut certain specified moral corners in their search for profit on behalf of the firm. Arising within a "hard law" legal environment in which the rules of corporate governance and fiduciary duty encourage calculated moral corner-cutting if the ratio of risk to reward is low enough, the legally unenforceable "soft law" of corporate ethics codes does at least *offer* to marginally soften the edges of capitalism by restraining some of the baser forms of rent- and profit-seeking by businesspeople.

However, just about every business executive with whom I have spoken on the subject has told me that there is another motive underlying the explosive development of the soft law of corporate ethics. The Enron scandal in 2001, the 2008 collapse of Lehman Brothers and AIG's liquidity crisis, the reckless lending and securitization practices that led us into the Great Recession: as we all know, corporate scandals and ethical lapses like these have periodically shaken the modern business world to its foundations, triggered public outrage, and produced a hue and cry for more government regulation of the corporate sphere. One of the most important collective goals of the movement to establish corporate ethics codes is to make a highly visible show of institutionalizing moral norms in order to defuse political demands for externally imposed corporate reforms.

Earlier I provided a sketch of the predominant view of CSR in business and legal circles. Distilled to its essence, this view holds that corporate managers "should" (legally and morally) do well by doing good only if it is not possible to do better by not doing good (or by doing bad). Seen from this perspective, the goal of maximizing shareholder value, which is already the basis on which the performance of most corporate officials is judged, becomes the defining characteristic of CSR as well. Seeking out and doing the *right kind* of social responsibility—the kind approved of in the firm's internal "ethics code"—not only will make the firm more money and potentially lessen its legal penalties in unrelated contexts—it will also advance your career.

Forgive me for saying so, but what keeps coming to mind in this context is Hannah Arendt's observation that Adolf Eichmann had internalized the stated goals of the Führer so completely that he was convinced "that nothing less than going beyond the call of duty will do" (1965, p. 137). For the more thoroughly the detailed abstractions of ethics codes—or of any other externally imposed norm for that matter—are accepted and internalized as our very own, the more blinkered and partial our gaze becomes, and the less able we are to notice what the codes do not want us to see. As Lisa Dodson's aforementioned study of the "moral underground" in corporate America illustrates, the ranks of management are not filled up with would-be Gordon Geckos and American Psychos[4] alone; they also contain a considerable number of decent human beings who are morally troubled by some of the particular things that their bosses have asked them to do in the pursuit of corporate profitability—things that do not necessarily fall under the prohibitions of a code.

The current craze for corporate ethics codes is best interpreted as yet another manifestation of the command-and-control mechanisms of corporate governance generally. As Ronald Coase (1937) so famously maintained, the invention of the corporate form can be viewed as an appropriate response to the problem of transactions costs. Large firms develop elaborate internal hierarchies mimicking the government bureaucracies of the welfare state because employing market solutions to each and every corporate decision would be far too costly when compared to the alternative of an enlightened, profit-seeking command-and-control system. While Coase's theory of the firm is not the only one that exists, it does have the advantage of highlighting the most important feature of our problem.

Just as routine economic decisions within the firm can be more efficiently managed by command-and-control principles than by costly case-by-case negotiations among individual market participants, so too ethical decisions would become very costly for the firm if each one had to be negotiated with an employee every time she felt a twinge of moral guilt on account of what her boss is telling her to do. Considered from the standpoint of the firm's directors and shareholders, it must seem much more efficient to control ethical situations in advance by in-house corporate ethics codes, thereby supplanting the individual moral sensibilities of corporate employees, than to allow employees the freedom to exercise autonomous moral judgment in each and every situation they confront during the workday. Philosophers like Kant might think that individual moral autonomy is the *sine qua non* of ethics, but if I understand them correctly, most businesspeople suspect that the suppression of individual moral autonomy (read "moral anarchy") in the boardroom and on the factory floor is the *sine qua non* of generating corporate profits.

The business ethics question par excellence: "who am I?"

Despite what I have just said, I believe there is something ethically significant—even monumental and potentially earth shattering—in the sheer social fact that

400 graduates of the Harvard Business School just took an oath promising to safeguard the interests of colleagues, customers, and society in pursuing their future careers in business. Harvard Business School Professor Rakesh Khurana recently remarked that just telling his students to maximize shareholder value "does not satisfy them anymore" (Bishop, 2009, pp. 67–68). My own experience in teaching the current generation of law students in America, and now in France, has been similar.

Going by what they say they want from law school, most of my students long to hear about justice and not just about legality; they want room to reflect on law from a moral point of view, and not just from the point of view of Holmes's notorious Bad Man. The latter "cares nothing for an ethical rule which is believed and practiced by his neighbors," but he "is likely nevertheless to care a good deal to avoid being made to pay money, and will keep out of jail if he can" (Holmes, 1920, p. 170). His point of view is a function of the distinction that I drew earlier between acting *because of* a norm (the Bad Man could care less) and acting *in conformity* with a norm (the Bad Man will conform to normative expectations only if doing so pays him more (or costs him less) than not conforming).

Of course, all of this could be a tragic illusion—a case of wishful thinking on my part. Perhaps Matthew Bishop (2009, p. 67) is right when he alleges that young people today, who face the worst job market in many decades, have come to see non-profit and government jobs as their best bet for getting any job at all and, therefore, have made the cold calculation that appearing to embrace the "values agenda" will be useful to them.

That said however, I believe the millennium generation's apparent "ethical turn," so to speak, represents something that cannot be so easily dismissed by those who think, however sincerely, that the only proper business of business is, well, business. Today's business students and law students may very well be displaying "naïvety," as Bishop (2009, p. 67) says. But so what? Given the right circumstances, it is just possible for today's naïvety to become tomorrow's consensus.

Whether a given consensus is actually good for humanity and all of the individuals who comprise it is another matter of course, and ultimately depends on how one evaluates the real, living world that it co-constructs each and every time a particular corporate decision is made and executed. To be honest, I cannot say whether the universal adoption by businesspeople of the Harvard MBA Oath would make for a better world. For me, there is too much uncertainty in how it would actually be applied to allow for a reasonable prejudgment on the question. What is more, it is hard to see how pledging allegiance to any abstraction—however noble it may sound—could ever reliably furnish us with a good conscience on account of what we do in *particular* situations to *particular* others in its name.

I do know one thing for sure, however. Properly understood, being ethical must never be conflated with the project of acting in conformity with externally imposed rules and customs. We who are alive in the twenty-first century bear (or should bear) tragic witness to the fact that following like sheep the rules and customs laid down by others has all too often led human beings to do terrible things to one another. Of course, it is quite true that we can always choose to delegate to others the power to construct the norms of our conduct. But the individual's ultimate ethical responsibility for what he or she actually does in the world can never be delegated in this way.

It seems to me that being ethical amounts to much more than paying hypocritical lip service to the question, *"Who am I?"* If the latter is not taken to be the genuine question lying at the very core of what is called "business ethics," then I, for one, want no part of it.

Notes

* An earlier version of this chapter was published in the *Journal of Law, Business & Ethics*, vol. 17, pp. 9–22 (2011), under the title "Asking the Right Question in Business Ethics."

1. This chapter was originally given as a keynote address on December 7, 2009, at a public program in Paris entitled "Revisiting Business Ethics." The program, sponsored by *France Amériques*, was attended by over 100 business leaders from Paris, and featured debate and commentary on the content of the address by four co-panelists: His Excellency Jacques Andréani, Ambassador of France to the United States; Catherine Delhaye, Director of Legal Affairs, Accenture; Christian Pardieu, Compliance Officer, GE Capital; and Edward Hadas, Assistant Editor of *Breakingviews.com*.
2. See, for example, *Katz v. Oak Indus, Inc.*, 508 A.2d 873, 879 (Del. Ch. 1986) ("It is the obligation of directors to attempt, within the law, to maximize the long-run interests of the corporation's stockholders.").
3. > *Act utilitarians* (also called *extreme* or *direct utiltarians* . . .) say that on each occasion we should do whatever act will produce the greatest good. *Rule utilitarians* (also called *restricted* or *indirect utilitarians*) say that we should obey those rules which would produce the greatest happiness if generally followed.
   >
   > (Lacey, 1986, p. 257)
4. *American Psycho* (2000) is a motion picture starring Christian Bale in the title role of Patrick Batemen, a wealthy, ethically challenged (to say the least) investment banker living and working in Manhattan during the 1980s.

Chapter 7

Social science

Senseless kindness and the politics of Cost-Benefit Analysis*

> Definitions determine the membership of a class the way golfers are admitted to the country club.
>
> William Gass (2012, p. 272)

What and why

Unlike physics and biology, which aspire to uncover the truth about underlying realities that everyday common sense tends to falsify or distort, the modern social science known as "Cost–Benefit Analysis" (CBA) finds itself in the odd position of seeking theoretical knowledge about ordinary opinions.[1] As the Greeks would have said, CBA sets out to acquire *epistēmē* about mere *doxa*: that is, it assembles theoretical knowledge on the subject of pre-theoretical, quotidian human opinions and choices. These everyday opinions and choices take the form of the revealed or supposed "preferences" of individuals about which goods (in the largest sense of the word) to keep or not to keep, to acquire or not to acquire.

CBA wants to know *what* people's preferences are so they can be measured and compared. It shows little, if any, interest in the question of *why* people have the preferences they have, or why their willingness to pay value (WTP) to achieve gains and their willingness to accept value (WTA) to compensate for losses are what they are at any given point in time. It is true, of course, that rational choice theory has always been aware, at least at some level of consciousness, that people's preferences are affected by the opportunities afforded them by their individual experiences and prevailing social and institutional arrangements—in short, by the currents and cross-currents of history's becoming. From the small (what we eat and wear) to the large (our political, cultural and religious institutions), different epochs and cultures produce different "opportunity sets" from which individuals are allowed or required to choose (Gravel, 1994, p. 454).

In light of the historical and social contingency of people's opportunities, some (albeit very few) rational choice theorists have called for CBA to take the "why"-question more seriously, perhaps by making it into an object of analysis, or, better still, a formal variable in the theory. Robert Higgs (1987, pp. 35–56), for example, asserts that rational choice theory ought to take account of the powerful influence of ideology on preference formation, while Michael Hechter (1992, pp. 1–2) observes (and bemoans) economists' relatively low level of theoretical sophistication about what he calls the "micro–macro link" connecting individual preferences to their social conditions.

However, despite these and other calls for CBA to broaden the scope of its inquiry, the field's mainstream practitioners by and large remain uninterested in the question of why people have the preferences they have. Indeed, some even go so far as to display their indifference to the historical contingency of institutions and opportunities as if it were an intellectual badge of honor.[2] For the practice of CBA, it seems to be enough that people simply appear (out of nowhere, so to speak) with measurable WTPs and WTAs that can be summed up and then brought into quantitative relationships that determine whether a given transaction or state of affairs does or does not satisfy one or more criteria of efficiency.

In thinking about CBA's theoretical and practical indifference to "Why?" it is important to remember that this question, though exceedingly common in everyday speech, is nonetheless ambiguous in the present context. In particular, the question "Why?" sometimes seeks factual information about the *causes and conditions* of a preference, and other times it inquires after the preference's *grounds*. The first kind of inquiry aims at a historical explanation; the second seeks a normative reason or justification.

For example, a person who says she wants to keep the Arctic National Wildlife Refuge (ANWR) free from all oil exploration may explain her preference by appealing to the fact that her parents raised her to love nature (a causal answer to "Why?") or by saying that drilling in ANWR is the morally wrong thing to do (a normative answer to "Why?"). Although CBA's indifference to the purely historical explanation of preferences can (perhaps) be defended on the basis of an academic division of labor that assigns causal questions to disciplines like history, sociology, and psychology, reserving so-called "economic" and "policymaking" questions to CBA, the roots of its indifference to the normative grounds of preferences lie much deeper. Whether consciously or unconsciously, CBA, like many modern social-scientific disciplines, has wholeheartedly appropriated Max Weber's central thesis that our environing world—the human world in both its natural and social dimensions—has become thoroughly disenchanted (Weber, 1978, vol. 1, p. 506).

The dominant tradition of political liberalism defines freedom negatively, as the mere absence of certain constraints on the exercise of personal choices. It does not concern itself with the value of whatever opportunities there are to choose from. It valorizes freedom to choose this product over that product, to live this way as opposed to that way, to attend this place of worship or that (or no) place of worship. But if one is free by this definition alone, how is one supposed to go about rationally choosing one's innermost *values* (the values that help ground every other choice) in a fully disenchanted world—a world in which all traditional modes for the grounding of one's values have lost their binding force? The theologian Reinhold Niebuhr's reflections about the quality of "modernity" in 1924 have if anything become more relevant to the postmodern (or post-postmodern) age we live in now:

> We do have a great many moderns who are emancipated from every kind of religious discipline without achieving any new loyalty which might qualify the brutal factors in human life. It is better that life incarnate have some ideal value, even if mixed with illusion (though anything with the spirit of love in it is not wholly illusion), than it should express nothing but the will to live.
>
> (Niebuhr, 2015, p. 53)

When it still thought of itself as "political economy" (Weber, 1958, p. 129), the discipline of economics actually cared about the problem of how the economic system (pertaining to the *material* reproduction of society) affects and interacts with the various normative systems that integrate individuals into the social order (the *symbolic* reproduction of society). The late John Kenneth Galbraith, for example, who made a point of describing himself as a *political* economist, once quoted with approval a colleague's opinion that "the economist, like everyone else, must concern himself with the ultimate aims of man" (*The Nation*, May 22, 2006, pp. 4–5). These days, however, economics as a specialized science seems to have conceptually severed the relationship between material reproduction and symbolic reproduction and has absolved itself of asking any questions about the legitimacy of the social order, including its possible pathologies (Habermas, 1984, vol. 1, p. 4).

Most economists today construe "rationality" in purely functional terms, as a mere means to economic equilibrium and individual rational choice. Economics as a discipline has lost its historical connection to the rational study and evaluation of the sociopolitical structures within which all equilibria and choices take place. CBA in particular has become a kind of semi-autonomous administrative system, and its connection to the life world is maintained at only one discrete point: the point at which CBA intervenes to *measure* individual preferences. The forces that shape those preferences go unexamined, with the result that CBA can contribute nothing to the study and development of the reality of the public sphere, where preferences are continuously being formed, dissolved, and reformed within what Hegel (1977, p. 27) called the "Bacchanalian revel" (*bacchantische Taumel*) of their ceaseless becoming-in-time.

As an empirical social science, CBA is configured in such a way that it lacks any mechanism for adjudicating the validity of people's preferences. It is therefore unsurprising that CBA fails to address the question of whether individual preferences are well-grounded in ethics, morality, or some other normative system. One might even go so far as to say that the very existence of CBA as a well-respected discipline in business, government, and academia tends to prove Nietzsche's thesis that in today's world "the highest values devaluate themselves. The aim is lacking; 'why?' finds no answer" (Nietzsche, 1968, p. 9).

Instead of *why*, we find the mere *what* of WTPs and WTAs: abstract entities extracted from unique (and thus incommensurable) particularities and crafted in advance to become pristine numerical quantities supremely suited for the task of scientific management and control. The radical abstraction of reality that is performed by modern social science, including especially CBA, underscores the fact that there is an intimate connection between CBA's methods and purely administrative modes of decision-making. Although each situation CBA analyzes is embedded in some particular context of a life-history and form of life, it "has to be subjected to violent abstraction, not only because it has to be subsumed under a law but also in order that it can be dealt with administratively" (Habermas, 1984, vol. 1, p. xxxiv).

Once its numerical data on preferences is collected, CBA's calculations lead directly to administration, bypassing the real events and processes that are constantly socializing and individuating the people whose lives will be affected by the decisions that administration makes. Perhaps this explains why some CBA practitioners have conceded that their criterion of economic efficiency "does not tell us 'the right thing to do' in a transcendent moral or spiritual sense" (Zerbe, 2001, p. 29). Implicit in the latter way of thinking is a contestable view about the nature of individual morality itself: namely, that moral actions are always deduced once and for all by individuals from personally chosen criteria that are immune both to rational criticism and to the messy historical processes in which individual preferences—including moral preferences—are constantly being formed and expressed.

Why and how

Although CBA's indifference to the question "Why?" in both its causal and normative senses is perfectly understandable, given CBA's history, the same cannot be said about its equally profound indifference to the question of *how* preferences are formed. The questions "Why?" and "How?" do not seek the same kind of knowledge. *Why* a thing is as it is concerns its antecedents or its grounds—its historical causes or its normative reasons—but *how* a thing is is not the same. Properly understood, a thing's "how" actually co-determines *what* it is.

The causal why of a thing is usually investigated by those who are concerned with general laws of human action and the useful explanations they afford, whereas the normative why is usually investigated by those who care about its legitimacy. In contrast, determining the *what-and-how* of a thing requires ontological investigation and aims toward a description rather than an explanation or a justification. That these different ways of making sense of the world sometimes find themselves in tension, or even at cross-purposes, is indicated by a remark of Wittgenstein's: "People who are constantly asking 'why' are like tourists who stand in front of a building reading Baedeker and are so busy reading the history of its construction, etc., that they are prevented from *seeing* the building" (Wittgenstein, 1980a, p. 40e).

Putting *why* aside for a moment, one could say that *what* and *how* are opposite sides of the same coin—different aspects of one and the same being or phenomenon. To borrow a distinction from the medieval Scholastics, the what-being (*essentia*) of, say, an individual preference for butter over guns, or guns over butter, is its determination as a present entity possessing such-and-such attributes, whereas its how-being (*existentia*) consists in its having a certain *mode* of existing—

a manner or style of persisting (and perhaps changing) through time (Heidegger, 1984, pp. 177–178). "What?" asks for a snapshot to be taken; "How?" wants a motion picture. "What?" seeks a static and eternally true proposition; "How?" aspires to unzip the surface of the real to investigate what lies beneath.

The inextricable link between the *what* and the *how* of preference formation has been convincingly demonstrated over and over again by behavioral economists. The academic discipline of behavioral economics was once considered marginal and exotic by mainstream economists. The latter had, and to some extent still have, a tendency to modify the phrase " 'survey evidence' with the adjective 'mere', which rhymes with 'sneer'," as Richard Thaler put it in his recent book *Misbehaving: The Making of Behavioral Economics* (2015, p. 47).

Nevertheless, the basic hypothesis of behavioral economics is that *how* a decision occurs can often affect *what* it is, and this hypothesis has been verified experimentally countless times. In an important early paper, for example, Tversky and Kahneman (1981) offer convincing experimental evidence that on average the way a choice is "framed" vitally affects the outcomes that people choose, even though the available choices are all demonstrated to be mathematically equivalent. It turns out that it makes a big difference if mathematically identical outcomes are described in terms of "lives lost" rather than "lives saved," or "chance of winning" rather than "chance of losing" (Kahneman, 2011, pp. 436–438). Behavioral economists have demonstrated that by manipulating the environment in which preferences are expressed—that is, manipulating the *how* of preference formation—they can often observe measurable differences in *what* those preferences are.

In theory and in practice, economists are able to measure what they call "revealed preferences" because WTPs and WTAs actually appear in consummated (and hence theoretically observable) transactions. Here people really do put their money where their mouths are, so to speak. But not all preferences are revealed in observable market transactions. Indeed, the discipline of CBA considers itself relevant to government decision-making precisely because the market has *not* provided a solution to the problems of public policy that it analyzes. The difficult task of developing a method for theorizing and researching people's WTPs and WTAs in the absence of actual transactions where all relevant preferences have been revealed and counted thus becomes particularly important for CBA. When one considers that CBA's entire *raison d'être* is to assist government in deciding whether and how to proceed with projects that will affect people's lives for better or worse, then this directly *political* application of CBA makes its *scientific* decisions about methodology all the more significant.

I will argue in this chapter that by theoretically recognizing preferences only insofar as they fit into pre-established functional units that are fit for quantification, CBA creates a kind of bureaucratic blindness to the spontaneous processes of opinion and will formation in reality. Another way to put this is to say that CBA cannot see or acknowledge the existence (let alone value) of surprise and idiosyncrasy in particular face-to-face encounters between human beings. Thismethodological blindness, in turn, makes it easier for decision-makers to decouple their political decisions from the particular, identity-forming contexts in which people's preferences actually arise. It also allows them to avoid making investments in public institutions that might make unscripted popular deliberation and discussion of competing political preferences more likely.

The phenomenon of senseless kindness

The term "senseless kindness" comes from a scene in *Life and Fate*, an epic novel about Stalinist repression and the Nazi invasion of the Soviet Union during the Second World War (Grossman, 1985). Its author, Vasily Grossman, was a Russian-Jewish novelist and war correspondent for *Krasnaya Zvezda*, or *Red Star*, the official newspaper of the Red Army (Grossman, 2005, p. vii). Although the manuscript was actively suppressed by the authorities, Vladimir Voinovich, one of the principal Soviet dissidents of the mid-1970s, managed to smuggle a microfilm copy abroad, and the novel was eventually published in 1980, 16 years after the author's death. The recent discovery and publication of Grossman's wartime notebooks (2005) has made it clear that many, if not most, of the war scenes in the novel are based on actual incidents that Grossman witnessed or learned about as a frontline correspondent. Grossman was embedded (as we would say today) with Soviet forces as they retreated in panic following Germany's invasion of the Soviet Union in June of 1941, as they fought from near-disaster to victory during the nightmarish battle of Stalingrad in 1942–1943, and as the Red Army made its slow but relentless advance from central Russia all the way to Berlin and the end of the war in May of 1945.

The phrase "senseless kindness" first appears in the context of Grossman's description of a punitive action aimed at a Russian village by a German military unit bent on "exact[ing] vengeance for the murder of two soldiers" (1985, pp. 408–409). An *Aktion* like countless others perpetrated throughout the Soviet Union by the SS and the Wehrmacht, this particular event contains a small but striking detail that underscores the bewildering complexity of human behavior.

The operation began late in the afternoon. The Germans entered the village, ordered its women to dig a large pit at the edge of the forest, and rounded up and held 20 male peasants for execution at daybreak the following morning. One of the women whose husband had been seized was also forced to quarter several German soldiers overnight in her hut. The next morning, as the Germans were getting their machine guns ready for the impending massacre, the eldest of them somehow pulled his trigger by mistake and shot himself in the stomach. His compatriots bandaged his wound as best they could, laid him on a cot in the woman's hut, and then went outside to begin shooting the captives. They left the woman alone in charge of the wounded soldier and motioned for her to watch over him. The novel describes what happened next:

> The woman thought to herself how simple it would be to strangle him. There he was, muttering away, his eyes closed, weeping, sucking his lips . . . Suddenly he opened his eyes and said in very clear Russian: "Water, Mother." "Damn

> you," said the woman. "What I should do is strangle you." Instead she gave him some water. He grabbed her by the hand and signed to her to help him sit up: he couldn't breathe because of the bleeding. She pulled him up and he clasped his arms round her neck. Suddenly there was a volley of shots outside and the woman began to tremble. Afterwards she told people what she had done. No one could understand; nor could she explain it herself.
>
> (Grossman, 1985, pp. 408–409)

Many other gratuitous and unforeseen particular acts of kindness appear in this book, and, in a good illustration of form following content, they seem to occur almost randomly during the course of the narrative.

To mention but one other example, there is a scene in which a captured German officer and his men are removing decomposing bodies from a basement in Stalingrad at the end of the battle in the winter of 1943 (1985, pp. 803–805). A woman in a crowd of Russian onlookers takes great delight in witnessing the obvious misery and suffering of the Germans, who have been forced by Russian troops to perform this heinous task. At one point the Germans bring out the corpse of an adolescent girl on a stretcher, and the woman collapses and wails in grief when she sees that it is the body of her daughter. Getting to her feet, the woman begins to stride angrily toward the captive officer, and a Russian guard lets her pass. Sensing that she is about to take vengeance, the crowd cannot take their eyes off her. The narrative continues:

> The woman could no longer see anything at all except the face of the German with the handkerchief round his mouth. Not understanding what was happening to her, governed by a power she had just now seemed to control, she felt in the pocket of her jacket for a piece of bread that had been given to her the evening before by a soldier. She held it out to the German officer and said: "There, have something to eat." Afterwards, she was unable to understand what had happened to her, why she had done this. . . . Much later still, lying on her bed, the woman remembered what she had done outside the cellar in Stalingrad, and she thought to herself, "I was a fool then, and I'm still a fool now."
>
> (Grossman, 1985, pp. 805–806)

The philosopher Emmanuel Levinas (2001, p. 80) was greatly impressed with *Life and Fate*, and not just because of its plot or its excellent writing. He was affected most of all by the many scenes and stories in the book depicting unaccountable acts of simple kindness and generosity passing from one person to another, most of which were performed under circumstances in which one might expect the opposite result owing to the presence of strong impulses of self-regard and self-preservation. Indeed, Levinas even went so far as to read the book as a proto-philosophical text full of meaning about the essential nature of human goodness—an interpretation occasionally confirmed by Grossman himself, as in this passage:

> This senseless kindness is condemned in the fable about the pilgrim who warmed a snake in his bosom. It is the kindness that has mercy on a tarantula that has bitten a child. A mad, blind kindness. People enjoy looking in stories and fables for examples of the danger of this senseless kindness. But one shouldn't be afraid of it. One might just as well be afraid of a freshwater fish carried out by chance into the salty ocean. The harm from time to time occasioned a society, class, race or State by this senseless kindness fades away in the light that emanates from those who are endowed with it. This kindness, this stupid kindness, is what is most truly human in a human being. It is what sets man apart, the highest achievement of his soul. No, it says, life is not evil!
>
> (Grossman, 1985, p. 409)

To distill a rich and variegated body of philosophical work to its essence, Levinas, like Grossman, believed that human goodness as such cannot be reduced to or explained by a person's compliance with ethical or legal norms. Nor can it be equated with an individual "preference" for goodness that could be quantified and compared with other individual preferences according to some sort of politico-scientific calculus. Levinas's work on ethics concerns itself primarily with elucidating the phenomenal irrationality of the ubiquitous small kindnesses that pass between strangers before reason has "explained" them by reducing them to calculations based on short- or long-term reciprocity.

How might the structure of this sort of human interaction be described? This question asks for a concrete phenomenological investigation of how eruptions of senseless kindness show themselves in the temporal flow of real human life.

To begin with, senseless kindness is always the product of a particular encounter between human beings who, suddenly and perhaps even unwillingly, find themselves standing face-to-face with one another. To use one of Levinas's most powerful images (1996, p. 33, 54), in the literal *nakedness* of the other's face can be glimpsed the phenomenon of distress on account of mortality. Derrida (2001, p. 171) speaks of this phenomenon in terms of the relationship between friends, both of whom know that one of them will probably outlive the other. It is on account of this mutual awareness of mortality that the friends become what Derrida evocatively calls "virtual survivors" in life. But in truth *every* face-to-face encounter between human beings (not just friends) can be haunted by the feeling that one will outlive the other.

I say that the phenomena of distress on account of mortality "can be glimpsed" to indicate the phenomenological truth that the inevitable death of the other is not necessarily (or even often) encountered as an *explicit* theme. Instead, the primordial experience of distress on account of the other's mortality shows itself as an existential *possibility* in every face-to-face relationship. Levinas describes the phenomenal structure of the possibility of this kind of encounter in vivid, almost lyrical terms:

> But that face facing me, in its expression – in its mortality – summons me, demands me, requires me: as if the invisible death faced by the face of the

> other – pure alterity, separate, somehow, from any whole – were "my business." As if, unknown by the other whom already, in the nakedness of his face, it concerns, it "regarded me" before its confrontation with me, before being the death that stares me, myself, in the face. The death of the other man puts me on the spot, calls me into question, as if I, by my possible indifference, became the accomplice of that death, invisible to the other who is exposed to it; and as if, even before being condemned to it myself, I had to answer for that death of the other, and not leave the other alone to his deathly solitude. It is precisely in that recalling of me to my responsibility by the face that summons me, that demands me, that requires me – it is in that calling into question – that the other is my neighbour.
>
> (Levinas, 1999, pp. 24–25)

It is important to understand that Levinas's description of the sort of interpersonal encounter that can lead to an eruption of senseless kindness is not an argument *for* senseless kindness, as if there were too little of it in the world and he wanted to encourage people to be nicer to one another. This way of putting it wrongly constructs the phenomenon in question as an event that one can plan for in advance on the basis of an ethical norm or individual preference that could be taught and learned, as it were, in Sunday school.

The phenomenal facts of the case are otherwise. The essence of senseless kindness consists in the fact that it stealthily comes upon or surprises the one who, all of a sudden, finds herself inexplicably acting selflessly and considerately toward another human being. Levinas's numerous accounts of the phenomenon of "facing" describe what sometimes (even often) *is* in daily life; they are not preachy lectures about what *ought to be*. Senseless kindness is something that just happens—albeit usually in small ways that fly under the radar of political and social theory—even if it is also true that the counter-phenomena of cruelty, greed, and selfishness are often more spectacular, and hence more visible to us.

The challenge to CBA posed by the phenomenon of senseless kindness

Senseless kindness should not be confused with compassion. In the context of our present inquiry, "compassion" names a feeling, whereas "kindness" names an activity. The two are not even genetically related, at least not necessarily: just as hatred does not always pass into violence, compassion does not always pass into kindness. Nor is every act of kindness preceded by an identifiable feeling of compassion.

Compassion as such has had a checkered career in post-Enlightenment Western thought. Reason-loving thinkers such as Kant (1996, p. 235) and Fichte (2005, p. 147) railed against it as an irrational affect that threatens to interfere with the performance of one's self-legislated ethical duties. Rousseau (1993a, p. 73), on the other hand, described irrational compassion (*la pitié*) as "the only natural virtue which even the most advanced skepticism has been forced to recognize." Rejecting Kant and Fichte on this score, and following the lead of Rousseau, Schopenhauer (2005, p. 85) became the first Western philosopher to bring compassion into play as a plausible "ultimate foundation" of ethics.

Kant (1996, pp. 560–561) (6:439–440) had argued that the phenomenon of conscience is evidence that the ego is split in two—that one's free but unknowable noumenal self is capable of laying down the law to one's knowable, causally determined phenomenal self, thus cutting off the influence of natural causes and initiating a brand new causal nexus. Kant also linked his famous duty-principle to a peculiar inner attitude of estimating the laws laid down by the noumenal self as if they were "divine commands," products of "a holy being (morally law-giving reason) distinct from us yet present in our inmost being" (1996, p. 561) (6:440). Schopenhauer noticed the implicit theology contained in this account of moral law-giving. He saw that if Kant's pseudo-theistic piety is removed from the equation, then what remains is the spectacle of a merely empirical self as it mumbles to itself in legalistic terms—in short, a fully determined and egoistic will that enjoys no more freedom than a falling rock or any other natural phenomenon.

Schopenhauer believed that the will is fully determined by its motives, which in turn are themselves fully determined by a person's character as situated within the infinite causal nexus produced by the sequential unfolding of events. The feeling that one has the freedom to do what one wills was for him an illusion. In a fully determined world, everything has a cause, including any motives that happen to present themselves, one at a time, to the mind, as well as the degree and extent to which those motives influence the will on any given occasion (Schopenhauer, 1999, p. 37).

Given his thesis of absolute determinism, it is little wonder that Schopenhauer turned to compassion as the "explanation" of ethics. If kind acts are thought of as *effects*, then they must have a *cause*. That cause he identified as the motive of compassion (*Mitleid*, translated literally as "suffering with") and the feeling of loving-kindness (*Menschenliebe*, translated literally as "love of humanity"). This motive-oriented approach is further confirmed by his identification of *Mileid* and *Menschenliebe* with the early Christian names for the virtue of loving-kindness (*agápē* in Greek, *caritas* in Latin).

Schopenhauer characterized the feeling of compassion as "the great mystery of Ethics," for he believed that only this feeling gives the will the chance to escape its predominant mood of egoism, if only for a moment (2005, p. 142). As Clark and Leiter (1997, p. xx) put it, Schopenhauer's neo-Kantian metaphysical dualism led him to endorse the view that:

> compassion, immediate concern for the welfare of another, possesses a higher worth than egoistic inclination because, rather than being a part of our natural equipment, it is a sign of our connection to a reality that goes beyond the phenomenal or natural world.

Schopenhauer's metaphysical views reflect what Chapter 2 called logical transcendence, or $A \rightarrow B$. They led him to want to "explain" ethics (B) by imputing it to its supposed cause (A): compassion conceived as a "natural" human feeling. But my purpose in drawing attention here to senselessly kind *actions*—as opposed to compassionate *feelings*—is not to explain them. Phenomenological research does not impute—it exhibits. Once exhibited, the sheer existence of a phenomenon can then become the factual basis, so to speak, for thinking about other, non-phenomenological, questions. One such question is *how* what CBA calls "revealed preferences" are (sometimes) actually formed and expressed.

The individual acts of kindness that Grossman describes as "senseless" in *Life and Fate* appear on their face to have been what Weber would have called *subjectively irrational*. That is, they lack any orientation as means to some subjectively valid end when viewed from the standpoint of the actors themselves. The subjective irrationality of these acts is indicated by the fact that immediately after they had performed them, the two Russian women mentioned earlier said they could not make sense of what they had done.

The existence of the phenomenon of senseless kindness threatens to subvert CBA's entire frame of reference. Trying to understand the sorts of behaviors that Grossman describes presents a difficulty that lies much deeper than the familiar question of whether it is legitimate for economists to make interpersonal comparisons of utility by transforming ordinal values into cardinal ones.[3] The real difficulty posed by the existence of the category of senseless kindness has to do with the very possibility of explanation according to criterion of rational choice itself. If human kindness can arise spontaneously from the unscripted particularities of each situation rather than from the conceptual generality of a "preference" that controls or explains every individual case that falls under it, then it would seem futile for the faculty of reason to try to "account" for this sort of primordial kindness as a phenomenon.

An unpredictable eruption of senseless kindness in what CBA would call a "market transaction" reminds us of the fundamental *uncertainty* of human action. It tends to confirm Hannah Arendt's trenchant observation "that we never quite know what we are doing when we begin to act into the web of interrelationships and mutual dependencies that constitute the field of action" (Arendt, 2005, p. 56). Despite (or perhaps because of) the ubiquity of the uncertainty to which Arendt refers, responsible decision-oriented technologies such as CBA are always seeking to achieve the most efficient and clearest possible technical solution to difficult social problems. As a result, such technologies by their very nature cannot see the point or value of studying any human behaviors that do not generate "data" that might contribute to some definitive solution to a pre-made problem.

Seen from this hyper-technological point of view, if the possibility of an unintended consequence (either positive or negative) can be foreseen, then its value can be calculated and incorporated into the analysis. And if this result cannot be foreseen—well then, it should be ignored precisely because of its incalculability. Economist Richard Zerbe has given a perfect description of CBA's general attitude toward any information that does not contribute to an efficient public policy solution. He puts what is at stake in terms of a competition between different *methods of decision-making*:

> If the government uses [the] KH or KHZ [criteria of efficiency] for evaluating all of its decisions instead of using some other criteria[,] it has the best chance of making *all* of the people in a society better off "at the end of the day."
>
> (Zerbe, 2001, p. 28)

This way of talking confirms that the social science discipline called CBA belongs to what Bernard Stiegler calls the modern "technocratic state." Such a state, Stiegler says, "no longer has as its aim either the encouragement of communicative action or the achievement of a critical distance toward purposive-rational action"; instead, the technocratic state's "activity consists in finding solutions to questions of a technical nature, those that escape public discussion" (Stiegler, 1998, p. 12).

By characterizing policymaking as a purely technical problem, CBA overlooks the possibility that other "methods" of policymaking might actually constitute *ends* and not just means—that they might express the kind of rationality that Weber calls *Wertrationalität*: behavior that is believed to possess intrinsic value or inherent rightness, even if it does not lead to policy outcomes that are efficient when measured by the sum of people's pre-behavior preferences (Brubaker, 1991, pp. 51–53). In short, CBA fails to consider the possibility that the coming-and-being-together of political discussion and mutual learning about a policy problem might be part of the good life itself, if not also a catalyst that can reshape the terms of the problem and people's feelings about it. Zerbe's above-quoted remark about competing "criteria" for decision-making is revealing. It suggests that CBA practitioners conceive of decision-making methods in terms of comparative *disutility*—costs that (regrettably) must be borne in the pursuit of solutions to problems the contents of which remain unaffected by the way in which they are decided.

Defining policymaking solely in terms of the relative costs of competing methods for making the mass of people in general better off in the future cannot explain a fact that is well known to any law professor who has ever tried, in good faith, to teach the insights of law-and-economics in the classroom. I am referring to the fact that many (even most) law students seem viscerally averse to reducing problems of decision-making—legal, political, or otherwise—to the *ex ante* calculation of costs and benefits according to a mathematicized criterion of efficiency. (For the careful empiricists among you, I am afraid I can only offer as proof of this fact more than a quarter century of my own experience in teaching contracts and torts to first-year law students, as well as a considerable amount of hearsay evidence from conversations with colleagues who tell me they have often witnessed the same kind of reluctance in their students.)

What can or should CBA do with a *preference to avoid the use of CBA itself* in favor of, say, deontological modes of decision-making such as Kant's Categorical

Imperative, or even just asking decision-makers to "follow the law" or "be fair" in a more or less evenhanded way?

Lon Fuller's well-developed procedural theory of natural law shows that people can have moral preferences for the *way* decisions are made that are at least as strong as their preferences for the contents of those decisions (Fuller, 1969). Since there is no reason in principle why CBA ought not to apply to procedures as well as to substance, the worrying possibility that this presents for the continued existence of CBA as a discipline is obvious. If the preference *for* exclusively deontological modes of decision-making (and *against* teleological methods such as CBA) is or becomes sufficiently widespread in society, and if the preference is backed up by a large enough aggregate WTP, then it would seem to follow from CBA's own methods and criteria that it ought to go out of business.

The acts of senseless kindness described in *Life and Fate* do not call for any political action, just as they do not preach anything that could be called an ethical doctrine. On the contrary: "The scenes of goodness in an inhuman world are disseminated throughout the book, without transforming it into a virtuous book for virtuous readers" (Levinas, 2001, p. 81). The many simple acts of kindness that appear in the course of the novel are "exterior to all system," as Levinas says, and they leave the mind to grasp (if it can) a kind of "ethics without ethical system" in which "the only thing that remains is individual goodness, from man to man." One can even interpret *Life and Fate* as an argument *against* any effort to rationalize or systematize the kind of behavior that the book celebrates:

> [Grossman] thinks that the "small goodness" from one person to his fellowman is lost and deformed as soon as it seeks organization and universality and system, as soon as it opts for doctrine, a treatise of politics and theology, a party, a state, and even a church. Yet it remains the sole refuge of the good in being. Unbeaten, it undergoes the violence of evil, which, as small goodness, it can neither vanquish nor drive out. A little kindness going only from man to man, not crossing distances to get to the places where events and forces unfold! A remarkable utopia of the good or the secret of its beyond.
>
> (Levinas, 1998a, p. 230)

CBA concerns itself with the formal and static structure of preferences conceived as "things" rather than with the fluidity of human phenomena as they show themselves through time (Sunstein, 2002, p. 20). Levinas undoubtedly would have been horrified at the prospect of any social-scientific effort to account for the phenomenon of senseless kindness by reducing it to a political factoid the numerical value of which could then be compared with the numerical values of other political factoids. He would have been horrified, in other words, by any description of ethics that reduced it to the expression of a well-formed "preference" for acting considerately toward others, either for its own sake or as a mere strategy for inducing social cooperation to achieve other ends.

Seen from the point of view of the ontologically particular, an "event" is always singular and never universal. It is always open to—indeed is inescapably nurtured by—what Alain Badiou (2003, p. 56) calls the "surprise of the unexpected." CBA attempts to smother the unexpected with an intervention that violently abstracts preferences from the unpredictable context of their formation. And there is no better example of this than CBA's interpretation of the phenomenon of human kindness as the expression of a well-formed "preference for altruism."

The "preference for altruism"

Calculated kindness versus senseless kindness

Recent CBA scholarship has made a determined effort to transform the so-called preference for altruism into a monetary value that can be measured in terms of the market-oriented categories of WTP and WTA. Zerbe (2001, pp. 24–26), for instance, argues that CBA should henceforth define as a "good" *any* value or outcome for which there is a willingness to pay money, and he criticizes the traditional economic literature for its arbitrary tendency to ignore the possibility that some (or many) people are actually willing to sacrifice their own interests to "purchase" more fairness and kindness toward others. On this question he is certainly correct, if only from the traditional academic perspective that values "objectivity" above all else. Any economic analysis that ignores "soft" goods like fairness that people are actually willing to pay for risks being accused of overt political bias. But notice: the "regard for others" that Zerbe identifies as a good must be theoretically capable of showing itself as a preference *before* the project or transaction whose net social value it is the job of the economist to ascertain. Otherwise, it could not figure into anyone's rational *ex ante* calculations about the proper decision to make.

Art performance critic Margaret Spillane tells a story about Samuel Beckett that nicely illustrates the category of such a well-defined *ex ante* preference for altruism:

> Beckett was well-known among Paris street people as an easy touch. Once while on a stroll with a friend, a beggar offered his tale of misfortune, and the playwright produced a generous offering. Shouldn't you consider the possibility, the friend asked, that the beggar was taking advantage of you? Replied Beckett: "I just couldn't take the chance."
>
> (Spillane, 2006, p. 22)

This amusing story is consistent with the commonly held view that some people are by nature more kindly than others, while some are by nature inclined more toward what Hobbes (1914, p. 87) calls "our natural Passions, that carry us to Partiality, Pride, Revenge, and the like." The view that every act of altruism is the ineluctable consequence of a constant character trait or disposition is dogmatic and pre-critical, however. Character is not always destiny. Just as the most compassionate person among us can sometimes act cruelly, so too even the most inveterate of rogues can sometimes surprise us by committing an unexpected act of kindness.

In contrast to the well-bounded, conscious, and even calculating preference for altruism displayed in the foregoing story about Beckett and the beggar, the sort of kindness that Grossman described in *Life and Fate* could not in principle show itself before the deed. It could not, by its very nature or definition, fall within the category of what CBA would call someone's *ex ante* set of preferences or utility function.

Senseless kindness displays a peculiar property in the way it comes into being: it does not implement an earlier preference for altruism, but rather *erupts* without prior warning in a way that squarely contradicts the actor's previous preference for the very opposite of altruism. This kind of behavior is "senseless" in the precise sense that it contradicts the subjective claims of instrumental reason, all of which argue against it on the basis of what is known about the actor's pre-behavior preferences. In short, you don't have to have a generally altruistic character, or even to have acted altruistically ever before, in order to experience this phenomenon. Even the biggest jerk imaginable is capable of manifesting it.

If one wanted to formulate that which the phenomenon in question "exemplifies" in terms of a social-scientific principle or natural law, then it would be just this: The formation and expression of individual preferences is *relatively* indeterminate and inconstant—relative, that is, to the classical CBA assumption that there is a determinate and constant connection between a well-formed *ex ante* preference and its immediate expression in this or that particular social context. The existence of the phenomenon of senseless kindness shows that preferring X at t_1 does not necessarily mean that one will prefer it at t_2, even in cases where the temporal separation between t_1 and t_2 is miniscule. The point is not just that people often change their minds about what they want. *The point is that they can, and do, change their minds and their behaviors as a consequence of being-with-others in particular and surprising ways.*

The other as a "transaction cost"

From the "*ex ante* point of view" that informs the modern quest for economic rationality, the possibility that this kind of unpredictable encounter might pop up to disturb an actor's well-thought-out plans and projects involves what CBA (if not the actor) would classify as a "transaction cost." In other words, mainstream economic theory interprets a previously unwanted face-to-face encounter between people as a burden rather than a benefit, and it counts the reduction of transaction costs as an a priori gain rather than the loss of an opportunity for something new and unexpected to emerge.

Mainstream economic theory nurtures a general political preference for market solutions to individual and social problems (Posner, 2011, p. 16). While the origin of this preference for markets is a normative commitment to efficiency as the proper end of social policy, the preferred means to this end—the market as such—empirically consists in people *coming together* in real or virtual face-to-face encounters. Indeed, the very existence of the discipline of CBA is based on the recognition that there can be significant barriers (transaction costs) that prevent otherwise willing people from coming together to achieve efficiencies. (Sunstein, 2002, p. 9). The idea that the law should mimic hypothetical market solutions when transaction costs prevent real market solutions is simply a corollary of economists' general preference for markets (Posner, 2003, p. 251). Since it generally considers the pursuit of government "projects" to be a second-best solution, CBA argues that public policy ought to be guided, or at least informed, by an analysis of the hypothetical things that people would willingly do with, and to, one another if there were no transaction costs (Zerbe, 2001, pp. 14–33).

The phenomenon of senseless kindness, together with the general principle of the relative social inconstancy of preferences that it illustrates, poses an acute challenge to this way of thinking. Senseless kindness implies that the coming-together process is not just, or at least not necessarily, a "cost." If we take this phenomenon as a symbol for the general thesis that something unexpected yet desirable (to the individual) can arise whenever human beings interact, it means that the coming together itself can be a transformative event.

Habermas (1984, vol. 1, pp. 17–20) contends that there is an intimate connection between coming together in discussion and the very concept of rationality itself. In earnest discussion about what is to be done, the participants make claims that they attempt to vindicate and criticize through arguments. As Habermas says, "in virtue of their criticizability, rational expressions also admit of improvement"; this implies that to be closed to argument—to be "deaf" to it—is to be irrational. In attempting to ground our own claims and preferences we learn from others, and in learning from others we expose ourselves to the possibility of change. Thus, says Habermas (p. 20):

> We call a person rational who interprets the nature of his desires and feelings . . . in the light of culturally established standards of value, but especially if he can adopt a reflective attitude to the very value standards through which desires and feelings are interpreted.

Habermas's point is that by bringing us to see certain aspects of a problem that we did not see before, the "coming together" of discussion changes us, and thus can change what we prefer.

Of course, not all instances of people coming together involve the prospect of rational and open-minded argumentation. In many routine economic transactions, an increase in transaction costs would admittedly burden the parties without any realistic chance of significantly changing them or their preferences: one thinks of such simple examples as paying bridge tolls and reconciling bank statements. If CBA limited the range of application of its theory to these kinds of human interactions, however, it would be of limited utility to policymakers trying to decide questions of a distinctly political nature, such as whether abortion should be made more or less available to women, whether the law should allow or disallow the cloning of human beings, and whether there should be more or less offshore drilling for oil.

In situations like these, one could argue that what we need is *more* discussion (more "transaction costs"), not less—more opportunity for people to test their preferences, and possibly change them, as a consequence of their interactions with others. To walk a mile in the other's shoes, as the saying goes, does not necessarily reveal an *ex ante* preference for altruism. Rather, the attitude that the saying recommends is a necessary precondition for any deliberation in the political sphere that aspires to become rational in the largest and most important sense of the word, namely, the rational evaluation of one's own ultimate ends in light of knowledge about the ultimate ends of others. Socrates famously said that the unexamined life is not worth living (*Apology* 38*a*). But one need not go as far as he does to conclude that at least an unexamined *preference* is not worth having.

If open discussion of the sort Habermas envisages is the quintessence of rationality, then the preferences of those who exhibit senseless kindness in *Life and Fate* undergo the kind of metamorphosis that is, if you will, pre-rational, and that is triggered by what CBA would call the "transaction cost" of a face-to-face encounter. All of a sudden there appears, out of nowhere, what CBA would undoubtedly recognize as a brand new set of preferences or utility function.

Before the Germans entered her hut, for example, the first Russian peasant mentioned above would probably have been "willing to pay" for all the enemy soldiers in her village, wounded and unwounded alike, to be strangled; indeed, she says as much herself, the very instant before she finds herself giving water and comfort to the gut-shot German who is lying on her cot (Grossman, 1985, p. 409). An intended course of action that threatens to become its own negation once the transaction costs of its implementation are incurred is, to say the least, a very curious kind of revealed preference. Although economists sometimes say that inefficiency arises only in dynamic societies (Zerbe, 2001, p. 66), the emergence of unexpected choices as a consequence of interpersonal contact seems to show that certain kinds of *efficiencies* can arise only when dynamic conditions change people's preferences. One way or another, one feels entitled to ask what the prospect of this kind of plasticity in preferences and behavior means for the concept of economic rationality itself.

Economic rationality and the problem of selecting the right "ex *ante*"

Economists tend to interpret transaction costs as something negative or bad—regrettable technical barriers that obstruct otherwise efficient transfers of resources. Conventional economic concepts of efficiency are predicated on the possibility of comparing alternative states of affairs according to some measure of individual welfare—usually a person's WTPs and WTAs in response to possible changes in her present situation. The most uncompromising of these concepts—and the starting point for constructing all other definitions—is "Pareto optimality," together with its corollary concept, "Pareto improvement":

> A Pareto optimum is a state of affairs such that no one can be made better off without making someone else worse off. A change in the economy is said to represent a Pareto improvement if at least one person is made better off as a result of the change and no person is made worse off.
>
> (Zerbe, 2001, p. 66)

To illustrate: if *A*'s WTP for a good owned by *B* is $100, and *B*'s WTA for this good is $90, then in the famously hypothetical "world without transaction costs" that was first introduced to economic theory by Ronald Coase (1960), *A* will acquire the good from *B* at some price between $90 and $100, and, in the absence of negative externalities—costs to others that the parties to this transaction do not have to bear—the resulting state of affairs will necessarily be a Pareto improvement over its predecessor. This conclusion follows mathematically from CBA's methodological decision to measure "better off" and "worse off" *solely* with reference to *A*'s WTP and *B*'s WTA, even though it is well known that a person's revealed preferences are in large part a function of her existing level of wealth (Adler and Posner, 2006, pp. 130–131). It is important to remember that CBA accepts the existing, legally maintained distribution of entitlements in society as a pre-given "fact" (Zerbe, 2001, p. 27). The result, according to economist Paul Heyne (1988, p. 56), is that "economic theory takes for granted, far more extensively than economists seem generally to recognize, the normative force of established rights and obligations."

The normative validity or acceptability of CBA's particular policy recommendations thus depends on not questioning the partly legal, partly empirical distributions of property rights that co-determine people's "psychological reference point," as Zerbe (2001, p. 83) puts it, for their subjective beliefs about ownership, and that therefore also underlie the relevant supply and demand functions. But the foregoing hypothetical example can also be used to illustrate another difficulty with the Pareto criterion of efficiency, even if one assumes that *A*, *B*, and everyone else in society possesses an unimpeachably fair share of wealth before ever coming into contact with one another in the market.

If, all of a sudden, it would cost the parties jointly more than $10 in transaction costs (travel expenses, negotiation costs, etc.) to complete this transfer, then economic theory predicts that it will not happen, since no price between $90 and $100 would defray the joint costs necessary to effectuate the exchange (Cooter and Ulen, 1988, p. 85). Given perfect information—a necessary condition of there being zero transaction costs in all other respects—*A* and *B* will both know that at least one of them will have to expend more in transaction costs to arrive at any deal than that party's expected gain from making the exchange. Hence they will not even attempt to reach a bargain, despite the fact that both of them would be better off if the underlying exchange were to occur. In *The Problem of Social Cost* (1960), Coase famously drew attention to cases such as this to illustrate his thesis that the existence of transactions costs sometimes (or often) leads to Pareto-inefficient allocations of resources.

When it comes to assessing the phenomenon of senseless kindness from an economic point of view, however, matters are not quite as straightforward as our hypothetical example suggests. The phenomenon of senseless kindness shows that there are real situations in which being made to incur otherwise cost-prohibitive transaction costs can transform the very opposite of an actor's original preference into the good that she *now* desires. It is as if a person's willingness to *sell* her last piece of bread suddenly and unaccountably became her willingness to *pay* something for that bread to be transferred to another. One might even generalize and restate this kind of situation as a formal paradox: There is a class of cases such that the circumstance of incurring the inefficiency of excessive transaction costs—owing to a prior miscalculation or to compulsion—leads to a transaction that nonetheless *becomes* efficient solely because the costs of engaging in it have produced a transformation of the parties' preferences.

Even more generally, one could say that the possibility of the socially unexpected *as such* puts into question the very nature of economic rationality. One need not be a sociologist to recognize that senseless kindness, coming as it does to disrupt prior preferences and redirect action away from their realization, makes visible the challenge that the interconnected phenomena of temporality and human sociality pose to the definition of the so-called "*ex ante*" in economic theory.

Richard Posner (2011, p. 51) correctly observes that "to an economist people who will not make exchanges that improve their net welfare are irrational." But it is also true that today's economic theorists do not assess an individual's net welfare in terms of universal criteria, or cardinal utility; they think that it is for the individual herself to decide which goods, or bundle of goods, will make her "best off" relative to her preferences (Cooter and Ulen, 1988, pp. 17–20). As I have noted already, recent economic theory has introduced the altruistic regard for others into CBA—a theoretical move that thankfully dispels the widely held misconception that the criterion of economic rationality is satisfied only by choices that maximize an individual's selfish material interests. After all, if I would be willing to pay for a more equal distribution of resources in society, despite the fact that my own monetary income might decline as a consequence, there is no non-dogmatic (or at least non-normative) point of view that can reproach my choice as irrational.

This relatively modest theoretical concession to the possibility of a WTP for altruistic ends is not the same as claiming, as John Rawls (1971, p. 151) does, that the concept of rational self-regard logically *entails* that social institutions be arranged so as to maximize the portion of the least well off in society. Modern economic theory purports to be value-neutral. It makes no claims whatsoever about which substantive values are or should be accepted as universally rational. Its presuppositions about the nature of rationality correspond to Max Weber's well-known schema of rational action: (1) an action is regarded as *subjectively rational* if it is directed toward a goal that the *actor* values, whatever that goal may be; and (2) an action is taken to be *objectively rational* only if the means the actor uses to achieve her chosen end costs her (net) no more than other available means would have done (Brubaker, 1984, pp. 53–55).

For CBA, as for Weber, "subjective rationality" is a purely descriptive category. A given actor just "has" whatever preferences she has, and for whatever reason she has them. Whereas the category of "objective rationality," although part of an external evaluation of the actor's conduct, is strictly limited to assessing the effectiveness of the technique the actor has adopted to achieve her particular end, *whatever it may be.*

To put this another way, CBA believes it is required to accept individual preferences as primordial givens for purposes of its analyses of net social welfare. As a matter of principle, WTPs and WTAs are supposed to be functions of what people just happen to prefer at any given point in time, and never functions of what a CBA analyst thinks they must or ought to prefer. In theory, the decision of a monk to get rid of all his money and possessions after taking a vow of poverty is just as "economically rational" as the average wage-earner's choice to work overtime in order to acquire more of the very kinds of things that the monk is so earnestly trying to give away.

The methodological stipulation that all preferences are radically subjective underscores how important it is for CBA to select the "right" point in time to sum them up, for people's preferences can and often do change with the passage of time and the accumulation of new experiences. If I prefer to pay $1 for an apple rather than a candy bar at t_1, and this point in time is taken to be the relevant *ex ante*, then my subsequent behavior at t_2 of using the money to buy a candy bar instead of an apple appears irrational. On the other hand, if we take t_2 as the relevant *ex ante*, then my *new* preference for a candy bar over an apple makes my act of purchasing it look rational. It all depends on which "when" the analyst selects.

The problem of selecting the right *ex ante* becomes even more difficult in the context of trying to give a theoretical account of the phenomenon of senseless kindness. Consider, for instance, the two specific examples of the phenomenon mentioned earlier. As of which *ex ante* should the Russian women's preferences (and hence their welfare) be determined: the *ex ante* that *precedes* the moment of facing the hated German soldiers toward whom the women will subsequently act "irrationally" by displaying senseless kindness, or the *ex ante* that all of a sudden bursts forth to reflect their new desire to be kind to the needy human beings whom they face, and that therefore shows their behavior to be "rational"? It is said that the proper purpose of CBA is "*to provide useful information to the decision maker, and not to furnish the decision itself*" (Zerbe, 2001, p. 16) (emphasis added). If this is so, then what "useful information" should CBA provide to the decision-makers in these cases, in as much as the possibility of an unpredictable social transformation of their preferences lurks just around the temporal corner, so to speak, of any given analysis of their *ex ante* WTPs and WTAs?

Method matters. The way we approach any given subject matter determines not just *how* we proceed but also *what* we look for and find. What CBA looks for and finds is a purely mathematical relationship between WTPs and WTAs. Calling these numbers themselves manifestations of individual preferences, CBA proceeds to sum them up and then recommend (or at least provide "information" about) hypothetical end states according to a test that most mainstream economists and lawyers accept as the definition of "economic efficiency": the Kaldor–Hicks (KH) criterion. While KH can be expressed in a variety of ways, for ease of exposition I will adopt the classical definition given by Boadway and Bruce (1984, p. 97): "State *a* is preferable to another state if, in the *other* state, it is *not* possible, hypothetically, to carry out lump-sum redistribution so that everyone could be made as well off as in state *a*."

Also known as the "potential compensation" and "wealth maximization" test, KH arose in response to the impracticability of using the Pareto criterion of efficiency as a tool of public policy (Zerbe, 2001, p. 4). The latter requires *both* that at least one person will be made better off by the move from the status quo to the proposed new state *and* that no one will be made worse off. Adding the notion of "potential compensation" to the mix assures that the winners in the new state are able, in theory, to compensate the losers for their losses, with net gains remaining that improve the winners' welfare relative to their previous positions. In other words, KH allows for efficient losers, so to speak, and is aimed at increasing net *social* welfare. This is why it is sometimes called the "wealth maximization" test.[4]

The questions posed earlier about certain instances of senseless kindness as depicted in *Life and Fate* expose the necessity of selecting the appropriate *ex ante* for purposes of applying the KH test to any given situation. A tool or criterion of public policy that asks *what* individuals would be willing to pay or accept for a change in the status quo is useless without a temporal reference point: a determination of *when* they would be willing to open their wallets or part with their possessions. Without a defensible criterion for selecting such a point in time, choosing one over the other would be wholly arbitrary. This observation about method shows that the above-noted definition of the KH criterion of economic efficiency contains an implicit philosophy of time and history. The notion of a "state" in which people "have" preferences not only presupposes the existence of a discrete point in time at which their WTPs (to change one state to another state) and WTAs (to let the change occur) can be measured—it also interprets time itself as a mere sequence of "states," each of which, when viewed in isolation, is static and fully determinable.

CBA refers to the original state-in-time of a given series of states as the relevant "*ex ante*" (Latin for "from before"). Since the problem that CBA wants to solve is whether a move from one state to another state would increase net social welfare, CBA answers the question, "Before what?" with the concept of the "project" (Zerbe, 2001, p. 16). A *project* consists of all of the payments and counter-payments that would have to be made to achieve the hypothetical end state under review—an idealized new state that either is or is not more efficient than the *ex ante* state, depending on how the numbers come out.

Thomas Kuhn's study of the structure of scientific revolutions (1970) famously shows that well-established scientific methods tend to assert their hegemony over every problem that falls within their domain, including new problems that seem to question the accuracy of their findings or the legitimacy of their conclusions. So it is with CBA's analysis of any public policy problem in which the "individual preference for altruism" plays a role. The typical account of a given project's efficiency or inefficiency begins with the stipulation that some people in society would be willing to pay, up to some maximum amount, for the project to proceed. Others are in a position to block the project because the existing distribution of entitlements requires that they be "bought off" (paid their minimum asking price) before the project can be done. Still others would be willing to pay, again up to some maximum amount, for the project not to proceed at all. All three sets of hypothetical payments must be quantified and compared.

At present, the practitioners of CBA take the socioeconomic significance of these hypothetical "factual" findings to be self-evident. They believe, for example, that if the sum of all individual WTPs in favor of a proposed project exceeds the sum of all individual WTAs to allow it to go forward plus WTPs to stop it, then society as a whole would be better off (relative to the total bankable preferences of its members) if the project were to proceed; if, on the other hand, the same process yields a negative sum, then the proposed project should be defeated. Or, as common sense would have it: if the project will increase the total size of the social pie, then do it; if it would cause the pie to shrink, then don't do it.

An important distinction is missing from this commonsensical interpretation of CBA's findings. There is a critical difference between the existence of a fact and the significance of the method that is used to ascertain and interpret all facts of its type. Thus, there is no doubt that CBA's "preference for altruism" can be a reasonably accurate description of some other-regarding behavior, such as the anecdote noted earlier about Samuel Beckett's reasons for giving money to a beggar. But if a preference for altruism is one kind of thing, then reducing all similar-looking behavior to a process in which individuals first decide to act by selecting from a "marketplace" of possible comportments, and then read off how to act on the basis of that selection, is something else altogether. In short, what is missing from CBA's let's-increase-the-size-of-the-pie interpretation of social welfare is any serious reflection on the difference between a fact and what Edmund Husserl, the founder of phenomenology, called the "meaning" (*Sinn*) of a fact.

The significance of market "facts": CBA's inherent antipathy to democratic politics

CBA is a *mathematical* social science. Simply put, this means that it determines and expresses its objects of inquiry—human preferences for and against projects that alter the status quo—in terms of numbers. It does this by counting up the number of fungible "dollar bids," so to speak, that it thinks would be made, both pro and con, if the project in question were to be put on the auction block in front of everyone in society. The discipline's basic regulative idea is that economic and political deductions based on these numbers (e.g., "\$2 is more than \$1, therefore the project would be inefficient") sum up or reflect, however roughly, all the particularities of people's needs, wants, and desires.

This arithmetical approach represents a radical transformation of the discipline of political economy into econometrics, and the ethical significance of that transformation should not be underestimated. The more the surface of reality is seen to be coated, so to speak, with an oil slick comprised of numerical relations, the greater is the temptation not to look at the painful particularities lying underneath. Social psychologists have called this phenomenon the "collapse of compassion," and perhaps its most notorious expression, attributed to Stalin, is "the death of one person is a tragedy; the death of one million is a statistic" (Payne, 2010). Although CBA's methodology contributes in its own special way to this insidious collapse, the discipline is hardly unique. It is part and parcel of modernity's general tendency to conceive of itself everywhere in terms of what Husserl called a *mathesis universalis*, a universal account of everything modeled on numerical relationships and modes of expression.

Husserl's analysis of the general social transformation of qualities into quantities began with the historical fact that modern algebra, following Descartes, had reduced the status of geometrical thinking from that of an origin for significant descriptions of spatial–temporal idealities to that of a calculating machine (1970, pp. 44–46). He noticed, for example, that modern algebra had replaced the ancient *idea* of a circle as an area that is inscribed by a straight line of determinate length as it rotates 360 degrees around a single point in two-dimensional space with the more rigorous and mathematically useful *formula* for a circle, $x^2 + y^2 = r^2$ (Downing, 1995, pp. 41–42). But note: the ancient idea of a circle, especially when supplemented by a Euclidean construction by compass and rule, immediately evokes a mental image; the formula for a circle does not.

It would be wrong to think of Husserl as a naïve mathematical Luddite. He fully conceded that the foregoing methodological change in the way geometry was practiced constituted a clear advancement in mathematical technique. But at the same time, he also observed that the change brought with it a major, and not altogether benign, transformation in the *meaning* of mathematics and calculation.

Kant (1998, p. 158) had attempted to demonstrate that the proofs of classical Euclidean geometry more or less correspond to, or mirror, our concrete intuitions of space. But in *The Crisis of European Sciences and Transcendental Phenomenology*, his last major work, Husserl (1970, pp. 43–46) showed how modern, algebraic geometry had overturned the traditional relationship between geometric proof and human intuition by making the concept of proof itself correspond to a set of purely numerical configurations. Husserl's interpretation of the significance of this ultimately technological "process of method-transformation" is worth quoting at some length:

> In algebraic calculation, one lets the geometric signification recede into the background as a matter of course, indeed one drops it altogether; one calculates, remembering only at the end that the numbers signify magnitudes. Of course one does not calculate "mechanically," as in ordinary numerical calculation; one thinks, one invents, one makes discoveries – but they have acquired, unnoticed, a displaced, "symbolic" meaning. . . . Like arithmetic itself, in technically developing its methodology [algebraic geometry] is drawn into a process of transformation, through which it becomes a sort of *technique*; that is, it becomes a mere art of achieving, through a calculating technique according to technical rules, results the genuine sense of whose truth can be attained only by concretely intuitive thinking actually directed at the subject matter itself. But now [only] those modes of thought, those types of clarity which are indispensable for a technique as such, are in action. One operates with letters and with signs for connections and relations (+, X, =, etc.), according to *rules of the game* for arranging them together in a way essentially not different, in fact, from a game of cards or chess. Here the *original* thinking that genuinely gives meaning to this technical process and truth to the correct results (even the "formal truth" peculiar to the formal *mathesis universalis*) is excluded.
>
> (Husserl, 1970, pp. 44–46)

In this passage, Husserl makes a very specific philosophical point that echoes a similar one made by Spinoza (1955, pp. 24–27) more than 200 years earlier, and that foreshadows some of the ideas that would also appear in Wittgenstein's mature philosophy of mathematics (Shanker, 1987, pp. 120–160). The point is really quite simple: the significance of mathematical propositions (what we call mathematical knowledge) depends upon more than just a correct series of calculations. A mathematical proposition may be proved, but it is not *understood* unless and until it can be viewed with perspicuity—unless and until concrete images give meaning to the symbols in the proof (Husserl, 1970, pp. 40–45). As Wittgenstein (1967, p. 45e) puts it:

> Perspicuity is part of proof. If the process by means of which I get a result were not surveyable, I might indeed make a note that this number is what comes out – but what fact is this supposed to confirm for me? I don't know "what is supposed to come out."

Taking Husserl's distinction between facts and the imagistic significance or meaning of facts as our clue, it becomes possible to interpret CBA as a quintessential manifestation of what Husserl's most famous student, Martin Heidegger (1977, p. 19), would come to call "the framework" (*Das Ge-stell*). According to Heidegger, *the framework* is none other than an entire orientation to being-in-the-world: it subjects the natural and social worlds to the imperatives of mastery and possession according to purely technological modes of thinking. It goes without saying that pre-modern humans also desired to master and possess elements of their environment. But only since relatively recently in human history have human beings sought to master and control everything on the basis of a universally correct set of procedures.

Imprisoned inside the complex lattices of the framework, modern human beings devote themselves to the planning and calculating of everything in the world, to such a high degree that reality itself is allowed to appear only within the horizon of what can be calculated (Heidegger, 1969, p. 35). CBA is but one manifestation of this global phenomenon. It projects a *mathesis universalis* over human relationships, and it identifies the essence of human rationality with calculation. In practicing CBA, the "I think" of the Cartesian subject (*cogito, ergo sum*) finds objectivity in purely arithmetical relations, in the comparison of relevant numerical data. Objectivity, as thus determined, permits conclusions to be drawn and political action to be oriented on the basis of criteria that present themselves as being completely objective and apolitical.

Among other things, this means that CBA does not conceive of a political project as the ongoing product of the complex and often chaotic give-and-take of interpersonal dialog and persuasion. The hypothetical project about which people are supposed to have measurable WTPs and WTAs does not have to be made up by them, and indeed it almost never is. Columnist and political commentator Eric Alterman recently noted that political campaigns are almost never about real public policy choices, but rather are about "offering hypothetical solutions that will likely never be tested by reality. Contradictions and compromises are simply wished away" (*The Nation*, August 3, 2015, p. 6). The project as CBA conceives of it is similar: it is a crude cartoon of a nonexistent state of affairs whose sketchy contents are usually determined by politicians or interest groups eager to peddle it to the public, and whose implementation will inevitably involve many contradictions and compromises that no one will ever put to *another* round of hypothetical "dollar bidding." CBA interprets the project as a hypothesis whose ideality is firmly secured in advance by some human agency or other so that it may then be sold to the highest bidders in a "market" that determines once and for all what should be done.

The quotation marks around the word *market* in the previous paragraph are meant to indicate that CBA's summing-up of WTPs and WTAs makes for a virtual rather than a real market, just as the "project" as such represents only a hypothetical state of affairs. The very *raison d'être* of CBA is to gather information about possibilities for which existing, real markets do not provide answers. CBA's virtual market, governed by a rigorously mathematical conception of efficiency, becomes the framework that decision-makers are supposed to impose on the concrete flow of historical time. It follows that CBA cannot be adequately understood if it is conceived of merely as a means—a simple "practical measure" for "practical people," as Richard Zerbe (2001, p. 1) puts it. However useful and pragmatic it may appear to be on the surface, CBA must also be understood ontologically—that is, as *a particular way of revealing what is real*. Its transformation of qualities into quantities does not simply apply a neutral method to pre-methodological "facts." Rather, CBA's stipulations determine in advance what counts *as* a fact.

Intellectually speaking, the conflict between politics and philosophy in Western thought, which began with Plato's account of the trial of Socrates (Arendt, 2005, pp. 5–39), reached its apogee with Hegel's critique of democracy. For Hegel, the radical separation of the individual from the state in the modern world means that democracy is impossible—that it implies or unduly risks a complete dissolution of the state into purely private interests, and therefore that the existence of a wise monarchical or tyrannical ruler is necessary to articulate the universal and preserve it from the interested onslaughts of the particular (Hyppolite, 1996, pp. 64–65). When democratic politics is seen from a jaundiced and mistrustful point of view such as this, it can always appear as a mere means in the service of the well-formed selfish ends of interested persons and groups (Kelman, 1987, pp. 247–249).

This point of view on democracy burdens all political interventions into civil life with the a priori suspicion that they will make most people worse off at the end of the day with reference to individual preferences that are themselves regarded as pre- or a-political. Ronald Reagan (1988) distilled this suspicion to its essence when he uttered the following infamous remark in one of his speeches: "There seems to be an increasing awareness of something we Americans have known for some time: that the ten most dangerous words in the English language are, 'Hi, I'm from the Government, and I'm here to help'."

In her book *The Promise of Politics* (2005), Hannah Arendt made the argument that politics, in the largest sense of the word, is not just a means but also an end in itself—that it is the never-ending endeavor of human beings learning to live together and share a finite earth. This thesis is completely foreign to CBA's way of thinking. Seen from Arendt's point of view, what CBA would call "transaction costs" in this sort of politics are not prima facie deadweight losses imposed from without on preferences that would otherwise exist without politics. On the contrary, the category of "political interactions" in her sense is what constitutes the very reality of individual opinions, at least when the phenomenon of preference formation is classified as a concrete, rather than an abstract, manifestation of human life.

If the ultimate nucleus of politics is supposed to consist of individuals and their choices, as some forms of democratic liberalism maintain, then it must also be recognized that "choices are manifest at particular points in time, but individuals have ongoing identities" (Kelman, 1987, p. 130). To express this point more precisely: the ontological truth of a person's unrevealed political preferences is not what her WTPs or WTAs are imagined to be at some arbitrarily selected moment in time. It is, rather, what her preferences are constantly *becoming* as a result of her ongoing interactions and experiences with others.

Arendt's extraordinary idea that genuine deliberative democracy can be an end in itself, rather than just another "method" of decision-making, gamely attempts to reconceive our relationships with others from a model of strife and competition to a model of discussion and cooperation among free people sharing the earth with others as members of a political community. This thesis, however idealistic and utopian it may appear to be when seen from the jaded standpoint of twenty-first century political experience, stands in the sharpest possible contrast to the presuppositions and tendencies of CBA. The contrast reveals a schism that is not only scientific or methodological, but also profoundly political and ethical.

The politics of CBA

Discussing the "project": a means or an end?

It is obvious that human interactions can have many positive, identity-forming effects that go far beyond whatever economically valuable projects they may happen to ratify or initiate. Undoubtedly most CBA practitioners would concede this point with respect to the kinds of relations that typically obtain between lovers, family members and friends, not all of which, by the way, are strictly "voluntary" or "chosen." But the existence of the phenomenon of senseless kindness, and more broadly, the principle of the relative inconstancy of preferences under which it falls, suggests a much larger range of applications for the general thesis that otherwise "costly" human interactions can have significant unscripted, project-altering effects on people's *ex ante* preferences.

According to our inherited view of the political situation in classical Athens, for example, human interactions and discussions in the *agora* were not regarded solely as means to previously established public or private ends. Conceiving of politics in this narrow, modern way would have contradicted the then-prevailing political ideology that it was impermissible to reduce free Athenian citizens to the unequal status of ruler and ruled. Citizens of Athens would have asked, suspiciously: pre-established by whom and on the basis of whose presumptuous assertion of authority? As Arendt (2005, p. 21) interprets them, "The Greeks understood the *polis* as the public-political realm in which men attain their full humanity, their full reality as men, not only because they *are* (as in the privacy of the household) but also because they *appear*." On this interpretation of the Greek ideal of popular democracy, the dialog of free citizens in the *agora* was a necessary step toward the formation of *wise* ends and *wise* citizens. It represented a commitment to what we might today call an unending process of "adult education."

The famous funeral oration of Pericles, as recounted by Thucydides (1982, p. 110)—one which he may or may not have actually given—makes this last point quite explicit. "*Instead of looking on discussion as a stumbling-block in the way of action,*" said Pericles, "*we think it an indispensable preliminary to any wise action at all.*" The thesis that public and private discourse is a *good* thing—that it is not a "stumbling block in the way of action," but rather a necessary precondition for wise action—can be expressed in modern economic terms by the proposition that discursive human interactions are *prima facie* net benefits rather than net costs. I am well aware that it is highly questionable whether Thucydides's account accurately depicts the real political conditions prevailing in mid-fifth century Athens. Be that as it may, however, it is more than a little interesting to note that the general bias of modern economists on the subject of human interactions is the exact opposite of the one that is expressed in the oration.

As I mentioned earlier, modern economic theory interprets project-oriented interpersonal discourse as a *cost* to be minimized rather than as a *good* to be encouraged. According to the standard economic account of transaction costs, the burden of dealing with others, if incurred, will reduce the net value of any resulting transaction. If the burden is not incurred, then this probably means that the underlying exchange would not have been mutually beneficial, or if it was, that the costs of getting together would have exceeded the deal's putative benefits. Either way, the event of interacting with others is conceived of as a stumbling block—perhaps a function of temporary technological limitations, like having to shop in a store instead of online, or at best a costly strategy for acquiring "information" (Harrison, 2003, p. 72).

The presumption that goal-related human interactions are costs rather than benefits is associated with Ronald Coase's enormously influential article *The Problem of Social Cost* (1960). One of the primary implications of Coase's work is that people often arrive at inefficient solutions to social problems "in order to avoid the cost of getting together," as Mitchell Polinsky (2003, p. 15) puts it. This implies that "getting together," at least with strangers and rivals, is something that rational human beings, like troglodytes, would prefer to avoid. Thus, law-and-economics scholars subscribe to the normative idea that legal decisions in disputed cases ought to facilitate private agreements in the future by reducing transaction costs, including "the need . . . to communicate information" (Baird, 2000, p. 61). This point of view tends to interpret human discourse in general as an unwanted burden—an unfortunate "obstacle to cooperation" (Cooter and Ulen, 1988, p. 101) rather than the possible origin of a different kind of cooperation, as in the case of senseless kindness.

CBA echoes the general antipathy to transaction costs that can be found in abundance in the law-and-economics literature. CBA practitioners imagine that we can always know our goals in advance of discussion with others if we are given the right amount of "information," and that this knowledge will automatically sanction the use of the most efficient means for achieving our goals. CBA's calculations cannot accommodate the possibility that our political goals might actually be "up for grabs" so long as we act as social beings during the *polis*-like activity of thinking, talking, and being with one another.

While I do not mean to suggest that we ought to return to the conditions of Athenian democracy during the Periclean era, unjustly built as it was on the backs of slaves and through the legal subordination of women (Kroger, 2004, pp. 919–920), I do want to criticize the thesis that human interactions are presumptively costs that should be avoided or minimized wherever possible. I want to suggest that what economic theory calls the "transaction costs" of human discourse is actually one of the very things that makes us into free and responsible agents in the first place. It also can be one of those face-to-face *ethical* experiences that allows our eyes to see what our hearts would not otherwise grieve over.

There seems to be an internal relation between the capacity for instrumental reason and the capacity for reaching inter-subjective understanding about things and events. An actor's successful use of instrumental reason in a social context implies the ability to make his point of view understood by others whose cooperative actions are necessary to achieve his ends. Habermas (1984, vol. 1, p. 14) calls the latter sort of ability "communicative action," and his analysis suggests that empiricist research traditions such as CBA have put the idea of communicative, social rationality into a kind of intellectual quarantine, leaving only instances of pure instrumental rationality (strategic offers and counteroffers, operational commands, etc.) to be analyzed and measured.

CBA's way of thinking about the relationship between preferences and entitlements rests on the belief that these two spheres are functionally autonomous from one another. It supposes that public institutions such as laws and regulations constitute an externally imposed mechanism within which bargaining in the private sphere transpires. By interpreting time as a succession of static "states," each one of which is chock-full of well-formed preferences, CBA cannot account for the reality of *how* preferences (if any) concerning legal arrangements change, or even how they stay the same. At best, it can impute change or constancy in the law to *what* people prefer, once this has been determined or stipulated by the analyst. Nowhere inside CBA's frame of reference does the possibility appear that legal rules and other public institutions might actually be *unscripted* projects that can include the kind of identity-molding, preference-altering communication with others that thinkers such as Habermas and Arendt imagine.

Communicative action of the latter sort cannot know in advance exactly where it is going. Nor can it guarantee in advance that CBA will be able to bless its outcomes as efficient. *That is its very point and value*, since efficiency requires evaluation according to a prior "state" that, however recently it may have been measured, may no longer be relevant to what people have *now* talked and behaved themselves into wanting. To say that people can talk and behave themselves into wanting something different than they did before they started being together with one another is obviously not the same as saying that this kind of behavior is irrational. On the contrary, human interaction, even if it is sometimes undesired before the fact, gives people the chance to achieve what I will call, with apologies to Kant,[5] *receptive spontaneity*.

Weber's classic metaphor of an iron cage (*ein stahlhartes Gehäuse*) of rationality (Weber, 1976, pp. 123–125) shows that absent ample room for unplanned spontaneity, a social system can become instrumentally rational to the highest degree without necessarily affording the people within it the chance to imagine and pursue a subjectively rational way of life (Sayer, 1991, p. 144). Witness the all-too-familiar phenomena in fully industrialized societies such as the United States and Japan of "living to work" (instead of the other way around), "the rat race," and the consumerist imperative of "keeping up with the Joneses."

Arendt aptly called the threat to receptive spontaneity that comes from modernity's hypertrophied need to seem instrumentally rational at all times the "tyranny of truth" (2005, p. 105). Consider the following rather chilling example of truth's tyranny, taken from the philosophical writings of Herbert Marcuse:

> A man who travels by automobile to a distant place chooses his route from the highway maps. Towns, lakes and mountains appear as obstacles to be bypassed. The countryside is shaped and organized by the highway: what one finds en route is a byproduct or annex of the highway. Numerous signs and posters tell the traveler what to do and think; they even request his attention to the beauties of nature or the hallmarks of history. Others have done the thinking for him, and perhaps for the better. Convenient parking spaces have been constructed where the broadest and most surprising view is open. Giant advertisements tell him when to stop and find the pause that refreshes. And all of this is indeed for his benefit, safety and comfort; he receives what he wants. Business, technics, human needs and nature are welded together into one rational and expedient mechanism. He will fare best who follows its directions, subordinating his spontaneity to the anonymous wisdom which ordered everything for him.
>
> (Marcuse, 1998, p. 46)

To update this anecdote, which was first published in 1941, just replace the man's highway maps with an electronic GPS device. I find this text chilling even (or especially) today because it so accurately reflects what passive sheep people have become to the wolves of their own habitual technological choices. Not only is the man's behavior in Marcuse's example perfectly rational in a technological sense, but the dissolution of all rationality into semi-spontaneous reactions to prescribed mechanical norms means that, from the standpoint of instrumental thinking, only a crank would insist on making journeys in some other, less efficient way. The cold, wet blanket of conformity to the "correct" thing to do makes any dissent that dares question its correctness from the standpoint of its ultimate personal or ethical meaning look like a symptom of mental illness, rather than the expression of an alternative vision of what being rational means. But the self-evident *ex ante* efficiency of the journey the man takes comes at a cost of its own. It loses him the chance to pursue a route meandering through villages and past farms that might actually have been more rewarding to him—indeed, that might have changed what he prefers, *or even who he is*, by virtue of the marginal increase in inter-human contact that it would have required of him.

Highly emblematic of our ever-increasing sheep-like submission to our own well-formed prior preferences is Google's recently announced strategy "to map every last hiking trail and park bench, and then make it easy to find" (*The Economist*, October 27, 2012, p. 9). This horrible strategy efficiently offers to transform the real world into an always-accessible digital world that every individual can use to program, *in advance*, all of his or her future movements in time and space. Even the calculated decision to make a "spontaneous" deviation from one's own previous hiking habits can be planned, again in advance. One need only move purposefully along the trail, smartphone held before one's eyes, toward the hitherto unvisited park bench that is conveniently indicated on the screen.

Suspiciously irrational, when seen from the hyper-efficient perspective of Google's mapping project, is the behavior of the *flâneur*—the aimless wanderer who is always eager to experience something new and unexpected, who might come to "prefer" the kind of experiences (or people) he never knew existed before he stumbled upon them by accident. Also suspicious to instrumental rationality, but nonetheless very real, is what Benjamin (1999, p. 449) calls "the intoxication of empathy" that only the *flâneur* is able to experience as a consequence of his casual, unscripted encounters with social inferiors—the kinds of people with whom a more instrumentally rational mind would never have associated.

Receptive spontaneity, as the term is used here, signifies the capacity to initiate new ideas, understandings, and actions as an unforeseen consequence of our interactions with others. The realm of this sort of spontaneity is the exact opposite of the realm of necessity that CBA constructs in determining the relation between individual ends and the means used for their accomplishment. For CBA, a person's preference for or against project *X automatically* links up with its means, either a measurable WTP to achieve *X*, or a measurable WTP to avoid it. Recall once again the stories of the Russian women in *Life and Fate* whose acts of kindness toward enemy soldiers surprised even (or rather, especially) themselves. CBA's way of thinking about human interactions excludes this sort of spontaneity from consideration. Speaking more generally, it excludes what both Grossman and Levinas considered to be the ultimate origin of all ethics: *the marvelous possibility of being surprised by one's own unplanned acts of kindness towards others.*

To be surprised by oneself

According to Coase (1988, pp. 174–179), the main point of his seminal article 'The Problem of Social Cost' (1960) was not to model reality as it is, but rather to demonstrate theoretically that transaction costs actually *are* incredibly important barriers to achieving KH efficiencies in the real world. His genius was to do this by imagining a world in which no pesky transaction costs *ever* intervened between human preferences and their efficient enactments. Earning him the Nobel Prize in economics in 1991, Coase's brilliant thought experiment also indirectly proves or implies something that is not listed in his prize citation, which justly praises him "for his discovery and clarification of the significance of transaction costs and property rights for the institutional structure and functioning of the economy."

Unmentioned in the citation is the fact that in a world where there are *literally* no transaction costs, people would never have any reason to change their preferences. Not only that, it would be a mystery how they ever could have come to have preferences in the first place. These conclusions seem to follow from the simple fact that in a Coasean world no "costly" interactions with other human beings could ever rise up to affect them. Why ask people anything if you already know what they will say? A stipulated preference in such a world would be like an unimpeded body moving in a perfect vacuum: it would go on forever.

The human capacity for receptive spontaneity would be utterly vestigal in a Coasean world. Ethically speaking, the "closed or solidified meanings" that are presupposed by someone's hatred of another person or class of persons (Nancy, 2014, p. 15) would remain forever closed and solidified, as would any "preference" he might have to harm them or let them suffer. The circle of his fellowship would be closed forever to strangers, whose concerns could not affect him because they are not by definition members of his well-bounded "opportunity set." He would remain permanently chained to his fixed wants and aversions, a mere tool of previously established preferences that he would be helpless to avoid or alter.

The foregoing thought experiment about the relationship between one's preferences and one's capacity for receptive spontaneity is an argument in favor of transaction costs. It is also an argument in favor of Arendt's surprising thesis that politics and freedom are actually the same:

> Only in the freedom of our speaking with one another does the world, as that about which we speak, emerge in its objectivity and visibility from all sides. Living in a real world and speaking with one another about it are basically one and the same. . . . Freedom to depart and begin something new and unheard-of or . . . the freedom to interact in speech with many others and experience the diversity that the world always is in its totality—most certainly was and is not the end purpose of politics . . . something that can be achieved by political means. It is rather the substance and meaning of all things political. In this sense, politics and freedom are identical.
>
> (Arendt, 2005, pp. xxx–xxxi)

Arendt's point is really quite simple: to be *completely* locked within oneself and one's desires is to exist without freedom, in the precise sense of existing without any reason to imagine or begin something new. Never surprised by anything, such a being would be perpetually enslaved to what is boringly familiar to it, like a zoo animal in a cage. It takes talking and being with others to imagine and create new things, new experiences—to disturb the given world and transform it into what it *can* become.

If we use the word *politics* as Arendt (2005, p. viii) does—as another name for the basic human phenomenon of "venturing forth in speech and deed in the company of one's peers, beginning something new whose end cannot be known in advance, founding a public realm (*res publica* or republic), promising and forgiving others"—then CBA's preference (or prejudice) against politics becomes clear. Indeed, it would not be too strong to say that this preference against politics exhibits hostility to freedom itself: not the ontologically impossible kind of freedom *of* choice that knows no community and emerges out of nowhere, but rather the kind of freedom *for* choosing that can only come to those who are able to conceive and begin something new as a consequence of their experiences with others.

By reducing the concept "human being" to a single preference-holding individual and the concept "humanity" to a mere multiple of this singularity, CBA renders itself incapable of accounting for or nurturing human freedom in the latter sense. CBA's methods and presuppositions thus represent more than just a set of semi-arbitrary scientific stipulations—more than just a disposable pragmatic yardstick, so to speak. CBA also constitutes a powerful ideology of human nature, one which pre-orients how we imagine individuals go about (and should go about, if they want to be considered "rational") forming preferences and making choices.

The methods of modern welfare economics were foreshadowed by Rousseau's (in)famous definition of the "general will" (*volonté générale*) as "the grand total of the small differences" in individual wills (Rousseau, 1993b, p. 202). In fact, CBA's faith in the utility of the idea of wealth maximization often eerily resembles Rousseau's confidence in the proposition that summing up "the pluses and minuses [in particular wills] that cancel one another" would produce a decision that "would always be good."

Good (or efficient) *when*, not to mention *at different times*? The question of "when" introduces the problem of change, which in turn raises the prospect of having to coerce the now-unwilling to participate in projects the experts had earlier confirmed as good or efficient. Given what we know about how real human beings behave, the wealth maximization criterion, like the concept of the general will, actually guarantees that coercion will be necessary—that some people will have to be "forced to be free," as Rousseau famously put it (1993b, p. 194). This is true even if (*pace* the KH test itself) compensatory payments are in fact made by the winners to the losers in the full amount of their pre-project maximum WTPs. For there is no guarantee that they will be satisfied *now* with that payment, or that it is not less than what their minimum WTAs would have been had they been originally treated as sellers rather than buyers—owners of entitlements that stand in the way of the project unless and until they are paid off.[6]

Like Rousseau's concept of the general will, CBA's calculations of what is or is not efficient for society as a whole are based on what Isaiah Berlin (2003, p. 48) called a "mythology of the real self, in the name of which I am permitted to coerce people." In the case of CBA, everyone's real self is a self-certain, clear-preference-holding monad that, when lumped together with other similar monads, comprises "society" or "the people." The state, as supreme political authority, can thus seem to base its projects not on naked acts of dictatorial will, not on the will of this or that interest group, but rather on what its white- or tweed-coated economic viziers tell it the people "as a whole" are willing to pay for.

"All things come to be through strife," said Heraclitus (1987, p. 49): a useful reminder that change—which is to say life itself—*always* comes at a "cost," if only the cost of learning to appreciate or desire something new. Without the prospect of change-inducing "costs," the people in Coase's world would lack the capacity to initiate anything new. Lacking spontaneity, they would also lack freedom. Knowing everything there is to be known, and requiring no costly human contact to realize their preferences, the denizens of Coase's world are like Leibniz's perfect monads, which "have no windows, by which anything could come in or go out" (Leibniz, 1934, p. 3).

A world without transaction costs is also a world without politics. A preference against politics is a kind of political theology, in the sense that it is a subjective value to which its supporters cling and for which they are prepared to struggle with others whose values are different. I confess that sometimes it seems to me that CBA aficionados actually believe that Coase's frictionless world is a sort of apolitical Eden from which human beings have fallen, and to which only their faith in the wisdom of CBA can restore them.

The *ends* that the state pursues through the application or threat of legal force are not the same as the *goals* of politics. Political goals, Arendt notes, "are never anything more than the guidelines and directives by which we orient ourselves and which, as such, are never cast in stone, but whose concrete realizations are constantly changing because we are dealing with other people who have goals." The *ends* of politics are altogether different:

> Only when brute force with its arsenal of means is introduced into the space between people—where until that point nothing has passed back and forth except speech, which is devoid of tangible means—do the goals of politics become ends. . . . If a political action that does not stand under the sign of brute force does not achieve its goals . . . that does not render the political action either pointless or meaningless. It cannot be pointless because it never pursued a "point," that is, an end, but has only been directed at goals, more or less successfully; and it is not meaningless because in the back-and-forth of exchanged speech—between individuals and peoples, between states and nations—that space in which everything else that takes place is first created and sustained. What in political language is called a "breakdown in relations" is the abandonment of that in-between space, which all violent action first destroys before it proceeds to annihilate those who live outside of it.
>
> (Arendt, 2005, pp. 192–193)

As harsh as it may sound to say it, the very existence of CBA as an institution represents a fundamental breakdown in political relations in Arendt's sense. It is the tip of the spear of state force in postmodernity, administered through legislation and government bureaucracies, both of which can use CBA's methods to legitimate whatever projects the numbers happen to favor. But as it seeks to guarantee the ends (political projects) with the means (a static determination of individual preferences), CBA ignores or fails to notice the fact that its means do not correspond to the particularities of human life.

Real human preferences are never essentially private. Individual intentions, interests, and desires are tied to language, culture, and experience, and thus are inescapably social and susceptible to change. Pretending merely to describe individual preferences, CBA actually constructs them as they would be if people never interacted with one another. That the resulting "information" can be cynically used and exploited politically is obvious. That it can *seem* democratic, in as much as it scrupulously counts everyone's "dollar bids" about a project without appearing to impose a solution from the outside, is equally obvious. What is less obvious, but nonetheless true, is that the objective information that CBA provides to policymakers is cloaked in a subjective and politically charged point of view on the true nature of human preferences.

This is hardly surprising, for history teaches us that an age usually gets the political institutions that it deserves. If bureaucratically managed decision-making on the basis of numerated individual preferences that are modeled as being immune to change is what is wanted, then CBA is just the ticket. On the other hand, if genuine democracy implies popular engagement in decision-making processes that never guarantee the result in advance, but always leave room for something new and unforeseen to emerge from the messy dynamics of human interaction, then it seems to me that CBA is part of the problem rather than a contribution to the solution. For there is nothing more dangerous to any robust conception of popular democracy, not to mention the ethics of the radically particular, than the belief that the determination of what the people want is safely in the hands of experts.

Notes

* An earlier version of this chapter was published in *Law and Inequality: A Journal of Theory and Practice*, vol. 25, pp. 147–202 (2007), under the title "Senseless Kindness: The Politics of Cost–Benefit Analysis."

1. This chapter was originally presented as an address in Seattle to economists and other social scientists attending the May 2006 Benefit–Cost Conference, subtitled "What Can We Do to Improve the Use of Benefit–Cost Analysis?" The conference was sponsored by the University of Washington's Daniel J. Evans School of Public Affairs and by the Program on Values in Society.
2. "It is quite true that economists take the existing system for granted in their work; it would make no sense to do anything else" (Heyne, 1988, p. 57).
3. In the present context, "ordinal" means a definite ranking of goods (1st, 2nd, 3rd, etc.) within a set of available goods whose order is determined by a *single actor's* particular utility function. "Cardinal" refers to an *absolute* ranking of goods (1, 2, 3, etc.) on the basis of some criterion other than a particular actor's utility function. Thus, the proposition "If they all cost the same, A prefers ice cream to broccoli, and broccoli to gruel" expresses something about A's ordinal utility, whereas "Ice cream is better than broccoli, and broccoli is better than gruel" is a proposition of cardinal utility that purports to be valid for all actors.
4. Whether the compensation actually occurs is not a requirement of the KH test as such, although Zerbe (2001, p. 18) has called for actual compensation to be included in CBA calculations to the extent that there is any willingness to pay it. Zerbe's modification of KH, primarily through his inclusion of the preference for altruistic goods within CBA, has led him and certain other economists to change the test's name to "KHM," for Kaldor–Hicks-Moral (Zerbe, Bauman, and Finkle, 2006, p. 449).
5. "If we call the *receptivity* of our mind to receive representations insofar as it is affected in some way *sensibility*, then on the contrary the faculty for bringing forth representations itself, or the *spontaneity* of cognition, is the *understanding*" (Kant, 1998, p. 193).

6. Coase's theory originally predicted that in an environment with zero transaction costs, all economic goods will inevitably wind up in the hands of those who value them most, as measured by their WTPs and WTAs, and that this will happen regardless of how and to whom the law *initially* distributes the goods in question. It has since been shown theoretically that this conclusion does not hold in cases where a person's WTA for a good that he owns exceeds his WTP for that good if he had to purchase it from another. This creates the so-called "offer-asking problem" for the analysis of economic efficiency (Kelman, 1987, pp. 145–148).

Chapter 8

Postscript

> The work is the death mask of its conception.
>
> Walter Benjamin (1996, vol. 1, p. 459)

The problem of the subject(s)

No one has ever been more disenchanted than Franz Kafka was about reason's pathetic attempts to forge an unbreakable link between personal identity and personal responsibility. On the one hand, the ethical imperative of taking responsibility for one's actions seems to require someone (some *one*, that is) to assume it. On the other hand, the one that should take responsibility *now*, in the present, is also a temporal being with a past and a future. Which is to say, a self has not one, but three, analytically separate times in which it might be called itself, and hence three different possible identities: a past self, a present self, and a future self. *He* (*Er*), Hannah Arendt's translation of a parable that Kafka wrote in 1920, illustrates this apparent contradiction by offering up the image of a man battling with two antagonists that are pushing on him from opposite directions:

> He has two antagonists: the first presses him from behind, from the origin. The second blocks the road ahead. He gives battle to both. To be sure, the first supports him in his fight with the second, for he wants to push him forward, and in the same way the second supports him in his fight with the first, since he drives him back. But it is only theoretically so. For it is not only the two antagonists who are there, but he himself as well, and who really knows his intentions? His dream, though, is that some time in an unguarded moment—and this would require a night darker than any night has ever been yet—he will jump out of the fighting line and be promoted, on account of his experience in fighting, to the position of umpire over his antagonists in their fight with each other.
>
> (Arendt, 1968, p. 7)

The man's situation in this parable resembles that of practical reason as it worries and frets incessantly over what should be done. Practical reason's present self knows that it owes everything that it has and is to its past self. The latter keeps pressing it forward from the origin, which can only be history in the largest sense of the word. On the other hand, practical reason also hopes its future self will be a better self, in every way, than it is now. This would-be better self thus keeps on importunely shoving it from its position ahead. It is frustrating and tiring to be repeatedly pummeled from opposite sides. The man's dream of ceasing his struggle to stand outside the fighting line as an umpire over his antagonists can thus be read to symbolize the traditional Western philosophical yearning for cognitive transcendence: the redemptive overcoming of a brutal reality through the heroic, truth-seeking efforts of a self-certain rational subject. "And what else is this [man's] dream and this region," asks Arendt (1968, p. 11) rhetorically, "but the old dream which Western metaphysics has dreamed from Parmenides to Hegel of a timeless, spaceless, suprasensous realm as the proper region of thought?"

In September 1917, 3 years before he wrote *He* and not long after he had been diagnosed with tuberculosis, Kafka decided to recuperate by moving for a few months to the Bohemian village of Zürau, where his sister Ottla worked on the farm of her brother-in-law Hermann. From the diaries that he kept there, Kafka later carefully extracted and individually numbered, on separate pieces of paper, 109 short, non-literary epigrams. Published posthumously in 1931 under the ungainly title *Betrachtungen über Sünde, Hoffnung, Leid und den wahren Weg* ("Reflections on Sin, Hope, Suffering, and the True Way"),[1] this collection of overtly metaphysical, or at any rate philosophical, texts has since come to be called, quite simply, *The Zürau Aphorisms* (Cisco, 2003; Kafka, 2006).

Foreshadowing the identity-deconstructing sentiments that Kafka would later put into the parable *He*, number 72 in this series of aphorisms is of particular interest to us here:

> *Es gibt im gleichen Menschen Erkenntnisse, die bei völliger Verschiedenheit doch das gleiche Objekt haben, so daß wieder nur auf verschiedene Subjekte im gleichen Menschen rückgeschlossen werden muß.*
>
> In one and the same human being there are cognitions that, however utterly dissimilar they are, yet have one and the same object, so that one can only conclude that there are different subjects in one and the same human being.[2]
>
> (Cisco, 2013, p. 72)

In Western thought, at least, the notion that the human mind is a kind of container for ever-changing perceptions and cognitions—but never for anything that could rightly be called a permanent "Self"—is most strongly associated with the philosophy of David Hume (1977, p. 149). But Kafka does not use the German term for the Self (*das Ich*) in this aphorism—he refers instead to different "subjects" (*verschiedene Subjekte*) contained in one and the same "human being" (*im gleichen Menschen*). The main subject, so to speak, of the aphorism is *subjects* in the human being, not the self or the soul. This allows the text to be read as an attempt to subvert a theory of human subjectivity that began with Descartes, reached its apogee in Kant, was historicized by Hegel and Marx, and then became thoroughly relativized by nineteenth- and twentieth-century social science and psychology.

The word "subject" comes from the Latin *subjectum* (literally "that-which-is-thrown-under"), which is itself a Roman translation of the Greek word *hypokeimenon* (literally "that-which-lies-underneath"). In the beginning, the concept of subject was identified with the ontological ground or foundation on which something (anything) stands. Later on, under the influence of medieval Christianity, the subject came to be personified as God, conceived of as the creator of the universe and the ultimate *subjectum* to whom all things refer, as Aquinas said, "as to their beginning and end" (*Summa Theologica*, I-I q. 1 a. 7).

Although the concept of subjectivity has changed meaning several times during the past two and a half millennia, the idea we have today that "the subject" refers primarily to an individual person can be traced to Descartes. His *Meditations on First Philosophy* (1984 [1641], vol. 2, pp. 1–62) is usually credited with having initiated the so-called "subjective turn" in Western philosophy. Descartes's principle of radical methodological doubt redirected thought's gaze, so to speak, from "outward" (nature and nature's God) to "inward," namely, to the thinking thing that is certain of itself (*res cogitans qua certum*). "Within the course of this change," observes Heidegger (2009, p. 119), "we can comprehend the shift of the concept 'subject'—from that which is permanent in things to that which is I-like—and of the concept 'object'—from that which is represented to the objective being of things."

The I that thinks (*ego cogito*) became for Descartes and his intellectual descendants "the first principle of philosophy" (Descartes, 1984, vol. 1, p. 127), the one being that is more in being than any other being. A century later, Kant's momentous "Copernican revolution" (1998, 110) in philosophy finally realized the revolutionary potentialities that had been previously unleashed by Cartesian subjectivism. Kant gave the human subject a systematic form that did not need to be derived from any authority beyond its own capacity for rigorous self-awareness. Elbowing the deity aside, with Kant's assistance the primitive Cartesian thinking thing (*res cogitans*) grew into a wholly new *subjectum* and ground of everything that is, or rather, of everything that can be thought about or experienced by human beings. In the guise of pure reason, Kant's transcendental subject became a fixed and abiding being, hardwired from birth with "forms of intuition," "faculties," and "categories" that allowed it to organize and make sense of its experiences.

Hegel, Marx, and the rise of "sociological" neo-Kantianism during the nineteenth century would come to subvert Kant's claim that the transcendental subject's forms of intuition, faculties, and categories of understanding are universal (Beck, 1967, p. 473). The various features of the transcendental subject's mental architecture began to look more like historically and socially contingent practices and habits rather than universal human attributes (Marcuse, 2011, pp. 180–181). Biology, neuroscience, psychology, anthropology, and behavioral economics began to poke and prod the Kantian subject, trying to find out what really makes it tick beneath all of its own flimsy self-interpretations and self-justifications.

Eventually, Kant's categories of understanding and the concepts they generate morphed into culturally determined patterns of thinking that just happen to prevail at this or that particular moment in history among this or that group of people. As a result of this displacement of the universal by the particular, the causes of patterns of thinking (historical, economic, psychological, etc.) not only jutted into prominence, but also rendered implausible the claim that any particular cultural pattern could constitute an objective, supra-historical ground of truth and knowledge. The transcendental subject became the historical subject, and philosophical epistemology became the sociology of knowledge.

It has become almost commonplace these days for members of the academic intelligentsia to assert that in a post-Kantian, post-Freudian, and postmodern world, "people have no essential identities outside of those constructed in symbolic discourses and practices" (Douzinas, 2000, p. 259). Kantian legalism—which also happens to be the legalism of mainstream jurisprudence—gives us "the notion of the human subject as a sovereign agent of choice, a creature whose ends are chosen rather than given, who comes by his aims and purposes by acts of will, as opposed, say, to acts of cognition" (Gaete, 1993, p. 125). But to put it mildly, the vociferous counterclaim that the ego is not *in fact* a master of its own house can be found everywhere in postmodern thought, which demotes the self from the status of a sovereign subject and author of its own destiny to that of an embodied entity that is constantly being subjected, so to speak, to historical, symbolic, and psychological forces. These forces seem to imprison the individual in heteronomy, and they cut the will loose from any ground that it could reliably "choose" on its own by acting autonomously, like God used to do, in the capacity of an ultimate *subjectum*.

It is important to remember that the historical diminishment of the rational subject from the status of a *ground* to the status of a *cause-cum-effect* (situated inside what Hegel (1975, p. 70) calls "the causal nexus") also diminished the status of language—most especially the language of normativity. Language is a human thing, and as such it can achieve no greater ontological and moral height than can the particular creatures who use it to babble and scribble to one another, or, for that matter, *to themselves*. The very moment the smarty-pants *cognizing subject* whispers "Do *X*" or "Don't do *X*" to itself it must fall asleep, like a narcoleptic, so that in the mode of the muscular *acting subject* it can now react, like one of Pavlov's dogs, to the stimulus of the words. We may call the latter's reaction a "correct understanding" of the words as they are received in the context of some contingent Wittgensteinian language-game, but who do we think we are kidding? The subject can indeed lay down the moral law as *X*, but it will always pick up and run with the *linguistic sign* "*X*" in ways that only social history can explain.

The most important ethical consequence of these historical developments is not, as is commonly supposed, the belief that intellectual honesty requires us to affirm that the norms of justice and morality are always (or usually, or often, or sometimes) relative to place and time—that "we see neither justice nor injustice which does not change its nature with change of climate," as Pascal put it (1941, p. 101) (*Pensée* no. 104). A norm—any norm—is just a bit of text, after all, unless and until it produces effects. The real problem with the demotion of the Kantian rational subject to a mere caused-and-causing being is the juridical presupposition that it is still identical to itself, however much diminished in status—still unified, however briefly, during the span of time that it takes for ethical responsibility to be affixed.

Like a golem that refuses to die, the *unity* of the Kantian subject has somehow managed to survive its many transformations right down to the present time, while all the while continuing to menace the ethical sensibilities of the living. Although the golem that began as Kant's transcendental subject still stumbles around in today's world, full of contents, the contingency and relativity of the contents themselves are not the most troubling thing about it. What troubles the ethics of justice most is the undead Kantian supposition that the subject is still an "it"—a unified being that can only interact with others by means of its contents, *whatever they are.*

Reenter Kafka's aphorism interpreted as a response to Kantian-style subjectivism. As Derrida notes (2008, p. 92), "Kant emphasizes the fact that 'I' signifies a consciousness that remains the same throughout all of its modifications." The unity of consciousness thus secured, Kant's critical philosophy famously holds that every rational being consists of *a* subject that is capable of knowing those perceptions (*Erlebnisse*) and cognitions (*Erkenntnisse*) of objects (*Gegenstände*) that appear to it in the form of inner phenomena, but that is also incapable of knowing the thing-in-itself (*Ding-an-sich*, or *Objekt-an-sich*) as it exists in the real, supersensuous (i.e., "noumenal") world (Kant, 1998, pp. 338–353). Kant believed that the rational subject's perdurence as a unity through time was a condition of the possibility of experience and knowledge, and therefore that it could be shown to exist by induction from the fact that we just do happen to experience and know things.

In opposition to the Kantian argument—which rests on the relatively weak logical reed of nonmathematical induction, as Nietzsche (1966, p. 22) mockingly points out—Kafka's aphorism no. 72 relies on two fundamental premises to assert that one *must* deduce (*rückgeschlossen werden muß*) that the subject is not identical with itself, and that it is in truth a multiplicity of subjects. These premises can be formalized as follows: (1) the obvious phenomenal fact that an individual's cognitions (*Erkenntnisse*) are variable through time, which Hume had also noticed, and (2) a commonsensically stipulated reality and self-identity of the very object (*das gleiche Objekt*) that any given subject happens to be cognizing.

Now Kant's theory of the subject–object relation is nothing if not subtle, although it is also true that he was not always perfectly consistent in the way he used the terms *Ding* (thing), *Gegenstand* (object), and *Objekt* (object) (Caygill, 1995, pp. 270–274). Rather than trying to enter into the complex maze of distinctions that Kant himself draws among these three terms (especially the latter two), it is far more interesting and productive simply to impose what Kantians might call a vulgar, reality-affirming interpretation on Kafka's text. For in his thinking about the real, Kafka was definitely not a Kantian.

This interpretation identifies the reference of Kafka's phrase *das gleiche Objekt* with what this book has already called the "ontologically particular," or the

Objekt-an-sich, as Kant sometimes puts it. *Pace* Kant, however, the aphorism can then be read to imply that the purely *phenomenal* Kantian "category" of unity applies to the *noumenal* pre-category (or non-category) of reality as such. The advantage of this interpretation for the journey we are taking here is obvious. It reinforces the existence of what Chapter 3 called "awareness without personhood or knowledge" and "what lies between the lines." It reconfirms the possibility that hidden ontological particularities, such as Levinas's "tears the civil servant cannot see" (1996, p. 23), are indeed real enough to reach out, so to speak, to affect our consciences and our ethical responses in ways that no *other* concept or category of reason can account for. And it will be recalled that Chapter 7 already raised this life-affirming possibility under the heading "senseless kindness."

On this reading, the aphorism still says that inside each one of us, there must exist not one subjectivity, but many different subjectivities. But at the same time, it does not also deny the unity of the *real* human being (*Menschen*). Rather, it denies the unity of that most cherished of all beings in Western epistemology, jurisprudence, and ethics: *the rational subject*. Thus construed, the thesis holds that different subjects exist inside one and the same person as they (the subject*s*) confront, or are confronted by, one and the same ontological particularity as it arises and then subsides within the sphere of the real. It is as if we all suffer from something akin to multiple personality disorder in the face of a tragic reality that, like Benjamin's mute and mournful nature (Benjamin, 1978, p. 329), keeps on speechlessly longing for our recognition—a surprising conclusion, perhaps, but still one that will serve to illuminate the last few steps we will be taking together in this book.

The completely broken heart

In this last section of the book, I, the author, will run the substantial risk of speaking to you, dear anonymous reader, directly from the heart—a heart that is not yet completely broken.

The older I get, the more I think my life resembles that of an insect walking on a wall. The mottled wall of the real, so to speak. The feeling is not necessarily unpleasant, though. Unlike Prufrock, who is stuck forever on the wall, left sprawling on the pin of a "formulated phrase,"[3] I seem to find myself, more and more, scuttering on and over wildly variegated patches that confound all my efforts to simplify them for purposes of comparison. How interesting, I think on many, many occasions; how distressing, on others; how horrifying, on others still. But I also sometimes wonder *who* is the me that is about to do (or avoid doing) justice and/or injustice in some ever-particular yet humanly opaque situation. Is the me (the "who") standing, here and now, on the verge of acting unjustly the same, or different, from the me that also simultaneously stands on the verge of doing what could be considered just? And if no formulated phrase can let me see the right outcome, then is there anything that could?

Nietzsche once said that the great danger of all direct questioning of the subject *about* the subject lies in the fact "that it could be useful and important for one's activity to interpret oneself falsely" (1968, p. 272). I find that every scrupulously honest account or phenomenology of the rational eventually leads to a description of the irrational (or pre-rational) ground of what is merely called "rational." In response to the query, "Who am I?" Derrida (2008, pp. 53–54) once asked, "What would ever distinguish the response, in its total purity, the so-called free responsible response, from a reaction to a complex system of stimuli?" The point of Derrida's question—and it is a non-rhetorical one—is deeply personal and ethical rather than remote and metaphysical. For him, as for me, "Casting doubt on responsibility, on decision, on one's own being-ethical, seems to me to be—and is perhaps what should forever remain—the unrescindable essence of ethics, decision, and responsibility" (Derrida, 2008, p. 126).

At the beginning of the book, I promised to give some kind of answer to the Fundamental Question, which, it will be recalled, is: *Is a life in the law—even one spent in the pursuit of justice—worth living, and if so, how can a disenchanted person come to bear the living of it without constantly having to engage in self-deception?* If this is the question, then *yes* and *through ethics* constitutes the book's ultimate answer.

Not ethics in the conventional philosophical sense of an inquiry into how people ought to act in general; not ethics in Schopenhauer's sense of the "feeling" of compassion; but ethics conceived in terms of individual, unscripted acts of kindness manifested in particular situations. Ethics in the sense used here might thus be described as the *principle* of remaining openly hospitable to the possibility of an *unprincipled* irruption of gratuitous, senseless kindness into institutions and situations that present themselves at first glance (and even second or third glance) as being doctrinally closed to that possibility.

No, that's not quite right either. A general principle of remaining open to being unprincipled is a bit of text, too, and I don't want to leave you with just *that*, not by a longshot. Not only is there no moral certainty in the world, but "its very assumption would be immoral, would falsely relieve the individual of anything that might be called morality" (Adorno, 1973, p. 243). Schopenhauer (2005, pp. 108–109) was therefore wrong to say that "boundless compassion for all living beings is the surest and most certain guarantee of pure moral conduct . . . Whoever is filled with it will assuredly injure no one, do harm to no one, encroach on no man's rights." He was wrong because unreasoning kindness, no more than reasonable sternness, can never guarantee that the totality of its effects will be beneficial, or that it will not be deployed (by someone) in the service of malevolent causes.

It is, of course, empirically possible that corresponding to every inflexible, rule-pettifogging Inspector Javert, ready as always to hound his Jean Valjean into an unworthy grave (Hugo, 1992), there is at least one soft-hearted Judge Hardy[4] who might mistakenly order the "compassionate release" from prison of a murdering psychopath. But until the relevant social science data can be assembled (assuming it can be), I can only respond to this supposition anecdotally, based on 68 years of living on this earth: I doubt very much that in the real world there is a 1:1 correlation between these two types of legal actors. Sadly, it has always seemed to me that for every Judge Hardy in the law there are 100 Javerts.

It is said that Spinoza searched for God and found him in a predicate of substance (Stevens, 1966, pp. 415–416). It would be fair to say that this book went looking for the ethics of justice without illusions and found it, not in a principle, but rather in a predicate of the particular.

In the middle of the nineteenth century, Marx described the massively destabilizing effects of capitalism on traditional social and economic relations in the following famous and oft-cited passage of *The Communist Manifesto*:

> All fixed, fast-frozen relations, with their train of ancient and venerable prejudices and opinions, are swept away, all new-formed ones become antiquated before they can ossify. All that is solid melts into air, all that is holy is profaned, and man is at last compelled to face with sober senses, his real conditions of life, and his relations with his kind.
>
> (Marx and Engels, 1998, pp. 38–39)

This passage has always seemed eerily appropriate to me as a way to describe the effect on individual ethical sensibility of the fact that, in the second decade of the twenty-first century, so very many of the highfalutin normative discourses of law and justice have been diminished in the popular imagination to the status of mere tropes that are manipulated by politicians and lawyers in the particular interests of those they serve. Unlike *The Communist Manifesto*, however, the writing in the present book has aspired to be more revelatory than revolutionary. My point has not been to offer therapeutic comfort or a path toward healing—some "*A*" leading to the "*B*" of an ethically sound regime of just social relations ($A \rightarrow B$)—to those beset by ethical trauma as a consequence of the current state of law and justice in the world. For anyone who cannot resist explaining the flower by the fertilizer, as Gaston Bachelard (1969, p. xxvi) puts it, the problems of ethics will never present themselves as genuine problems of how to live in the now, in just this particular situation. If I have sought to accomplish anything that could plausibly be called political, then it must be said that I have tried my best to accentuate and increase the ethical crisis that this book has identified.

David Mathiessen's recent book *In Paradise* (2014) is a novel depicting a modern Zen retreat held at the site of one of the former camps in Auschwitz, of all places. It makes for painful reading. To paraphrase the character of the rabbi in the novel (p. 162), it seems to me now that it is no longer enough for the heart to break on account of losing the illusions that once made its pathetic, enchanted view of law and justice possible. Instead, the heart must *completely* break, without re-growing a new carapace of cherished symbols and images to protect it against the arrival of the particular.

Notes

1. The title was selected by Max Brod, Kafka's friend and literary executor.
2. Michael Hofmann's alternative translation is more fluid, but misleadingly substitutes "perceptions" for *Erkenntnisse* and "person" for *Menschen*: "The same person has perceptions that, for all their differences, have the same object, which leads one to infer that there are different subjects contained within one and the same person" (Kafka, 2006, p. 71). The more literal Kaiser/Wilkins translation shown in text ("cognitions" for *Erkenntnisse* and "human being" for *Menschen*) is more faithful to the original usages of these terms in German, especially when read in the context of German philosophical discourse.
3. From T.S. Eliot's poem "The Love Song of J. Alfred Prufrock":

   > And I have known the eyes already, known them all – / The eyes that fix you in a formulated phrase, / And when I am formulated, sprawling on a pin, / When I am pinned and wriggling on the wall, / Then how should I begin / To spit out all the butt-ends of my days and ways? / And how should I presume?
   >
   > (Eliot, 1934, pp. 11–16, 13).

4. Judge James K. Hardy is a fictional character in the "Andy Hardy" series of movies, 15 of which were released by MGM from 1937 to 1946. Judge Hardy, played by the actor Lewis Stone, had a grandfatherly demeanor, a wry sense of humor, and a very soft heart, especially when it came to rescuing his son Andy, played by Mickey Rooney, from his many ill-advised adventures and legally questionable dealings. A good example of his compassionate nature is exhibited in *Judge Hardy and Son* (1939), wherein the judge, moved by the plight of a destitute elderly couple, enlists Andy in an ultimately successful effort to keep them from losing their home. As far as I know, the Judge's compassionate acts in the movies never went awry in the manner suggested in text. But of course, that does not prevent his character from being used as a whipping boy to illustrate Spinoza's unfortunate thesis that pity or compassion (*commiseratio*) is both "evil and unprofitable" (*per se mala et inutilis*) in someone who lives according to the guidance of reason (1955, p. 224) (Prop. 50).

References

Adler, M & Posner, E 2006, New Foundations of Cost–Benefit Analysis, Harvard University Press, Cambridge, MA.

Adorno, T 1973, *Negative Dialectics*, trans. EB Ashton, Routledge, London.

Agamben, G 2012, *Remnants of Auschwitz: The Witness and the Archive*, trans. D Heller-Roazen, Zone Books, New York.

Agamben, G 2000, *Means without End: Notes on Politics*, trans. V Binetti & C Cesarino, University of Minnesota Press, Minneapolis, MN.

Agamben, G 1998, *Homo Sacer: Sovereign Power and Bare Life*, trans. D Heller-Roazen, Stanford University Press, Stanford, CA.

Agamben, G 1993, *The Coming Community*, trans. M Hardt, University of Minnesota Press, Minneapolis, MN.

Al-Aayed, SH 2002, *The Rights of Non-Muslims in the Islamic World*, trans. A Alosh, Dar Eshbelia, Riyadh, Saudi Arabia.

Alduy, C 2014, "The Battle for the Soul of France" *The Nation*, March 24, pp. 17–21.

American Bar Association 2007, *Model Rules of Professional Conduct: Preamble and Scope.* Available from: *www.americanbar.org/groups/professional_responsibility/publications/model_rules_of_professional_conduct/model_rules_of_professional_conduct_preamble_scope.html* [April 7, 2015].

Antisocial Personality Disorder Symptoms, 2014. Available from: *http://psychcentral.com/disorders/antisocial-personality-disorder-symptoms/* [July 12, 2015].

Aquinas, T 1948, *Introduction to Saint Thomas Aquinas*, Ed. A Pegis, Modern Library, New York.

Arendt, H 2005, *The Promise of Politics*, Ed. J Kohn, Schocken, New York.

Arendt, H 2004, *The Origins of Totalitarianism*, Schocken, New York.

Arendt, H 2003, *Responsibility and Judgment*, Ed. J Kohn, Schocken, New York.

Arendt, H 1993, *Essays in Understanding, 1930–1954*, Ed. J Kohn, Harcourt Brace, New York.

Arendt, H 1968, *Between Past and Future*, Penguin, New York.

Arendt, H 1965, *Eichmann in Jerusalem: A Report on the Banality of Evil*, rev. ed., Viking Press, New York.

Auden, WH 1972 [1940], "In Memory of W.B. Yeats" in *The New Oxford Book of English Verse: 1250–1950*, Ed. H Gardner, Oxford University Press, Oxford.

Austin, JL 1975, *How to Do Things with Words*, 2nd ed., Harvard University Press, Cambridge, MA.

Bachelard, G 1969, *The Poetics of Space*, trans. M Jolas, Beacon Press, Boston, MA.

Badiou, A 2003, *Infinite Thought*, Eds. & trans. O Feltham & J Clemens, Continuum, London.

Bainbridge, S 2002, *Corporation Law and Economics*, Foundation Press, Mineola, NY.
Baird, D 2000, "The Law and Economics of Contract Damages" in *Chicago Lectures in Law and Economics*, Ed. E Posner, Foundation Press, Mineola, NY.
Balbus, I 1977, "Commodity Form and Legal Form: An Essay on the 'Relative Autonomy' of the Law" *Law & Society Review*, vol. 11, no. 3, pp. 571–588.
Balkin, JM 1998, *Cultural Software: A Theory of Ideology*, Yale University Press, New Haven, CT.
Beck, L 1967, "Neo-Kantianism" in *The Encyclopedia of Philosophy*, 8 vols. Ed. Paul Edwards, Macmillan, New York, vol. 5, pp. 468–473.
Beckett, S 2011, *The Letters of Samuel Beckett 1941–1956*, Eds. C Craig et al., Cambridge University Press, Cambridge.
Beckett, S 2009, *The Letters of Samuel Beckett 1929–1940*, Eds. M Fensenfeld et al., Cambridge University Press, Cambridge.
Bender, L 1993, "A Lawyer's Primer on Feminist Theory and Tort Law" in *Feminist Legal Theory: Foundations*, Ed. DK Weisberg, Temple University Press, Philadelphia, PA, pp. 58–74.
Benjamin, W 1999, *The Arcades Project*, trans. H Weiland & K McLaughlin, Harvard University Press, Cambridge, MA.
Benjamin, W 1996, *Selected Writings*, 4 vols., Ed. M Jennings, Harvard University Press, Cambridge, MA.
Benjamin, W 1994, *The Correspondence of Walter Benjamin: 1910–1940*, Eds. G Scholem & T Adorno, trans. M Jacobson & E Jacobson, University of Chicago Press, Chicago, IL.
Benjamin, W 1978, *Reflections: Essays, Aphorisms, Autobiographical Writings*, trans. E Jephcott, Shocken, New York.
Benjamin, W 1968, *Illuminations: Essays and Reflections*, trans. H Zohn, Shocken, New York.
Bennett, W 2013, *The Book of Man: Readings on the Path to Manhood*, Nelson Books, Nashville, TN.
Berger, P & Luckmann, T 1967, *The Social Construction of Reality*, Doubleday, New York.
Berlin, I 2003, *Freedom and its Betrayal: Six Enemies of Human Liberty*, Princeton University Press, Princeton, NJ.
Bernard of Clairvaux 1839, *Opera Omnia*, vol. 1, Apud Gaume Fratres, Bibliopolas, Paris.
Bishop, M 2009, "A Hippocratic Oath for Managers: Foreswearing Greed" *The Economist*, June 4, pp. 67–68.
Blackstone, J 1979 [1766], *Commentaries on the Laws of England*, facsimile 1st ed., vol. 2, University of Chicago Press, Chicago, IL.
Blinder, A & Fausset, R 2015, "Kentucky Clerk Who Said 'No' to Gay Couples Won't Be Alone in Court," *The New York Times*, September 2. Available from: *www.nytimes.com/2015/09/03/us/kentucky-rowan-county-clerk-kim-davis-denies-marriage-license.html* [September 18, 2015].
Bloch, E 1988, *Natural Law and Human Dignity*, trans. D Schmidt, MIT Press, Cambridge, MA.
Boadway, R & Bruce, N 1984, *Welfare Economics*, Basil Blackwell, Oxford.
Borradori, G 2003, *Philosophy in a Time of Terror: Dialogues with Jürgen Habermas and Jacques Derrida*, University of Chicago Press, Chicago, IL.
Bouwsma, OK 1986, *Ludwig Wittgenstein: Conversations 1949–1951*, Eds. JL Craft & R Hustwit, Hackett, IN.
Breyer, S 2005, *Active Liberty: Interpreting Our Democratic Constitution*, Vintage, New York.
Brigham, E & Ehrhardt, M 2010, *Financial Management: Theory and Practice*, 13th ed., Cengage Learning, Stamford, CT.

Broadway, N & Bruce, N 1984, *Welfare Economics*, Basil Blackwell, Oxford.

Brown, D 1972, *Bury My Heart at Wounded Knee: An Indian History of the American West*, Bantam Books, New York.

Browne, T 1658, "Hydriotaphia Urne-Buriall, or, A Brief Discourse of the Sepulchrall Urnes Lately Found in Norfolk." Available from: *http://penelope.uchicago.edu/hydrionoframes/hydrion.html* [October 9, 2015].

Brubaker, R 1984, *The Limits of Rationality: An Essay on the Social and Moral Thought of Max Weber*, Routledge, London.

Buber, M 2000, *I and Thou*, trans. R Smith, Scribner, New York.

Camus, A 2008, *Notebooks 1951–1959*, trans. R Bloom & IR Dee, Chicago, IL.

Camus, A 1965a, *Notebooks 1942–1951*, trans. J O'Brien & A Alfred, Knopf, New York.

Camus, A 1965b, *Notebooks 1935–1942*, trans. P Thody, Modern Library, New York.

Camus, A 1955, *The Myth of Sisyphus and Other Essays*, trans. J O'Brien, Vintage Books, New York.

Camus, A 1947, "Neither Victims nor Executioners," *Politics*, no. 3, pp. 141–146. Available from: *www.unz.org/Pub/Politics-1947jul-00141* [February 9, 2015].

Carrington, P 1984, "Of Law and the River," *Journal of Legal Education*, vol. 34, pp. 222–228.

Cassirer, E 1963, *The Question of Jean Jacques Rousseau*, trans. P Gay, Indiana University Press, Bloomington, IN.

Caygill, H 1995, *A Kant Dictionary*, Blackwell, Oxford.

Chapin-Pinotti, E 2013, *John Adams: Non-Fiction Readings: Interactive Common Core Workbook*, Lucky Willy Publishing, Plymouth, CA.

Chekhov, A 2003 [1892], *Ward No. 6 and Other Stories*, trans. C Garnett, Barnes & Noble Classics, New York.

Churchland, P 2013, *Touching a Nerve: The Self as Brain*, Norton, New York.

Cicero, MT 1999, "On the Laws," in *On the Commonwealth and On the Laws*, Ed. J Zetzel, Cambridge University Press, Cambridge, pp. 105–175.

Cisco, M 2013, "Kafka's *Zurau Aphorisms*," *Glossator*, vol. 8, pp. 1–114. Available from: *https://solutioperfecta.files.wordpress.com/2013/11/g8-cisco2.pdf* [November 28, 2015].

Clark, M & Leiter, B 1997, "Introduction" in *Daybreak: Thought on the Prejudices of Morality*, Ed. *F* Nietzsche, trans. RJ Hollingdale, Cambridge University Press, Cambridge, pp. vii–xxxiv.

Clausewitz, C 1984 [1832], *On War*, Eds. and trans. M Howard & P Paret, Princeton University Press, Princeton, NJ.

Coase, R 1988, *The Firm, the Market, and the Law*, University of Chicago Press, Chicago, IL.

Coase, R 1960, "The Problem of Social Cost" *Journal of Law and Economics*, vol. 3, pp. 1–44.

Coase, R 1937, "The Nature of the Firm" *Economica*, vol. 4, no. 16, pp. 386–405.

Coleman, J & Leiter, B 1996, "Legal Positivism" in *A Companion to Philosophy of Law and Legal Theory*, Ed. D Patterson, Blackwell, Oxford, pp. 241–260.

Cooter, R & Ulen, T 1988, *Law and Economics*, Scott Foresman, Glenview, IL.

Critchley, S 2014, *The Ethics of Deconstruction: Derrida and Levinas*, 3rd ed., Edinburgh University Press, Edinburgh, UK.

Cross, R 2014, *Medieval Theories of Haecceity*. Available from: http://plato.stanford.edu/entries/medieval-haecceity/ [November 29, 2015].

Crowe, D 2004, *Oskar Schindler: The Untold Account of his Life, Wartime Activities, and the True Story behind the List*, Westview Press, Cambridge, MA.

Cutts, M 2000, "Clarity in EC Legislation," *Clarity*, vol. 45, pp. 11–12.

D'Amato, A 1989, "Aspects of Deconstruction: The 'Easy Case' of the Under-Aged President," *Northwestern University Law Review*, vol. 84, pp. 250–256.

Dawkins, R 2006, *The God Delusion*, Houghton Mifflin, Boston, MA.

de Sélincourt, B 1911, *William Blake*, Duckworth, London.

Demetz, P 1968, "Introduction" in *Illuminations: Essays and Reflections*, Eds. W Benjamin & H Arendt, trans. H Zohn, Schocken, New York, pp. vii–xiii.

Derrida, J 2014, *The Death Penalty*, vol. 1, trans. P Kamuf, University of Chicago Press, Chicago, IL.

Derrida, J 2008, *The Animal that Therefore I Am*, Ed. M-L Mallet, trans. D Wills, Fordham University Press, New York.

Derrida, J 2001, *The Work of Mourning*, Eds. P-A Brault & M Naas, University of Chicago Press, Chicago, IL.

Derrida, J 1997 [1967], *Of Grammatology*, corrected ed., trans. GK Spivak, Johns Hopkins University Press, Baltimore, MD.

Derrida, J 1990, "Force of Law: The 'Mystical Foundation of Authority'" trans. M Quaintance, *Cardozo Law Review*, vol. 11, pp. 919–1045.

Derrida, J 1989, *Of Spirit: Heidegger and the Question*, trans. G Bennington & R Bowlby, University of Chicago Press, Chicago, IL.

Descartes, R 1984, *The Philosophical Writings of Descartes*, 2 vols., trans. J Cottingham, R Stoothoff & D Murdoch, Cambridge University Press, Cambridge.

Diamantides, M (Ed.) 2010, *Levinas, Law, Politics*, Routledge-Cavendish, London.

Dodson, L 2009, *The Moral Underground: How Ordinary Americans Subvert and Unfair Economy*, The New Press, New York.

Donnelly, J 1984, "Cultural Relativism and Universal Human Rights," *Human Rights Quarterly*, vol. 6, no. 4, pp. 400–419.

Douzinas, C 2000, *The End of Human Rights: Critical Legal Thought at the Turn of the Century*, Hart Publishing, Oxford.

Downing, D 1995, *Dictionary of Mathematical Terms*, 2nd ed., Barron's, Hauppauge, NY.

Dreyfus, H & Kelly, S 2011, *All Things Shining: Reading the Western Classics to Find Meaning in a Secular Age*, Free Press, New York.

Dumas, A 2003, *The Count of Monte Cristo*, Bantam Books, New York.

Dunn, J 2014, *Breaking Democracy's Spell*, Yale University Press, New Haven, CT.

Duns Scotus 2005, *Early Oxford Lecture on Individuation*, trans. A Wolter, Franciscan Institute, St. Bonaventure, NY.

Dworkin, R 1991, "Pragmatism, Right Answers, and True Banality" in *Pragmatism in Law and Society*, Eds. M Brint & W Weaver, Westview Press, Boulder, CO, pp. 359–388.

Dworkin, R 1986, *Law's Empire*, Harvard University Press, Cambridge, MA.

Easterly, W 2006, *The White Man's Burden: Why the West's Efforts to Aid the Rest Have Done So Much Ill and So Little Good*, Penguin, New York.

Einstein, A 1916, "Die Grundlage der allgemeinen Relitivitätstheorie" *Annalen der Physik*, vol. 49, pp. 769–782.

Eliot, TS 1934, *Selected Poems*, Harcourt Brace Jovanovich, New York.

Elster, J 1985, *Making Sense of Marx*, Cambridge University Press, Cambridge.

Entessar, N 1988, "Criminal Law and the Legal System in the Revolutionary Iran" *Boston College Third World Law Journal*, vol. 8, pp. 91–98.

Eskridge, W 1988, "Interpreting Legislative Inaction," *Michigan Law Review*, vol. 87, pp. 67–137.

Etxabe, J 2013, *The Experience of Tragic Judgment*, Routledge, Abingdon, UK.

Fichte, JG 2005, *The System of Ethics: According to the Principles of the Wissenschaftslehre*, trans. D Breazeale & G Zöller, Cambridge University Press, Cambridge.
Finnis, J 1984, "The Authority of Law in the Predicament of Contemporary Social Theory" *Notre Dame Journal of Law, Ethics & Public Policy*, vol. 1, no. 1, pp. 115–137.
Fish, S 1991, "Almost Pragmatism: The Jurisprudence of Richard Posner, Richard Rorty, and Ronald Dworkin" in *Pragmatism in Law and Society*, Eds. M Brint & W Weaver, Westview Press, Boulder, CO, pp. 47–81.
Fish, S 1989, *Doing What Comes Naturally: Change, Rhetoric, and the Practice of Theory in Literary and Legal Studies*, Duke University Press, Durham, NJ.
Folk Archive 1997, *The Preacher and the Slave (Joe Hill)*. Available from: *www.folkarchive.de/pie.html* [January 30, 2015].
Foucault, M 2008, *The Birth of Biopolitics: Lectures at the the Collège de France 1978–1979*, Ed. A Davidson, trans. G Burchell, Palgrave Macmillan, New York.
Foucault, M 2007, *Security, Territory, Population: Lectures at the the Collège de France 1977–1978*, Ed. M Senellart, trans. G Burchell, Palgrave Macmillan, New York.
Foucault, M 2005, *The Hermeneutics of the Subject: Lectures at the Collège de France 1981–1982*, Ed. F Gros, trans. G Burchell, Palgrave Macmillan, New York.
Foucault, M 2003, *"Society Must Be Defended": Lectures at the Collège de France 1975–1976*, Eds. M Bertani & A Fontana, trans. D Macey, Picador, New York.
Foucault, M 1980, *Power/Knowledge: Selected Interviews and Other Writings 1972–1977*, Ed. C Gordon, trans. C Gordon et al., Pantheon, New York.
Foucault, M 1972, *The Archaeology of Knowledge and the Discourse on Language*, trans. AMS Smith, Pantheon, New York.
Frank, M & Broschard, D 2006, "The Silent Criminal Defendant and the Presumption of Innocence: In the Hands of Real Jurors, Is Either of Them Safe?" *Lewis & Clark Law Review*, vol. 10, no. 2, pp. 237–285.
Frege, G 1948, "Sense and Reference" *The Philosophical Review*, vol. 57, pp. 209–230.
Freud, S 1962, *Civilization and its Discontents*, trans. J Strachey, WW Norton, New York.
Fried, C 1981, *Contract as Promise: A Theory of Contractual Obligation*, Harvard University Press, Cambridge, MA.
Friedman, M 1970, "The Social Responsibility of Business Is to Increase its Profits" *The New York Times Magazine*, September 13. Available from: *www.umich.edu/~thecore/doc/Friedman.pdf* [April 7, 2015].
Fukuyama, F 2014, *Political Order and Political Decay: From the Industrial Revolution to the Globalization of Democracy*, Farrar, Strauss & Giroux, New York.
Fukuyama, F 1993, *The End of History and the Last Man*, HarperCollins, New York.
Fuller, L 1969, *The Morality of Law*, rev. ed., Yale University Press, New Haven, CT.
Fuller, L 1958, "Positivism and Fidelity to Law – A Reply to Professor Hart," *Harvard Law Review*, vol. 71, no. 4, pp. 630–672.
Fuller, L 1948, "What Law Schools Can Contribute to the Making of Lawyers," *Journal of Legal Education*, vol. 1, pp. 189–204.
Gaete, R 1993, *Human Rights and the Limits of Critical Reason*, Dartmouth, Aldershot, UK.
Gass, W 2012, *Life Sentences: Literary Judgments and Accounts*, Ed. A Alfred, Knopf, New York.
Genet, J 2003, *Prisoner of Love*, trans. B Bray, New York Review Books, New York.
Glendon, MA 2001, *A World Made New: Eleanor Roosevelt and the Universal Declaration of Human Rights*, Random House, New York.
Goethe, JW 1964, *Goethe: Selected Verse*, Ed. & trans. D Luke, Penguin Books, London.
Gordon, R 1984, "Critical Legal Histories" *Stanford Law Review*, vol. 36, pp. 57–125.

Gramsci, A 1989, *An Antonio Gramsci Reader: Selected Writings, 1916–1935*, Ed. D Forgacs, Schocken, New York.

Gramsci, A 1971, *Selections from the Prison Notebooks*, Eds. & trans. Q Hoare & G Smith, International Publishers, New York.

Gravel, N 1994, "Can a Ranking of Opportunity Sets Attach an Intrinsic Importance to Freedom of Choice?" *American Economic Review*, vol. 84, no. 2, pp. 454–458.

Graves, R 1955, *The Greek Myths*, 2 vols., Penguin, Baltimore, MD.

Grayling, AC 2013, *The God Argument: The Case against Religion and for Humanism*, Bloomsbury, New York.

Greenwald, G 2014, *No Place to Hide: Edward Snowden, the NSA, and the U.S. Surveillance State*, Metropolitan Books, New York.

Grossman, V 2010, *The Road*, Ed. R Chandler, trans. R Chandler et al., New York Review Books, New York.

Grossman, V 2009, *Everything Flows*, trans. R Chandler et al., New York Review Books, New York.

Grossman, V 2005, *A Writer at War: Vasily Grossman with the Red Army*, Eds. & trans. A Beevor & L Vinogradova, Pantheon, New York.

Grossman, V 1985, *Life and Fate*, trans. R Chandler, Harper & Row, New York.

Guyer, P & Wood, A 1998, "Introduction" in *Critique of Pure Reason*, Ed. I Kant, Ed. & trans. P Guyer & A Wood, Cambridge University Press, Cambridge.

Habermas, J 2003, *Truth and Justification*, Ed. & trans. B Fultner, MIT Press, Cambridge, MA.

Habermas, J 1984, *The Theory of Communicative Action*, 2 vols., trans. T McCarthy, Beacon Press, Boston, MA.

Harper, D 2012, *Online Etymology Dictionary*. Available from: *www.etymonline.com/index.php?allowed_in_frame=0&search=diversity&searchmode=none* [April 7, 2015].

Harrison, J 2003, *Law and Economics in a Nutshell*, 3rd ed., Thomson West, St. Paul, MN.

Hart, HLA 1961, *The Concept of Law*, Oxford University Press, Oxford.

Harvard Business School MBA Oath, 2009. Available from: *http://mbaoath.org/mba-oath-legacy-version/* [August 13, 2015].

Hayek, FA 2007 [1944], *The Road to Serfdom: Text and Documents*, Ed. B Caldwell, University of Chicago Press, Chicago, IL.

Hechter, M 1992, "The Micro–Macro Link in Rational Choice Theory" *Perspectives: Theory Section Newsletter*, July, pp. 1–3.

Hegel, GWF 1977 [1807], *Phenomenology of Spirit*, trans. AV Miller, Oxford University Press, Oxford.

Hegel, GWF 1975 [1812], *Hegel's Logic*, trans. W Wallace, Oxford University Press, Oxford.

Hegel, GWF 1967 [1821], *Philosophy of Right*, trans. TM Knox, Oxford University Press, Oxford.

Heidegger, M 2015, *The Beginning of Western Philosophy: Interpretation of Anaximander and Parmenides*, trans. R Rojcewicz, Indiana University Press, Bloomington, IN.

Heidegger, M 2010a, *Country Path Conversations*, trans. B Davis, Indiana University Press, Bloomington, IN.

Heidegger, M 2010b, *Phenomenology of Intuition and Expression*, trans. T Colony, Continuum, London.

Heidegger, M 2009, *Logic as the Question Concerning the Essence of Language*, trans. WT Gregory & Y Unna, State University of New York Press, Albany, NY.

Heidegger, M 2008, *Basic Concepts of Ancient Philosophy*, trans. R Rojcewicz, Indiana University Press, Bloomington, IN.

Heidegger, M 2005, *Introduction to Phenomenological Research*, trans. D Dahlstrom, Indiana University Press, Bloomington, IN.
Heidegger, M 2002, *The Essence of Truth: On Plato's Cave Allegory and Theaetetus*, trans. T Sadler, Continuum, New York.
Heidegger, M 2000, *Towards the Definition of Philosophy*, trans. T Sadler, Continuum, London.
Heidegger, M 1999, *Contributions to Philosophy (From Enowning)*, trans. P Emad & K Maly, Indiana University Press, Bloomington, IN.
Heidegger, M 1998, *Pathmarks*, Ed. W McNeill, trans. T Sheehan, Cambridge University Press, Cambridge.
Heidegger, M 1995, *Aristotle's Metaphysics ? 1–3: On the Essence and Actuality of Force*, trans. W Brogan & P Warnek, Indiana University Press, Bloomington, IN.
Heidegger, M 1994a, *Basic Questions of Philosophy: Selected "Problems" of "Logic,"* trans. R Rojcewicz & A Schuwer, Indiana University Press, Bloomington, IN.
Heidegger, M 1994b, *The Fundamental Concepts of Metaphysics: World–Finitude–Solitude*, trans. W McNeill & N Walker, Indiana University Press, Bloomington, IN.
Heidegger, M 1991, *The Principle of Reason*, trans. R Lilly, Indiana University Press, Bloomington, IN.
Heidegger, M 1984, *Nietzsche, Volume II: The Eternal Recurrence of the Same*, trans. D Krell, Harper & Row, New York.
Heidegger, M 1977, *The Question Concerning Technology and Other Essays*, trans. W Lovitt, Harper & Row, New York.
Heidegger, M 1976, *The Piety of Thinking*, trans. J Hart & J Maraldo, Indiana University Press, Bloomington, IN.
Heidegger, M 1975, *Early Greek Thinking*, trans. D Krell & F Capuzzi, Harper & Row, New York.
Heidegger, M 1971, *Poetry, Language, Thought*, trans. A Hofstadter, Harper & Row, New York.
Heidegger, M 1969, *Identity and Difference*, Ed. JG Gray, trans. J Stambaugh, Harper & Row, New York.
Heidegger, M 1962, *Being and Time*, trans. J Macquarrie & E Robinson, HarperCollins, New York.
Heidegger, M 1959, *An Introduction to Metaphysics*, trans. R Manheim, Yale University Press, New Haven.
Heraclitus 1987, *Fragments*, trans. TM Robinson, University of Toronto Press, Toronto.
Herodotus 1997, *The Histories*, trans. G Rawlinson, Everyman's Library, New York.
Heyne, P 1988, "The Foundations of Law and Economics: Can the Blind Lead the Blind?" *Research in Law and Economics*, vol. 11, pp. 53–71.
Higgs, R 1987, *Crisis and Leviathan: Critical Episodes in the Growth of American Government*, Oxford University Press, Oxford.
Higham, TF & Bowra, CM (Eds.) 1938, *The Oxford Book of Greek Verse in Translation*, Clarendon Press, Oxford.
Hitchens, C 2007, *God Is Not Great: How Religion Poisons Everything*, Twelve, New York.
Hobbes, T 1914 [1651], *Leviathan*, J.M. Dent, London.
Holmes, OW 1920 [1897], "The Path of the Law" in *Collected Legal Papers*, Harcourt, Brace, New York, pp. 167–202.
Honderich, T 1995, *The Oxford Companion to Philosophy*, Oxford University Press, Oxford.
Hong, H & Liskovich, I 2015, *Crime, Punishment and the Halo Effect of Corporate Social Responsibility*. Available from: *http://papers.ssrn.com/sol3/Papers.cfm?abstract_id=2492202* [July 5, 2015].

Horkheimer, M & Adorno, T 2002, *The Dialectic of Enlightenment: Philosophical Fragments*, Ed. GN Noerr, trans. E Jephcott, Stanford University Press, Stanford, CA.

Hugo, V 1992 [1862], *Les Misérables*, trans. C Wilbour, Modern Library, New York.

Human Rights Committee 1993, *Summary Record of the 1196th Meeting*, U.N. Doc. CCPR/C/SR.1196.

Human Rights Committee 1992, Consideration of Reports Submitted by States Parties under Article 40 of the Covenant: Second Periodic Reports of States Parties Due in 1983; Addendum, Islamic Republic of Iran, U.N. Doc. CCPR/C/28/Add.15.

Hume, D 1977 [1738], *A Treatise on Human Nature*, Everyman's Library, New York.

Husserl, E 1990, *The Idea of Phenomenology*, trans. W Alston & G Nakhnikian, Kluwer, Dordrecht, The Netherlands.

Husserl, E 1970, *The Crisis of European Sciences and Transcendental Phenomenology*, trans. D Carr, Northwestern University Press, Evanston, IL.

Husserl, E 1962, *Ideas: General Introduction to Pure Phenomenology*, Collier Books, New York.

Hutton, W 2015, *How Good We Can Be: Ending the Mercenary Society and Building a Great Country*, Little, Brown, London.

Hyppolite, J 1996, *Introduction to Hegel's Philosophy of History*, trans. B Harris & J Spurlock, University of Florida Press, Gainesville, FL.

James, W 1904, *The Principles of Psychology*, 2 vols., Henry Holt, New York.

Jankélévitch, V 2005, *Forgiveness*, trans. A Kelley, University of Chicago Press, Chicago, IL.

Jeffries, D 2008, *Hell's Cartel: I.G. Farben and the Making of Hitler's War Machine*, Metropolitan, NY.

Judt, T 2012, *Thinking the Twentieth Century*, Penguin Press, New York.

Kafka, F 2006, *The Zürau Aphorisms*, trans. M Hofmann, Schocken, New York.

Kahneman, D 2011, *Thinking, Fast and Slow*, Farrar, Straus & Giroux, New York.

Kant, I 2000, *The Critique of Judgment*, trans. JH Bernard, Prometheus Books, Amherst, NY.

Kant, I 1998, *The Critique of Pure Reason*, trans. P Guyer & A Wood, Cambridge University Press, Cambridge.

Kant, I 1996, *Practical Philosophy*, trans. M Gregor, Cambridge University Press, Cambridge.

Kant, I 1993, *The Philosophy of Kant: Immanuel Kant's Moral and Political Writings*, Ed. C Friedrich, trans. C Friedrich et al., Modern Library, New York.

Keats, J 1818, *Letter to his Brothers*, December 2. Available from: *www.mrbauld.com/negcap.html* [August 20, 2015].

Keizan 2001, "Transmission of Light" in *Classics of Buddhism and Zen*, trans. T Cleary, Shambhala, Boston, MA, vol. 4, pp. 1–225.

Kelman, M 1987, *A Guide to Critical Legal Studies*, Harvard University Press, Cambridge.

Kennedy, D 1986, "Freedom and Constraint in Adjudication: A Critical Phenomenology" *Journal of Legal Education*, vol. 36, no. 4, pp. 518–562.

Kierkegaard, S 1993, *The Diary of Sören Kierkegaard*, Ed. P Rohde, Citadel Press, New York.

Kojéve, A 1980, *Introduction to the Reading of Hegel*, trans. J Nichols, Cornell University Press, Ithaca, NY.

Kolakowski, L 2013, *Is God Happy? Selected Essays*, Basic Books, New York.

Kripke, S 1982, *Wittgenstein on Rules and Private Language*, Harvard University Press, Cambridge, MA.

Kroger, J 2004, "The Philosophical Foundations of Roman Law: Aristotle, the Stoics, and Roman Theories of Natural Law" *Wisconsin Law Review*, vol. 2004, pp. 905–944.

Kuhn, T 1970, *The Structure of Scientific Revolutions*, 2nd ed., University of Chicago Press, Chicago, IL.

Lacan, J 2007, *The Other Side of Psychoanalysis: Book XVII*, trans. R Grigg, WW Norton, New York.

Lacey, AR 1986, *A Dictionary of Philosophy*, 2nd ed., Routledge, London.

Leff, A 1979, "Unspeakable Ethics, Unnatural Law" *Duke Law Journal*, pp. 1229–1249.

Leibniz, G 1934, "The Monadology" in *Leibniz: Philosophical Writings*, trans. M Morris, Dent, London, pp. 3–20.

Leiter, B 2002, *Nietzsche on Morality*, Routledge, London.

Leslie, E 2007, *Walter Benjamin*, Reaktion, London.

Levinas, E 2003a, *Humanism of the Other*, trans. N Poller, University of Illinois Press, Urbana, IL.

Levinas, E 2003b, *On Escape*, trans. B Bergo, Stanford University Press, Stanford, CA.

Levinas, E 2001, *Is It Righteous to Be? Interviews with Emmanuel Levinas*, Ed. J Robbins, Stanford University Press, Stanford, CA.

Levinas, E 1999, *Alterity and Transcendence*, trans. M Smith, Columbia University Press, New York.

Levinas, E 1998a, *On Thinking-of-the-Other Entre Nous*, trans. M Smith & B Harshav, Columbia University Press, New York.

Levinas, E 1998b, *Otherwise than Being, or Beyond Essence*, trans. A Lingis, Duquesne University Press, Pittsburgh, PA.

Levinas, E 1996, *Basic Philosophical Writings*, Eds. A Peperzak et al., Indiana University Press, Bloomington, IN.

Levinas, E 1989, *The Levinas Reader*, Ed. S Hand, trans. A Orianne et al., Blackwell, Oxford.

Levinas, E 1987, *Autrement que savoir*, Editions Osiris, Paris.

Liddel, HG & Scott, R 1843, *A Greek–English Lexicon*. Available from: *http://stephanus.tlg.uci.edu/lsj/#eid=1&context=lsj* [April 7, 2015].

Lilla, M 2015, "Slouching Toward Mecca," *New York Review*, April 2, pp. 41–43.

Lindroos-Hovinheimo, S 2012, *Justice and the Ethics of Legal Interpretation*, Routledge, London.

Löwy, M 2005, *Fire Alarm: Reading Walter Benjamin's "On the Concept of History,"* trans. C Turner, Verso, London.

McCloskey, M 2009, *Visual Reflections: A Perceptual Deficit and Its Implications*, Oxford University Press, Oxford.

McDougal, S, Laswell, H & Chen, L-C 1977, *Human Rights and World Public Order: The Basic Politics of an International Law of Human Dignity*, Yale University Press, New Haven, CT.

MacKinnon, C 1983, "Feminism, Marxism, Method, and State: Toward Feminist Jurisprudence," *Signs: Women in Culture and Society*, vol. 8, pp. 635–638.

Mannheim, K 1985 [1936], *Ideology and Utopia: An Introduction to the Sociology of Knowledge*, trans. L Wirth & E Shils, Harcourt Brace Jovanovich, San Diego, CA.

Marcuse, H 2011, *Philosophy, Psychoanalysis and Emancipation*, Eds. D Kellner & C Pierce, Routledge, London.

Marcuse, H 1998, *Technology, War and Fascism*, Ed. D Kellner, Routledge, London.

Marens, R & Wicks, A 1999, "Getting Real: Stakeholder Theory, Managerial Practice, and the General Irrelevance of Fiduciary Duties Owed to Shareholders" *Business Ethics Quarterly*, vol. 9, no. 2, pp. 273–293.

Margaronis, M 2015, "Greece Stands Up" *The Nation*, March 23, pp. 13–16.

Martel, J 2012, *Divine Violence: Walter Benjamin and the Eschatology of Sovereignty*, Routledge, London.

Marx, K 1964, *Early Writings*, Ed. & trans. TB Bottomore, McGraw-Hill, New York.

Marx, K 1959, *Basic Writings on Politics and Philosophy*, Anchor Books, Garden City, NY.

Marx, K 1906, *Capital: A Critique of Political Economy*, vol. 1, trans. S Moore & E Aveling, Modern Library, New York.

Marx, K & Engels, F 1998 [1848], *The Communist Manifesto: A Modern Edition*, Verso, London.

Massey, C 1992, "Faith Healers" *Law and Social Inquiry*, vol. 17, no. 4, pp. 821–829.

Mathiessen, D 2014, *In Paradise*, Riverhead Books, New York.

Matt, D 1996, The Essential Kabbalah: The Heart of Jewish Mysticism, HarperCollins, NY.

Matthews, W 1995, *Time and Money*, Houghton Mifflin, Boston, MA.

Meaney, T 2015, "The Great Chastening" *The Nation*, March 23, pp. 27–32.

Melville, H 2004, "Bartleby the Scrivener: A Story of Wall-Street" in *Great Short Works of Herman Melville*, Ed. W Berthoff, Perennial Classics, New York, pp. 39–74.

Mendelson, E 2014, "The Secret Auden" *New York Review*, March 20, pp. 4–7.

Mill, JS 1895, *Utilitarianism*, E.P. Dutton, New York.

Miller, A 1958 [1949], *Death of a Salesman*, Viking, New York.

Miller, J 2015, "Liberalism as Fighting Faith" *The Nation*, May 4, pp. 35–39.

Mills, CW 2008, *The Politics of Truth*, Oxford University Press, Oxford.

Moore, GE 1993, *Principia Ethica*, rev. ed., Cambridge University Press, Cambridge.

Nancy, J-L 2014, "Hatred and Solidification of Meaning" *Law & Critique*, vol. 25, no. 1, pp. 15–24.

National Association of Corporate Directors (NACD) 1995, *Report of the NACD Blue Ribbon Commission on Director Compensation: Purposes, Principles, and Best Practices*. Available from: *www.nacdonline.org/* [July 27, 2015].

Nguyen, S 2014, "Making Organizations Moral" *Harvard Magazine*, November/December, pp. 11–12.

Niebuhr, R 2015, "Leaves from the Notebook of a Tamed Cynic" in *Major Works on Religion and Politics*, Ed. E Sifton, Library of America, New York, pp. 1–133.

Nietzsche, F 1992, *Ecce Homo: How One Becomes What One Is*, trans. RJ Hollingdale, Penguin Books, New York.

Nietzsche, F 1968, *The Will to Power*, Ed. W Kaufmann, trans. W Kaufmann & RJ Hollingdale, Vintage Books, New York.

Nietzsche, F 1966, *Beyond Good and Evil*, trans. W Kaufmann, Vintage Books, New York.

Nietzsche, F 1927a, "The Genealogy of Morals" in *The Philosophy of Nietzsche*, trans. H Samuel, Modern Library, New York, pp. 617–807.

Nietzsche, F 1927b, "Thus Spake Zarathustra" in *The Philosophy of Nietzsche*, trans. T Common, Modern Library, New York, pp. 3–368.

Nishida, K 1990 [1921], *An Inquiry into the Good*, trans. M Abe & C Ives, Yale University Press, New Haven, CT.

Norris, C 1988, "Law, Deconstruction, and the Resistance to Theory" *Journal of Law and Society*, vol. 15, no. 2, pp. 165–167.

Nozick, R 1974, *Anarchy, State, and Utopia*, Basic Books, New York.

Okin, S 1991, *Justice, Gender and the Family*, Basic Books, New York.

Oppen, G 2007, *Selected Prose, Daybooks, and Papers*, Ed. S Cope, University of California Press, Berkeley, CA.

Orwell, G 2012, *Diaries*, Ed. P Davison, Liveright Publishing, New York.

Orwell, G 2010 [1937], *The Road to Wigan Pier*, Oxford University Press, Oxford.

Orwell, G 1961 [1949], *Nineteen Eighty-Four*, New American Library, New York.

Orwell, G 1954, "Politics and the English Language" in *A Collection of Essays*, Doubleday, Garden City, NY.

Parmenides of Elea 1984, *Fragments*, trans. D Gallop, University of Toronto Press, Toronto.
Pascal, B 1941, *Pensées and the Provincial Letters*, trans. WF Trotter & T M'Crie, Modern Library, New York.
Payne, K 2010, *Why Is the Death of One Million a Statistic?* Available from: *www.psychologytoday.com/blog/life-autopilot/201003/why-is-the-death-one-million-statistic* [November 23, 2015].
Penelhum, T 1967, "Personal Identity" in *The Encyclopedia of Philosophy*, Ed. P Edwards, Macmillan, New York, vol. 6, pp. 95–107.
Perkins, T 2014, "Progressive Kristallnacht Coming?" *Wall Street Journal*, January 24. Available from: *www.wsj.com/articles/SB10001424052702304549504579316913982034286* [February 10, 2015].
Pew Research Center 2015, *America's Changing Religious Landscape: Christians Decline Sharply as Share of Population; Unaffiliated and Other Faiths Continue to Grow*. Available from: *www.pewforum.org/2015/05/12/americas-changing-religious-landscape/* [May 16, 2015].
Phillips, DZ 2005, "Voices in Discussion" in *Religion and Wittgenstein's Legacy*, Eds. DZ Phillips & M von der Ruhr, Ashgate, Aldershot, UK, pp. 89–95.
Pinsky, R 1994, "Translator's Note" in *The Inferno of Dante*, Farrar, Straus & Giroux, New York.
Polinsky, M 2003, *An Introduction to Law and Economics*, 3rd ed., Aspen, New York.
Posner, R 2011, *The Economic Analysis of Law*, 8th ed., Aspen, New York.
Proust, M 1934 [1913–1927], *Remembrance of Things Past*, 2 vols., trans. CKS Moncrieff, Random House, New York.
Rand, A 1992, *Atlas Shrugged*, Signet, New York.
Rawls, J 1999, *The Law of Peoples*, Harvard University Press, Cambridge, MA.
Rawls, J 1985, "Justice as Fairness: Political not Metaphysical" *Philosophy and Public Affairs*, vol. 14, no. 3, pp. 223–251.
Rawls, J 1971, A *Theory of Justice*, Harvard University Press, Cambridge, MA.
Raz, J 1984, "The Obligation to Obey: Revision and Tradition" *Notre Dame Journal of Law, Ethics & Public Policy*, vol. 1, no. 1, pp. 139–155.
Reagan, R 1988, *Remarks to Representatives of the Future Farmers of America*. Available from: *www.presidency.ucsb.edu/ws/?pid=36169* [April 8, 2015].
Rieff, D 2015, "Philanthrocapitalism: A Self-Love Story: Why do super-rich activists mock their critics instead of listening to them?" *The Nation*, October 1. Available from: www.thenation.com/article/philanthrocapitalism-a-self-love-story/ [April 11, 2016].
Rorty, R 1997, *Achieving Our Country*, Harvard University Press, Cambridge, MA.
Rousseau, J 1993a [1755], "A Discourse on the Origin of Inequality" in *The Social Contract and the Discourses*, trans. GDH Cole, Everyman's Library, New York, pp. 31–125.
Rousseau, J 1993b [1762], "The Social Contract" in *The Social Contract and the Discourses*, trans. GDH Cole, Everyman's Library, New York, pp. 179–305.
Ruggie, J 2010, "Report of the Special Representative of the Secretary-General on the issue of human rights and transnational corporations and other business enterprises" U.N. Doc. A/HRC/14/27. Available from: *www.ohchr.org/EN/Issues/TransnationalCorporations/Pages/Reports.aspx* [November 4, 2015].
Sartre, J-P 2009, *Portraits (Situations IV)*, trans. C Turner, Seagull Books, London.
Sartre, J-P 1956, *Being and Nothingness: An Essay on Phenomenological Ontology*, trans. H Barnes, Philosophical Library, New York.
Sayer, D 1991, *Capitalism and Modernity: An Excursus on Marx and Weber*, Routledge, London.
Scalia, A & Garner, B 2012, *Reading Law: The Interpretation of Legal Texts*, West, St. Paul, MN.

Schauer, F 1985, "Easy Cases" *Southern California Law Review*, vol. 58, pp. 399–440.
Schelling, FWJ 2000 [1811–15], *The Ages of the World*, trans. J Wirth, SUNY Press, Albany, NY.
Schopenhauer, A 2005 [1840], *The Basis of Morality*, trans. A Bullock, Dover, Mineola, NY.
Schopenhauer, A 1999 [1839], *Prize Essay on the Freedom of the Will*, Ed. G Zöller, trans. EFJ Payne, Cambridge University Press, Cambridge.
Schopenhauer, A 1969 [1818 & 1844], *The World as Will and Representation*, 2 vols., trans. EFJ Payne, Dover, Mineola, NY.
Schumpeter, 2009, "The Silence of Mammon: Business People Should Stand Up for Themselves" *The Economist*, December 17, p. 37.
Seavey, W 1964, *Handbook of the Law of Agency*, West Publishing, St. Paul, MN.
Sen, A 2009, *The Idea of Justice*, Harvard University Press, Cambridge, MA.
Seneca 1928, "On Mercy" in *Moral Essays*, vol. 1, trans. J Basore, William Heinemann, London, pp. 356–449.
Shanker, SG 1987, *Wittgenstein and the Turning-Point in the Philosophy of Mathematics*, State University of New York Press, Albany, NY.
Sinclair, U 1994 [1935], *I, Candidate for Governor: And How I Got Licked*, University of California Press, Berkeley, CA.
Smith, A 1937 [1776], *The Wealth of Nations*, Modern Library, New York.
Solomon, R & Murphy, M 2000, *What Is Justice? Classic and Contemporary Readings*, 2nd ed., Oxford University Press, Oxford.
Sorel, G 1999 [1908], *Reflections on Violence*, Ed. J Jennings, Cambridge University Press, Cambridge.
Spengler, O 1996 [1918/1922], *The Decline of the West*, 2 vols., trans. C Atkinson, Alfred A. Knopf, New York.
Spillane, M 2006, "Beckett at 100" *The Nation*, May 15, p. 37.
Spinoza, B 1955, *Ethics Preceded by On the Improvement of Understanding*, Ed. & trans. J Gutmann, Hafner Publishing, New York.
Spiro, J 2015, "How to Write a Code of Ethics for Business." Available from: *www.inc.com/guides/how-to-write-a-code-of-ethics.html* [November 8, 2015].
St. Augustine's Press 2013, *All Within the State, Nothing Outside the State, Nothing Against the State.* Available from: www.staugustine.net/blogs/rectify-names-a-blog-on-publishing/e2809call-within-the-state-nothing-outside-the-state-nothing-against-the-statee2809d-january-14-2013/ [April 11, 2016].
Stanford University Libraries n.d., Available from: *http://web.stanford.edu/dept/SUL/library/prod/depts/dp/pennies/1860_alger.html* [October 12, 2015].
Stern, F 2015, "How We Got to Where We Are" *New York Review*, May 7, pp. 54–57.
Stevens, W 1990, *The Collected Poems of Wallace Stevens*, Vintage Books, New York.
Stevens, W 1966, *Letters of Wallace Stevens*, Knopf, New York.
Stiegler, B 1998, *Technics and Time*, trans. R Beardsworth & G Collins, Stanford University Press, Stanford, CA.
Stone, J 1964, *Legal System and Lawyers' Reasonings*, Stanford University Press, Stanford, CA.
Sunstein, C 2002, *The Cost–Benefit State: The Future of Regulatory Protection*, American Bar Association, Chicago, IL.
Terence 1976, *The Comedies*, trans. B Radice, Penguin, New York.
Terry, L 2000, "A Survey of Legal Ethics Education in Law School" in *Ethics in Academia*, Eds. SK Majumdar et al., Pennsylvania Academy of Science, Easton, PA, pp. 61–74.
Thaler, R 2015, *Misbehaving: The Making of Behavioural Economics*, WW Norton, New York.

The History Channel 1984, *Morning in America Video.* Available from: www.google.com/ #q=reagan+it%27s+morning+in+america+again [April 11, 2016].

Thoreau, H 1937 [1854], "Walden; or, Life in the Woods," in *Walden and Other Writings of Henry David Thoreau*, Ed. B Atkinson, Modern Library, New York, pp. 1–297.

Thucydides 1982, *The Peloponnesian War*, trans. R. Crawley, Random House, New York.

Trilling, L 2008 [1950], *The Liberal Imagination: Essays on Literature and Society*, New York Review Books, New York.

Tversky, A & Kahneman, D 1981, "The Framing of Decisions and the Psychology of Choice," *Science*, vol. 211, no. 4481, pp. 453–458.

UNESCO 1991, "Universal Declaration on Cultural Diversity". Available from: *http://portal.unesco.org/culture/en/ev.php-URL_ID=35232&URL_DO=DO_TOPIC&URL_SECTION=201.html* [April 7, 2015].

United States Holocaust Memorial Museum 2007, *Auschwitz through the Lens of the SS: Photos of Nazi Leadership at the Camp*. Available from: *www.ushmm.org/information/exhibitions/online-features/collections-highlights/auschwitz-ssalbum* [April 2, 2015].

Varden, H 2010, "Kant and Lying to the Murderer at the Door . . . One More Time: Kant's Legal Philosophy and Lies to Murderers and Nazis," *Journal of Social Philosophy*, vol. 41, no. 4, pp. 403–421.

Veitch, S 2007, *Law and Irresponsibility: On the Legitimation of Human Suffering*, Routledge-Cavendish, Abingdon, UK.

Waismann, F 1979, *Wittgenstein and the Vienna Circle: Conversations Recorded by Friedrich Waismann*, Ed. B McGuinness, trans. J Schulte & B McGuinness, Basil Blackwell, Oxford.

Weber, M 1978, *Economy and Society*, 2 vols., Eds. G Roth & C Wittich, trans. E Fischoff et al., University of California Press, Berkeley, CA.

Weber, M 1976, *The Protestant Ethic and the Spirit of Capitalism*, trans. T Parsons, Scribner, New York.

Weber, M 1958, *From Max Weber: Essays in Sociology*, Eds. & trans. HH Gerth & CW Mills, Oxford University Press, New York.

Weber, M 1949, *The Methodology of the Social Sciences*, Eds. & trans. E Shils & H Finch, Macmillan, New York.

Weinberg, J 1964, *A Short History of Medieval Philosophy*, Princeton University Press, Princeton, NJ.

Weinberg, S 2015, *To Explain the World: The Discovery of Modern Science*, HarperCollins, New York.

Weissbrodt, D, Ni Aoláin, F, Fitzpatrick, J & Newman, F 2009, *International Human Rights: Law, Policy, and Process*, 4th ed., LexisNexis, San Francisco.

Wiley, T 1992, *Original Sin: Origins, Developments, Contemporary Meanings*, Paulist Press, Mahwah, NJ.

Williams, T 2004, *A Streetcar Named Desire*, New Directions, New York.

Wittgenstein, L 2005, *The Big Typescript TS 213*, Eds. & trans. GG Luckhardt & M Aue, Blackwell, Oxford.

Wittgenstein, L 1993, "A Lecture on Ethics" in *Philosophical Occasions: 1912–1951*, Eds. J Klagge & A Nordmann, Hackett, Indianapolis, IN, pp. 36–44.

Wittgenstein, L 1980a, *Culture and Value*, Ed. GH von Wright, trans. P Winch, Basil Blackwell, Oxford.

Wittgenstein, L 1980b, *Wittgenstein's Lectures 1930–1932: From the Notes of John King and Desmond Lee*, Ed. D Lee, Rowman & Littlefield, Totowa, NJ.

Wittgenstein, L 1978, *Philosophical Grammar*, Ed. R Rhees, trans. A Kenny, University of California Press, Berkeley, CA.

Wittgenstein, L 1975, *Philosophical Remarks*, Eds. & trans. R Hargreaves & R White, University of Chicago Press, Chicago, IL.
Wittgenstein, L 1974, *Tractatus Logico-Philosophicus*, trans. DF Pears & BF McGuinness, Humanities Press, Atlantic Highlands, NJ.
Wittgenstein, L 1960, *The Blue and Brown Books: Preliminary Studies for the "Philosophical Investigations"* 2nd ed., Harper & Row, New York.
Wittgenstein, L 1953, *Philosophical Investigations*, trans. GEM Anscombe, Macmillan, New York.
Wolcher, L 2008, *Law's Task: The Tragic Circle of Law, Justice and Human Suffering*, Ashgate, Aldershot, UK.
Wolcher, L 2005, *Beyond Transcendence in Law and Philosophy*, Birkbeck Law Press, London.
Zerbe, R 2001, *Economic Efficiency in Law and Economics*, Edward Elgar, Cheltenham, UK.
Zerbe, R, Bauman, Y, & Finkle, A 2006, "An Aggregate Measure for Benefit–Cost Analysis" *Ecological Economics*, vol. 58, pp. 449–461.
Žižek, S 1999, *The Ticklish Subject: The Absent Centre of Political Ontology*, Verso, London.

Index

For Product Safety Concerns and Information please contact our EU representative GPSR@taylorandfrancis.com Taylor & Francis Verlag GmbH, Kaufingerstraße 24, 80331 München, Germany